Artificial Generation

Photogenic French Literature and the Prehistory of Cinematic Modernity

CHRISTINA PARKER-FLYNN

Rutgers University Press
New Brunswick, Camden, and Newark, New Jersey, and London

Library of Congress Cataloging-in-Publication Data

Names: Parker-Flynn, Christina, author.
Title: Artificial generation : photogenic French literature and the prehistory of cinematic modernity / Christina Parker-Flynn.
Description: New Brunswick : Rutgers University Press, [2022] | Includes bibliographical references and index.
Identifiers: LCCN 2021009096 | ISBN 9781978825062 (paperback) | ISBN 9781978825079 (cloth) | ISBN 9781978825086 (epub) | ISBN 9781978825093 (mobi) | ISBN 9781978825109 (pdf)
Subjects: LCSH: French literature—19th century—History and criticism. | Motion pictures and literature | Motion pictures—Philosophy. | Representation (Philosophy) | Modernism (Art)
Classification: LCC PQ283 .P273 2022 | DDC 840.9/007—dc23
LC record available at https://lccn.loc.gov/2021009096

A British Cataloging-in-Publication record for this book is available from the British Library.

∞ The paper used in this publication meets the requirements of the American National Standard for Information Sciences—Permanence of Paper for Printed Library Materials, ANSI Z39.48-1992.

www.rutgersuniversitypress.org

Manufactured in the United States of America

Artificial Generation

For my greatest creations, Marlowe and Elvin

Contents

Illustrations

Artificial Generation

Introduction

Modernity's Reori-gene-ation

In one of his earliest writings on the cinema, film "prophet" Louis Delluc declares that the "cinema surpasses art by being life."[1] Delluc was a prophet in the Old Testament sense because he was gifted with an extraordinary capacity for comprehending film's most minute and beautiful details and, more important, his eloquent judgments confirmed his belief in the film as a unified work, "an entity"[2]—a being and, in some sense, a generative life force. To connote the art and glory of the cinema, he uses the French neologism *photogénie*, a term replicated and refined by French film critic and director Jean Epstein just a few years later in his essay "On Certain Characteristics of Photogénie" (1924). According to the *Dictionnaire vivant de la langue française*, the term's earliest usage was to connote the production of light, but Epstein's refinement of the term in relationship to the cinema exploits the (gene)rative behavior at the heart of *photogénie*, which only exists as a reproduction (on film).

The Photo Genes of Nineteenth-Century Literature

Befitting Delluc's consideration of cinema as life force, Epstein first describes "as photogenic any aspect of things, beings or souls whose moral character is enhanced by filmic reproduction," allowing the term to define "the cinematic property of things."[3] Cinema is an enigma that, Epstein rhetorically questions, could be seen as art, pictorial writing, or even an extension of human sight as "a sort of telepathy of the eye," but while batting around possible ways to determine the character of cinematic language, Epstein comes to define its most essential component—its animistic tendency, its ability to bestow a "semblance of life" to the objects it defines.[4] Conjugated in the future imperative, Epstein's *photogénie* is not a state of being but a machinery of generation, a generator of beings and of "a new reality." "Everything is alive" in Epstein's cinema, and film images—momentary flashes of this "fecund" *photogénie*—may equally represent "cells of the noblest tissues."[5]

However, I must rewind to an even earlier usage of the term "photogenic" by English scientist and inventor William Henry Fox Talbot in the 1830s, a crucial historical period regarding the emergence of precursory, photographic thoughts and technologies, and the same literary period from which this book begins its study. Experiments with a camera lucida and rudimentary drafting aids, spirited by his desire to reproduce on paper the loveliness of the Lake Como landscape, triggered Talbot to imagine how wonderful it would be "if it were possible to cause these natural images to imprint themselves durably, and remain fixed upon the paper."[6] Talbot named the process whereby the object of a first drawing or image can be reproduced on transparent paper as a re-presentation "photogenic drawing," which ultimately served as the historical and representational basis for photography. After on-and-off refinements of method, by 1841 Talbot patented the calotype—a more fixed image developed onto paper through the use of silver chloride—named from the Greek καλός (*kalos*) meaning "beautiful" and τύπος (*tupos*) meaning "impression." Illustrating a relationship to or production by light chemically reacting to a light-sensitive surface, Talbot wrote in his notebooks that "if the paper is transparent, the first drawing may serve as an object, to produce a second drawing, in which the lights and shadows would be reversed."[7] The necessary reversibility of the image in its photographic inscription—the negative needed to produce a positive (image)—equals what will amount to a constant reversibility of past and future, dead and living, male and female in the culturally inflected textual and cinematic studies in this book's chapters. It also syncs directly with the reversibility of subject and object, as "the camera, celebrated from the first as objectivity incarnate, also came to serve as one of modernity's most powerful emblems of the subjectivity of perception and of knowledge."[8]

At this particular moment in cultural history, new modes of representation emerged through technological evolution—from photogenic writing to the daguerreotype, photography, and phonography—and resulted in traditional modes of representation, most specifically literature, being threatened by their own replication as *something else*. Accordingly, the mid-nineteenth century's economy of literary representation becomes equally an economy of simulation wherein literature imitates, or copies, the effects of these emerging forms of representation, specifically photography and its prefiguration of the cinema. As French literature shed the traditional values Romanticism placed on nature, it began to reform itself according to increasingly visual and artificial edicts dictated via the simultaneous emergence of newfound, man-made technologies, forming the foundation for its own subjectivity of perception. In turn, the literature of modernity reached great heights of heterogeneity, as an amalgamation of these newly invented representational modes permeated texts at the level of composition, resulting in literature's newfound, and often unconscious, optical model.

Examining the relationship between these hybrid, representational mediums at this crucial moment in cultural and technological history, I will present a photogenic literary imperative in the nineteenth century, specifically through French texts written under the influence of Aestheticism and Symbolism, both movements influential to Jean Epstein's notion of *photogénie.* Intimately related to Walter Benjamin's idea of the "optical unconscious," or how photography mediates our experience of the world in unconscious ways, *photogénie* also operates analogously to Plotinus's philosophy of The One, which "flows into something other than itself."[9] *Artificial Generation* uses Epstein's concept of *photogénie,* itself a generator of beings, to consider and reveal this "new reality" befitting a literary form constantly in photo-genic replication, and as an index to open the question to the emergence of a proto-phenomenological form of cinema's photogene in nineteenth-century French literature.

This photogenic aesthetic, as I define it, is a method of literary reproduction, or generation, that required literary works to replicate an illusion of life and its sensations in ways directly related to broader transitions into the cinematic age. As culture and technologies evolved, further influencing literary composition, this photogenic aesthetic became ever more pronounced. Moreover, as a key part of this evolution in representation, a wide-scale reconditioning of artistic subjectivity also occurred, specifically around the reemergence of the artificial woman—the figure of and for the replication of photo-genes, as I will claim—a notion that hearkens back to long-standing expressions of mythological, masculine subjectivity through the figuration and reconfiguration of the female. This is underscored by the obsessive interest of artists and writers throughout the nineteenth century in reforming and refashioning important female figures that symbolize and/or problematize man's origins. Twentieth-century image production in the cinema—particularly its centering on the figure of the artificial woman—finds antecedents in nineteenth-century literary Aestheticism (*l'art pour l'art*) and Symbolism, both of which sought to complicate what is essential in nature, specifically by artificializing the woman, the figure for natural reproduction. This quest for masculine artistic subjectivity, directly informed by this photogenic literary aesthetic and continuously mythologized through the artificial woman, becomes a filmic drive by the turn of the century.

In "The Myth of Total Cinema," French film theorist André Bazin affirms that it is not the technical savants who invented cinema, but that the real primitives and primogenitors of the medium are the nineteenth-century men "obsessed by their own imaginings." A convergence of these various obsessions thus creates what he calls "the myth of total cinema."[10] In a palimpsestic way, the literature penned by these nineteenth-century authors functions as the ghostly, ever-present writing that one can detect underneath the cinema and its workings.

One of Bazin's prime examples of writing "in which inventors conjure up nothing less than a total cinema that is to provide that complete illusion of life" is the French Symbolist novel *L'Ève future*—the focal text in chapter 2—in which Auguste Villiers de l'Isle-Adam writes about Thomas A. Edison creating a film from successive photography and lampascope reflection, two years prior to the historical Edison's experiments in animated photography.[11] Indeed, I have reproduced this book's stem title from its all-caps usage in Villiers's novel: "ARTIFICIAL GENERATION (already much in vogue during recent years) seems destined within a century to fulfill the secret purpose of our species," Villiers speculates about the process of reproduction that disarticulates biological reproduction, thus reproducing "electro-human" creatures of the page—and, in the future, of the screen (98).

The chapters in part II of this book explore a generational line of textual experiments in photo-genic representation, works that all suitably offer primordial film moments. What is at stake in these narratives is not only the theme of artificial women but also the question of artificial generation itself. For the purposes of this book, its titular phrase "artificial generation" holds a doubled meaning, indicating not only the artificial generation of female figure(s) within the text but also the generation of artists who retreated into the artificial ideals of *l'art pour l'art*, Aestheticism, Symbolism, and Decadence—movements that best characterized the reverberations of this myth.

Yet despite the plural "imaginings" that Bazin espouses as the basis for a movement toward total cinema, he also gestures multiple times toward an idée fixe at the center of the cinematic pursuit and its "automatic fixing of the image."[12] The idea of an idée fixe can be traced back to composer Hector Berlioz's *Symphonie fantastique: Episode de la vie d'un artiste*, a symphony marked by a recurring and persistent theme that surfaces in various forms in all five movements. Berlioz wrote the symphony in Paris in 1830, the year of the July Revolution, and the same period from which this book begins its explorations in chapter 1. The symphonic piece tells the story of an artist so obsessed with his beloved that he poisons himself with opium (Berlioz seemingly wrote it partially drugged on opium as well). This "fixed" idea, which Bazin uses as a metaphor for the photograph capturing a fixed image, is not only a structural component (the recurring refrain that creates "movement" through the piece) but also a thematic one (the woman as love object). Of cinema, Bazin inquires how "the invention took so long to emerge, since all the prerequisites had been assembled and the persistence of the image on the retina had been known for a long time."[13]

Metamorphosis, Myth, and the Pygmalion Paradigm

From this fixed image in the mind of prior generations, *Artificial Generation* explores the duality of still life, both the male artist's fixation on artificial women (fixed, as in no longer reproductive, and in marking an object permanence) and its direct relation to the fixedness of images at a time of temporal and cultural upheaval—the overcoming of the transitory nature of modernity through the imprint of more permanent, photo-genic forms. Undertaking the project of exploring the "myth" of cinema requires an affirmation that the idée fixe of the female beloved is actually transformed into a photo-genic woman, a muse that most literally produces and emits light, a figure generated out of an imaginative assembly of reproductive technologies that have animation as their ultimate goal, and cinema in their sight(s).

Two major elements seem to be at stake in Bazin's idea of total cinema that are of structural relevance here, specifically myth and metamorphosis. In Bazin's conception of the cinematic as a complete and perfect representation of reality, he calls its "guiding myth" the accomplishment of "a recreation of the world in its own image"—thus granting the cinema a godlike status in both language and divine reproductive potential. Indeed, in decades prior Epstein had declared the cinema animistic and polytheistic, marked by the worship of itself as the god-like process of rendering things multiple ad infinitum. Befitting my future analysis in chapter 2 of a novel that offers a "future Eve," I would attach the importance here to Epstein's suggestion that the cinema creates a new aspect of the world in such a way then "proving superior to man," itself metaphorically positioned as a future Adam "who seems constitutionally unsuited to capture a continuous event in four dimensions all by himself."[14] In truth, the cinema is predicated on an originating event that temporally precedes it, so the most suitable myth at the heart of the movement toward total cinema proves to be that of the genesis of humankind, the story of Adam and Eve. Indeed, this extraordinarily comprehensive etiological myth will be a necessary intertext through my readings in this book, most specifically in chapter 2, along with other biblical narratives that themselves are reproduced by and after God's generation of man and woman, including Ecclesiastes in chapter 2, and the Song of Songs and story of Salome (beheading of John the Baptist) in chapter 3.

Bazin mentions another myth—that of Icarus, who "had to wait on the internal combustion engine before descending from the platonic heavens"—which is, at the same time, a metamorphosis. In Ovid's telling of the tale in the *Metamorphoses*, Icarus flies too close to the sun with wings fashioned by the mechanical artistry of his father, Daedalus, and thus the tale may be read as Ovid's way of stressing the fatal dangers of art's seemingly magical, and morphological, properties. Indeed, I myself have fashioned the clay of this project out of readings of the *Metamorphoses*, this book returning to the most compelling "myth" at the intersection of mimesis and animation, Ovid's story of Pygmalion, to start questioning, as I do here, what it means that Pygmalion's imitative "ivory girl" is better than the real thing—a copy both mimetically similar and yet different from the original. Nineteenth-century French authors returned habitually to the long-established Pygmalionesque paradigm as a means to assert particularly modernized and artificial conceptions of literary reproduction and to respond to the need for reconditioning artistic subjectivity, largely because of the particular anxiety emerging from the necessary impulse toward hybridizing any sense of boundaries between impossibly discrete fields of reproductive aesthetics. On the one hand, this literary trope, as well as the nineteenth century's photogenic aesthetic, emulates the *ars adeo latet arte sua* used by Ovid's Pygmalion to describe his feminine masterwork—*art lies hidden by its own artifice.* On the other hand, it reaches toward the future by predicting the "illusion of life" offered by cinema at the turn of the century.

The artist of the nineteenth century finds himself convincingly bestowing life through a composite art form, no singular art form being able to reproduce the multiple sensations necessary for the illusion of life. He chooses to engender as symbol of this movement, in line with the Ovidian tradition, an artificial replacement of she who gave him life—woman. Examining the cycle of love and loss in the Ovidian parables of Pygmalion and Narcissus as characteristic of artistic reproduction, both tales illustrate the complicated issue of artificial representation by defining love as an artificial determination and signaling the frightening, ever-reversible shift between persons and things, bodies and images, subjectivity and objectivity. Narcissus misrecognizes his self-reflection as someone other than himself, and despite the description of his effigy's statuesque resemblance, it proves far more fleeting than a statue. Despite the artificial generation of what I call feminine supplements,[15] like Pygmalion's statue, this rejection of female nature by replacement with a photo-genic woman yields de(gene)rative—and filmic—results.

On the most simplistic level, Pygmalion's story seems to be a happy one: he sculpts a statue of a woman, which comes to life and becomes his beloved. But the original story in Ovid's *Metamorphoses* offers a certain complexity of this tale of artificial generation. Pygmalion embarks on his artistic endeavor of sculpting a female figure as a form of repudiation, in response to the preceding story of a sexual perversion. After denying the divinity of the goddess Venus, the Propoetides, daughters of Propoetus of Cyprus, are transfigured into "the first / Strumpets to prostitute their bodies' charms" (10.236–237). Their life-giving, sexual function vitiated, in consequence, they turn into cold, lifeless stone: "As shame retreated and their cheeks grew hard, / They turned with little change to stones of flint" (10.238). Finding himself "horrified / At all the countless vices nature gives / To womankind," Pygmalion rejects natural women and remains celibate until he carves a sculpture "more beautiful / Than ever woman born" (10.241–243, 10.247–248). He falls in love with his sterile statue, this daughter of artifice, remarking upon the incongruous and deceptive lifelikeness of his masterwork. At first, we might be persuaded to read Pygmalion's myth as a story of animation of the inanimate, especially if we consider that, in the panoply of metamorphoses that constitute Ovid's text, it is the only transformation of a thing into a person rather than a person into a thing. However, at the feast of Venus he does not request the direct animation of the statue. Instead, Pygmalion prays for his bride to be "the living likeness of my ivory girl" (10.274), a likeness of his artificial reproduction of woman—*a copy of a copy*.

Ovid elucidates his own aesthetic, creation fantasy through the tale of Pygmalion; as Douglas F. Bauer asserts, "the happy resolve of the Pygmalion episode is unique," perhaps because this story justifies the durability and dexterity of artistic reproduction. When the sculptor debates the lifelikeness of his statue upon its creation, Ovid describes the effect through the epigrammatic "ars adeo latet arte sua"—art (*ars*) lies hidden by its own artifice. What is at stake, then, is the idea of an art that hides itself from itself, an art that pretends to be something else. Indeed, the phrase's chiastic structure emblematizes the condition sine qua non here; it indicates a level of artistic reproduction that reaches such elevated heights that one cannot distinguish the difference between real and illusion, between form and the simulation of form, thus transmitting an inversion wherein the signifier powers over the signified. In other words, the copy supersedes the original, most specifically regarding the question of woman. There *is* a clear difference between real women (the Propoetides) and artificial woman (the statue come to life), and clearly Pygmalion prefers the woman who was not born but made, "the body he had formed" (10.258). Even more surprisingly, Ovid allows this aesthetic deception to end with a magically positive transformation of the statue into a "real" woman Pygmalion can love. In fact, Ovid permits Pygmalion's aesthetic progeny to somehow bear his biological offspring as "she" begets Paphos nine months afterward.

I would suggest further that Pygmalion's tale of artistic reproduction is already a re-presentation of an earlier metamorphosis in Ovid's text, the tale of Narcissus. In similar fashion, Narcissus has fallen prey to the inability to negotiate the difference between original and copy, misrecognizing his own image reflected on the water's surface. He leans down to quench his bodily need to drink from the river, and a need of another kind suddenly presents itself, love. Ovid writes, "As he drank he saw before his eyes / A form, a face, and loved with leaping heart / A hope unreal and thought the shape was real" (3.415–417). His misinterpretation of his reflection, this "phantom of a mirrored shape," invites a mediation of Narcissus as a preemptory figure for the artist. In his fifteenth-century treatise on painting *Della Pittura*, Leon Battista Alberti argues for an evaluation of Narcissus as an artist figure and attributes the origins of painting to this tragic figure who falls in love with his own creation. "What is painting," Alberti asks his reader, "but the act of embracing by means of art the surface of the pool?"[16] Pygmalion's desire for a statue produced with his own hands repeats the same gesture as Narcissus's forbidden desire for his own image. As Paul Barolsky notes on the doubling of the tales of Pygmalion and Narcissus in the *Metamorphoses*, "A clue to the fact that Ovid's thinking about Pygmalion is related to his contemplation of Narcissus resides in the detail of Narcissus so charmed by his own image that he is still as a 'marble statue.' If he resembles a statue, then so does his creation, which, like Pygmalion's, is also a sculpture."[17]

Remarkably, both tales not only invoke the identical theme of selfsame love but also use the same literal material in their respective destruction and reconstruction of faith in this concept of artificial generation. Ovid remedies the tragic end of Narcissus, who "as wax melts before a gentle fire . . . So by love wasted, slowly [he] dissolves / By hidden fire consumed," by transubstantiating the melted wax of Narcissus's body into the wax that forms the body of Pygmalion's female likeness (3.488–490). After returning from the feast of Venus, Pygmalion touches his statue and soon finds that the body's material "yielded to his hands, as in the sun / Wax . . . softens and is shaped" (10.274, 10.284–285). Seemingly, Ovid repairs the breach caused by Narcissus's unrequited love for his own fleeting image by granting Pygmalion the power to resurrect his own self-reflection as a sturdy, ivory statue.

In J. Hillis Miller's *Versions of Pygmalion*—the title of which immediately betrays the inherent sense of multiplicity seated within the tale, and accordingly reproduced outside of it—he writes that for the statue "Galatea, to see at all is to see Pygmalion, and to be subject to him," quite "as if Narcissus' reflection in the pool had come alive and could return his love."[18] The tale of Pygmalion takes this trajectory one step further, however, because rather than just deal with the complicated relationship between a person and his reflection, the Pygmalion story adds a layer of complexity by illustrating the relationship between a person and the likeness of his already lifelike work of art. I suggest the importance of this because it prefigures the mechanized sense of artificial reproduction that will become increasingly relevant in the nineteenth-century texts that re-produce Pygmalionesque scenarios, texts that themselves seem to replicate via their photo-genes.

Yet both tales illustrate the complicated issue of artistic representation by defining love as an artificial determination and signaling the frightening, ever-reversible shift between persons and things, bodies and images, subjectivity and objectivity. Narcissus misrecognizes his self-reflection as someone *other* than himself, and despite the description of his effigy's statuesque resemblance, it proves far more fleeting than a statue. His beloved image is fashioned out of an absence. "What you see is nowhere," Narcissus is scolded, for the image he loves is "nothing itself" (10.434, 437). He designates his own otherness by addressing his reflection as "you," and his misrepresentation of self as other triggers the inevitable death of his human form, and his subsequent metamorphosis into a flower. Pygmalion treads no more cautiously in his own moment of Narcissistic recognition: after his heart begins to desire "the body he had formed," he touches it and "believes / The firm new flesh beneath his fingers yields" (10.258). What for Narcissus seemed to be the misrecognition of self as other is for Pygmalion more a matter of fantastical delusion. The sculptor treats the statue like a woman, bringing "it" gifts that "girls delight in," when suddenly "it" transforms into a "she." Ovid writes, though "lovely she looked" in her nakedness, Pygmalion decides to adorn her with jewelry and "laid her on a couch of purple silk," "cushioning her head, / As if she relished it" (10.268, 270, 271–272).

If looking at the cycle of love and loss in the parables of Pygmalion and Narcissus as characteristic of artistic reproduction, I find it striking that although they both fall in love with selfsame, self-made images that are artificially gendered, it is also difference, and the attempt to overcome it, that defines these scenarios. Narcissus falls in love with his selfsame reflection in the water, but his inability to recognize this sameness, his misrecognition of the image not as a reflection of his body but as other from his self, leads to the fatality of his human form. In effect, Pygmalion abolishes sexual difference—which the figures of the Propoetides illustrate as abominable—by re-producing woman as a body made of stone—female only in/as art form. Yet despite the artificial generation of feminine supplements like Pygmalion's statue, this rejection of female nature only yields degenerative, or pathogenic, results. And so, the generation of artificial women spawned by Pygmalion's Galatea across the aesthetic tradition proves deviant as well, fitting reflections of the ultimate deviancy of the author, whose adoption of the fecund gaze of the *photogénie* seems to equal the metaphoric usurpation of female, biological reproduction. What results is possibly an unconscious queerness in these texts I will analyze; from the mummy to the machine, many of the artificially generated or preserved literary figures in post-1830s French literature operate as allegories for the destruction of gender binaries, as well as aesthetic categories.

Whereas Alberti sees Narcissus as the root figuration of the artist, he might actually fit more squarely as an actor or, more specifically, a foundational figure for my photogenic concerns. The double, as Hillel Schwartz assesses in *The Culture of the Copy*, is endemic to theater, the human being onstage as double as can be, obligated to invent false emotions and apprehended images.[19] In his seminal writing on the subject in relation to film, Epstein defines the photogenic actor as, at heart, a reproduction of Ovid's Narcissus; upon first seeing themselves onscreen, "they thought they were someone else. Whether an actor or not, each of us is confounded when gazing at himself as seen by the camera lens."[20] Just as Narcissus fatally misrecognizes his own photogenic image—literally and necessarily produced by light—on the surface of the water, all humans are fated to misrecognize their cinematic doubles. The fleeting image on the "pool's deceptive surface" that serves as the "illusion that deceives him" operates as extraordinary analogue to the cinematic image.

Italian poet and playwright Gabriele D'Annunzio, who largely worked in the Decadent style so closely associated with French Symbolism, was one of the first to offer an early full-fledged version of the cinema by heralding the cinematic impulse at the heart of Ovid's *Metamorphoses*, suggesting the poet as precursor to the medium's inventiveness and power of animation. Indeed, classicists of late have offered studies of Ovid's relationship to film studies, including Paula James's

Ovid's Myth of Pygmalion on Screen (2011), which charts a breathtaking array of films with Pygmalion subtexts from silent cinema to *Lars and the Real Girl* (2007);[21] and in *Ovid on Screen: A Montage of Attractions* (2020), Martin M. Winkler examines affinities between classical and modern texts and images that he defines as "cinemetamorphoses."[22] While the germ of cinematic visuals can be discerned in the tale of Narcissus, I would suggest that the cinema's "Pygmalion effect" proves more notable both in academic discourse and regarding the interests of this book. Senior Curator at the Museum of Modern Art Roxana Marcoci proposes that "Within the history of representation, the myth of Pygmalion is a parable not only of the relationship between model and copy but of the mechanical creation of a world in movement," quite specifically located in the cinema[23]; art historian and past director of the Cinémathèque française Dominique Paini suggests, in his work on sculpture, that the Pygmalion complex lies at the heart of the invention of film; while in his book *The Pygmalion Effect*, Romanian art historian Victor Stoichita examines the history of this phenomenon in art, concluding with an analysis of Alfred Hitchcock's *Vertigo* (1958) as "The Original Copy," per his section title[24]—a gesture this book will repeat in its examination of Hitchcock in chapter 5.

Reori-gene-ating; or, the Will to Copy

I would like to re-originate the concept of *photogénie* and suggest that this Pygmalion effect at the root of the cinematic enterprise is due largely to a possible reading of Ovid as an ancient photo-genic engineer, first on the level of what we might call differential mimesis. Mimesis, from the ancient Greek μιμεῖσθαι, "to imitate," ranges widely in critical meanings, which include measures of representation, mimicry, and even self-expression. Pygmalion's creation of a statue as an imitation of a real woman serves as a traditional example of the mimetic representation of the real, or nature, in art. But what does it mean that Pygmalion's "ivory girl," the imitation, is better than the real thing? So much better, in fact, that she magically becomes real at the story's end, thus replacing the real. How is Pygmalion's copy both the same mimetically and yet different from the original? "Indeed," as Elisabeth Bronfen writes in *Over Her Dead Body*, "the Greek verb *mimesthai* is fraught with ambiguity, given that it refers both to the creation of a new object and the copy, or imitation of a pre-existing one."[25] The cinema, too, reverses the traditional conceptual binary that privileges the original over the copy, human over artistic reproduction.

The answer might be found by reuniting with Jean Epstein's conception of *photogénie*, specifically that it offers a virtual embodiment for the spectator wherein the projected film operates as interface between viewer and material film. I would like to reconceive the photogenic more specifically in consideration of how these protocinematic texts actually embody screen women, the figure of the medium through which I see the photo-gene getting replicated. Indeed,

Epstein's *photogénie* is mimetic by definition, only accessible in and as a cinematic reproduction of an image, therefore always a copy. *Photogénie* "hinges upon the existence of a gap between resemblance and difference," and therefore becomes interchangeable, in theory, with the concept of metamorphosis, taking on a sense of plasticity akin to that defined by Soviet filmmaker Sergei Eisenstein as a continuous variability of forms—possibly why film theorist Mary Ann Doane acknowledges that *photogénie* is often considered "theoretically incoherent," that which is inarticulable, exceeds language, "and hence points to the very essence of cinema specificity."[26] As I will show throughout the book's chapters, the photogene of nineteenth-century French literature, housed in the figural body of the artificial woman, is in constant replication. Beyond sameness and difference, what is truly at stake for these photogenic stories is the necessity to stimulate and simulate life and its origins. Differentially mimetical, then, because these photogenic texts will simulate woman as a congruous de-realization of the real.

Epstein's concept of *photogénie* is largely inspired by French literary movements such as *l'art pour l'art*, prompted by Théophile Gautier's preface to his novel *Mademoiselle de Maupin* (1835), and later in the literary generational line, Symbolism. What the chapters in part I will do, then, is expose the "flashes" of what might inform Epstein's later theory, but which I will be examining as indicative of a newfound literary simulation—a virtual reality, in essence—and synesthesia. The depth of amalgamation that occurred within literary representation during this era is a key aesthetic tradition that continues to inform movies and contemporary culture today; more important, it demonstrated how humans were becoming more photogenic outside the pages of literature as well. Accordingly, the aesthetes—Théophile Gautier and Oscar Wilde among those I will be discussing at length—equally became synesthetes. From the ancient Greek, meaning "to bring the senses together," synethesia can often lead to, or represent, a sensory overload. In the reverse, this development within the literature of nineteenth-century France seemed a somewhat unconscious response to an explosion of complex senses, specifically born of the industrialization and urbanization of Paris and beyond, and the mechanization of reproductive technologies. Adapting to the experience of new perceptual phenomena, these literary minds produced in their aesthetic endeavors a sense of synesthesia that projected the future "life" of the cinema.

Artificial Generation explores how these early literary endeavors (screen texts) and then films (texts on-screen) embrace and reproduce the cultural and technological heritage of antiquity and its necessary confrontation with modern transience and those optical models that emerge in post-1830s Paris. This sense of cultural and possibly aesthetic progress requires a paradoxical directive, to both make new and return to the old. As with Andreas Huyssen's concept of the authentic ruin, which emerged specifically as a product of modernity, these photogenic texts achieve a subjective effect through the re-presentation of a ruin that renders visible "devastations of time."[27] Indeed, the fixedness of modernity's necessary ruin of representation not only helps remythologize modern life's newfound and endless multiplicity but also guarantees that the characteristically fleeting moments will soon, and somewhat magically, be "fixed" by the cinematic endeavor.

The cinematic effect bears striking similarity to that of Pygmalion, both relying on an essential negotiation between stasis and movement embodied in the ambulatory statue, the flash of the mysterious *photogénie* on-screen, and the moving photographic images that create cinema. The potentiality of cinema for Epstein resides in its state of *becoming*, those aspects enhanced by filmic reproduction specifically mobile and in perpetual flux. Movement, according to Henri Bergson, is reality itself, and as critic Alexander Bakshy affirms, "The only real thing in the motion picture is *movement* without which all its objects would appear as lifeless shadows."[28] Movement is also absolutely definitional of modernity, hence the near sense of differential mimesis between modernity and the cinema; as Malcolm Turvey offers with emphasis, "modernity is undoubtedly a precondition for the emergence of film."[29] Likewise, these texts written by the artificial generation of the nineteenth century, as I define the lineage, carry essential photo-genic material that migrates through the twin souls of modernity and the cinema.

Organization of the Book

In part I, I trace a particular photo-genealogy of the critical cinematic obsession with female automatons, animated statues, excavated mummies, and dancing bodies to a constellation of the affective forms of French literary modernity in the nineteenth century. Writers Théophile Gautier, Auguste Villiers de l'Isle-Adam, and Oscar Wilde prepared the conceptual ground for the emergence of film on a psycho-cinematic level, making material—even if they were not yet fully materialized—the new modern aesthetics and technologies by imprinting them in their notably photo-genic texts. To grasp the conditions that make cinematic art possible, one must interrogate its literary and cultural ancestors. In the course of analysis, I will question how, for instance, these texts re-produce visual paradigms from Ovid's Pygmalion (and Narcissus) in ways specific to cultural evolution in the nineteenth century. What is at stake in an artistic subjectivity marked by this demand to bear artificial women as their Symbolic progeny? More specifically, how and why are these figures so photo-genic—generative of film form as well as so thematically relevant to protocinematic stories?

Many studies claim Charles Baudelaire as the master of nineteenth-century French literary modernism, but "The Literary Afterlife," the first chapter here, begins with a close analysis of the heterogeneous literary imaginings of Théophile Gautier, *maître* to Baudelaire and a figure criminally underaddressed as critical to the emergence of a new aesthetic imperative with seeing (psycho-cinematically) at its root. In my reading of Gautier's fantastic tale "La Morte amoureuse" (1836), and further discussion of his other mummy and Egyptological fictions, I will assess the unique, dual influence of two mediums that developed concurrently with Gautier as an artist, photography and archaeology—both representational modes participating in this new culture of virtuality. Through what I refer to as the author's aesthetic of resurrection, Gautier's version of the fantastic—from the Greek *phantasticus*, meaning "to have visions"—functions as pre-Freudian psychoanalytic case study and, like psychoanalysis itself, partially constructs the hetero-optical foundation of the aesthetic of French modernity. The chapter ends with meditations on Gautier's spirited, aesthetic defense of photosculpture in the 1860s, focusing on the technology's invocation of mechanical multiplicity, its future relevance in twenty-first-century hypotheses on cybernetics, and, most important, Gautier's critical claim that photosculpture's authenticity and supreme value lie in its ability to produce *a statue whose original does not exist* ("une statue dont l'originale n'existe pas").

The book's second and most axiomatic chapter argues that Villiers's Symbolist novel *L'Ève future* (1886) epitomizes modernity's book of genesis, a re-generation of the biblical Eve under the auspices of modern technology that presents its reader with an incongruous composition of a prehistorical figure and a modern, futurized woman. The novel essentially rewrites Milton's *Paradise Lost*—itself a literary reproduction of the biblical book of Genesis, the narrative basis for human procreation in the Christian tradition—in order to confront the myth of likeness between the first man and woman and transfigure these relevant concerns into its reproduction of (real) woman as her (mechanical) likeness. The book's fictional Thomas Edison operates allegorically as a vehicle for the set of modern, reproductive technologies—the stereoscope, phonograph, telephone, electrical connections, color and successive photography—that encompass the book's notion of artificial generation as the production of "une vivante reproduction," a living likeness, which in *Artificial Generation* I clearly re-produce, a foundational sentiment regarding cinema's future, moving images, replicated from the photo-genes of the *andréïde* (in the first usage of the neologism in French literature), or female automaton, that Edison invents in Villiers's novel. Prominent film theorists and scholars such as Raymond Bellour and Annette Michelson use the book's depiction of the process of archaic cinematic projection, a film that Edison creates of the character of Evelyn Habal "miraculously caught in color photography," as indicative of an aesthetic prediction[30]; for Michelson, the literary scene operates as "the fantasmatic ground of cinema itself."[31] More consciously than the optical unconscious that emerges in Gautier, Villiers's novel illustrates how the quest for masculine (literary) subjectivity becomes a photographic drive by the end of the nineteenth century. Accordingly, the relevant intersection of the singularity of the statue and its newfound, mechanically reproductive status will be further discussed specifically in relation to the Venus de Milo and the Statue of Liberty.

Just as Ovidian poetics represented a crucial moment in Roman intertextuality, nineteenth-century Salomania—the cultural swell of collective desire among European artists and authors to reproduce the biblical story of Salome—cultivated a breathtakingly heterogeneous display of artistic reproduction. Especially for the French Symbolists, the figure of Salome became a limitless source of adaptation and a central figure of artificial generation, specifically through ekphrasis as the literary vivification of an art object, and later and most significantly dancing her way into cinematic modernity. Chapter 3 analyzes Oscar Wilde's *Salomé* (1891), written specifically in French and borne in and through his relationship with French Symbolism, as the apex of artifice and a cornerstone text of artificial (de)generation. In *Degeneration* (1895), Max Nordau specifically reproached artistic movements including Aestheticism, Symbolism, and Decadence—of which Wilde was for him the chief representative—for causing an infection of the artificial, emerging as an adverse effect of modernity that caused this necessarily heterogeneous sense of art and literature, texts signifying promiscuously rather than in regard to any stable referent or natural, "original" source. By specifically writing the play in French, using the language as another instrument through which to express himself, Wilde coordinately represents the heterogeneous aesthetic and mechanical forms of reproduction that preoccupied French literature from the emergence of Gautier's *l'art pour l'art* movement, of which Wilde considered himself a descendant: as he writes in *De Profundis*, "Like Gautier I have always been one of those *pour qui le monde visible existe*."[32] *Salomé* demonstrates Wilde's own mythopoeic faculty, an artificialization of the Salome myth through his anti-Arnoldian dictum of portraying the object in all its as-it-can-be-ness—a central foundation for Jean Epstein's theory of the *photogénie*. Indeed, the root of mimesis is symbolic representation, and Wilde's literary and linguistic mimicry in *Salomé* proves that his intention for the piece was a form of artificial generation as simulation, a surface resemblance, or the tendency to assume the form of *something else*—a gesture toward his writing it in a "foreign" language, and forward to the cinematic image. I will explore a bevy of intertextual relationships relevant to the text, most specifically by examining the way Salomania as an adaptive network gets reinscribed through other important realizations of the text, most notably in regard to illustrations done by Aubrey Beardsley for the play's Bodley Head version, and the importance of the French actress Sarah Bernhardt as its creator through performance. Opening up a network of ever-fluctuating, somewhat virtual realizations of *Salomé* will allow me to consider the something-else-ness of the play as indicative of the heterogeneity at the root of artificial generation, but also means to consider the play, an illustrated text in multiple ways, as integrally connected to early cinema. Ultimately, this chapter will offer a reading of *Salomé* as an emblem of aesthetic re-generation, its textual system modeled on a re-production of the lyric quality of desire and love as "generative force" in the biblical Song of Songs, which shares the same preoccupation as the story of the Garden of Eden yet represents its inversion—a paradise regained.

In part II, *Artificial Generation* illustrates how this core literary mode of artistic subjectivity and the "gene" of the photogenic woman get continually replicated by twentieth-century filmmakers. Over the course of its two chapters and epilogue, part II delineates how early to contemporary film reimagines and replicates the same themes, figures, and major elements that were charted in chapters 1 through 3, thus effectively repeating the gesture of reproduction on which this book's theoretical premise rests.

In chapter 4, "Statuesque Cinema," the lineage of this diverse interaction between mediums will be traced, beginning with an exploration of the "Egyptomania" that defined cinema's birth and that informs the earliest mummy films that are thematically indicative of cinematic animism—and some, direct adaptations of Gautier's stories. Early filmic works of George Méliès and Thomas Edison will be discussed as cinematic metamorphoses, specifically those of the magician-cum-filmmaker Méliès, who made the first Pygmalion and Galatea film, one of many reasons Winkler considers the filmmaker Ovid's possible twin soul, "offering a hermeneutic perspective on the medium's own birth, namely the passage of inanimate to animated."[33] Reproductions of statues and Salomes in early film will be examined, specifically Loie Fuller's film experiments in movement, fabric, and lighting that invented a uniquely sculptural cinema that epitomized the French Symbolist project—and that of cinema's new art of motion—of "a continually changing spectacle of metamorphosis."[34] Fuller, like dancer Isadora Duncan, quested toward the equivalent synesthesia of male authors in the prior century, becoming a sort of "*ekphrastic* machine," an embodiment of textuality that transcribes itself "from one medium to another."[35] A more literal ekphrasis, doubled over, occurs in the chapter's discussion of Russian American actress and filmmaker Alla Nazimova's adaptation of *Salomé*, which marries the text and images of Wilde and Beardsley, respectively. Adapted from Villiers's *L'Ève future* and an integral text of cinematic modernity, Fritz Lang's *Metropolis* (1927) offers a most indelible image of the female android as moving sculpture, the vertical dimensions of the film's modern cityscape representing modern, industrialized anxieties and operating as the connective tissue for the book's last chapter.

The Pygmalionism in and of the cinema fully crystallizes in chapter 5, "See-Through Woman," through an examination of Alfred Hitchcock's *Vertigo* (1958), his only film adapted from a French novel, inspired by what the director called his "Symbolist dreams." Primarily a balance disorder wherein one experiences the sensation that the environment moves when in fact no movement occurs, vertigo operates metaphorically for Pygmalionism, which then doubles for the cinema as an artistic medium predicated on the illusion of movement and life. The film reenacts with striking similarity the cinematic embodiment of woman as the site for the conversion of absence into presence, lack into "representational plentitude," and death into life, ultimately reproducing the literary photo-gene examined in part I as a necessarily cinematic story.[36] At its root, *Vertigo*'s main determination is the impulse to be possessed (stilled) by representation, bearing close relation to Hitchcock's own predilection for modernist art and sculpture: the visual perception and multiplicity of profiles of the sculptural cohere with the analyses in this book's first, literary chapters and establish a basis for examining the woman as work of art in Hitchcock's film. Yet, ultimately, Hitchcock structures the film's narrative around willful and visual misrepresentation—a fundamental and theoretically resonant aspect in Hitchcock studies, according to Slavoj Žižek—of its symbolic, interpretive system.[37] The vertiginously swirling spiral graphics by Saul Bass that epitomize the film from its opening credits operate metaphorically for the machineries of cinematic history, indicative of what Hillel Schwartz deems the "kinestructs" of a new kinesthetic (like Bernhardt's performance of death spirals and the "seductive spirals of vamps" like Salome) and as generative of the "hermeneutic spiral" of the film's endless proliferation of interpretations.[38] And going back to the beginning, a direct repetition of what Gautier in "La Morte amoureuse" calls the "two spirals entangled and confounded" that serve to define this modern, bicephalic—and cinematic—life.

To close, the epilogue asserts that the newest lineage of cinematic replicants in *Blade Runner 2049* (2017) operates as cells interlinked within the literary and aesthetic replication crisis that *Artificial Generation* has charted from the 1830s. Just as the original *Blade Runner* (1982) film takes a mythopoeic approach to the book of Genesis, its sequel perpetuates the most essential question of biological production as the premise of its mystery, offering a miraculously procreative artificial woman—the replicant Rachael—as a re-production of one of the most important maternal figures in the Bible and descendant of Eve, reading her as Rachel from the book of Genesis. Along with an examination of the film's intertextual network, specifically designed through Vladimir Nabokov's novel *Pale Fire*, a literary forefather for the technological idea of hypertext, I will establish how *2049* belongs to this very same aesthetic lineage. I will discuss the relevance of the cinematic re-production of Rachael (Sean Young) from the original film to its sequel, outlining the special effects process used to create a "digitally generated human," and offer my ultimate reading of Rachael's scene of resurrection in this film as a copy in and of *Vertigo.*

Part 1

Literary Simulations

1

The Literary Afterlife

Théophile Gautier's Aesthetic of Resurrection

> It's important to read a book, but also to hold the book, to smell the book . . . its perfume, its incense, it's the dust of Egypt.
> —Ray Bradbury

By the 1830s, new modernizing forces emerged—aesthetic forms, visual paradigms, technological apparatuses—and inflamed the hybridization of France's literary models. As an artist, Théophile Gautier served as a somewhat unwitting emblem of this transformative aesthetic. Though most famous for his seemingly homogeneous, selfsame literary project of *l'art pour l'art,* Gautier led an intellectual life characterized by a heterogeneous intertextuality among various modes of artistic production: journalism, painting, letters, storytelling, travel writing, ballet and art criticism, and so on. As Charles Baudelaire famously claimed of his *maître* and the object of his dedication for *Les Fleurs du mal* (1857), wherever an artistic product, Gautier was ever-present, ready to describe it or ascribe to it as if, I might add, he were an artistic product himself.[1] For Gautier, like other French writers at the decline of Romanticism who supported the concept of a *fraternité des arts*, artistic genres were no longer forms to be locked into without flexibility. Before his career in letters, Gautier trained as a painter under Louis

Rioult, albeit unsuccessfully; from the 1830s through the 1860s, he wrote a number of *contes fantastiques* (fantastic tales) while also working in journalism. A practitioner of literary and visual arts, he became an influential art critic, writing reviews of ballets as well as commentaries on culturally evolving technologies, like photosculpture, which emerged later in the century, and which this chapter will discuss more fully by its end. The question of generic artistic form for Gautier was, then, always perpetually distracted by a sense of heterogeneity seemingly inherent in the aesthetic of French modernity; as Baudelaire vividly suggests, "The spirit of Théophile Gautier, poetic, picturesque, meditative, had to love this form, to caress it, and to dress it in the various costumes that are most to his liking."[2] Accordingly, Gautier's literary and critical endeavors were influenced by his artistic talents of transposition, supplementing a restricted prosaic depiction with multifaceted sensibilities, dressing his art in different costumes akin to the sculptor, the painter, and even the daguerreotypist.

His aesthetic operating as an unconscious reformation, or even deformation, of literary and aesthetic form, I will argue that Gautier develops a pre-Freudian, psychoscopic literature, and that notably, his aesthetic output matures concurrently and subsequently mates with the sensibilities of the daguerreotype, the archaic blueprint for modern photography. As an artist, Gautier himself develops contemporaneously with photography's invention and evolution. Frenchman Louis-Jacques-Mandé Daguerre commercially invented the image-making medium, perfecting the process between 1835 and 1839, when he finalized the patent for the "daguerreotype" in his name. In 1837, Daguerre presented to the chief curator at the Louvre his very first daguerreotype as proof of his invention, a still-life composition of the interior of a cabinet of curiosities, which features numerous sculpted heads as well as a marble bas-relief of a Romanesque Galatea by Jean Goujon, one of the greatest sculptors of sixteenth-century France (figure 1.1). Daguerre, like Gautier, started out as a painter, and he introduced his invention as a "canvas." The advent of photography, "when aesthetic experience was firmly rooted in Romanticist tenets of originality, brought into focus the critical role that the copy plays in the perception of art."[3] In 2010 at the Museum of Modern Art, Roxana Marcoci curated *The Original Copy: Photography of Sculpture, 1839 to Today*, an exhibit founded on the quite specific category of mechanically produced visual images of sculptures, to "consider how one medium has been implicated in the creative reproduction and analysis of the other."[4] The earliest photographs, then, function as artifacts that attest to a necessary encounter between the ancient statue and the modern, automatic image.

In this broader visual culture of France around the 1830s—a crucial moment in the mechanization of man's vision—art, literature, and photography cannot be considered as disparate fields; indeed, they share parallel interests in simulation and reproduction. Of significance, Daguerre viewed the daguerreotype as "not merely an instrument which serves to draw nature" but one that "gives her the power to *reproduce herself*."[5] That a photo produced an automatic copy of

FIG. 1.1 *L'Atelier de l'artiste*, the first surviving daguerreotype by Louis-Jacques-Mandé Daguerre (ca. 1837) uses sculptural art, including a bas-relief of Galatea, as subject of its still life.

the art object caused many Romantic artists anxiety over the loss of art's singularity, provoking some, like Baudelaire, to criticize the medium's encroachment on the world of imagination, while others, like American author Edgar Allan Poe, "took pleasure in the fact that the daguerreotype could capture . . . ciphers of his own imaginative sensibility."[6] One of the earliest daguerreotypes in *The Original Copy* exhibit, attributed to Daguerre's assistant Alphonse Eugène Hubert, is presented under the title *Nature morte, bas-reliefs et sculptures dont la Vénus de Milo* (1839; Still life, bas-reliefs, and sculptures with the Venus de Milo): the image shows a sculpture in the left foreground, ancient bas-reliefs in the background, and the Venus de Milo on the right side.[7] But Geoffrey Batchen makes the point that the Venus in this daguerreotype is not the original statue but a reproduction, further complicating the issue of technological reproducibility and creating a mise en abyme effect of meaning at the very primal level of these technological mediums—the copying of flat images, as well as three-dimensional sculptural bodies. Around 1836, according to Batchen, Achille Collas introduced a sculptural reducing and copying machine that was able to produce a less-than-half-size version of the canonical statue.[8] These "reproductions of reproductions," as Batchen calls the first photographs that took sculpture and statues as their main visual components, become "historical documents" that function as monuments "formed and tempered as they were through artistic subjectivity"—aesthetic records specific to/in 1830s France. Of significance, as I will argue, this concept is specifically yet unconsciously illustrated in Gautier's *fantastique*.[9]

Photography and archaeology were mediums developing in the nineteenth century as vehicles for the preservation of artifacts both real and virtual, revolutionizing the culture's grasp of temporality and radically changing the image culture of the period.[10] As Eric Downing writes, "The truth value of a photograph seemed a fleeting one indeed, without much staying power, and it tended to produce a correspondingly ephemeral sense of history and, more pointedly, self-image. The subject was no longer thought of as a single, sustained, or constantly true identity; it became a series of possibly disconnected and always changing images or truths."[11] Downing's "subject" in the age of photographic reproduction transforms into an "it" in the preceding quote, indicating that artistic subjectivity upon the advent of photography becomes equally a question of visual objectivity, signaling the decade's repetitious encounter with the Pygmalionesque rendering of woman into an art object. Although archaeology and photography might be considered representational modes of the real, they also provided and promoted the century's newfound access to an "extra-aesthetic 'real'" by participating "in the proliferation of a new culture of virtuality, or inauthentic images and simulacra."[12] For photography, this meant the endless, mechanical reproducibility intrinsic to the image. Archaeology, on the other hand, provided snapshots of past civilizations through their unearthed ruins, a portal to myriad societies past that served equally as a reminder of the sense of modernity's transient sense of time.

Gautier fortifies the cult of modernity in ways immediately equivalent to the aforementioned, in understanding modernity as a "perpetuation of faith in Antiquity into the modern world."[13] As discursive possibilities, both photography and archaeology allowed Gautier to produce culturally relevant, optical aspects of meaning in his fiction, further permitting and even emboldening the male artist's mastery of the female subject precisely as visualized object. This chapter explores Gautier's aesthetic of resurrection through a close reading of one of his earliest fantastic tales, "La Morte amoureuse" (1836), published concurrently with the arrival of the earliest daguerreotypes in France. As in the *nature morte* images transferred between painting-sculpture-daguerreotype, Gautier's "La Morte" deals with the ever-reversible association between the dead and the living—past and present—thus emblematizing that during an era associated with the rise of technology, modernity's new optically oriented mode of literary representation seeks refuge somewhat unexpectedly in the relics of an ancient past. It bears mentioning that the title of this story corresponds to what painters refer to as *la nature morte* (still life), which not only invites the story's inevitable connections with more visual, plastic mediums of art but also dictates an imperative in the oscillations between still and moving, living and dead. In turn, Gautier's aesthetic hybridization within his literature becomes an indicator of three other key and intentional ambiguities within his story's narrative, discussed in great detail in the following sections: the vacillation of gender, a temporally fluctuating conception of modernity as a transposition of the ancient, and the ever-reversible association of life and death that functions as an underlying premise for theories on photography and film in the following century.

Optical Introductions

In 1830, at only eighteen, Théophile Gautier published his first book, *Poésies*, a collection of forty-six poems; it was not, however, a particularly auspicious start to his literary career. It was a year of radical change in France, historically and culturally, during which the July Revolution caused political unrest and social turbulence that persisted throughout the decade. Published at that time, *Poésies* attracted little attention whatsoever, at least not until the long poem "Albertus" was rereleased in 1832. Yet Gautier made himself part of the literary unrest that paralleled France's political and cultural upheaval. In February 1830, Victor Hugo's revolutionary, Romantic drama *Hernani* was set to open at the Théâtre-Français. To demonstrate his opposition to dramatic classicists, who would be filling the boxes at the theater that night, Hugo organized a nonviolent insurgence of his own. He gathered his loyal disciples as a "Romantic Army," dressed in eccentric costumes to vex the classicists and to announce themselves as a new artistic force to be reckoned with. Wearing his long hair over the shoulders of a crimson waistcoat (the color of defiance), Gautier led these aestheticized "troops" toward shocking the conservative audience and imprinting an indelible image in French cultural history.[14]

In *Optiques: The Science of the Eye and the Birth of Modern French Fiction*, Andrea Goulet posits that 1830 is also a particularly important year in the evolution of French literary models, calling it "a marker for the advent of modern visual culture."[15] Certainly, Goulet is not alone in arguing that this specific period in time marked a revolutionary point in artistic and visual models. In "Modernizing Vision," Jonathan Crary asserts that by the 1820s there emerges "a model of autonomous vision" that privileges "the body as a visual producer," collapsing the previous perspectival models of vision just as it begins to equally "collapse the distinction between inner and outer upon which the camera obscura depended."[16] Goulet understands this visual epistemology as "a sort of protophenomenology" that maps itself onto the development of modern fiction; her literary analyses focus largely on the realist literature of Honoré de Balzac, whose multivolume collection depicting French society through the first half of the nineteenth century, *La Comédie humaine*, saw its first volume published in 1830. Indeed, nineteenth-century French writers like Baudelaire were cognizant of Balzac's gift for visual, material observation and its translation into his literary work. Baudelaire asserts that the author's most admirable contribution to the French novel's evolution is his ability to animate his characters with his own vitality and ardor, making him a subjective observer turned "visionary" author."[17] Yet Baudelaire makes these considerations of Balzac's literary trademarks in order to illustrate how they get far surpassed by those of Théophile Gautier, to whom Baudelaire's essay is devoted; though Balzac's art finds itself inspired by the muse of modern society, Gautier's muse lives in a more ethereal world.[18]

Ethereal because, to borrow from Baudelaire, Gautier represents an earlier yet no less archetypal painter of modern life. He renders modernity through an aesthetic of resurrection, which produces, or reanimates, images more alive than art itself. A liminal artist, Gautier offered a perhaps irrationally yet directly proportionate relationship between past and progress—ancient and modern art—through the still–ness of female sculpture-cum-mother of man's photographic subjectivity. Gautier's most magical and vivifying turns in fiction exist, as one might expect, in his *contes fantastiques*. Young writers disillusioned by France's politics, like Gautier and friend and contemporary Gerard de Nerval, found inspiration in dark Gothic forms, especially the bizarre tales of the German writer E.T.A. Hoffmann. Hoffmann pioneered tales of fantasy as generic forms that allowed for the illumination of the darker side of Romanticism while also providing a literary space for the exploration of the fantastical and the unnatural.[19] It was the perfect medium for Gautier's muse, who empowered the author to create *une seconde réalité* (a second reality) that inebriated his readers, capable of resuscitating defunct cities and resurrecting the dead.[20] The literary powers Gautier wielded in the service of an ethereal muse were so fantastic indeed that the female figures he reproduced repeatedly over the century were equal parts earthly and extraterrestrial, artificially generated and generating women quite specifically made of stone. Gautier and many of his contemporary writers were particularly fascinated with "stone women," which appeared in vast numbers in the nineteenth century "as antique examples of the ideal feminine."[21]

In an autobiographical essay, Gautier acknowledges his Pygmalionesque propensities toward painting, admitting that "the first female model did not seem beautiful, and disappointed me singularly, inasmuch as art renders nature most perfect. . . . As in this first impression, I have always preferred the statue over the woman and marble over flesh."[22] Indeed, Gautier's writings obsessively returned to this foundational mythology for artistic subjectivity; at his death, he left unfinished a fantastic ballet named *La Statue amoureuse*, "a scenario in which a statue of the goddess Venus comes to life before the sculptor who has professed his love for her," a clear descendant of a lineage of animated statue works of the Romantic era, such as *La Fille de marbre* (1847) and *Néméa* (1864), both ballets by Arthur Saint-Leon.[23] Though Gautier's statuary predilection inflected the desire for a time-honored solidity of stone, it also assimilated itself to more modern and specifically visual, fleeting forms of aesthetic representation. A comment oft reproduced as emblematic of the author, Gautier famously remarked that he was a man for whom, above all, *le monde visible existe* (the visible world exists)—a sentiment Oscar Wilde will importantly reproduce for his own by the end of the nineteenth century.

Originally published in two parts for the *Chronique de Paris* under the direction and mentorship of Balzac, "La Morte amoureuse" tells *une histoire singulière et terrible*, but it begins—like many good acts of mourning, or of cinema—at the end. Romuald, the tale's narrator, answers an anonymous demand of his fellow *frère*, to know whether or not he has been in love. Indeed he has, but his love affair already lost, the male speaker must resurrect his dead love, *la morte amoureuse*, as a fantastical vision—a memory from the ashes: "My story is a strange and terrible one . . . I scarcely dare even now to disturb the ashes of that memory. . . . I remained a victim of a most singular and diabolical illusion" (5). Romuald laments the aftereffects of this diabolical romance from the very beginning of his tale: "Poor country priest though I was, I led every night in a dream—would to God it had been all a dream!—a most worldly life, a damning life, a life of Sardanapalus" (5–6). The poor priest is thus equated to the subject of a painting—specifically, Eugène Delacroix's *La Mort de Sardanapale* (1827)—from the onset.[24] Delacroix's painting depicts the last king of Assyria as he peers apathetically upon his subjects, mainly nude women presumably from his harem. They are about to be set ablaze and murdered in a decree set forth by the king himself, who will also die by his own hand now that he faces military defeat. The scene of the painting is both maniacal and orgiastic, leading Delacroix's Romantic generation to reflect on Sardanapalus as a libidinous lunatic. But in his preface to *Mademoiselle de Maupin*, published at about the time he was writing "La Morte amoureuse," Gautier tells his reader to be wary of such judgments on virtue: "I would prefer to give, like Sardanapalus, that great philosopher who has been so misunderstood, a handsome premium to the man who should invent a new form of pleasure. . . . *Mon Dieu!* What an idiotic thing is this alleged perfectibility of the human race that is being dinned into our ears!" In "La Morte," Romuald will become a carbon copy of Sardanapalus, a man who partakes in the sensual delights: woman, wine, and other licentious activities. And though interpreting this structure traditionally would lead us to assume that the woman represents the profane, wickedness may be closer to godliness than one might expect within the realm of Gautier's fantastic. While the male figure is equated to a painting, the emergent female figure will be the invocation of "a new form of pleasure" in the visual and aesthetic realm. This oscillation between ineffective forms of "good" and "evil" gestures toward the literary uncanny, often characterized by an ambivalence equivalent to the seemingly contradictory poles of monstrous and ideal conjured up by Gautier's chimeric ideal—or, more relevantly, between real and illusion.

We must use the term "uncanny" in a pre-Freudian way here because he would not lay claim to it by way of his explorations within the "fertile province" of aesthetics and literature until 1919, when he illustrates its function through his reading of E.T.A. Hoffmann's equally Pygmalionesque story "Der Sandmann" (1817).[25] According to Freud, what the uncanny presents, foundationally, is the meeting with something that is both familiar/*heimlich* and unknown/*unheimlich*—an encounter that produces an acute form of anxiety because the uncanny takes the *shape* of something that has undergone repression and since reemerged from it. Gautier's fantastic tales, however, perpetuated the idea of the chimera as an ever-reversible myth of differential mimesis, and thus a deformation of literature in the face of newfound, precinematic technologies. In French, the word *fantastique*, from the Greek *phantasticus*, means "to make visible" or "to have visions."[26] Gautier famously strove for an illusory, aesthetic ideal that he aptly coined *la chimère*, the word's contradictory meanings matching the uncanny quality of his fantastic fiction. Born from the name for the Greek mythological creature with a lion's head, a goat's body, and a serpent's tail, a chimera came to connote a variety of grotesque monsters across centuries of literature and painting. In seventh-century England, the word adopted a wholly different character, meaning "imaginary," "fanciful," "visionary," and "ideal." In a figurative sense, however, a chimera can be any number of things with an incongruous composition.

Automatic Woman: Seeing Is Believing

In "La Morte amoureuse," Romuald discovers the object of his affection, and Gautier's *chimère*, when, during his ordination ceremony at Easter, he lifts his head by chance and finds a woman. Virtually close enough to touch, Clarimonde it seems was actually at a "considerable distance": "The charming creature appeared in bright relief against the background of that darkness, like some angelic revelation. . . . What eyes! With a single flash they could have decided a man's destiny. They had a life, a limpidity, an ardor, a humid light which I have never seen in human eyes; they shot forth rays like arrows, which I could distinctly *see* enter my heart" (10–12). On a day when a Christian subject should be the mirror through which the divine is reflected, Romuald instead succumbs to the brilliant, penetrating eyes of a competing female presence, revealing man's "destiny" and seeming to "flash" like the bulb of a camera—a perverse substitute for the vows Romuald is meant to take in the same instant. Gautier overturns the ritualistic necessities of the Christian faith and replaces God with the equally captivating yet distanced cult of *beauté*—now hybridized within a photographic unconscious.

To be historically specific, gentleman scientist Joseph Nicéphore Niépce spent the 1810s and 1820s trying to reproduce and render permanent the images seen in the back of the camera obscura. Around 1816, using sheets of silver-coated paper, he successfully reproduced a nonfixed photographic image that he called a "retina," essentially a negative that vanished in broad daylight. Turning to light as the essence of the photographic infrastructure, Niépce experimented into the

1820s with all sorts of chemical compounds to discover their (re)action in light, including resin of Gaïacum and, with more success, bitumen of Judea—a natural tar used in antiquity. He called the process *héliographie*, writing of/with the sun, and in 1827 officially captured what many consider the world's first photograph. In some respects, Gautier's description of Clarimonde functions as an afterimage of Niépce's discovery of heliography in the decade prior. Struck by her "radiating light," Romuald closes his eyes in order to "not be influenced by external objects," as if he were the sheet of pewter resisting an image's sunlight etching. Yet upon reopening his eyes, he "still beheld her, all sparkling with prismatic colors, and surrounded with such a penumbra as one beholds in gazing at the sun" (10).

Indeed, Romuald recounts the bizarre events that compose his story of lost love through portraits of the woman, or the lovers, that operate like protocinematic scenes, or even as "stills" that are sutured together to offer the illusion of (narrative) movement. Film is as much about the interruptions between frames as anything, and the fantastic the irruption of the supernatural within everyday life; the two modes mesh in this tale of artificial generation, "La Morte" functioning as an early screen text.

Gautier's mysterious *femme* turns out to be either angel or demon, or "maybe both," the juxtaposition serving to prove the woman is certainly not human and therefore not subject to the ravages of time.[27] Pointedly, the story tells us so, that "assuredly she never sprang from the flank of Eve, our common mother" (12). The immediate anxiety Romuald experiences upon this *boulversement* of time wherein "every successive minute seemed [to me] at once but a second and a century" signals an eminent danger and a break in the literary narrative—and, perhaps, a breakaway from the literary realm and into a primitively cinematic one (13–14). The fear directly overturns the order of time, or at least causes it to still, just as photography does, and now one minute resembles not only a second but an eternity (of image preservation) as well.

Here, instead of raising his eyes to God, Romuald lifts his gaze and catches sight of a different figure of immortality in the form of Woman in/as film. And if she embodies an artistic ideal, it is far more potent than that which is accessible in a simple poem or a painting, in troublesome excess to any notion of genre, or literature itself. As her name suggests at its French root, Clarimonde epitomizes the light of the world, usurping the position of the Divine in his own house. The fate of Gautier's country priest is that he has become the "plaything" of a seemingly cinematic *illusion magique*, a woman cast through the darkness "in bright relief," "herself radiant, and radiating light," like a projector or an image on-screen (10). Romuald's slowly warming discovery that his exceedingly lively love is for an inhuman "dead one" is made in what seems to be a death chamber, wherein "a bluish flame flickering in a bronze pattern filled all the room with a wan, deceptive light, here and there bringing out in the darkness at intervals some projection of furniture or cornice" (19).

The female figure in "La Morte" becomes a dialectics of the unconscious, photographic optics of Gautier's *fantastique*. Romuald admits to knowing woman not as a subject but as a thing (*quelque chose*); he can only comprehend woman as a representation, admitting, "I knew in a vague sort of way that there was something called Woman" (8). Upon the eve of his ordination, Romuald gets initiated into, in the words of Walter Benjamin, "the principles of the art of seeing," entering into "a covenant with his eyes" with the mysterious Clarimonde, an invocation of the book of Job 31:1 (9). Romuald metaphorically acquires the faculty of sight not in the service of spiritual enlightenment but as an internal figuration of the artist and a delusion that mimics the spectator's positionality in the early dioramas created by Daguerre. No doubt that Gautier was creating within his literature, through his ability to resuscitate dead cities in palpably visual ways, a space strikingly similar to how Daguerre—who started out as a professional scene painter for the theater—used painted pictures as the backdrops for his early dioramas. A precinematic medium that arrived in Paris around 1822, the first dioramas created a binary experience that led spectators to become an essential component of the "scene," often strolling through the ruins of an ancient city unable to discern between reality and illusion. They also gave rise to darkened auditoriums perfectly paralleled with Clarimonde's dark chamber in "La Morte." Hereafter, Romuald gains the power (*puissance*) of artistic vision as an unconscious figuration of a photographic eye and, seemingly, the control of an all-seeing spectator. Every detail of the feminine figure emerges instantly, and not inconsequently, at the very moment he mentally forgoes the possibility of permanently sacrificing self to the worship of an inexcusably invisible God. Instead, Romuald lifts his eyes for the first time, shocked into the ability to create a visible world all his own, "as though scales had suddenly fallen" from his eyes, "like a blind man who unexpectedly recovers his sight" (10). Romuald is born into "a new order of things" by an automatic woman likened in the story as "a singular optical effect"—performed by actions either unconscious or occult, nonetheless wedded to the emerging technologies of the period. The allure of mechanical imagery comes not just from the illusion of reality it provides but rather from the way that new media create new visions.[28] Clarimonde opens portals to Gautier's second reality—a seeming precursor to Surrealism and its obsessions with female muses like Gala and Gradiva, as well as the cinema—wherein suddenly life makes itself visible to Romuald under a totally novel aspect. In other words, Romuald starts to see somewhat cinematically, born into this new dis-order of reality, things now seemingly under the sway of the female as projector and projected image.

Like Gradiva for the Surrealists, Gautier's *revenante*, Clarimonde, operates as a symbolic mediator between real and illusion, and as the inciter of man's newly fortified vision in the aesthetics of modernity. A literary screen woman, she represents unearthed civilizations as the premise for a perceptual phenomenon emerging at the advent of photographic reproduction. Indeed, at the turn of the twentieth century, Freud takes German author Wilhem Jensen's *Gradiva* (1903) as the privileged text to demonstrate the revival of desire; his essay "Delusions and Dreams in Jensen's *Gradiva*" illustrates the effects of taking classic archaeology through the intermediary of literature as a model for the formation of psychic identity, a probing into the realm of the unconscious. In Jensen's text, subtitled "Pompeiian Phantasy," young archaeologist Norbert Hanold, previously sheltered by his "science" from the living female sex, is instead only interested in women made of stone. Hanold retains the belief in the reality of a dream wherein he encounters a light-footed female sculpture come alive on the very site (and at the very moment) of the destruction of Pompeii.[29] This "being in love" with something "past and lifeless" reanimated symbolizes "an echo of his forgotten childhood memories," ultimately revealing the unconscious economy of the mind. Most notable, though, is the sense of delusion inherent in the Gradiva figure, and specifically in Hanold's anxiety dream of her.[30] Indeed, the animation of Pygmalion's sculpture into a woman directly resembles the unconscious confusions between life and death, animate and inanimate inherent in the Gradiva myth.[31]

In the ordination scene of "La Morte," we can trace the invocation of the Pygmalion myth, but in reverse—the uncanny reversal of animation in Gautier's Clarimonde. Let us consider the full trajectory of her visual development in the text:

> She was rather tall, with a form and bearing of a goddess. . . . she seemed a diademed queen. Her forehead, bluish white in its transparency, extended its calm breadth above the arches of her eyebrows. . . . There was a delicacy and pride in the regal outline of her nostrils bespeaking noble blood. Agate gleams played over the smooth lustrous skin of her half-bare shoulders. . . . As the ceremony proceeded the features of the fair unknown changed their expression. . . . Never was deeper anguish painted on human face than upon hers. . . . the mother bending over the empty cradle of her child, Eve seated at the threshold of the gate of Paradise. . . . All the blood had abandoned her charming face, leaving it whiter than marble; her beautiful arms hung lifelessly on either side of her body as though their muscles had suddenly relaxed, and she sought the support of a pillar for her yielding limbs almost betrayed her. (11–18)

The male literary subject literally vivified through this self-manufactured woman, Gautier illustrates an immediate, entropic exchange that occurs between the two. As the blood drains from Clarimonde's face, rendering it as white as a statue's, Romuald experiences a new surge of life, "rising within me like a subterranean lake, expanding and overflowing; my blood leaped fiercely through my arteries" (21). This scene not only emphasizes the power of the gaze but also illustrates vision as an exchange of vitality, a question of entropy. Literally, woman has been subsumed into art, turned into stone in some strange gender reversal of the

Medusa effect. At first, he resists the desires awakened within him by the *fascinante*—she who visually captivates or, here, almost literally captures—and follows through with becoming a priest. On a nightmarish evening while asleep at his new presbytery, Romuald is awakened by a monstrous messenger who delivers the newly appointed priest to the confines of Clarimonde's deathbed. In an attempt to avert the arousal of temptation, Romuald refuses to look at the dying body of his beloved, seemingly in fear that her death might be transferred: "Without daring to cast my eyes upon the bed, I knelt down . . . thanking God that He had placed the tomb between me and the memory of that woman" (38). His desire is not to see but to be blind and, instead, fix the (idea of) woman in memory, letting her stay sanctified in death.[32] But just as soon as he believes he has escaped his seduction, when he thinks that averting his eyes has saved him, something literally starts to stink: "That chamber bore no semblance to a chamber of death. In lieu of the fetid and cadaverous odors which I had been accustomed to breathe during such funereal vigils, a languorous vapor of Oriental perfume . . . floated through the tepid air" (38). Rather than invoke fear and anxiety regarding death, this smell—an intoxicating fragrance of the Orient and the intrusive sign of the fantastic—suggests other worlds and seductions.

Other worlds and seductions were a feature of life for French authors of the time. Controversy over the opium trade in the nineteenth century led to increased awareness of the use of intoxicants in Europe, especially in the form of opium (morphine), as well as hashish and cocaine. Gautier was no stranger to the drug economy in this age of intoxication, documenting his personal experience with hashish and opium in Le Club des Hachichins (1846), a piece written for the fittingly titled *Revue des deux mondes* about an elite group who would gather to discuss experiences and experiment with hashish, first brought back to Paris after Napoleon's expedition to Egypt in 1798. French physician Jacques Joseph Moreau credits himself with introducing Gautier to cannabis, and through him an introduction was made to other literary greats like Hugo and Baudelaire, who were also members of the club.[33] Gautier further testified to his familiarity with the drug through his fantastic tales, like La Pipe d'opium (1838), in which the effect of opium creates a communal relationship between two lovers made impossible without the aid of the intoxicant. But while many authors found themselves resorting to artificial stimulants as recourse to the active imagination—insistent on the "visionary" quality they produced in their literary work—Gautier eventually parted ways with the group after a dozen or so sessions, ironically insisting that one only needs "natural dreams" to create, rather than the influence of any artificial agent.

Opium use, in particular, has a long and transnational history. Egyptian civilization promoted the use of opium as a sleep aid, and the ancient Greeks had numerous gods that were portrayed wreathed with or carrying poppies, including Nyx (the goddess of night), Thanatos (the god of death), and Hymnus (the god of rest and oblivion). Egyptian Pharaohs were even buried with opium artifacts. Introduced into England by the Romans, opium extract was later made into morphine, named after Morpheus, god of sleep; the term finds its origin in the Latin *somniferum*, which means "sleep bringing." In "La Morte," sleep performs the same task as an intoxicant, evidenced in Gautier's repetitive image of Romuald getting drunk after "gorgées du sommeil," which consequently stimulates dreams in which Clarimonde is the main attraction (101). The intoxicant not only is essential in the transcendence of reality and the evocation of the ideal but also proves to be a fundamental component to literature itself. Specifically, fantastic fiction often uses sleep as a necessary frame story for the representational dreams of ancient Egypt. Gautier uses literature as an opiate replacement in the way it opens up the space for readers to exist apart from the material world and insert themselves into his second reality, which in some sense already dictates itself as a copy.

Gautier manifests another "second" reality in his fantastic tale "Le Pied de momie" (1840), which blends the representation of the ancient ideal with that of the cabinet of curiosities, the visual subject matter of Daguerre's earliest exhibited daguerreotype. In this story, a man visits a bric-a-brac shop where he purchases the mummified foot of an Egyptian princess for a paperweight; after bringing it home, he becomes aware of a vague whiff of *parfum oriental* that titillates his olfactory senses, an intoxicating scent that even four thousand years could not dissipate, the heat of the room warming scents like bitumen and myrrh "in which the *paraschistes*, who cut open the bodies of the dead, had bathed the corpse of the princess."[34] The *parfum oriental* emitted by the mummified foot here, the scent of the embalming herbs, re-presents the exotic scent pervading Clarimonde's death chamber in "La Morte." It is the smell of that which preserves the lifelikeness of the dead—embalming fluid, an odor that, like ancient Egypt itself, has the "solidity of granite" (*solidité du granit*).[35] Like the scent emanating from her chamber, Clarimonde proves stronger than both the edicts of religion and the edicts of time, indicating that this final farewell coincides in the literary with the moment of enchantment.[36] Scent, as Benjamin affirms, "is more privileged to provide consolation than any other recollection . . . because it deeply drugs the sense of time."[37] As much as she promises an eternity of love to Romuald in the church, the vision of her in the most perfect *immobility* seduces him into a world of eternal life as never-ending death, a death that cannot be escaped because of its eternal presence: a stench that never goes away.

This scent not only allows the narrator to ascend consciousness in the real, rendering him separate from the mortal world, but also causes him to split from himself. In Clarimonde's death chamber, Romuald lets "a sigh of regretful anguish" escape only to have it return: "It seemed to me that someone behind me had also sighed, and I turned around to look. It was only an echo" (39). Like Ovid's Narcissus, Romuald does not even recognize that the sigh of regret that echoes is his own. Instead, it seems to come from a mysterious other. The reader of Gautier, like that of Ovid, finds themself confronted "with the rather puzzling image of a speaker who does not hear himself speak" when his sigh is echoed back in its sameness.[38] No simple repetition, instead this suggests a splitting of consciousness, something previously repressed coming back to life. Hilda Nelson discusses Gautier's penchant in his fantastic narratives to explore *l'anéantissement*, the sensation of getting rid of the subject's "I" in order to allow otherness to surface.[39] Gautier plays with the contradictory situation of being and not-being in this sense, and in this scene. Indeed, the echo does not need to come out of the embodied Clarimonde, in the way that Ovid has Narcissus's words Echo-ed from his female counterpart. Romuald believes mistakenly that it is the echo of someone else before he realizes that it is his own voice that reverberates.

The doubling of Romuald's sigh signals a splitting of subjectivity, the echo of the sigh representing the unconscious, or even desire in general. Desire and speaking consciousness have had a problematic relationship, it seems, from the first encounter of the lovers in the church. The fascinating conundrum there was that Romuald has a mouth that cannot utter words because Clarimonde controls them, yet she does not have a voice to physically utter them. Clarimonde's lullaby, the intoxicating hymn of a seemingly maternal sort of love, flows out of her eyes and an invisible mouth, plunging Romuald into a state of horrid delirium wherein his words are rendered invisible as well: "Though fully awake, I felt like one under the influence of a nightmare, who vainly strives to shriek out the one word upon which life depends" (15). The sudden presence of Woman, as idealized object, has stripped Romuald of the ability to be his own speaking subject; despite being ready to renounce God upon the sight of her, he cannot utter the words to deny his holy pledge. He has become a horror film spectator, writhing in agony over the impossibility of helping the victimized on-screen.

Even more interesting, the dialectical tension arising between Romuald and the female figure portends that which occurs between spectator and screen image, the illusion of fullness on-screen of which the spectator is not realistically a part. In addition, the conflation between the phantom figure and her life-giving properties—offered through the seemingly entropic exchange in the ordination scene—is evinced later in the nineteenth century through the numerous names used for marketing archaic cinematic projectors. For instance, Charles Francis Jenkins projected what is oft considered the first motion picture through what he called a Phantoscope, which also comes from the Greek root *phan-* meaning to make visible or to appear, bearing similarity then to all manner of ghostly visions and imperatives: phantoms, phantasmagoria, and, of course, fantastic fiction. The Phantoscope was the first projector to allow for each still image to be projected long enough so that viewers could register the pictures individually while still enjoying a fluid moving representation. After further development of the technology (and a rift over the rights), Jenkins and his financial partner, Thomas Armat, created what was then called the Vitascope, after being sold to Thomas Edison and marketed as his "greatest marvel," an improved version of the Phantoscope that uses light to cast images. Herein, these all too similar inventions bear the same etymological trace and afterimage of Gautier's own life-giving ghost.

Love among the Ruins

Gautier introduces France to its first "vampire femelle," according to Jean Bellemin-Noël, an instrument of eroticization that turns a priest, in the span of three mysterious nights, into a libertine.[40] When Romuald presses his lips against Clarimonde's, a kiss we fear (and he hopes) has come too late, Clarimonde opens her eyes and sighs in equivalent measure to his earlier one. As if resurrected and brought back to life, she envelops him in her arms, a mother unwilling to let go. Her invitation for him to sleep on her bosom brings itself to fruition through the power of the stench, inebriating Romuald to the point where, fully intoxicated, he faints on the chest of "la belle morte." After an episode that lasts three immeasurable days, Romuald lies in his bed in the presbytery, unable to speak and without memory of the time lapse (99). With a voice like the Last Judgment's trumpets, his church mentor, Abbé Sérapion, warns Romuald that "the great courtesan Clarimonde" had died at the close of an "orgy" akin to those at Cleopatra's banquets. He acknowledges that she is the figurative generator *of stories*: "There have always been strange stories told of this Clarimonde. . . . They used to say that she was a ghoul, a female vampire; but I believe she was none other than Beelzebub himself" (48). The *undead*, an organizing metaphor for the disorganization of narrative space and time, equates here to the ghostly return of that which refuses to die. The vampirism located here operates more as a functional screen for the quest for immortality, indeed, an incredibly and equally seductive concept.[41]

Despite Sérapion's warning, one night soon afterward Romuald submits himself to the luxurious intoxication of sleep. After barely the first "sips" of sleep, Romuald is revisited by Clarimonde in a space that intimates a dream, and for the three years that follow, he lives a double life as priest of a country presbytery and as a "jeune seigneur," residing in Venice as Clarimonde's lover. Yet, their amorous, vampiric relationship takes on a symbiotic quality more like that of mother and child than partners—giving and taking desire, love, and blood in seemingly equal measure. She whispers to her supposedly unconscious lover before pricking/penetration, "Sleep, my only treasure . . . my child! I will do thee no harm; I will only take of thy life what I must to keep my own from being forever extinguished" (68). Rather than aberrant, their relationship is characterized by an essential reciprocity, their lives intertwined just like the "two spirals entangled" that represent his "bicephalic life" (61). Jean Bellemin-Noël claims that this reminds us of what we thought we had forgotten: that all the first relationships with the maternal body have a secret structure that places them under the sign of reciprocity, or interpenetration.[42] Clarimonde epitomizes the forgotten primal mother, the figurehead of battling man's ever-present fear of inevitable death.

It remains difficult, however, to accommodate the fullness of the mythological vampire, considering the delicate nature of Clarimonde's blood acquisition. With the aid of a mirror reflection, Romuald realizes that his lover taints his wine with some sort of intoxicating powder in order to induce a deeper sleep so she may drink his blood. Pretending to have drunk from his cup, Romuald remains conscious, permitting the witnessing of his (supposed) victimization. He sees that Clarimonde's bloodletting is downright civilized, done using a delicate, golden pin she pulls from her hair. The reader finds this form of exsanguination shocking precisely because it is so gentle; rather than invoking violence, Clarimonde truly makes her blood conquest a tender endeavor. She performs the procedure with gentle kindness, accompanied by her own tears when in fear of causing him harm. We must, then, ask ourselves the very rhetorical question that Sérapion poses to Romuald—in what century are we living?—to discover that Clarimonde's power hails not only from her evocation of the past as a visual present but also from her disconnection with the temporal firmament. What initially appears to be a vampire story turns out to be something much more.

The origins of the vampire myth lie in the cults of ancient civilizations; more specifically, there exists a compelling link between vampires and their source, Egyptian mythology. Accordingly, the vampire trope is already a copy, simply another disguise that hides from view what Clarimonde really represents: mommy, but, more important, mummy. Although Nicholas Daly suggests that Gautier's "Le Pied de la momie" was one of the first stories to explore the fictional possibilities of the mummy, "La Morte amoureuse" opens up the same space of Egyptian eroticism four years earlier. While sources that discuss "La Morte" as mummy fiction and/or Clarimonde as a mummy are limited to nonexistent, it seems unavoidable given Gautier's repetitious, fictional encounters with ancient Egypt in his writings through the 1850s.

In accommodating the "importance of interpreting signs by presenting archaeology as a matter of reading,"[43] we discover that "La Morte," though written before ancient Egypt became his powerful and overt muse of choice, provides strong precedent for Gautier's later preoccupation with the mummy as trope and the creation of a literary, and almost literal, model akin to what art historian Aby Warburg called "the afterlife of antiquity."[44] Avid believers in the afterlife, Egyptians regarded death simply as a change of (bodily) matter: the human body would metamorphose into its spiritual double, which dwelled with the mummy in the tomb after the body perished. Gautier accomplishes his own literary metamorphosis by aesthetically reanimating the dead woman, "La Morte," in order to resurrect her as modern muse, as *revenante*, or she who returns—an animated corpse. In fact, almost the entirety of his literary project may be devoted to this reversible rendering of the woman as objet d'art in the same spirit that Pygmalion carves his ivory girl. Everything is put in place to describe the woman into immobility, as in a painting, and render her comparable to an inanimate object.[45]

Revisiting Clarimonde on her deathbed, we may unbury further significance of the mysterious archaeological space. The Oriental perfumes that pervade the room suggest the scent of embalming fluids, like the scent that emanates from the mummified foot in Gautier's "Le Pied de la momie." The scent signals the disorder of the supernatural and causes an immediate intoxication that borders on delirium. Not only does it effect Romuald's change of mental state but this fragrance of revitalization, conversely, becomes the stench through which the story literally begins to go to hell:

> The air of the alcove intoxicated me.... My arteries throbbed... and the sweat poured from my forehead in streams, as though I had lifted a mighty slab of marble. There, indeed, lay Clarimonde.... With her, death seemed but a last coquetry. The pallor of her cheeks, the less brilliant carnation of her lips... her beautiful hands, purer, more diaphanous, than the Host, were crossed on her bosom in an attitude of pious rest and silent prayer.... I do not know whether it was an illusion or a reflection of the lamplight, but it seemed to me that the blood was again commencing to circulate under that lifeless pallor, although she remained motionless. (41–43)

Our earlier interpretation of Romuald's echoing sigh over the body of Clarimonde as evidence of a splitting self remains valid, but the scenic details—the Oriental scents, the woman's body "covered with a linen wrapping of dazzling whiteness," her hands crossed "in an attitude of pious rest"—suggest something other than the deathbed of a mortal or a coffin for a vampire's repose. God has not put the tomb between the two lovers after all, as Romuald hoped. Instead, his voice has seemingly echoed through the hollowness of this architectural void as tomb.

Romuald's arduous journey into this room is an archaeological voyage, a tomb raid that leaves him face-to-face with a mummy. If Clarimonde originates from someone other than Eve, she belongs to Mother Egypt, representing Isis, "the Goddess from whom all becoming arose," with a causal link to Cleopatra, Isis's most infamous priestess.[46] The cult of Isis became enormously popular under the Roman Empire, which used her figure, through scriptures and hymns, as the archetypal model for the Virgin Mary. Accordingly, this invocation of an eroticized encounter with the mummified body of a figure linked to Isis puts Romuald in contact with the highest Mother, an ideal exalted by its prehistorical and archaic character. Essential to the Egyptian death-rebirth cycle, Isis can guarantee immortality as she represents time incarnate.

Modern, literary representations of ancient Egypt in the nineteenth century often utilized its mystery as mirror image of the self, or as a thematic possibility for the re-creation of self through archaeological metaphor.[47] After three days in an unconscious swoon, Romuald escapes the deathbed scene with a life now split in two. His next three years are spent in limbo between two selves, priest and lover, perpetually unable to discern where reality begins or illusions ends. His entire existence now bears a hallucinatory quality. At first, Clarimonde may have captured Romuald's gaze as the *fascinante*, but returning to the scene, we realize that as *revenante* she has also left on him a different mark: "As I was about to cross the threshold a hand suddenly caught mine—a woman's hand! I had never till then touched the hand of any woman. It was cold as a serpent's skin, and yet its impress remained upon my wrist, burned there as though branded by a glowing iron. It was she. . . . My face presented the wildest aspect imaginable; I blushed and turned pale alternately; dazzling lights flashed before my eyes" (18). Clarimonde represents the hybrid femme fatale, part seductress and part serpent, in a perverse return to the most archaic of female demons. One of the oldest symbols of female power and divinity, as well as the sacred animal of Isis, serpents were considered immortal because they were believed to renew themselves by shedding old skins. The quality of immortality promised by the undead vampire transfers to the serpent, Egyptian symbol of immortality as regeneration and infinite resurrection. Clarimonde may, above all, reproduce herself, automatic then in both ancient and modern mythological senses.

The representation of ancient Egypt in such fiction becomes "vampiric" in character; it "breaks into the present and lures the souls of willing victims into the past," just as the serpent-woman here hearkens back to the myth of the lamia, the foundation for the modern conception of the vampire.[48] In Christian tradition, lamias were spoken of as snakelike she-devils, witches able to transform themselves into snakes. But the original concept of the lamia turns up within the Egyptian tradition.[49] A precursory figure to Isis, Neith has become synonymous with all sorts of beginnings, proved through one of her metaphoric monikers, Self-Made. Associated with primeval water and the invention of mummification, Neith preemptively evokes her own birth. That is to say, she invented birth, and so her own creation remains unrevealed and unknowable. Neith symbolically imparts the same ideal that sparked most of Gautier's literary endeavors—to create a singular artistic engagement with beauty through literature that plays out as a male artist's immaculate, and deceptively modern, conception. One may then sterilize the messiness of birth as equivalent to the disarray of the modern world, the bending of desire under the weight of common drudgery, by invoking a beginning as pure and ancient as that of the goddess Neith. As the importance of matrilineal descent declined in ancient Egypt, so too was Neith worship suppressed and eventually driven out of the land, a symbolic parallel to the abjection of the archaic mother. In "Le Fétichisme dans l'amour," Alfred Binet suggests a transposition of the fetish from religion; from the word *fetisso*, the fetish can be viewed as the enchanted object that held sway over individual destiny, *fatum*. And, as Baudelaire declares in his essay on Gautier, the taste of beauty is for him a predestined fate.[50] The mummy and its relation to the Egyptian deities directly represent these parameters of fetishism; as Freud admits in *Moses and Monotheism*, the mother deities were probably developed in order to compensate for the limitations placed on the matriarchy.

The "impress" left on Romuald, as if burned there by a branding iron, produces trouble seeing—or, to be more emphatic, the troubling anxiety of seeing, an unconscious ciné-optics that emerges here and replaces God as a structure of belief. Film theorist Christian Metz proposed the cinema as a system of belief, and that it, like Romuald's relationship with Clarimonde, offers the feeling of directly witnessing "an almost real spectacle," that the filmic mode is that of presence and thus "to a great extent it is *believable*."[51] What is fairly real is that Clarimonde imprints Romuald in the same way, according to Metz, that a photograph imprints something that was but no longer is.[52] Clarimonde's "dazzling lights," like a camera, flash before his eyes. Romuald is correct that her death chamber is nothing of the sort; instead, it represents the dark chamber of the camera obscura, and he operates as the light-sensitive surface, upon which the transitory nature of modernity may be rendered momentarily still and visually splendid.

Mummy fiction opens up a space in which fantasy, part image and part object, is "allowed to enjoy momentary ascendancy over the subject, only to be expelled from the narrative."[53] Within this literary space the fetishized mummy, a threshold figure for the living dead, offers a narrative strategy for exploring the oscillation of gender as well. Romuald's immortal love is for a woman whose real nature is covered up and already expelled, a woman who is *nature morte*.[54] In *Creativity and Perversion*, Janine Chasseguet-Smirgel remarks on how the "practice of embalming, by the Egyptians in particular, exactly produces a fetish. Make-up is applied to the putrefying body, which is then decorated with jewels, dressed up with a golden mask, and made into a god."[55] The mummy rises above nature and into the realm of art by masking her natural (dead/unnatural) qualities and going under the cover of makeup. Such artifice, according to Baudelaire, presents us (or the poet at least) with the most dependable method of overcoming the cruel hideousness that nature has to offer, cosmetics and fashion as means toward "a sublime deformation of Nature, or rather a permanent and repeated attempt at her *reformation*" (33). All the practices adopted by women to "make divine their fragile beauty" immediately approximate the human being to the statue, for Baudelaire, and become a "kind of duty" women have to devote themselves "to appearing magical and supernatural" (33). Being made up, by that which Gautier calls "la toilette éternité" in *Le Roman de la momie*, further disguises the fact that female figures in his works are not only invoked from the past but also dead.

The immobility of the woman painted into a frame, mummified or chiseled in marble, grants aesthetic preservation from the feared decomposition of the body. It is also death, which does not discern on the basis of gender, that the mummy as fetishized object is meant to combat. As Elisabeth Bronfen asserts in *Over Her Dead Body*, the body of the dying woman becomes "a cipher for the mutually constitutive relation between decomposition . . . and representational composition (as re-composition of the ultimately absent, decomposed body)."[56] In his literary development of the cult of the visual, Gautier conceives his aesthetic of resurrection by perversely reviving the dead as emblematic of the ideal, an ironic reversal of art's vampiric effect.

Feminine Supplements

There is mention of only one "woman" in "La Morte" before Clarimonde—Romuald's mother. In the church, when he admits to knowing only vaguely that there was such a thing called "woman," Romuald continues by explaining that he was "of perfect innocence. Twice a year only I saw my infirm and aged mother" (8). Marked by a sterile quality, his experience with his mother must be buried; now that he prepares to enter the brotherhood, his earthly connections with his mother must be suppressed. In the realm of psychoanalysis, which Gautier's literature prophesies by decades, the mother figure evokes an equivalent problematic for the boy child who must escape the castration complex and enter into the state of normative heterosexuality.[57] One perverse possibility for the boy to reject this threat of his own castration, as mirrored to him through the sight of the mother's already castrated genitals, is to endow a substitute object and symbol (a fetish) with the value of the phallus, which he cannot do without—thus, to overcome sexual difference with a visual (feminine) supplement.[58]

Gautier resuscitates his own foot fetish—the most popular—in "Le Pied de momie," wherein he doubles fetish objects, the mummy's foot taking on meaning only inasmuch as it remains already fractured from the woman's body. The narrator purchases the embalmed foot of the divine princess Hermonthis in order to own a piece of her to use as a paperweight, evoking a charmingly bizarre effect. Permanently detached from her body, the relic takes on a "special" and spectral life of its own, forced to define itself in terms of market value. After the apparition of Hermonthis appears with only one foot, she requests the other to keep herself "intact." But her severed limb informs her (yes, it talks!) that such an exchange will prove impossible, telling his princess that he has already been bought and paid for. Of course, the time-traveling young Hermonthis does not have the five louis to purchase the foot and rectify her fractured corporeal state; she cannot barter by modern terms, but she does find other means. Instead, she literally takes the narrator by the hand and, together, they return in time to visit her father, the Pharaoh. As the narrator recounts the beginning of the journey, "The Princess Hermonthis still held my hand, and graciously saluted the mummies of her acquaintance." Here, too, the female character makes time travel possible, mutating temporarily, and overturning reality in favor of the possibility of a fantastic voyage, made in order to unearth this objet d'art. The princess's predicament of not owning her foot is representative of mastery over desire: the narrator promises the Pharoah that he will give back her foot if, in exchange, he can have her hand (in marriage), a part that becomes highly invested with equal, fetishistic value.

Written at approximately the same historical time as "La Morte," Gautier's *Mademoiselle de Maupin* too "is full of the cultivation of the superficial, of logical relationships that move horizontally, not vertically, from art to art, or among variations of a theme, or with tantalizing instability between two poles: male and female, living and dead, flesh and fabric."[59] Originally intended to be a historical novel about the real-life cross-dressing French opera starlet, the book later gets characterized as a literary treatise of a heroine whose transvestism makes possible the transgression of heterosexual imperatives. The figure of Mlle Madelaine de Maupin acts as narrative strategy, an exploration of the literary possibility of a "third sex" as she identifies, who has the body and soul of a woman, the spirit and strength of a man. In fact, Gautier frequently employs the word *chimère* in the novel not only to represent male protagonist d'Albert's dream of rendering tangible and "ours" this elusive mistress Beauty—"to possess you, to actually be you"—but also to describe this third sex, directly linking the desire to produce an aesthetic ideal by way of excavating the female relic into the impossible dream of gender fluidity (169). As d'Albert plainly admits, "My dream, a chimera, would have to be both sexes in turn, to satisfy this dual nature" (318). Naomi Segal contends that the novel is exceptional for a number of reasons, most notably because "it sets forth with unusual frankness the man's desire to be a woman."[60]

In "La Morte," the new life that Clarimonde allows Romuald to live is the enchanted life of an image-fetish, "in reality an afterlife, like the survival of an embalmed corpse."[61] If the male protagonists of Gautier's supernatural tales want to know the ancient world, it is the artificial woman who brings him into the "Kingdom of Mothers," according to Natalie David-Weill, to the place where time is immobilized.[62] In "La Morte" the pair of lovers embark on a journey, one night unspecified in time, which greatly resembles the one undertaken by Princess Hermonthis and her young French suitor in "Le Pied." Clarimonde fetches Romuald from a deep sleep (or, perhaps, from within the dream procured in a deep slumber) in order to embark on a journey to a faraway land, to begin their life together as libertine lovers in Venice. Interestingly enough, before they can depart, before he can enter a world dominated by love and leisure, Romuald must change into clothes presented to him by Clarimonde. Once he is dressed, she holds up a Venetian mirror and asks him what he thinks, to which he reflects: "I was no longer the same person, and I could not even recognize myself. I resembled my former self no more than a finished statue resembles a block of stone. . . . I was handsome, and my vanity was sensibly tickled by the *metamorphosis*" (58, emphasis mine). This Venetian mirror essentially reflects back to Romuald the statuesque image of his newly formed self.[63] Just as the real woman disappears behind the disguise of makeup, here the clothes literally make the man—"The spirit of my costume penetrated my very skin"—while Clarimonde watches with an air of maternal pleasure over he who becomes her artistic product, *son oeuvre* (59).

Into the Dust: Doubles, Desexualization, and Disintegration

Baudelaire famously claimed that Gautier was unique, *sans doublure*—a word that is used in modern times to denote one's stand-in or body double in cinematic endeavors. The double, which has an inevitable connection with mirror reflections, functions originally as an insurance against the destruction of the ego. In "The Uncanny," Freud would later directly illuminate the connection between the theme of the double and the Egyptian mummy. "This invention of doubling as a preservation against extinction," Freud acknowledges, links the "same desire [which] led the Ancient Egyptians to develop the art of making images of the dead in lasting materials."[64] This desire produced the very idea, then, of mummification in the spirit of self-preservation. Gautier uses the other, the Orient—and his aesthetic mistresses as fetishistic surrogates, newly mated with mechanized visions of the early nineteenth century—to escape modern, quotidian life and as an unconscious mechanism for a second reality, in and of seeing.

Yet this resurrection of the Egyptian body implies a grander liaison between the sexes as well. The *ba*, the physical manifestation of the deceased, was often depicted as a bird with the head and facial features of the deceased party, with no implication as to the sex of the person. Freud observes the "androgynous structure" of Egyptian goddesses, distinguishing that this "combination of male and female sex characters, was an attribute not only of Mut but also of other deities like Isis and Hathor . . . like Neith of Sais . . . all these hermaphrodite divinities are expressions of the idea that only a combination of male and female elements can give a worthy representation of divine perfection."[65] Freud makes similar claims in his study of Leonardo da Vinci when he observes the young boy's childhood fantasy of vultures. The resultant totality, like the fetish, guards against the inevitable awakening to sexual difference by the young boy (like da Vinci in Freud's study) who recognizes that "the penis could be missing," a revelation that "strikes him as an uncanny and intolerable idea."[66] Gautier too learns to duplicate himself, to abandon himself to the chimeras of his imagination that appear as a dangerous sort of vertigo—"un vertige dangereux"—prefiguring my discussion in chapter 5 of Alfred Hitchcock's *Vertigo*.[67]

The metamorphosis of Romuald that begins with his first transgression in the church develops throughout the story as the fantastical journey of a priest who lives a double life as libertine fop. Fantastic literature, indeed, proves particularly suitable for the task considering the additional etymology of the "fantastic," which has also been used historically to describe someone foppish in attire.[68] The artificial reproduction of woman functions as the catalyst for a more important alteration of gender: the exposure of the femininity of man. Literary female supplements, like Gautier's *fascinante* Clarimonde, assume the role of figment of the artist's fascination insomuch as he may map this bewitching femininity onto his own body within the safe space of literature. By the end of the tale, Romuald can no longer recognize himself, not only because he has been refashioned by the female figure (literally dressed in her clothes) but also because he looks like one, admitting to being both materialized and feminized—perhaps one in the same—in the same instant.

Throughout his literary career, Gautier would frequently conjoin archaeological objects and metaphors with the dandified/artificialized male subject. Gautier depicts Lord Evandale, the protagonist in *Le Roman de la momie* (1857), as conforming to the rules of the highest dandyism oddly enough at the very moment he crosses the threshold into the mummy's tomb, the perversions of fetishism and narcissism intertwining. This might make perfect sense, considering that "psychoanalysis understands fetishism as a complicated and particular form of defense against reality . . . a perceptual denial of the difference between presence and absence . . . it is often extended to a denial of differences of all sorts, including those between organic and inorganic material and between living and dead people."[69] In "La Morte," Clarimonde represents a buried, aesthetic ideal as well as a desexualized yet hetero-sexed figure for the archetype of origins, mother Eve. Here, Romuald's perceptual desire to see and reproduce her extends into the creation of his own self-image, or his birth of self—his mirror stage, as it were. The female figure, or Other, functions as the screen through which man validates his own narcissistic importance inasmuch as she reflects "the fantasy of an idealized corporality located at the very intersection of the differences between the sexes."[70] Romuald dresses up in clothes that refashion him as his feminine other, as one of the resemblances sought in modernity's modes of artificial generation: man's very resemblance to woman.

Gautier's archaeological/literary exploration of the Egyptian landscape resurrects antiquity as both temporal firmament and safe haven through which the male subject may seek solace from his anxiety-ridden modern existence. In his book *Le Regard de Narcisse* on the works of Gautier, M. C. Schapira proposes that Gautier's trademark and this combat between good and evil are coupled, through imperceptible allusions, by another struggle—the recognition of an originally divided self.[71] Ironically, *singulière*, the most repeated word in "La Morte," gets seemingly nullified in lieu of the fact that no facet of this "unique" story remains sacred: Gautier uses the same duplicitous formula for most of his fantastic tales, implying that these dreams of stone might be more universal than exclusive. Although not set in Egypt, Gautier's "Arria Marcella" similarly, and perhaps more blatantly, exposes the intersection of literature as (both public and private) archaeology and psychoanalysis by the agency of yet another past-dressed man (*homme vêtu à l'antique*). In the story, Gautier again uses the resurrection of the ancient world as the preferred means of dissolving the burden of modernity, overcoming the flow of time and attaining life in the literary possibility of finding oneself face-to-face with one's "retrospective" chimera. Arria Marcella, the female figure in the story, resembles Clarimonde quite literally at the level of Gautier's repetitious language, both described as cold as a serpent's skin, or the marble of a tomb. Like Romuald, Octavian finds the uncharted disorder bewitching: "I do not know if you are a dream or a reality, a phantom or a woman . . . if I am the plaything of a prestigiously vile sorcery, but what I do know well is that you will be my first and last love" (199–200). We might call the literary connection between the search for the aesthetic ideal and the birth of the modern subjectivity herein more blatant, at least retrospectively, because the ideal woman who haunts the imagination of Octavian rises from the ashes of Pompeii, like Jensen's/Freud's/Dali's Gradiva. Reviving this ruined civilization symbolizes what would become by the end of the century, in terms of psychoanalysis, the attempt at reifying the already psychically fragmented subject. Gautier did not have access to any consciously psychoanalytic vocabulary, but his narratives often journeyed into the dark, ancient recesses as a representation of what Freud would later name the unconscious. And for Freud, "Archaeology and psychoanalysis announce the same fundamental paradox: each is a way of engaging and articulating what remains alive—in effect immortal—and continues to determine our humanness, yet seems dead and buried and lost forever, permanently forgotten."[72]

In his musings in the essay "Photography and Fetish," Christian Metz believes it necessary "to consider psychoanalysis as the founding myth of our emotional modernity."[73] If we are reading "La Morte" as if it were a pre-Freudian case history, it terminates with the inevitable return of the sense of loss and mourning that characterized the story's opening. This might be the most telling aspect of the story's predisposition to what would later be known as the unconscious, and specifically a ciné-optical unconscious. As Jacques Lacan would later theorize through his seminars and writings, the process of psychoanalysis is much like Orpheus's quest into the underworld. He represents psychoanalysis "less as the discovery of the lost secrets of the unconscious," as Freud does with the archaeological metaphor, and more as "the endless re-discovery of the unconscious *as lost*," a past that "dis-members."[74]

At the end of "La Morte," Abbé Sérapion mutates into a diabolical, almost inhuman figure, set upon combating Clarimonde in order to restore Romuald to the living, to remove him from the phantasmagoric world of the prearchaic cinema of his mind.[75] When the two men venture to unearth Clarimonde's unholy grave, in quite the reversal of expectations, the monstrous refracts itself upon the male figure of authority: "There was something grim and fierce in Sérapion's zeal . . . his great aquiline face, with all its stern features, brought out in strong relief by the lantern-light, had something fearsome in it" (73). As he catches sight of the "impure courtesan" who is specifically referred to as a "corpse" here, Sérapion—in an act Romuald calls an abominable sacrilege—throws holy water on her, causing her previously statuesque body not only to be dismembered but, more specifically, to actually disintegrate. Her body crumbles into "dust," becoming "a shapeless and frightful mass of cinders and half-calcined bones" (75).

In medical discourse and Egyptian mummification, the transformation of her body into dust carries a powerful connotation. Indeed, the final scene of the story suggests an entirely new economy and a metaphor of incorporation markedly divergent from the trope of vampirism. If Sérapion can be considered as a medical figure/analyst, we must also regard him as a doctor administering another type of cure—mummy as remedy. As early as the sixteenth century, fraudulent cadavers, or contraband mummies, were plucked from their graves on Egyptian soil and brought to Venice (the site of Romuald and Clarimonde's mysterious liaisons) to be sold to Europe on the black market, so that European people could cure their myriad ailments with the superior properties a dead body would offer a living one.[76] The broken fragments of mummies were often made into powder and administered as a cure for diseases as varied as epilepsy and cataracts. It seems that the mummy became misappropriated as medicine, the powder of dead bodies being used to cure living ones, due to various lapses and misunderstandings in translation. In fact, the translation of the work of the familiarly named Arab physician Sérapion the Younger (1070), who wrote at length on the use of *mumia* (a word that later became the English term for "mummification") as medicinal cure-all, became one of the main reasons for this misunderstanding that resulted in medical treatments all the way through the nineteenth century.[77]

When the bones of Clarimonde's body crumble into dust, we not only confront the image of a once well-preserved, now immemorialized death but also must read the desiccation of her bones as Romuald's cure, and the necessity of her ruin to modern artistic representation. Abbé Sérapion must disintegrate the bones of woman in order to "cure" man of his perversion, satisfying the Promethean desire to strive toward an aesthetic ideal. The eater—Clarimonde as a metaphoric "drinker of blood and gold"—becomes the eaten in this perverse parody of an antidote. Romuald is left as the mourning, material double of this dematerialized woman, interiorizing her as if her dust impregnates him with his own "vast ruin" (75). And he leaves his *frère* with this final piece of advice: "Never gaze upon a woman" (76). The spectacularity of "La Morte" lies in Gautier's uncovering of woman in/as archaeological object: his conception of modernity held not within the ruins of a city long buried but in the ruin of woman internalized in and by man.

Waking the Dead

By the middle of the nineteenth century, early photography used the dead as its main subject matter; Niépce's first engravings on pewter were image reproductions of Jesus and the Virgin, and the long exposures necessary for the completion of Niépce's earliest heliographs, which often took upwards of twenty-four to forty-eight hours of development, meant the "still" subject could be seen more sharply than a living one. These "stone pictures," early photographs "appeared larger than life," according to Hillel Schwartz, "iconic faces burned for hours into sacred stone: bitumen of Judea."[78] From the original still-life photographs, later by Daguerre, a clear trajectory develops to the foundational use of thanatography prominent through the Victorian era. These deathbed photographs were often a person's only, and final, memorialization; the body would be propped up, rendered cosmetic with rosy coloring, or even had eyes painted on in order to give the dead subject the illusion of life in their final moment captured. Other important genres of early photographs include spectral photographs, where phantoms were seemingly rendered visible through the photographic exposure, or "hidden mother" photographs, where a barely obscured mother would be seen in the background, possibly wrapped in fabric (mommy as mummy, of course), so that the child operated as the main subject of the photograph.

In the decades following the publication of "La Morte amoureuse," Gautier became an unlikely advocate for another art form that combined the still image and the illusion of life. Invented in 1861 by François Willème, photosculpture emerged as a cutting-edge technology "whose function it was to mass-produce statues and statuettes" through volumetric photoproduction.[79] His photosculpture methods required a multiplicity of the model's profiles, mimicking the mechanical multiplicity, or adherence to the copy, that characterized many of the period's technological advancements. A complicated process that requires the participation of five artists and technicians, photosculpture reproduces a model, plastic or living, as a statuary in relief. In an article in the *Moniteur universel* (1864), Gautier argued against then popular opinion to assert that this new method of sculpting with light would allow the artist to unveil the ideal more readily than traditional methods. Now, Gautier recognized, is a time to leave the bright rotunda for the dark room where such photosculptures could be miraculously made, the product of what he called the "wonderful eye" in what operates like a virtual camera.[80] Using language reminiscent of Narcissus's story in Ovid, he grants photosculpture the privilege of attaining an aesthetic ideal he was already motioning toward in his *contes fantastiques* of the 1830s onward: "That this ancient dream of fixing the fleeting image in the mirror would have been realized was already marvelous enough . . . but the sunlit sculptor! The disconcerted imagination refuses to believe such a prodigy."[81] Consciously acknowledging these photographic means, which he considers near magic, Gautier's aesthetic concerns over *singularité* translate into the unique ability to copy, mimic, and aesthetically reproduce in such a photographic fashion a statue whose original does not exist ("une statue dont *l'originale n'existe pas*," emphasis mine).[82]

Retreating to Willème's photosculptural methods, modern media scholar and theorist Alexander Galloway constructs a broad critical engagement in cybernetics and "parallel media." In his 2012 talk at the Winchester School of Art, "The Cybernetic Hypothesis," Galloway advances an alternate history of cybernetics that uses photosculpture as a landmark development from which we can chart a "genealogy" that illuminates the ways in which time and space become automated, helping us understand modern information models and three-dimensional imaging.[83] The infrastructure of what is selected and what is repressed in these different kinds of historical media becomes the groundwork of a cinematic mode of mediation too, despite Galloway's theory lending to a pre-cybernetic mode of visual analysis. Friedrich Kittler's theoretical variations actually lean more directly toward cinema and the inherent connections he saw between discrete units of electronic imaging and the narrative segmentation of film.[84] Kittler also believed that the positions vacated by Romantic writers who worked in fantastic fiction—as I contend that Gautier was one of the most preeminent—were soon to be filled by the cinema and its screenplay writers, who would convert such imaginary realms into reel appearances on the cinematic screen.[85]

The next chapter will continue to chart our own "genealogy," focused on the work of French author Auguste Villiers de l'Isle-Adam, a man who Gautier rejected as a real-life son-in-law, yet who nevertheless became Gautier's aesthetic disciple.

2

Book of Genesis

The Villi-fication of Woman in *L'Ève future*

The story of Thomas A. Edison and his Eve-of-the-future, Auguste Villiers de l'Isle-Adam's novel *L'Ève future* (1886) represents modernity's book of genesis, a re-generation of the biblical Eve under the auspices of modern technology. Behind both narratives is an almost identical premise—to create a righteous companion for man. And while Eve's body is generated from Adam's own rib, the body of Villiers's future Eve is equivocally man-made. In creating his future Eve, Villiers's Edison uses modern technologies he invents and advances, notably phonographic and photographic recording devices, as a somewhat satirical means of creating a more agreeable companion to address male psychic needs. Through these ever-constant creation fantasies, the male artist may psychically reverse the adverse effects precipitated by original sin and may access a literary refuge from the ever-fragile state of being human, born of woman. Deviating from the traditional embodiment of woman as daughter of Eve, Villiers's novel presents the reader with the incongruous composition of a prehistorical figure (Eve) and a modern, futurized "woman" (future Eve). The book not only develops a new and improved copy of a woman who resembles man and who is *reproduced* rather than reproducing, but also simultaneously establishes a modern, female symbol derived from an archetypically mythic and primitive woman.

Accordingly, this chapter engages first with the most striking and apparent paradox on which the novel is predicated, the incredible transformation of both sexual and temporal difference into "une similitude éblouissante," a stunning likeness (84). I examine how Villiers uses Edison as propagandist for man's collective desire in the nineteenth century to reclaim an Eve-of-their-own, one who reflects their proper desires at this particular cultural moment. The concept of a technologically produced likeness of life—*une vivante reproduction*—embodies the main theoretical thrust of the novel, causing it to act as a historical precondition for modern, cinematic projection, preconditioned through the figure of the artificial woman.

Literary Genealogy and Technological Reproducibility

> The garden like a lady fair was cut,
> That lay as if she slumbered in delight
> And to the open skies her eyes did shut;
> The azure fields of heaven were 'sembled right
> In a large round, set with the flowers of the light,
> The flowers de luce, and the round sparks of dew,
> That hung upon their azure leaves did show
> Like twinkling stars, that sparkle in the evening blue.
> —Giles Fletcher

Conventionally, an epigraph might function as an inscription, placed at the beginning of the text in order to direct and authorize a reading. In *Deviant Modernism*, Colleen Ramos writes, "Like the inscriptions on monuments and coins, epigraphs declare the text's lineage, for the epigraph's power to frame or orient the interpretation of the text is the result of its claim to reinscribe the intentions of the [poem's] 'first' author."[1] *L'Ève future*'s litany of epigraphs offers Villiers a strategy by which revolutionary, literary reproduction is staged. Although born of a lineage of male-authored literature, Villiers's novel also becomes its own origin, a cornerstone text in the representation of artificial generation, both part of this important, cultural lineage and the imperative on the process of creating new ways of being.

Villiers opens the first chapter of *L'Ève future* with the preceding epigraph, a stanza from Giles Fletcher's long allegorical poem "Christ's Victory and Triumph" (1610). Though epigraphs were commonly used in nineteenth-century literature, one becomes aware instantly that *L'Ève future*'s first epigraph is *too* common and, indeed, that Villiers's exploitation of the literary device merits closer attention. Nadine Satiat, the editor of the novel's Flammarion edition, informs us that as readers we may be experiencing a case of déjà vu, and not just the customary recognition of an epigraph's original source text. Rather, it seems plausible that Villiers consciously committed to purloining the epigraphy; he inscribes not from the original poem's stanza inasmuch as he re-presents a selection of Fletcher's poem that had already been made into an epigraph by

American author Edgar Allan Poe. Satiat footnotes that indeed, Villiers borrowed the citation from Poe, who had used it as an epigraph for his story "The Domain of Arnheim," a text Villiers most likely read in Charles Baudelaire's translation of it in *Histoires grotesques et sérieuses*.[2] Though by definition an epigraph is already a replication of a selection of text, Villiers re-repeats the very gesture of inscription by appropriating an epigraph that had already been made memorable by Poe as an epigraph. Villiers's inscription is not extracted directly from the original text but from Baudelaire's translation of Poe's inscription of Fletcher's stanza. It is a copy (of a copy of a copy) of the original.[3]

In further defiance of expectations, Villiers's novel does not rely on this sole epigraph to frame the text as a whole, unveiling another reproductive dilemma. Instead, each chapter has its own introductory inscription. Written in seventy-four chapters constituting six books, the novel presents an assemblage of seventy-six epigraphs from a veritable array of sources: literary texts, proverbs, and philosophical and religious treatises.[4] The epigraphs range widely in intent as well as source. Some are quite specific and poignant, extracted from the primary text (for instance, book 4, chapter 4's "And it's hard work being a beautiful woman!"—Charles Baudelaire). Others are oddly vague, oftentimes employing ellipses to indicate the idea's sweeping, open-ended nature (for instance, book 1, chapter 13's "A nothing . . ."—A common phrase). Some epigraphs even present difficulties, according to Villiers's biographer A. W. Raitt, regarding their credibility (for instance, book 1, chapter 14's "You have devoted friends: still . . . if you turn your back?"—Goethe).[5] Even more striking, then, is that Villiers's novel challenges the very potential of a first author through its reliance on a monstrous multitude of literary authorities. A labyrinthine text, *L'Ève future* announces itself as a riddle on the structural and narratological level from the onset, radically calling into question the very idea of a textual origin by epigraphically reinscribing the authority of so many "first" authors.

This heterogeneity of epigraphic citation is countered and paradoxically complemented by what Villiers proudly called the "homogeneity in the composition" of his novel. Despite the book's multitude of textual precursors, Villiers intended to make its theme rather circumscribed and unique. To present *L'Ève future* as homogeneous in any way may seem anomalous, even this early in the discussion. To address this seeming contradiction, and to better understand what he means exactly by "homogeneity," I offer the letter written to Jean Marras in 1879, in which Villiers boasts of the novel's development in its early stages, a work whose publication he believes will "create something of a sensation." It "will chill the blood and storm the citadels of dreams! Never, never would I have believed myself capable of so much perseverance in the analyses!—of so much homogeneity in the composition, of so much astounding imagination, things, the new and magnificent evocation of which no one before me, do you hear, has dared to attempt."[6] Despite Villiers's grandiloquent tone, this letter reveals that, instead of being a consequence of composition, the unique "sensation" produced by the novel is rather its precondition. Villiers seems most exhilarated and perhaps fulfilled by the fact that he, as author, was able to reproduce such "an avenging and brilliant book." The prolific reproduction of epigraphs snatched from such an assortment of mostly male-authored texts acts as a barely concealed expression of Villiers's submerged anxiety of reproduction.[7] The use of a borrowed epigraph, as well as the profusion of epigraphs in general, emblematizes the notion of perverse, literary reproduction—the enigmatic question at the very heart of *L'Ève future*.

After years of struggling for literary validation in Paris, Villiers made his breakthrough with *L'Ève future*, the idea for which originated in a short story entitled "Miss Hadaly Habal," published on an unknown date before he began to compose the novel.[8] In the winter of 1878–1879, Villiers worked incessantly and under some extreme financial hardships on the now book-length project, under its striking, original title, *L'Andréïde paradoxale d'Edison*. Villiers managed to "create something of a sensation" in the original title, or at least the "magnificent evocation" of an entirely new word. Although the French word *androïde* existed over centuries to connote a creature made in man's likeness, Raitt maintains that Villiers pioneered the neologism *andréïde* to connote a specifically female, technological being. The word *paradoxale* used to modify the noun undoubtedly proves superfluous, for the etymology of the word *andréïde* demonstrates the most rebellious and inescapable paradox of the novel. From the prefix *andro-*, meaning "male," and *-oid*, meaning "like" or "having the nature of," this word signifies a being that resembles a man, but is not. The modifier *paradoxal(e)*, a feminized adjective to modify a feminine noun, indicates this being is female. The etymological turn of the word *andréïde* reveals that Villiers's literary creation acts as a modern substitute for the autochthonous woman who resembled man, usurping the female reproductive function and artificially generating it as an aesthetic mode.

L'Ève future rests upon many philosophical paradoxes, but the greatest is the faulty premise of similitude, or homogeneity, between male and female (desire), mythologized through God's first human creations, Adam and Eve. Rather than resign itself to the authority of its literary patronage, the novel uses epigraphic intertexts to prepare for its ultimate disobedience to the traditional concept of paternity as symbolized by mankind's first author, God. By the time Villiers's text was serialized in *La Vie moderne* in 1884, he had given the story an entirely different and more evocative title, *L'Ève future*, to indicate that his anomalous literary creation springs forth from Eve, Western religion's prototype of woman. As the book of Genesis dictates, God creates man in his likeness, "formed . . . of the dust of the ground, and breathed into his nostrils the breath of life; and man became a living soul."[9] In effect, this makes man the first-order reproduction of God's image. However, soon thereafter, God realizes that "it is not good that the man should be alone" and decides to create "an help meet for him."[10] God puts Adam to sleep in order to take his rib and "made he a woman and brought her unto the man."[11] God subsequently determines that Eve "shall be called Woman because she was taken out of Man."[12]

The borrowed epigraph at the onset of *L'Ève future* thus acts as a figuration of Eve in the Garden of Eden—a distorted replica. Daring to make an autonomous decision to eat of the Tree of Knowledge causes Eve to fail at resembling man on the level of desire, as it seemed was God's intent. And so, Eve comes to signify a miscarried attempt at man's perfect similitude. As a second copy of God and a distorted duplicate of man, she becomes a symbol for sin in Christian theology and Western mythology. Villiers's novel directly confronts the myth of likeness between man and woman by acknowledging that man's companion, although fabricated from his own body, inversely becomes an entirely other species. Woman, like Villiers's first epigraph, symbolically represents a copy with no compulsory reference to its original. In the novel's preface, Raitt contends, rather than fear measuring his work against the grand myths, Villiers wanted his text to reflect man's rebellion against God.[13] All the allusions to diabolical pacts that Villiers reiterates in his epigraphs, and within the primary text, establish the framework for the narrative—that what is at stake in this techno-literary enterprise is the entire human condition. Rather than invoking distance, the theoretical complexity of Villiers's relationship to literary history and mythology—the novel's lineage of artifice, and its relations to the generations that came before and that follow—actually serves to heighten the humanity behind what seems to be a most inhuman story.

When the story begins, inventor Thomas Edison receives an unexpected visit from his British friend Lord Ewald. Despondent, Ewald is on the verge of suicide because he has fallen hopelessly in love with the singer Miss Alicia Clary, his heart locked in "the pillory of this freak" (44). Attracted to her because of her resemblance to the divine marble of the *Venus Victrix* statue, Ewald soon discovers that her apparent mystique conceals little more than her loathsome materiality. Ewald confides to Edison, "I recognized, myself, though too late, that this was a sphinx without an enigma" (38). Edison offers his latest scientific invention as a cure for Ewald's dilemma; in his underground laboratory, Edison has created an *andréïde*, a new Eve, and he proposes to bestow her with the outward appearance of Ewald's beloved Alicia. He urges Ewald to postpone suicide for three weeks in order to wait for the completion of this Ideal-as-woman. Edison details the scientific principles behind the creation of the *andréïde* Hadaly over the course of the first half of the novel. Through the use of technologies at his disposal, Edison replicates Alicia's likeness and transfers it to his invention: the principles of photosculpture allow Hadaly to take on Alicia's physical likeness, while two gold phonographs reproduce Alicia's voice, in recitation of a catalog of words composed by male artists over the course of history. Edison acknowledges that Hadaly's creation can be easily and rationally explained. Though nothing but a "Being in Limbo," ultimately Hadaly will become magical in her value, "an unexpected human relic" that will renew hope for humankind (181).

Edison admonishes Ewald for not being aware that his love for Miss Alicia Clary is nothing but an illusion—overpowered by her beauty, Ewald desires nothing less than a "phantom"—and so Edison suggests to him, why not trade "illusion for illusion," expelling Alicia's troublesome otherness in favor of Hadaly's obedient artificiality? Edison establishes the stakes behind his Faustian challenge; if Ewald dares, he can affirm the very "being" of Hadaly, just "as you affirm the being . . . of all the illusions that surround you. And then you will judge in your own intimate conscience." Edison continues, "whether this auxiliary Creature-Phantom which leads you back to the love of life doesn't really merit the name of HUMAN more than the living specter whose sorry so-called 'reality' was never able to inspire you with anything but the desire for death" (68). Here, Villiers ruptures the category of the human, revealing the intricate relationship between man and his mechanical Eve. Villiers alludes to the fact that to understand our own humanity we must paradoxically measure ourselves against the nonhuman, or the posthuman. This revelatory reaffirmation of life reflected by the nonliving will renew Ewald's desire to live—at least momentarily.

At the end of the novel, seduced and duped by Alicia's charms yet again, Ewald comes to discover in horror that this ever-more-convincing Miss Alicia Clary is none other than Hadaly, a more sublime representation of the original. But as one might expect, happiness does not ensue. Instead, the novel ends on a final note that makes definitive its thematic resurgence against a higher paternal power, emphasizing the inevitable futility of such attempts at amending nature and the divine order. Aboard the steamer the *Wonderful*, Ewald and Hadaly leave America to begin their life together in Scotland. Tragically, the ship catches fire and Hadaly perishes. Alicia, also a passenger, dies when the lifeboat meant to bring her to safety capsizes. Edison learns of the story from the newspaper, and his disenchantment is cemented when he receives a telegram from Lord Ewald. In it, Ewald tells Edison that he cannot withstand the loss of the archetypal Hadaly and bids him a final and definitive "Adieu."[14] Indeed, the novel's final gesture reveals to Edison that he could never have succeeded in replacing God's divine creation with his own, and the book ends with an immense and interrogatory silence.[15]

(P)reproduction: The Manufacture of History

The first line of the novel reveals what, besides literary language, grants the internal authority to reconfigure the myth of Adam and Eve in the realm of future possibility—electricity: "Twenty-five leagues from New York, at the heart of a network of electric lines, is found a dwelling surrounded by deep and quite deserted gardens" (7). Rather than endow divine light as the creator and source of the novel, Villiers forges history anew, thwarting God in favor of Electricity, the most omnipotent power of the industrial age. In the original French,

Villiers's use of the phrase "fils électriques" is a camouflaged yet still compelling demonstration that the power of redemption belongs to the new generation—modern, electric sons taking over the role of God. The word *fil* objectively indicates a wire used as an electric conductor, but in the plural the word *fils* means son.[16] This reading is further bolstered by the male surnames in the story—Edison, meaning "son of Edward," and Anderson, from "son of Andrew"—which emphasize lineage and paternity. By the same token, *L'Ève future*'s first line of text visualizes Edison's home in Menlo Park, New Jersey, "a dwelling surrounded by deep and quite deserted gardens," as the site of modernity's new and improved Eden. Villiers conducts the reader outside the hubbub of New York along these very *fils électriques* to the source of their electrical power, pausing before the plot commences in order to display the inventor and his surroundings. Once inside the gates of his veritable compound, we find Edison solitary and pensive, almost godlike in Villiers's depiction of him. But as Villiers warns in his "Advice to the Reader"—prominently situated before the novel's dedication "To the Dreamers, To the Deriders"—the "modern legend" operates as something "distinct from anything existing in reality," not "the engineer, Mr. Edison, our contemporary," but "above all 'The Sorcerer of Menlo Park'" who belongs in the literary world as a symbol (3). Although readers have frequently been perplexed by the novel's seemingly overt, misogynistic premise of creating a simulacrum of a woman more advantageous than the real thing, Villiers does not confine himself to turning only women into technological symbols. From the onset the author advises the reader that a speculative, literary exaggeration of Edison's mythical persona was of greater use to him than the real man himself, and that the inventor in his novel is "somewhat distinct from anything existing in reality" (3).

On the narrative level, Edison operates as a symbolic surrogate for the historian, especially at the novel's outset when he mourns the impossibility of bearing phonographic witness to landmark events in history. In *L'Ève future*'s third chapter fittingly titled "Les Lamentations d'Edison," Edison regrets, "What a latecomer I am in the ranks of humanity! Why wasn't I one of the first-born of the species?" (9). Although Edison hesitates to make any direct gestures of usurpation toward God, affirming the "life-creating cliché *Fiat lux*!," he complains of his powerlessness over both capturing and validating history, moments that have since "fallen forever into the abyss" (9, 10). Edison intermittently dreams of historical phenomena that his phonograph could have recorded and thus preserved: for example, the trumpets of Jericho or the "morning melody of Memnon" (10). But of all the historic milestones to phonographically record, Edison deems the moment immediately *preceding* the creation of Eve quintessential: "I would have been lurking behind some secret thicket in Eden—first of all that sublime soliloquy, 'It is not good for man to live alone!,'" and then 'Ye shall be as gods!'" (9). In effect, Edison's performative repetition of God's words reinstates the question concerning man's solitary existence upon his creation in order to respond with a revolutionarily different answer. Returning to the precise moment Eve can be reconfigured, the novel prepares its own enigmatic relationship with the notion of "recording," which will prove to be as paradoxical as the novel's conception of a "real" woman. Although Edison bemoans his inability to phonographically record and thus authenticate man's past, he also authorizes a rerecording of Eve, albeit one unfaithful to the original.

Edison acknowledges the impossibility of aural proof to act as reliable, historical testimony. Talking to himself—in essence, representing the lonely man in the Garden of Eden preceding the creation of Eve—Edison complains "that while the phonograph was reproducing sounds, it was unable to represent the sound, say, of the fall of the Roman Empire. It can't record an eloquent silence, or the sound of rumors. In fact, as far as voices go, it is helpless to represent the voice of conscience" (10). The phonograph alone cannot faithfully reproduce the experience of life, full of secrets and the aural void of consciousness as much as audible sound; it lacks the faculty to locate man's extralinguistic experience. In order to appease his fellow man, Edison knows he "must invent a machine that replies before one has even addressed it" (11). His presupposition, that a conglomeration of technologies would be necessary to produce the truest replica of life, appropriately foreshadows his *chef d'œuvre* of inventions, the *andréïde* Hadaly. Edison's will to simulate history mirrors his scientific project of using this "surprising agent we call Electricity" to reproduce "all the *illusion* of life" in an "Imitation Human Being" (61). Peculiarly, Edison's fulminations over being unable to authenticate history technologically prompt him to become the architect of man's prehistory. Through the proposition of an instrument (the exact "kind" of machine or techno-being remains unclear at the story's beginning) who replies before being addressed, Villiers advances a solution to nineteenth-century France's anxieties over the curious relationship between history and industrial progress. Subsequently, Villiers manufactures history symbolically by envisioning a being that quizzically repeats, or copies in the future, what has already been said in the past. One can never be too late (*trop tard*) for what will endlessly be repeated. And so, Hadaly represents the reliable capture of man's mythological history, the new Eve of Edison's puzzling, prehistoric future.

Re-production: A Virtual Impression

L'Ève future's foremost investment lies in the role played by Eve throughout literary tradition and art history, superseding any reliance on religious mythology. In one of the novel's most religiously charged scenes, Edison delivers a sermon about his ability to resurrect Eve as a profoundly new indexical sign suitable to modernity, in effect, vowing that he can offer a better solution to man's solitary existence than God did. Edison conjures "woman" neither from the earth's clay nor from man's body. Instead, he discloses the power of technology as most divine creator: "*I will duplicate the living woman in a second copy, transfigured according to your deepest desires!* I shall endow this Shade with all the songs of that Antonia described by the tale-teller Hoffmann, with all the passionate mysticism of Edgar Poe's Ligeia, with all the burning seductions of that Venus conceived by the mighty musician Wagner! . . . I promise to raise from the clay of Human Science as it now exists, a Being *made in our image*, and who, accordingly, will be to us WHAT WE ARE TO GOD" (64). Creating a woman for man through technological rather than religious intervention indicates a shift in material, from the lime of the earth from which Adam's body was formed to the man-made "clay of Human Science." This artificial genesis still coincides with that of all time, to create a companion in man's perfect semblance—a being made in one's image. Hence, to bring to life a companion based on his own handmade processes indicates that man can act as God in this chain of signification or, as may interest us more precisely, as author: the Antonias, the Ligeias, the Venuses, and the Hadalys alike operating as the symbolic daughters of Eve.[17]

Though the novel's mindful intertextuality causes us to recognize both its place within and perverse challenge of literary genealogy, the concept of perverse reproduction in *L'Ève future* encompasses nineteenth-century cultural and technological discourses of reproduction as well, Edison functioning allegorically as a vehicle for the set of modern technologies representative of the notion of artificial generation. Villiers represents Edison as a technological historian defined by the very attributes of his most famous invention, the phonograph—as a recorder. On the novel's first page, Villiers describes Edison not by telling us who he is as much as by showing us whom, or what, he resembles:

> Edison is forty-two years old. A few years ago his features recalled in a striking manner those of a famous Frenchman, Gustave Doré. It was very nearly the face of an artist *translated* into the features of a scholar. The same natural talents, differently applied; mysterious twins. At what age did they completely resemble one another? Perhaps never. Their two photographs of that earlier time, blended in the stereoscope, would evoke an intellectual impression such as only certain figures of the superior races ever fully realize, and then only in a few occasional images, stamped as on coins and scattered through Humanity. (7)

Villiers's offering of French artist Gustave Doré and Edison as "mysterious twins" implies that, despite the cross-cultural context, the two men could be of the same familial lineage. In consideration of their likeness, Villiers suggests that one could have been copied, *traduit*, from the other. The author also purports that this visual likeness extends to their occupations. One an American engineer and the other a French artist, their aptitudes being *congénères*, from the original French meaning "equivalent" or "of the same species," indicates that these seemingly disparate men evolved from the same cultural gene pool. Note that perhaps Villiers chooses Doré as Edison's mysterious twin because of their twin preoccupations with the representation of man's point of origin, the story of Adam and Eve. A French engraver, illustrator, and sculptor, Doré rose to artistic prominence after he was commissioned to illustrate a new English Bible (1866); his later works included illustrations for an oversize edition of Poe's "The Raven" and John Milton's *Paradise Lost*. Villiers may have found the artist additionally provocative here because in the 1870s, *Art Journal* accused Doré of inventing rather than copying.[18]

Submitting the quoted passage to the ill-logic of Genesis, we truly arrive in a new Eden. Villiers replaces the first couple, Adam and Eve, with a second copy of the couple in his new Edenic myth—Edison and Doré, or scientist and artist: though homo-geneous in outward gender, heterodox in their modern occupations. In Genesis, reproduction between the first man and woman is the direct result of (their expulsion from) the Garden of Eden. Here, Villiers reverses the order: reproduction can only take place inside Edison's "Eden." I would suggest that at the moment their two photographs are placed side by side in the stereoscope, producing an "intellectual impression" like the imprint of faces on money, reproduction occurs. After cultivating an interest in the new art of photography, physician, poet, and Harvard professor Oliver Wendell Holmes Sr. marveled at the invention of a process of visual representation that separated the form of objects from their physical matter, producing bodies in their "superficial aspect."[19] In his article "The Stereoscope and the Stereograph" (1859), Holmes coins the term "stereograph" to connote the three-dimensional, illusionistic photographs that had become fashionable during that decade. The stereoscopic image is composed of two pictures mounted next to each other and viewed through a set of lenses.[20] The intellectual imprint produced from the blending of the men's faces in the aforementioned passage supersedes the type of imprint made on a coin because the stereoscope specifically produces a three-dimensional image. When observing the pictures through the viewer, the pair of images merges into one because the left and right eyes see a slightly different version of the same scene. Consequently, this creates the illusion of depth necessary to imbue the image with its seeming three-dimensionality. This photographic mating of the two men's faces in Villiers's novel produces not a person but a virtual impression.

The stereoscopic image contains, in miniature, some of the questions most central to the novel; as Holmes writes, "Many persons suppose that they are looking on miniatures of the objects represented, when they see them in the stereoscope."[21] So here, to use the stereoscopic image as a miniature of the larger thematic questions at work in the novel is to again invoke the sense of mise en abyme that pervades *L'Ève future*. First, this image displaces the value and usurps the function of an epigraph, acting as the internal authority for the story. Indeed, something "like the inscriptions on . . . coins" dictates the lineage of this text, but instead of being an inscription of selected, borrowed literature, here it is more specifically an internal, technological reproduction that bears resemblance to the facial inscriptions on money.

In other words, the concept of a technologically produced likeness of life—*une vivante reproduction*—embodies the main theoretical thrust of the novel as it presents a preconditional blueprint for cinematic projection. Further, this stereoscopic image encapsulates the concept of a genealogy begotten solely by men, signaling the primary reproduction between men—that of Eve, "daughter of God and Man," as Milton refers to her in *Paradise Lost*. While myths have traditionally been generated from various classes of organic life, *L'Ève future* acts in the reverse.[22] The organic life of man aids in the creation of a new and improved generative tool—technology—that takes the helm of generating a new class of life. In this way, technology offers a site at which this symbolic staging of "generation" occurs. The term is doubled over to comprise the process as well as the product—the generating of a new generation. This conjures up the striking image evoked by the real-life Thomas A. Edison, who told a *New York Graphic* reporter interviewing him in 1878, at the time he invented the phonograph: "I've made a good many machines, but this is my baby [the phonograph], and I expect it to grow up to be a big feller, and support me in my old age."[23]

Les Fil(le)s de Milton: Daughters of Invention

At the very end of "The Stereoscope and the Stereograph," Oliver Wendell Holmes conveys his interest in technologies of representation inasmuch as they function in a far greater capacity than mere "toys" or a "charming novelty," arguing that within these very technologies a "new epoch" will emerge of "human progress," continuing to mimic the desires of "He who / 'never but in uncreated light / Dwelt from eternity' / took a pencil of fire from the angel standing in the sun,' and placed it in the hands of a / mortal."[24] These last lines come from the beginning of book 3 of John Milton's *Paradise Lost* (1667). Incidentally, Villiers's recasting of Eden as Edison's workshop in *L'Ève future* becomes consciously intertwined with the Milton reference as well, specifically in the novel's third book, "L'Éden sous terre." That Villiers sections his novel into "Books" also makes it structurally similar to Milton's epic poem. Of this book's five chapters, two of them—"Chant des oiseaux" (Birdsongs) and "Électricité" (Electricity)—commence with epigraphs from *Paradise Lost*. The epigraph that prefaces "Èlectricité"—"Hail, holy Light, offspring of Heaven first-born!"—originates from the beginning of book 3 of Milton's poem as well, the first fifty-five lines of which constitute what is commonly called "The Prologue of Light" (232, 96).[25] The setting of this part of the poem, the transition from the darkness of hell to the light of the heavens, occasions Milton to "speak of his blindness" to his readership. John Milton suffered from problems with his eyesight and by 1652 was rendered blind, presumably by glaucoma.[26] The loss of sight fully tortured Milton, but never so much as in relation to his writing of *Paradise Lost*, though luckily, his blindness did not thwart his composition of the epic poem. Romantic artists both literary and visual revered Milton as an authority not least for his thematization of artistic creation and as offering a figural representation of wisdom even at moments of (literal) blindness. Numerous Romantic poets, including William Blake and Samuel Taylor Coleridge, approached Milton and his poetry as a strategy for contextualizing their own poetic endeavors. Biographical elements of Milton's life, especially his blindness, also served as functional allusions for Romantic artistic undertakings. Many painters throughout the long nineteenth century depicted scenes of a blind Milton reciting his epic poem to his daughters, who acted as his personal scribes, notably including Swiss-born Henry Fuseli, who exhibited the "Milton Gallery" in London (1799–1800), a catalog of forty works reflecting on the author's poetic works, and Eugène Delacroix, a leading figure of the French Romantic school referenced in chapter 1, who painted *Milton dictant le paradis perdu à ses filles* in the late 1820s.

Having equally regarded Milton as an erudite literary genius, Villiers directly appropriated this recurrent Romantic theme in a Symbolist vein in a short story entitled "Les Filles de Milton," which was left unfinished and was published posthumously. About a year after the publication of *L'Ève future*, Villiers embarked upon researching and documenting Milton's life explicitly at the Bibliothèque Nationale in order to compose the story.[27] The tale, in which Villiers artistically capitalizes on Milton's blindness in a similar fashion, has a powerful and perplexing moral import for our reading of *L'Ève future*. The story commences with conversation between Milton's wife and one of his daughters, who denounces her father's vain and solitary preoccupation with literature. Milton's daughter bewails: "O vanity! To think that he imagines that this 'Paradise Lost' will endure in the memory of posterity. . . . We shall be in rags soon; but he is blind, and it is of his verses, not his daughters, that he is proud" (111). In rebellion over her father's disinclination to pay attention to practical matters, like bread for the family to eat or his own daughters' futures, she determines to no longer obey his edicts. Subsequently, Milton enters the scene, "feeling his way along the wall with the end of his cane," and demands his family scribes not change his words, and not interrupt him unless he stops himself (114). Instead of being faithful "recorders," however, his daughters are busy at their *toilettes de nuit*. When they finally commit to the task of transcription, they solicit Milton to *recommencer*, to begin anew. However, the story ends with Milton's decree that "it is too late," he has already forgotten (119). Villiers fictionalizes this recurring scenario to explicitly portray the anxiety over the potential loss of man's literary masterpieces, which are destined to fall into nothingness, *le néant*. His fear mirrors Edison's early lamentations in *L'Ève future*, echoing one of man's greatest fears—being too late, a serviceable metaphor for death. Edison deplores what a latecomer he is to man's history, pontificating on how many mysterious sounds were known to our predecessors, "which for lack of a convenient machine to record them have now fallen forever into the abyss" (10). In place of a woman who may reproduce/*reproduire*, Villiers's *L'Ève future* posits one that will record/*retenir*—just like a machine.

In the entirety of "Les Filles de Milton," Villiers's fictional Milton speaks aloud only one direct line from the actual text of *Paradise Lost*. Notably, this is the same line Villiers uses as the epigraph for the chapter of *L'Ève future* entitled "Èlectricité," "Salut, lumière sacrée, fille du ciel née la première . . ."; both his uses of the citation in French are, however, misquoted. In the context of "Les Filles de Milton," we discover that Villiers's main distortion of the citation—describing the *lumière sacrée* as a daughter, *fille* in French, rather than a gender-neutral offspring in Milton's original usage—discloses his philosophical intentions. An evident breach occurs in Villiers's story between Milton's real *filles* and the *fille du ciel* that licenses his poetic product. In the story, Milton's daughter complains that the author's pride resides with his descendent poems rather than his flesh-and-blood daughters. The poet's preference for self-generated verse over his biological heirs proves that the most exalted flesh is that made of words, that which is *printed*. Accordingly, the connotation of the word *fille* shifts, from the biological *filles de Milton* to the symbolic daughters of Milton's poetic genius, particularly Eve from *Paradise Lost*. Milton's daughters' failure to conscientiously record his masterpiece, as imagined by Villiers, may be symbolically repaired through the crafting of artificial women.

Villiers takes up a cause similar to Milton's, passed down through generations of literature and art, of defining male identity by addressing how this identity was first and continuously thereafter imperiled by its complicated and mercurial identification with woman. The second epigraph Villiers uses in *L'Ève future*, for the chapter "Birdsongs," comes directly from Eve's speech of personal subjection in book 4 of *Paradise Lost*. Although Milton envisages Eve in this speech calling Adam her "author and disposer," it is she who ultimately writes Adam's all too human future.[28] This is the precise dilemma for which *L'Ève future* extends a hypothetical resolution. In a Judeo-Christian reading of the biblical text, man's female companion directly causes his Fall from divine perfection by eating first from the Tree of Knowledge, the only act forbidden in the Garden of Eden. Milton's Adam laments his abject state as perhaps a fault of Nature, which in the creation of Eve "from [my] side subducting took perhaps / More than enough." In turn, she exhibits "Too much of ornament, in outward show / Elaborate, of inward less exact" (*Paradise Lost* [*PL*], 8.536–539). Adam admits that he succumbs to Eve's artifice, blinded by woman's seductive "ornament" worn in her prototypal state. In Milton's version of the myth, woman ensnares male narcissism on the level of being his "Best image" (5.95). Adam's misrecognition of the copy (Eve) for the original (himself) creates the impetus for Milton's literary re-creation of man's regression to his most fragile state, being human. Now bifurcated into two different sexes, male identity is uncertain, malleable, and ultimately called into question. Duped by nature, Adam senses "the link of nature drew me, flesh of flesh" (9.913–914). Forced to make woman's intentions his own causes Adam to eat the fruit, committing the same sin as his selfsame image. He tells Eve, "what thou art is mine. / My own in thee" (9.957–958). The moment of narcissism occurs transitively when Adam first gazes at Eve, compelling him to fall in love with his duplicated image, "in delight / Both of her beauty and submissive charms" (4.497–498). Adam consequently falls prey to the same fatal reflection that composed Narcissus's sin: "I now see / Bone of my bone, flesh of my flesh, my self / Before me: *Woman* is her name, of Man / Extracted" (8:494–497). However, while Narcissus commits the fault of taking his own image for someone else, Adam misapprehends inversely someone else as his own image.

It may be that Adam not only misrecognizes Eve as his "Best image" but further commits his own sin in Milton's poem: falling in love. In book 8 of *Paradise Lost*, Adam seems willing to believe in Eve's naivete, remaining steadfast in his dedication to her, despite not having what he calls "proof enough" of her character. He finds himself "only weak / Against the charm of beauty's powerful glance" (8:532–533). In fact, it seems that the copy here overpowers its original. Adam acknowledges what will prove to be his faulty urge to submit himself completely to Eve's intentions as "best" when in fact he is guided only by her perfected appearance: "when I approach / Her loveliness so absolute she seems / And in herself complete so well to know / Her own that what she wills to do or say / Seems wisest, virtuousest, discreetest, best" (8:546–550). Illogically, Milton's Adam equates beauty with goodness, or "Best image" with most virtuous intention. His falling in love with Eve, a riddle as perplexing as Narcissus falling in love with his own imago, endangers his own sense of self:

> O fairest of Creation, last and best
> Of all God's works, creature in whom excelled
> Whatever can to sight or thought be formed,
> Holy, divine, good, amiable, or sweet! . . .
> How can I live without thee, how forego
> Thy sweet convérse and love so dearly joined
> To live again in these wild woods forlorn?
> Should God create *another Eve* and I
> Another rib afford, yet loss of thee
> Would never from my heart. (9:896–899, 908–913, emphasis mine)

Within Milton's poetic re-creation, Adam yields to Eve not on the level of logic but on the level of love. However, he persists in mistakenly considering Eve a mere copy of himself by indicating the future possibility of "another Eve," another copy. In her act of delinquency, Eve makes herself a most troublesome original.

After taking "their fill of love" by sealing their mutual guilt with the act of sex in book 9, Adam alters his view of Eve considerably as a result of their newfound sexual difference, for as they "Soon found their eyes how opened and their minds / How darkened" (9:1053–1054). Accordingly, they reach for tree leaves to cover up their loins, the evocative symbol of their shameful act (eating the fruit/sex) as well as the symbol for the guilt inherent in their newfound acknowledgment and understanding of sexual difference. In the end, Adam admits to Eve that his only offense was "overmuch admiring / What seem'd in thee so perfect . . . which is become my crime / And thou th' accuser" (9:1178–1179, 1181–1182). It is possible to read Eve's ostensible perfection as one and the same with her ostensible likeness to Adam. "[O]vermuch admiring" what then seemed to Adam so perfectly congruous with his own divine creation leads to the fallacy that ends in their discord. In Milton's depiction, Eve conveniently becomes the eternal literary referent for man's fallen state.

Future male literary depictions of Eve and her daughters are subject to the fearful foundation provided by Adam's final sentiment: "Thus it shall befall / Him who to worth in women overtrusting / Lets her will rule!" (9:1182–1184). The discourse of female monstrosity born of the parable of Adam and Eve represents the flip side of divinity as well as that which divinity encapsulates, immortality. Ushering in human mortality is the most significant trespass of woman against man. Milton's Adam bewails to Eve that he "might have lived and joyed immortal bliss" if he had not chosen "rather death with thee" by partaking in her sin (9:1166–1167). God condemns Adam to return to his original state, from dust to dust. Eve's twofold punishment corresponds to her crime as well. Woman becomes indebted to bear the biological fruit of mankind and to subdue her own desire in order to reflect only the desires of her husband, or, as Genesis reads, "In sorrow thou shalt bring forth children; and thy desire shall be to thy husband, and he shall rule over thee."[29] Authorial control over the re-production of woman signifies man's attempt to regain command over his own identity, which in the nineteenth century as in ancient times is threatened by the very idea that the being made in his image is always already irretrievably different. The immortality of artistic production counterbalances, at least metaphorically, the mortality man faces since his expulsion from Eden. Villiers can simultaneously and paradoxically position Eve as both the signifier of sin and, by re-producing her in the future, the medium to psychically erase it.

The dual punishments of the Fall, death and procreation, attest to the cyclic, mortal existence forced upon humankind. Accordingly, Villiers's literary projection of the male author's *filles*, specifically their failure to accurately record and preserve, acts as a thinly veiled substitute for his anxiety regarding his own subjective point of origin—his mother. As A. W. Raitt recounts, *Revue illustré* editor René Baschet received an unexpected visit from Villiers in 1887. Purportedly arriving "pale and dramatic" over the exhumation of his mother's remains, Villiers needed money to have her reburied. To earn the 800 francs needed, he proposed the following story: "Milton, blind, is dictating *Paradise Lost* to his daughters. . . . The daughters leave the work they are doing, and go to the window to see the handsome soldiers marching past. And while they are there, the poet continues dictating magnificent lines . . . which will be lost forever."[30] Threatened with the exhumation of his mother's remains, Villiers associates the inability to safeguard her memorialization with powerlessness in the recording and preservation of history, which, like the composition of *Paradise Lost* in his story "Les Filles de Milton," would be lost without a faithful "recorder." As Modris Eksteins writes, "The Faustian notion of 'becoming' rather than 'being' became the central logic of the century, the historian became the indispensable explicator of this logic."[31] This mirrors the function of Edison in *L'Ève future*—a historian made nearly infallible with technology by his side. Mother acts as an allegorical symbol for man's recuperative history and for reproduction. But by usurping her function—by giving birth to his own mother Eve as a blasphemous Eve-of-the-future—Villiers ensures a maternal betrayal on a literary level.

Villiers perpetuates what, in the wake of *Paradise Lost*, becomes an enduring fantasy of literary parthenogenesis: he embarks upon a project of substituting aesthetic productivity in place of biological reproduction. *L'Ève future*, a perplexing book about the technological re-production of another Eve, functions as a treatise on perverse reproduction, on one hand by its protestation over a literary "first" author, and on the other hand through its rejection of a biological origin, woman as mother "Nature." Of course, Eve functions appropriately as the archetypal figurehead for biological maternity. "Woman" in Villiers's novel is transformed into "this new electro-human creature, TOMORROW'S EVE, if you will, who with the aid of ARTIFICIAL GENERATION (already much in vogue during recent years) seems destined within a century to fulfill the secret purpose of our species" (98). The novel disarticulates humankind's reliance on biological reproduction in order to instead promote artificial generation as the means to reproduce literary daughters and, through them, to unravel the secrets of our species. In fact, Villiers had exclusive information regarding the production and uses of these new technologies. A regular attendee at Nina de Villard's Parisian salons in the 1860s and 1870s, popular with the more bohemian men of letters, Villiers met and became close friends with Nina's lover and fellow member of the literati, Charles Cros, who alternated his writing of poetry, which he hoped would evoke sensations, with theoretical work in photo and sound recording: Cros authored the "original" idea for recording sound (paleophone) months before the phonograph's "invention" by Edison; he also published an early theory of color photography, another of his conceded inventions. In actuality, Cros supplied Villiers with in-depth knowledge of these technological developments that he used to bring such specific life to Hadaly's mechanical body. Notably, Cros also penned a short farce called *La Machine à changer le caractère des femmes*, and when the play was acted Villiers found himself fittingly playing the leading role.[32]

Although Villiers's novel never explicitly engages with Mary Shelley's *Frankenstein; or, the Modern Prometheus* (1818) intertextually, both novels pay homage to *Paradise Lost* as their fundamental father.[33] Like Villiers, Shelley joined the force of electricity to the aim of creating life, choosing Milton's reproduction of the original act of divine creation as the model subject for a literary birth myth, *L'Ève future* echoing and imitating the nexus of *Frankenstein*'s narrative structure, which "prepares us to confront Milton's patriarchal epic, both as a sort of research problem and as the framework for a complex system of allusions."[34] Like Victor Frankenstein, Villiers's Edison represents the creator and source of a "new species" of symbols. (No doubt, acknowledged or not, Villiers creates his novel from the germination of an idea born of woman (author).) Edison's phonograph—like the galvanization experiments that inspired Shelley to conceive of (literary) reproduction as corporal animation by electrical means—serves as an example of a technical means of representation, supplementation, and reproduction of life (voice). Indeed, Villiers embarked upon writing *L'Ève future* in the exact year (1878) that Edison exhibited the phonograph at the Paris Exposition; an article in *Engineering* that year upheld, "It is impossible altogether to resist a feeling of wonderment, recalling to one's mind perhaps the feelings of Pygmalion or the hero of *Frankenstein*" when confronted by Edison's new invention. The phonograph compelled even the general public at the time to identify its capabilities with mythical, and literary, predecessors: "Of all the startling powers of the phonograph, there is none perhaps so extraordinary as its capability of reproducing, years after, the voices of those who are no longer on the earth."[35] While Villiers believed *L'Ève future* to be exceedingly original—"the new and magnificent evocation of which no one before . . . has dared to attempt"—his Promethean endeavor, built upon a framework of epigraphs sewn together, nevertheless reflects the cobbled-together limbs of Frankenstein's dead thing, and what it comes to symbolize: the monstrous maternity of (the) artificial generation.

Most commonly used to designate a female infant or child, as opposed to the word *fils*, which means son, the French word *fille* has important, ancillary connotations. Though also used for a young woman, *une jeune fille*, in the nineteenth century the word became a popular term used for a prostitute of varying degrees. In the latter half of the century, Parisian officials established methods of registration and classification for working girls in order to manage and monitor the sex trade, which was not about to dissipate under current demand, the social anomaly profoundly irresistible for bourgeois men. For instance, many women joined a *maison de tolérance* and would become either a *fille à numero* by putting her name in the brothel keeper's book, or a *fille en carte*, given a personal registration card to present to the authorities. As Alain Corbin confirms in his book *Women for Hire*, "Registration indicated not the adoption of a profession, for prostitution could not be regarded as such, but of the state of being."[36] Unsurprisingly, Villiers's recasting of woman as technological symbol reflects mid-nineteenth-century social anxieties over the decline of marriage and women's self-commodification, concerns bound to larger forces at work, like the emergence of industrialism and the postrevolutionary apprehension over the very concept of history.

In the later 1850s, historian Jules Michelet interrupted work on his massive historical tome *Histoire de France* to write two books on women, *L'Amour* (1858) and *La Femme* (1859). In sum, Michelet presents a manifesto on marriage, love, and society, summoning mankind to reproduce woman by reinforcing man's duty of heritage. He beckons to his fellow brethren, "creators, manufacturers, the true sons of Prometheus," to embody their mythological forebears, affirming, "We do not want a ready-made Pandora; we prefer to make one for ourselves."[37] Michelet surmises that to achieve social salvation and marital bliss, man must literally create his other half, relying on the irresistible *génie* (which in Villiers becomes *photogénie*-like) of invention. In his suitably titled chapter "No Life for Woman without Man," Michelet asserts that to "break that vicious circle in which we revolve, in which woman prevents us from creating woman," one must take for a wife a woman "having as yet received *no definite impress*."[38] Instead, he volunteers the daughter as the "second love"—possibly corresponding to Gautier's second reality—to restore man's future, the allegorical prototype of *fille*-cum-woman and his proof of life. His own feminine progeny in this twistedly incestuous affirmation of the ideal, and equally perverse reordering of the family, man's second love can provide him with the next generation of suitable, female companions. Framing the ability to love, and the possibility of social restitution, as a question of making rather than finding—"love, in these modern times, loves not *what it finds*, but *what it makes*"—Michelet equates man's wish of regulating the obedience of a wife with the necessity of producing a (better) copy of her, his own daughter as "adorable ideal" that ensures the reinstitution of his waning male authority.[39] Man must avoid, according to Michelet, women who have already received a definite impress, *une empreinte définitive*; instead, he must marry a woman he impresses himself—his own printed woman.

This spirit was not lost on Villiers, who directly replicates Michelet's notion of woman-as-symbol as the cornerstone of his narrative. In *L'Ève future*, Miss Alicia Clary's profane bourgeois sensibilities and her willingness to do anything to increase her *prix* as a performer suggests a metaphoric woman of ill repute. Even though Villiers's attitude toward science remains ambivalent, there is nothing ambiguous about the author's condemnation of the bourgeois sensibility incarnated through Alicia; her self-prostituting, performative awareness serves as the evocative emblem of monstrosity in the novel. Conversely, Villiers depicts Edison as a Promethean and Pygmalionesque avatar, one of Michelet's "true sons of Prometheus," in his aspirations to surpass divine creation—to become father to modernized men by his dream of creating a new breed of Eves, who will replace the obsolete and imperfect ones.[40] If each successive scientific invention endeavors to replace the obsolete invention of old, why not apply the same formula to anything passé and inadequate—even if that antiquated invention is a woman? As Marie Lathers contends, Edison lays claim to the ability to nullify feminine deviance by creating a simulacrum of the flawed woman conveniently void of all of the nuisances he sees real women offering, like their own consciousness and agency.[41] Rather than defy nature and humanity, Edison's experiment instead seeks to rectify what he sees as monstrous within female nature—to establish instead an artificial generation of women.

Womanproof: To Begin Anew

> Vanity of vanities, saith the Preacher, vanity of vanities; all *is* vanity.
> What profit hath a man of all his labour which he taketh under the sun?
> *One* generation passeth away, and *another* generation cometh: but the earth abideth for ever.
> . . .
> The thing that hath been, it *is that* which shall be; and that which is done *is* that which shall be done: and *there is* no new *thing* under the sun.
> Is there *any* thing whereof it may be said, See, this *is* new? it hath been already of old time, which was before us.
>
> —Ecclesiastes 1:2–1:4, and 1:9-1:10

In his early lamentations in the novel, Edison reopens the question of man's solitary existence by parroting the words of God upon his creation of Eve.[42] I suggest that both his performative reiteration of these biblical words and the narrative return to the precise moment Eve can be reconfigured allow the novel to prepare its own enigmatic relationship with the notion of "recording" as well as reproduction. In short, Hadaly will represent an artificial copy of Edison's view of humankind, a being that represents a catalog of masculine citation and the embodiment of male history—thus, a tool for man's self-preservation.

In the course of his monologic discourse in book 1, chapter 9, "Snapshots of World History," Edison actually usurps the authority of another important biblical pronouncement. He bemoans the lost visions, proclaiming, "Yes, yes, everything fades, it's true; even discolorations on collodion, even scratches on steel plates. Vanity of vanities, all is vanity, to be sure!" (23). Here, Edison recites the first line of Ecclesiastes from the Old Testament, excerpted in the epigraph to this section. Believed to be written by Qohelet, son of King David, the book of Ecclesiastes muses on the futility inherent in the worldly endeavors of man, a great portion of the book reflecting indirectly on the inevitably of death. Instead of reiterating the words and denoting their original author, Edison reproduces these sentiments from Ecclesiastes as his own, thus severing them from their original context. Villiers reflects upon this notion of vanity in numerous and distinct ways within *L'Ève future* as well as other texts, including a short story entitled "L'annonciateur," which he inscribes with the epigraph "Habal habalim, vêk'hol habal!"—a transliteration of the original Hebrew version of that most famous of lines in Ecclesiastes: vanity of vanities, all is vanity. From the Hebrew word *habal*, meaning "vanity," Villiers names Evelyn Habal, the direct prototype of Alicia in *L'Ève future*'s backstory. Her name, encapsulating both the figure of

Eve and the notion of *habal*/vanity, establishes her as a paradigmatic figure for the novel's attempted, artificial re-generation.

More conspicuously, Villiers names book 5, chapter 2, "Nothing New under the Sun," also from Ecclesiastes, and further inscribes the chapter with an epigraph taken from that biblical book: "This is also vanity" (134). In the chapter, Edison preaches to Ewald that in passionate love there is nothing but vanity built on infinite illusions perpetuated, maladies heaped atop mirages and phantoms. He insists he can answer Ewald's need to "aimer zéro" (love degree zero) with his *andréïde*, which represents "nothing but the first hours of love, immobilized, the hour of the Ideal made prisoner" (135). In order to convince Ewald that *l'andréïde* Hadaly will be more true to the enterprise of loving a "real" woman, Edison expounds on the inextricable connection between the human condition and endless reproducibility. We can hear the echo of Villiers's own epigraphic usage and authorial strategy when Edison insists that people are constantly *reciting*, "In actual truth, there's not a single word that isn't a repetition: and you don't need Hadaly to find yourself, every so often, in close conversation with a phantom" (138). Edison divulges that all words are recitations, that all men are nothing but parrots, and that everything is a reproduction, a copy—thus, affirming Qohelet's proclamation that, despite the vain enterprises of men, *there is no new thing under the sun*.

Venus Transference

Although Hadaly represents the apotheosis of artificiality, she is not as *new* as one might think. In fact, Hadaly is *une redite*, a rewriting of two antique female figures: the God-made companion Eve and the man-made archetype of beauty and ideality asserting its prominence in nineteenth-century France, the Venus de Milo (figure 2.1).[43] As with the figure of Eve, the history of this specific art object reflects the cultural moment's obsession with "the incorporation of the antique ideal into modernity's technological constructions of woman and, furthermore, the confrontation between traditional ('classical') views of art and the bourgeois will to copy most notably evident in the rise of photography."[44] As Marie Lathers notes, out of numerous possible archetypal Venuses, Villiers settled on the *Venus Victrix*, or the Venus de Milo, which had been discovered on the island of Milos in 1820 and subsequently replaced the *Medici Venus* as "the French archetype of ideal feminine beauty" after being installed in the Louvre by Louis XVIII.[45] The revival of interest in the Venus figure, brought about through the archaeological excavation of the statue as artifact, analogizes these very reverberations of the antique feminine ideal as modern icon in literature and art. The Paris Salon of 1863 marked a climactic moment in this cultural obsession over Venus representations; so many Venus paintings were exhibited there that Théophile Gautier himself christened it "The Salon of Venuses."[46] Because Venus was the perfect vehicle for "the expression of 'the ideal' in art, her representation also brought with it anxieties about the power of masculine

FIG. 2.1 Photographic reproduction of the renowned Venus de Milo sculpture, discovered on the island of Melos in 1820 and afterward installed in the Louvre Museum, Paris.

creativity."[47] Accordingly, Jennifer Shaw suggests that the Salon of 1863's veritable fixation on Venus representations was "symptomatic of a need to assert the primacy of masculine creativity and control, both of which were perceived, consciously or not, as under threat."[48] Man's appropriation of a generative image—like the fertile Venus or primordial mother Eve—provided means for the articulation of his own generative power. Nineteenth-century French literature exploited the notion of the woman as an unknown masterpiece, signified by the mysterious *Venus*, in order to refashion the incomplete masterpiece that is man into a more fully realized subject and modern artist.

That Miss Alicia exhibits the visual splendor of a humanized *Venus* is both the cause of her attractiveness and the nexus of Lord Ewald's downfall. Though her resemblance to the famous Venus statue is to be envied and adored, Villiers presents the humanization of such a divine image as utterly disturbing, monstrous. Understanding love from the standpoint of reproduction induces a shift in perspective that shows Alicia as a freak of the nature that formed her. Acknowledging the disharmony, that "between the body and the soul of Miss Alicia" there was nothing but "absolute *disparity*," Ewald finds this mismatch between her body (divine) and her soul (too human) so distressing that, on his own, he can find no other alternative to consider except suicide (31). Edison categorizes Alicia's resemblance to a work of art as a sign of degeneracy and further conjectures that falling in love with this de-generated image has caused Ewald to contract a disease, compelling his inclination toward self-immolation.

In a book that symbolizes technological reproduction as the highest power, this "natural" projection of an ideal artistic image upon a mortal woman—the imprint of stone on her flesh—proves to be *maladive*, the basest instance of monstrosity. Additionally, Alicia's own self-love and self-worth directly conflict with Ewald's desires; he declares that if Alicia were deprived of her thoughts, he then might be able to understand her. After all, the "marble *Venus*, in fact, *has nothing to do with thinking.* The goddess is veiled in stone and silence" (41). Ewald's conundrum is doubled over to reflect man's foremost misfortune, being the human descendant of mother Eve. He inquisitively demands, "How to understand a Venus Victorious who has found her arms again in the dark night of time, and reappears in the middle of the human race" (41)? In other words, how does one negotiate a creature so heterogeneous, the divine trapped in the earthly, and woman-made? Alicia, functioning as a symptom of a "bizarre" lineage of female degeneracy, becomes the necessary warrant for Edison's project of artificial generation. While the novel's original title illuminates a gendered paradox, inherent in the concept of the *andréïde*, suggesting that herein artificial reproduction is monstrous, the novel instead shows that the mechanical body of the *andréïde* replaces the true aberration. In a curious reversal of the narrative trajectory of *Frankenstein*, Villiers's fictional Edison is compelled to replace God's version of woman (Eve) with his own (future Eve) not as part of an ill-conceived scheme to usurp nature but in order to correct "some dreadful mistake of the

Creator's" (44). A hybrid of base sentimentality and external beauty, Alicia turns out to be the novel's most veritable monster—not the product of artificial reproduction but its very cause.[49]

Given that Venus symbolized art itself at this point in France's cultural history, Ewald's inability to reconcile the disparity between the Venus statue and Alicia symbolizes Villiers's meta-literary occupation with the irreconcilable differences between real women and their artistic depictions.[50] But the gulf between Ewald and Alicia only becomes impossibly widened when Ewald attempts to amend the incongruity of Alicia and her doppelgänger statue by bringing them face-to-face in the Louvre: "I got the idea—sacrilegious, even crazy, I agree—of confronting this living despondency with the great marble who is, as I told you, her image—the *Venus Victorious* herself." At the moment of *reconnaissance,* Alicia looks at the statue with surprise and declares, "Look, it's *me*!" while adding, "But I have arms, and besides I'm more distinguished looking." Once outside the museum she indelicately asks, "*Well, if they spend all that money on this statue—then—I may do well too?*" (46). Alicia perceives her completeness as a human body—she possesses the arms the *Venus* lacks—as an extension into her value as a subject. She presumes that if a statue without arms costs as much as it does, then inevitably she, a Venus with all her parts, should fetch a fair amount of success as a performer on the stage. This far too facile, subjective identification on the part of Alicia yields Ewald's permanent unease as a subject. Subsequently, he succumbs to a state of vertigo (the word used in the original French is, importantly, *le vertige*) brought forth from the abyss betwixt his own lofty ideals and Alicia's all too bourgeois self-identity.[51]

Ewald's imaginary call for someone to separate Alicia's soul and body gets answered by Edison, who takes the inverse of the problem as its solution, and his equation—scientific, mathematical, and cinematic—for creating the ideal woman. While the ultimate result of these technological revisions of Alicia will be Hadaly—the ultimate theorem of the animation of the inanimate—the first step is paradoxical Pygmalionism, the actual rendering of Alicia back into the statue from which she was imaginarily modeled. Edison will reproduce the external image of Alicia onto a mechanical body in order to reproduce her in the form of the *andréïde*. Alicia, who already resembles the *Venus*, will be made back into a statue as an original; her image will be transferred by means of the techniques of photosculpture onto the body of the *andréïde*, a living statue more exact to its model.[52] But Edison must dupe Alicia to pose for a statue in her likeness by appealing to her bourgeois vanity and taking advantage of her ignorance of the art world. In order to gain full access to Alicia's image, Edison convinces her that having oneself made in marble is à la mode, and that stage performers are indeed replacing their portraits with statues.

Via Edison, Villiers further fictionalizes Eve by metamorphosing her from being to pose, destabilizing any value of the primordial human mother except as an artificial role for Alicia to play. Edison convinces Alicia that her own likeness in a statue is necessary because "a magnificently beautiful statue of the singer predisposes the audience in your favor, sets the crowd to talking, attracts the interest of directors. So you must pose as Eve; it's the most distinguished pose of all. No other artist, I dare say, will dare to take the role or sing the part, after you've made it yours, of *Tomorrow's Eve*" (177). Villiers's concept of an Eve-of-the-future markedly suggests a complete transformation of Eve's value as a figure, from human being in the biblical book of Genesis to the referential and entirely artificial likeness of woman—a Symbol, and a theft of woman's image through modern technology (photosculpture).[53] Alicia relinquishes her agency as an actress to the directorial control of Edison/Ewald. From his perspective, Edison repairs the breach, Ewald's stereoscopic failure to achieve the superposition of the *Venus* and Miss Alicia by placing them side by side at the Louvre.

Although the novel aims at the vision of a female made supplementary to the male subject, one of Villiers's most powerful contributions to this shifting mythology will be the novel's illustration that a stable sense of identity, like Alicia's faulty self-recognition in the *Venus Victorious*, is mythical. *L'Ève future* suggests that in order to supplement the vicarious male identity, literature requires the establishment of woman not as *identité* but as *identique* (to man). When Ewald inquires about what the reproduction of woman's identity entails. Edison's response, both emphatic and comical, suggests a total dissolution of the term, replacing any viability of woman's identity in favor of her identicality:

> —You can reproduce the IDENTITY of a woman? You, a man born of woman?
>
> —She will be a thousand times more identical to herself . . . than she is in her own person! Yes, I assure you since not a day passes without changing some outlines of the human body, and the science of physiology demonstrates to us that the body changes *completely* all of its atoms, every seven years approximately. Does anybody's body really exist at any given point? Does one ever resemble oneself? When this woman, and you, and I, were just an hour and twenty minutes old, did we resemble what we are tonight? The very idea of resembling oneself! What is this, a prejudice out of the ice age, or the time of cavemen? (65)

In Edison's iterations, identity is the most mythical and elusive of concepts. In revolt, his project of artificial generation, to create from the clay of human science a new Eve, operates as a most transparent metaphor for Villiers's own extrafictional project, unified in the desire to reify the always already fractured status of universal male subjectivity. Edison divulges that man's plight is unchanged from ancient to modern: "He feels that he is alone, in the entire universe, is not a finished product. . . . By an impulse both natural and sublime, he asks himself *where he is*; he tries to reconstruct his own starting point" (111).

The Algebra of Identity

Despite his satiric tone intermittently adopted toward technology, Villiers admired equally the "proof" it offered his literary quest for an extraliterary, extrasensory ideal. As Raitt asserts in the book's preface, Villiers was forever fascinated by the idea that scientific methods could one day furnish irrefutable proof of the supernatural and of the world beneath that of appearances.[54] Outward appearances, in particular, had already become loathsome to Villiers by the mid-1880s; he had spent the good part of his life fighting to uphold the integrity of his noble name but nevertheless ended up as financially impoverished as he was depleted psychically by modernity's progress. Once inspired to write the novel, Villiers worked unremittingly during the winter of 1879, often under the most desperate conditions, "in the icy horror of a room in the rue de Maubeuge, which had been emptied of its furniture, lying on the floor flat on his stomach and diluting in water his last drops of ink," according to friend and French playwright, Gustave Guiches.[55] By 1886, the year of *L'Ève future*'s publication, Villiers and literary friends Leon Bloy and J. K. Huysmans banded together to form the Council of Paupers, what Raitt calls a "mutual aid society, as well as an unofficial club for the vituperation of all that they hated in the modern world."[56] Accordingly, *L'Ève future* equivocates on the value of industrial progress, at one moment lauding technology's powers, while at another seemingly admonishing men's overvaluation of scientific progress.

However, Villiers's foray into his science fiction project also attests to a more personal disappointment, a failed engagement to Miss Anna Eyre Powell in 1873–1874. In sum, the Faustian wager Lord Ewald makes with Edison in the novel may be the distorted mirror image of Villiers's own terribly Faustian contract with a mysterious matrimonial agent named La Houssaye, giving him "a signed promissory note for two hundred thousand francs, payable upon marriage to the person to whom" he would soon be introduced.[57] Upon their meeting, the precarious engagement became a dream come true against all odds. Anna, an Anglo-Irish heiress with money in her background and some training as a singer, had an interest in acquiring a French husband of noble birth.[58] A letter written by Villiers to a good friend, French author and poet Stéphane Mallarmé, gives the scope of his enchantment with his soon-to-be bride: "I have fallen in love very late in life and it's the first time that I've been in love. How can I compare what is incomparable? I love an Angel *whose like is positively not to be found anywhere under the sun!* She is *the last one*, my dear friend, there can never be anyone better!"[59] But what Villiers believed was the incarnation of a beautiful dream soon became one of his grandest miseries. Although accounts of what went awry differ, John Payne, poet friend of Mallarmé and Villiers's contact during his visit with Anna in England, offered the following in a letter to Mallarmé: "I fear (as I have always feared) that the unfortunate outcome is the fault of the girl, a somewhat hysterical young person and a *poseuse*."[60] All accounts, according to Raitt, confirm that Anna Eyre was a romantically minded young lady who became a singer in Paris—on the surface level, a possible prototype for Alicia Clary.

The concept for Villiers's new, industrial Eve rests on a compilation of proofs—personal histories as well as mathematical theorems—that reveal the motivation toward her conception as well as the means to create her. Conceivably, Villiers identified with Adam's misplaced trust in Eve, the "last and best" of God's creations in *Paradise Lost*, just as Villiers calls Anna both his first love and "the last one" in his letter cited earlier. After being duped by Eve into committing original sin, Milton's Adam inveighs against not having "proof enough" of her once-seeming virtuousness. Likewise embittered, Villiers directly answers the call of Adam by writing the novel as a theorem for a new Eve, or a new Anna, to more adequately alleviate man's loneliness and proffer renewed happiness. The ultimate proof is Hadaly, the new and improved love object in the age of technological reproduction; in the reverse, the ultimate love is proof itself. Edison offers both mathematical and photographic proofs within the novel as mitigative blueprints for artificial woman.

Edison's most consequential mathematical trial for Hadaly begins with the story of an already deceased Edward Anderson, an inventor and friend who had fallen victim to the charms of a theater performer named (Eve)lyn Habal, whose name, discussed earlier, suggests she embodies the plight of Ecclesiastes—vanity.[61] The undoing of Anderson frightens Edison so drastically as to influence him to create a female simulacrum before Ewald ever comes to visit, in a curious temporal reversal that mimics Edison's desire to reproduce a future Eve just before the Eve of the past was even created. In the same manner that the myth of Adam and Eve acts as the foundation of Milton's *Paradise Lost*, the Anderson-Evelyn tale acts as the primary narrative impetus for the Ewald-Alicia story, which unfolds in the real time of the novel. In brief, the background story goes as follows. One night at the theater Anderson falls for the charms of theater performer Evelyn; Edison's telling of the story not surprisingly suggests Anderson's innocence in the matter. As a result of their tepid affair, Anderson leaves his wife and children, loses his job, and falls into debt as well as psychic disrepair. Anderson ultimately ends his own life, and his death incites Edison to undertake his *andréïde* project, which he now employs to prevent Ewald from meeting the same fate as Anderson. Edison explains, "I had assembled these proofs that my unhappy friend had never held in his arms anything but a sad phantom, and that underneath all her paraphernalia the hybrid creature of his passion was as false as his love itself—to the point, in fact, of being nothing but *the Artificial giving an illusion of life*" (122). Edison draws from scientific reasoning that there must be "thousands of episodes *almost* identical with this one," of men being destroyed (122). Edison undertakes this project because the fear instilled by the Anderson-Evelyn prototype story threatens the livelihood of men collectively. Neither Anderson nor Ewald is an original.

After presenting the Anderson-Evelyn story as testament, Edison concludes that he can use science to discover the secret of love. He tries to quell what he sees as the now collective epidemic brought upon man, and to act as universal savior of men, by reducing the problem to a simple mathematical proof, or what Sylvie Jouanny calls the novel's "l'algèbre de l'identité."[62] Edison claims quite matter-of-factly, "Miss Evelyn represented the X of an equation which could, after all, hardly have been more simple since I knew both terms of it: Anderson, and his death" (109). The foundational mathematical terms derived from the Anderson-Evelyn story are understood accordingly: woman with consciousness (+1) negates male identity (−1), thus negating man's control over her image. Edison recognizes that man cannot make a positive identity out of a negation already inherent in the subjectivity of woman. In place of Anderson's all-too-real passion for this hybrid creature, Edison crafts an equally artificial hybrid, but of a scientific sort instead. He builds the blueprint for the *andréïde* upon a revised attempt at providing man with love degree zero: negate consciousness in woman (−1) by projecting (both psychically and photographically) male desire on female form (+1) = Hadaly, or the Ideal.[63]

Protocinematic Woman and the Dance of Death

Edison turns Evelyn into a symbol (x) in an algebraic equation, but even more tellingly, he transfigures her into a photographic proof, making a trial print of her in order to visually investigate woman for her symbolic re-production into Hadaly/the Ideal.[64] The photographic proof Edison creates to illustrate Evelyn, the sad chimera, not only strips the performer of her ability to disillusion duplicitously but also provides Edison with the very technological platform to replace woman with a simulacrum. In the chapter entitled "Danse Macabre," Villiers narrates the process of an archaic cinematic projection, a film that Edison takes of Evelyn before her death in order to illustrate the seductress's true nature:[65]

> A long strip of transparent plastic encrusted with bits of tinted glass moved laterally along two steel tracks before the luminous cone of the astral lamp. Drawn by a clockwork mechanism at one of its ends, this strip began to glide swiftly between the lens and the disk of a powerful reflector. Suddenly on the wide white screen within its frame of ebony flashed the life-size figure of a very pretty and quite youthful blonde girl.
>
> The transparent vision, miraculously caught in color photography, wore a spangled costume as she danced a popular Mexican dance. Her movements were as lively as those of life itself, thanks to the procedures of successive photography, which can record on its microscopic glasses ten minutes of action to be projected on the screen by a powerful lampascope, using no more than a few feet of film. (117)

Rather than being drawn to Evelyn dancing, Villiers's reader instead marvels over the technological reproduction of the dance made possible by Edison's rudimentary application of successive photography. Evelyn's real skin no longer holds any fascination after being turned into an illusive representation that is miraculously photochromatic—an image that provides a fitting foreshadowing of the *andréïde*, a being literally enrobed in photochromatic skin. From the protocinematic mechanization of woman's image, Edison contrives the concept of a mechanical woman. In the chapter entitled "L'Épiderme," he explains to Ewald the scientific equation of fitting Hadaly with mechanically produced skin, which he contends will be as true as nature. "Our colored projectors, then, imprint on this mock skin . . . the exact tints of the nudity being reproduced," Edison explains, and "served to give vitality." With conviction, he asserts that the cinematic copy of woman will be indistinguishable from the living woman, that the process will "render the copy and the original indistinguishable" (162). This passage further suggests, in its capitulation of the origins of cinematic projection and its conflation with the representation of the woman, that woman symbolizes more than mere object of the camera's lens.

The very representation of the female establishes the psychic substratum for the cinema as a modernized, mechanical means of representing the ideal. This shift in focus from the dance onto the actual filmic/photographic procedure "announces the conflation of women's bodies and the mechanical, cinematic images that will come to characterize mass culture."[66] The process of successive photography mechanizes Evelyn; to be sure, the living Evelyn is no longer of consequence.[67] But here, the novel predisposes Ewald to loving Hadaly by forcing the reader to recognize that Edison, seemingly "lost in a romantic reverie," falls in love with the very *idea* of a photographic, artificialized woman (117). Annette Michelson offers that Villiers's novel stages the female body not merely as voyeuristic object of desire but more vigorously as the substratum of cinema itself. In relation to the novel's entanglements with the cinematic body and the possible conflation of body, text, and theory, Michelson affirms that these "acts of magic perpetrated upon the female subject, as by Edison and Méliès in the films of the primitive period" permit "the obsessive reenactment of that proleptic movement between analysis and synthesis, which will accelerate and crystallize around the female body in an ultimate, fantasmatic mode of representation *as* cinema."[68]

However, the primitive film within the narrative also authorizes a negation of the female performer's illusory power by capturing what Edison would conversely call "*la vraie*" of the living woman's fakery. In other words, the male projection of the filmic female image overturns the power and agency of Evelyn's own force of self-representation and identity as a theater performer. Though such women act as good re-presenters in the novel, they are still bad copies. Immediately after the pleasurable film of Evelyn dancing and singing, Edison shows Ewald one of an entirely other character: "The first filmstrip leaped from its track; the image disappeared from the screen. A second heliochromic band quickly replaced the first and began running as quick as light before the reflector. On the screen appeared a little bloodless creature, vaguely female of gender, with dwarfish limbs, hollow cheeks . . . and wrinkled features" (118). By capturing these indelible images of Evelyn Habal stripped of her feminine ornamentation, Edison believes that he handily proves that the actual woman under the makeup and mirage is monstrous: a shriveled-up, bloodless imp of a figure, vaguely female in gender. The "real" woman is not real at all but a chimerical monster, an apparition drained of all blood and life, only vaguely representative of a woman. Making her the object rather than the subjective force of the performance by technological means, Edison uses this photographic, cinematic proof of what he sees as Evelyn's hideousness, in order to begin his sensible assault on Ewald's insensible enchantment with Alicia and to reveal the true monstrosity that is (Eve)lyn.

Mythologized through the artificial woman, the quest for masculine literary subjectivity becomes a photographic drive by the turn of the twentieth century. As a result, the ideal woman in *L'Ève future* not only is objectified by the eye of the camera and rendered static but also symbolizes the photographic process itself, the lens through which man sees his ideal self by subjugating woman, rendering her a photographic object. Edison amplifies the appropriateness of photographic reproduction for his project by showing that, in both the case of the "living" woman (Alicia) and his future Eve (Hadaly), man's love is nothing but a matter of projection. As film theorist Raymond Bellour suggests in "Ideal Hadaly," "Instead of acting as a mirror, and 'naturally' refracting everything, Alicia becomes this 'creature of death' who destroys both look and thought 'in her horrible *camera obscura*.'"[69] Lord Ewald's disequilibrium caused by this woman as animated duality parallels what Bellour suggests is the impossibility, in completing the camera obscura metaphor, of Ewald striking the "optimum distance where he would be reflected by the mirror-body of the love object."[70] In fact, the narrative remodeling of woman from Alicia to Hadaly corresponds to the reformation of the photographic process, from the rudimentary capabilities of the camera obscura to the sophisticated aptitude of the cinematic apparatus for the representation of illusory life.[71] As Jonathan Crary proposes, by the early 1800s "the rigidity of the camera obscura, its linear optical system, its fixed positions, its categorical distinction between inside and outside . . . were all too inflexible and unwieldy for the needs of the new century."[72] The inability to find within Alicia the true projection of Ewald's desire mirrors the impossibility of striking a harmonious distance from the camera obscura, an inefficiently obsolete technology.

Here I return necessarily to the dilemma of Narcissus, and the impossibility of taking one's projected image as love object, for Edison's labor for love makes possible this impossibility. As Pygmalion does in Ovid's *Metamorphoses*, Edison allows man to partake in an illusory existence wherein his beloved is an artificialized and feminized object of his own psychic, subjective projection. He triumphantly proclaims to Ewald, "Her 'consciousness' will no longer be the negation of yours. . . . You will be able to evoke in her the radiant presence of *your own, your individual passion*, without having to worry, this time, that she gives the lie to your dream!" (133). Edison sees that both Anderson's Evelyn Habal and Ewald's Alicia Clary function as *chimères*, hollow shells of being, and that man's love for these real women is nothing but an illusion: "In short, it's the objectified projection of your own soul . . . that you CREATE in your living woman, and *which is nothing but your own soul reduplicated in her*" (68). The objectivity of the photographic apparatus as it is employed in *L'Ève future*, as Bellour asserts, "is merely an apparent dialectic of illusion. The external image, the simulacrum which it reproduces, depends on the internal, mental image which can alone make it true for the mind."[73] In this context, a photographically objectified woman becomes a subjective supplement for modern man—an extension of his psychic needs as well as an extension of his technological advancements.

While in my early examination of the *andréïde* I determined the figure to be a woman, in fact, Hadaly functions only as symbol of an ideal femininity inaccessible through any of the real women in the novel. Both Alicia as actress and Hadaly as *andréïde* function as performers; Alicia, however, has control over her representations while Hadaly does not. Hadaly *only acts like a woman*. She bears no genetic markers of femininity and is not equipped with any sexual organs—reproduced, but not reproductive. Acting like an actress is just another way Hadaly represents the second copy within a technologically enhanced environment wherein the copy supersedes the model. Mostly, Hadaly resembles women, either in the way she passively mimics Alicia's physical appearance or stands in as modernity's indexical Eve, woman-as-symbol fulfilling man's aforementioned desire to reconstitute her from a being with identity to being identical. Unlike Eve or Miss Alicia, though, Hadaly is unmistaken about her role. As she sheepishly acknowledges in her efforts to please Ewald, "Here I am asking you questions, just like a woman; and a woman is what I must not become: I should change!" (200). Built to act like woman, never meant to be one; in actuality, Hadaly is a second copy, like the novel's first epigraph—for the real appeal of Alicia is her resemblance to the *Venus Victorious*. A copy of what is already a copy, Hadaly becomes a copy without an original, or, in turn, "she" becomes an original produced from a copy.[74]

Villiers's ultimate symbolic offering, Hadaly will be the first, the original, and the last of an entirely other species within the novel, an original without a copy—that is, until she becomes the foundation for modern cinema. The novel depicts the technological reproduction of an ideally photo-genic woman using technologies that make endless reproduction possible, and in this paradox we may ascertain the novel's intended and impossible veracity. Artificial generation expropriates biological reproduction, the *andréïde* body being made sterile a deliberate indication. Void of any reproductive organs and wielding a dagger to enforce her chastity, Hadaly represents the blockage to any sense of natural reproduction. Like Frankenstein's wretch, she is the first and last of an entirely other species, bestowing artificial life and expiring the real.

Returning to the stereoscope as a reading strategy allows us to look further into the complex intermix of female characters in Villiers's novel. All of the female characters are of little consequence by the novel's climax because they become fragmented and fused into Hadaly.[75] Her represent-ability acts as the very locus of her power as a "woman," her ability to represent a multitude of female characters while retaining "une empreinte definitive" (a definite imprint) of none. Ewald perpetuates Edison's Faustian victory at the novel's end by falling in love with Hadaly, unaware that she is not Alicia. Ewald proves further that his love is predicated upon Hadaly's identicality to Alicia and not any true identity on the part of the woman. When at this moment of horrifying misrecognition he asks her, "Who are you?," Hadaly must admit that she is no one, specifically because she is a multiplicity, the embodiment of reproduction as an Idea and the representative of (film) Theory itself (194). She tries to make Ewald understand that her identity is as shape-shifting as his very desires: "I have so many women in me, no harem could contain them all. Desire them, and they will exist! It's up to you to discover them within me" (199). Herein, the conceptualization behind Hadaly turns out to be even more enigmatic for the reader. While she ostensibly contains within her all these "other feminine potentials," Hadaly merely represents the entire corpus of men's experience and understanding of womanhood.

Hadaly represents artificial intelligence, then, on two levels. First, she is the product of the artificial intelligence that creates her: technology constructs her body—two golden phonographs as lungs, photochromatic skin. More notably, she becomes the sum of man's knowledge: literature designs her speech—by means of the phonographic recordings made by her lungs, Hadaly speaks the words already written by famous authors. However, love, too, is required, for without a forlorn lover Edison would never have been able to give life to the eternal feminine Ideal. In response to Ewald's query, Edison explains what Hadaly stands for: "A particular intelligence? No. INTELLIGENCE, yes" (65). Not a singular being, Hadaly represents the Symbolist's version of being-in-the-world. If the artificial is the novel's truth, then Hadaly represents its *Veritas*. Man's shared literary ambition to understand his origins through artificial re-creation is equally a quest for knowledge and mastery. Though Villiers's literary invocation of her is partly contemptuous, Hadaly answers the call for both, validating the novel as a book of genesis. Hadaly functions as a tropological symbol of the very thing she lacks: a navel, of women and of woman.[76] *L'andréïde* represents modernity's symbolic and technological point of origin.

The ultimate promise Edison makes Ewald at one of the turning points of the novel is that man can regain his lost paradise through this double projection, both psychic and photographic. Accordingly, man can replace woman with an eternal, technological symbol of the feminine. However, the problem seems to dictate that woman was, in fact, never an original, and always a copy. To define her accordingly forces us to realize why woman provides the ultimate provocation for the male author's ventures into technological reproducibility at this point in the cultural history. As Lathers argues, in "*L'Eve future*, femininity itself is the non-existent original, the copy that no woman can embody, and that Villiers and Edison try so desperately to (re)construct."[77] Edison reveals to Ewald the key equation in order to revolutionize the concept of woman—technological reproduction between men: "Come, my lord, between the two of us, we form an eternal symbol: I represent Science and the omnipotence of its delusions; you are Humanity with its paradise lost" (71). Strangely, *L'Ève future* reaffirms the quality of the human life born of Adam and Eve in a most inhuman and curious range of substitutions: *andréïde* for female love object, man for mother. But Edison steadfastly asserts that these most unnatural stand-ins will, in turn, allow Ewald to regain his ability to be happy and to be human.

Vanité-Veritas-Vanitas . . . and *Liberté*

The novel consciously returns to what I have suggested to be its textual prototype, the book of Genesis, but not until its very last chapter when, despite all attempts to repel and defeat time, it is too late.[78] The "Fate" of the novel's last chapter—"And it repented the Lord that he had made man on the earth, and it grieved him at his heart. And the Lord said, I will destroy man whom I have created"—symbolizes the ultimate punishment for mankind's transgression of the divine.[79] That which man tries so vehemently to escape inevitably returns. Edison reads a newspaper story that reveals the fate of Lord Ewald, Hadaly, and Alicia aboard the steamer the *Wonderful*, en route back to England. The ship's rear cargo area catches fire, ignited by an unknown cause and further incited by strong winds off the water. Perhaps in an act of divine retribution, the mythological fire stolen by Prometheus, translated into the fire of electricity used to create Hadaly, serves to destroy them all by engulfing their ship in flames. The news story continues, telling of a "strange incident" that occurs as the ship's captain ushers women and children onto the lifeboat: "A young Englishman, Lord E****, seized a capstan bar and tried by main force to rush into the flames where the chests and boxes were already burning fiercely . . . he shouted that he wanted to save from the flames a chest containing an object so precious" that he offered an enormous but completely useless sum of money (218–219). The news story also includes a list of lives lost when the first lifeboat capsizes: the first name listed is "Miss *Emma-Alicia Clary, artistique lyrique.*" At the very moment Edison flings this newspaper aside, he receives a telegram from Ewald, which reads: "My friend, only the loss of Hadaly leaves me inconsolable—I grieve only for that shade. Farewell" (219). Unfazed by the death of Alicia, Ewald mourns only for the loss of his Ideal, the reader left to presume that Ewald reverts to his only option, death, after losing his artificial love object—his proof of life.

A fuller examination of Hadaly in the book illustrates that she acts as the bearer of death, "a kind of messenger of death herself, metonymic of its realm, not only artificial Eve, but an artificial Eurydice as well."[80] Throughout the text, Hadaly is dressed in death's splendor. She travels aboard the *Wonderful* in a coffin, inscribed with her name on the front plaque. Indeed, Ewald had actually pronounced his wish for his perfect woman early on as a dead woman, who still retains the appearance of her living human features: "What I would really like would be to see Miss Alicia dead, if death didn't result in the effacing of all human features" (46). It is instead "the presence of her form" that Ewald desires, and in this way Hadaly responds to his need, a living snapshot of man's history, an artificial form divorced from innate matter and substance. But this equation also means death, not just *la morte* Alicia and the death of the maternal function, but the destruction of the male artist, who will perish for having been led so astray by his own vanity.

Although Hadaly is created indirectly as a response to the feminine *vanité* inherent in the figures of Evelyn Habal and Alicia Clary, she comes to represent its irresistible return as the male artist's *vanitas*. A seventeenth-century genre of Dutch still-life painting named through the Vulgate translation of *Ecclesiastes*'s "vanity of vanities," *vanitas* works incorporated symbols of mortality or mutability, the most prominent being the skull, aesthetic reminders of human vanity and the futility of life. Hadaly, rather than embody the traditional concept of *vanitas* as still-life painting, instead makes death into a modern, moving picture. Once seeming to be the "magnificent evocation" or artificial generation of life by men, the novel only ends up reinscribing, through a variety of exchanges, the conceit from which it sought asylum: from the *vanité* of the female performer, to man's illusory discovery of *veritas* within the mechanical feminine, to the futility of a modern, cinematic *vanitas* of which *L'Ève future* becomes apotheosis.

Although Alicia poses for a statue as tomorrow's Eve, Hadaly may actually represent a very real statue that was installed in 1886, the very year of the novel's publication—the Statue of Liberty. When first introduced both to Ewald and to the reader, Hadaly stands as if by a tomb, shrouded in darkness and holding up a lantern at the entrance of the passage to Edison's laboratory as underground Eden. Designed by French sculptor Frédéric Auguste Bartholdi, *La Liberté éclairant le monde* was first imagined as a colossal woman holding up a lamp as lighthouse, to stand at the entrance to the Suez Canal; Bartholdi spoke with the leader of Egypt to propose the work at the Paris World's Fair in 1867, but it never came to fruition. Instead, over the next two decades the *Liberté* statue was designed and eventually assembled for her final position on what was then named Bedloe Island in New York City's harbor, just over the river from Thomas Edison's real-life laboratory in New Jersey. Yet before the actual installation of the unique art object, the image of the statue was mechanically reproduced with abandon. In the mid-1870s, an illuminated transparency of *Liberté* was displayed at a fundraising dinner; by 1876, her electrically illuminated torch was displayed at the Philadelphia World's Fair; and by 1877, she turned into a diorama at the Jardins des Tuileries. Statuettes were mass-produced, photographs of her were printed

FIG. 2.2 Frontispiece of Leon Bloy's "La resurrection de Villiers de l'Isle-Adam," representing a proposed funerary sculpture of the author being symbolically brought back to life by his ideal woman, done in rough draft maquette by Frédéric Brou.

in magazines, and souvenir photographs of a statue that did not yet exist were mass-produced for individual ownership, bringing Bartholdi's original concept for the State of Liberty "deep into the heart of mechanical reproduction, where it has been ever since."[81]

The Statue of Liberty was also one of the earliest images to be used for the competitive selling of electrical light by French designers and graphic artists.[82] French graphic artists through the 1880s and 1890s reproduced numerous images, all seemingly generated by *Liberté*, which conflated femininity, electricity, and modernity, including cover art for periodicals like *La Lumière électrique*, books, and other sorts of promotional materials. Her original design to emit light was used to sell her as the evocation of the "dazzling form" of French genius displayed for their American friends—specifically, she became the utmost symbol of a particularly electrified sense of modernity that also advanced the image of Paris as the city of light.[83]

Most important, the real Thomas Edison had a significant relationship with the statue. Its head and shoulders were on display at the 1878 Paris Exposition, attended by American patent lawyer Grosvenor Lowery, who sent a file on the subject to Edison hoping to inspire his "renewed experimentation with the practical application of electric light."[84] Edison would actualize many of his own electrical exchanges with France in the reverse: his lamps were largely responsible for the lighting of the 1889 Exposition Universelle in Paris, where his inventions occupied an acre of space in the Hall of Machinery, capped off with a painting of Menlo Park as the center of "rays of light" projecting outward to all parts of the globe, like the rays intended to beam from the seven points on the statue's crown in her original design as lighthouse. One can only imagine the prospect of Edison's intended use of his phonographic technologies to install a "monster disc" in the Statue of Liberty so that she might speak—just as Hadaly does in *L'Ève future*—an idea he introduced in 1878 upon his patenting of the technology.[85]

In 1906, French writer Leon Bloy published "La resurrection de Villiers de l'Isle-Adam," a pamphlet aimed at convincing people—and, most specifically, the real Thomas Edison—to contribute funds for the erection of a funerary statue of Villiers by Frédéric Brou.[86] As the frontispiece of Bloy's text, the statue depicts the deceased author in his casket, its lid being lifted by his Ideal Woman (figure 2.2). This powerful image restores Villiers to life as a work of art—a strange mise en abyme between the real, historic Villiers and his characterization of Alicia/Hadaly as a living work of art—and also symbolically restores the dream dashed at the end of his novel. But the sculpture, only done in rough draft maquette by Brou, remained unfinished, only to be formally abandoned.

And to this call, Edison never responded.

3

Salomania

The Unnatural Order of (Beautiful) Things in Oscar Wilde's *Salomé*

By the time Oscar Wilde actually published his first textual edition of *Salomé* in 1893, it was a copy born of such a heterogeneous multiplicity that many critics derided the work, written by an author so fierce about his own authenticity, for representing *absolutely nothing original*—except, as some insisted, an irredeemable sense of utter depravity. Though Wilde purported himself publicly as the autonomous master of his literary works, his texts often proved to be influenced greatly, if covertly, by myriad relationships, whether literary intertexts or religious scripture, art movements, or fads in fashion. Quite simply, his *Salomé* was limitless in her adaptive otherness long before she arrived on the printed page or in any theatrical performance.[1]

Wilde's adaptation of Salome's story, complexly and essentially multiple, will be assessed less as a fixed text and more so as a constantly moving network of relations and significations, the dancing figure emblematic of the play's "ongoing whirl of dialogical transformation, of texts generating other texts in an interminable circuit of recycling and transformation."[2] Film theorist Robert Stam discusses film adaptation, or literature through film, in terms of broad intertextual networks, a like foundation for my exploration of Wilde's play, the central work to be discussed within this nebulous adaptive network "with no clear point of origin."[3] An inexhaustibly endless, aesthetic regeneration of the figure, French

Symbolism's Salomania is an auspiciously apt bridge to discuss textual adaptation and re-generation, especially considering, as I will do in chapter 4, that Salome became a prodigiously important model and mode for film adaptations of the early twentieth century.

The French Connection: Adapting Oscar Wilde

Wilde planned to stage *Salomé* with actress Sarah Bernhardt in the lead role during the summer of 1892, but soon into the London rehearsals the Lord Chamberlain's licensor of plays banned its performance based on old English law prohibiting the depiction of biblical characters onstage. Before the official ban, Wilde, who seemed to expect this level of censorship, threatened indignantly, "If the Censor refuses *Salome*, I shall leave England to settle in France. . . . I will not consent to call myself a citizen of a country that shows such narrowness in artistic judgment."[4] This exclamation proves unfaithful to itself almost automatically in that it seems to be, as was most everything Wilde said and did throughout his artistic career, a performance. The type of performance this represents, in particular, is Wilde's phantasmatic and desired re-production of himself as a French artist, rather than an Irish writer bound to a singular, national identity. Indeed, Wilde claimed himself part of this particular lineage of nineteenth-century French authors—from Gautier to Flaubert to Baudelaire, determined as essential figures in this book's artificial generation of writers—gesturing directly toward "the romantic movement in France in 1830" as his psychic birthright, as if to performatively gain "a genetic and literary filiation."[5] Idealized and mythologized in this way, Paris represented a paradise of artistic opportunity that Wilde yearned for and ascribed to, believing that to be a true artist one would have to "be presumptively French."[6] Wilde suggests transferring himself to "another fatherland" in order to gain access to the one he loves: "There is but one Paris, *voyez vous*, and Paris is France."[7]

Yet his desire to ingratiate himself and his work into the French Symbolist tradition existed far earlier than the historical occasion of the play's censorship, Wilde thus re-presenting the very desire that incites *Salomé*'s generation as he re-presents himself as French (like his text). That Wilde chose to write the play in French, a tongue foreign to him, indicates his intent that the piece's language be alienated, as well as adaptive, from the very start. In an interview published in 1892, Wilde admitted, "I have one instrument that I know I can command, and that is the English language." But Wilde found himself intrigued by "another instrument to which I had listened all my life," expressing his desire "to touch this new instrument to see whether I could make any beautiful thing out of it."[8] In February 1893, Wilde wrote a letter to Florence Balcombe Stoker (his first young love, who later became the wife of *Dracula* author Bram Stoker) asking her to accept a copy of *Salomé*, which he calls "my strange venture in a tongue that is not my own, but that I love as one loves an instrument of music on which one has not played before."[9] Indeed, Wilde compares the French language—the uttermost signifier of his aesthetic ideal, next to Greek—to an object of desire, constructing a fantastical relationship to it by writing *Salomé* in French.[10]

Much historical debate has questioned whether or not Wilde wrote *Salomé* unequivocally for actress Sarah Bernhardt. Kerry Powell argues, for instance, that by writing the play in French, Wilde hoped to reserve the title role for "the one actress who in his view had the necessary histrionic panache and vocal distinction to succeed in it."[11] This suggestion is bolstered by the fact that Bernhardt "did not know English—despite having had lessons, hoping to act in Shakespeare in his own language—and performed, like the rest of her ensemble, entirely in French."[12] As soon as Bernhardt read the play, she agreed to portray the title character, a role she probably believed was written expressly for her. "At a party at Henry Irving's she remarked to Wilde that he should write a play for her one day," to which Wilde replied with irony, "I have already done so."[13]

The play's performance necessitated a voice—possibly the archetypal musical instrument—which the golden-voiced actress considered to be her most powerful artistic medium; as Bernhardt writes in *L'Art du théâtre*, the voice "fixes the attention of the public, it is she who binds the artist to the audience."[14] After seeing her first nightly performance of *Phèdre* in London in June 1879, a peculiarly Pygmalionesque Wilde commented that it was "not until I heard Sarah Bernhardt in *Phèdre* . . . that I absolutely realized the sweetness of the music of Racine."[15] Before the production's ban, Wilde witnessed Bernhardt bring the character to life in rehearsal; he admitted feeling that hearing his "own words spoken by the most beautiful voice in the world has been the greatest artistic joy that it is possible to experience."[16] The eros of the artist here depends upon Wilde's Pygmalionesque exultation, of hearing his words vivified by the most beautiful voice—the actress of actresses reciting what will constitute, as I will explore later in this chapter, Wilde's own climactic song of songs. A tragedy, *Salomé*'s musicality—born from its biblical intertextuality, aesthetic aims, and performance by Bernhardt—will make it, nevertheless, an artistic triumph.

But when *The Times* in February 1893 wrote offhandedly that Wilde composed the play for Bernhardt, he responded swiftly to the editor that the "fact that the greatest tragic actress of any stage now living saw in my play such beauty . . . always will be, a source of pride and pleasure to me. . . . But my play was in no sense of the words written for this great actress. I have never written a play for any actor or actress, nor shall I ever do so. Such work is for the artisan in literature, not for the artist."[17] Many critics, like Powell and Nicholas Frankel, affirm that this disclaimer by Wilde is simply not true. In fact, Wilde did capitalize on his relationships within the theatrical, literary, and social scenes in London as well as in France, and Paris specifically. As Frankel points out, Wilde's own letters offer proof that he had George Alexander and Herbert Beerbohm Tree in mind when writing *Lady Windemere's Fan* and *A Woman of No Importance*.[18] In addition, Powell contends that "impostures of originality were not unusual with Wilde, who portrayed himself as an artist set apart, one for whom it was unthinkable to be influenced by another dramatist or the requirements of a fashionable actor."[19] On the other hand, it mattered little that many of Wilde's texts were informed by real people; more relevant was the fact that these people were reproduced as fictional personalities and caricatures, all cast through Wilde's artistic imaginations as performative, aesthetic likenesses—endless adaptations. Quite the reversal of Villiers's artistic goals in *L'Ève future* this is, in effect, Wilde's unnatural order of things.

While writing *Salomé* in French might have been prompted by having the Divine Sarah play the lead role, there exists another, less dubious motivation for Wilde: his embrace of French aestheticism. Wilde affirms his own allegiance to the artificial generation of writers this book has been tracing, acknowledging the debt for his own artistic subjectivity by parroting Gautier's self-realization discussed in chapter 1: "Like Gautier I have always been one of those *pour qui le monde visible existe.*"[20] His use of the French language seems to suggest his thinly veiled desire to ingratiate himself even more fully into the French literary *fraternité*, to throw himself quite garishly into the Salomania captivating an entire generation of French artists and authors.

The daughter of Herodias, who by dancing incites the beheading of John the Baptist in the Bible, was the most infamous and degenerative daughter artistically disseminated throughout the latter half of the nineteenth century. In *Salome and the Dance of Writing*, Françoise Meltzer charts the periods during which Salome becomes an object of interest, illustrating how her popularity during the Middle Ages fades until the nineteenth century, upon the publication of Heinrich Heine's *Atta Troll* in 1842. Gustave Flaubert's novel *Salammbô* (1862) excites the Salome frenzy, compelling Symbolist author Stéphane Mallarmé to compose the poem "Hérodiade" (1869) and painter Gustave Moreau to add Salome to his already existing catalog of femmes fatales, which included Helen of Troy, Cleopatra, and the Sphinx. In 1876, Moreau exhibited two paintings at the Salon Palace of the Champs Elysées that were inspired by Flaubert's novel: *Salomé dansant devant Hérode*, done in oils, and *L'Apparition*, done in watercolors.[21] From Flaubert's young, Far Eastern girl depicted in *Salammbô* dancing on her hands, Moreau conceptualized Salome dancing at Herod's request in order to satisfy her mother's self-serving purposes, requiting the wrongs done by John the Baptist's slanderous condemnation of her and ultimately securing his head on a silver platter. Moreau's paintings fortified the stamina of the Salome promulgation in the aesthetic world by naming the daughter of Herodias properly. In turn, his paintings inspired a bevy of literary copies and ekphrases, even another by Flaubert, who had rejoined what by the 1870s became a representational maelstrom via his tale "Hérodias" (1877). Moreau's paintings inspired French author Joris-Karl Huysmans immensely too, who directly internalized them within his novel *À Rebours* (1884). Huysmans's novel enacts an ekphratic representation of Moreau's *Salomé* paintings wherein the novel's protagonist, Des Esseintes, reflects unequivocally on the dancing girl as the paintings' subject as much as on Moreau's inspired paintings as objets d'art.

The swelling, collective desire to re-produce Salome's story was nothing short of a mania, engulfing the multitude of European men of art and letters. Her mimetic representation became emblematic of the French artistic *fraternité*, and she, like a token to be redeemed only by the "true" artist, was passed among authors, painters, and composers—a secondhand plaything. This feverish and perpetually repetitive encounter of artist-subject and feminized object ensured a dangerous similitude between art and life, male and female, finally reaching an apex of blurred boundaries in Wilde's version.

By the spring of 1892, Wilde's manuscript circulated widely amid an audience of French Symbolist writers and poets who lent their editorial talents, thus becoming an object of its own mania, as eroticized and disseminated as the titular subject of the drama. In his 1929 autobiography Wilde's lover, Lord Alfred "Bosie" Douglas, declared that Wilde wrote the play in English originally and that his translating it into French, with the assistance of Pierre Louÿs and André Gide, was all part of "a rather ridiculous pose."[22] Frankel points out that all surviving drafts of Wilde's *Salomé* are written in French in his own hand, so Douglas's claim that Wilde wrote it in English originally is untrue. However, the idea that writing the play in French was part of a "pose" is worth taking seriously because Wilde did solicit the editorial assistance of many fraternal Symbolists; for instance, Louÿs's handwritten corrections survive on the second draft manuscript, now preserved at the Rosenbach Foundation in Philadelphia, and Marcel Schwob corrected proofs of the play in 1892. Frankel writes, "As Douglas's account makes abundantly clear, the point is not *what* the symbolists altered so much as *that* they altered Wilde's work—that *Salomé* was at this early stage in its history a thoroughly homosocialized work."[23] And despite, or perhaps because of, the text's emphasis on its own inclusion in this fraternal society, many Symbolists were led to praise the play's queerness and detachment, qualities that had come to characterize the literature of French modernity.

Posing as Wilde

Before maturing into an artist in his own right, Wilde paid homage to a great number of famous fin de siècle actresses, including Lillie Langtry, Ellen Terry, and Bernhardt. Wilde greatly admired these female self-fashioners and looked upon them as inspiring objects of affection, reveling in the freedom of heterogeneous artistic expression accessible through their powers of represent-ability. While Villiers regarded the duplicitous woman as a problem needing to be directed and controlled, Wilde saw the poseuse as a solution. One of the earliest caricatures of Wilde, Alfred Thompson's "The Bard of Beauty" for *Time* published in April 1880, shows the author holding a plate in each hand, one offering a sonnet inspired by Terry, and the other a platter with a triolet for Bernhardt

FIG. 3.1 Caricature of Wilde, "The Bard of Beauty" by Alfred Thompson, published originally in London's *Time*, April 1880; from the Oscar Wilde collection at the Williams Andrew Clark Memorial Library.

(figure 3.1). It has taken me many years—since my own archival work in the Williams Andrew Clark Memorial Library collections, which house this particular illustration—to realize how Salome-like Thompson's depiction of Wilde is here. Long and lithe, with a pleasantly curved corporeality, Wilde holds out two platters, each containing the head of one of the lovely actresses, circularly framed in cameo.

Since his days at Oxford, Wilde passed as both artist and model, playing multitudinous characters, encompassing the delightful parts he cast himself in, as well as the more tragic roles others cast for him. In fact, Wilde's initial emergence on the literary scene was not so much the consequence of any text he authored, becoming a fast celebrity when in 1882 he embarked on his American lecture tour, entitled "The English Renaissance," an adapted homage to Walter Pater's *Studies in the History of the Renaissance*, which was widely considered, especially by Wilde, the golden book of Aestheticism. Previously, Wilde was merely a cultish figure of Aesthetics in England who had published a small book of poems. At the behest of booking manager Richard D'Oyly Carte, Wilde was dispatched on his lecture tour simultaneously with the U.S. run of Gilbert and Sullivan's opera *Patience*, propelling him into the position of spokesman: though Wilde was not the original model for the aesthetes in the opera, which satirized the Aesthetic movement, he became the poster child of the movement subsequently.[24] Soon after the tour ended, on July 23, 1883, the *New York Times* wrote under its "Current London Gossip" column that Wilde "was not a lecturer before he went out, nor an art critic of any newspaper, nor a journalist, nor anything . . . and when Gilbert & Burnand (of *Punch*) burlesqued a *something in art that does not exist*, they elected Oscar to the position of their puppet. He accepted the satire, and no doubt fancied that he was unconsciously or otherwise the representative of some sort of an art craze" (emphasis mine). It bears noting that Bernhardt's own American tour (1881–1882) set the foundation for Wilde's, which commenced the same year hers ended. In fact, she initiated the idea for D'Oyly Carte to even employ Wilde on his own lecture tour, as alleged by Wilde himself.[25] "An artist who became her own model, Bernhardt was one of the great self-fashioners of her age," critic John Stokes upholds, "although for a time she did have a rival, Oscar Wilde."[26] While visiting Niagara Falls, Wilde could only be persuaded to wear the obligatory yellow rain slicker, required to view the site from below, upon hearing that Bernhardt had agreed to wear it during her own prior visit.[27]

During his American tour, Wilde posed for a series of photographs taken by acclaimed American photographer Napoleon Sarony. These photographs, now the most recognizable images of the author, formed the legal basis for understanding photography as a work of art, causing Wilde, unwittingly, to become the model for aesthetic hybridity based in the imperative of photographic reproduction. Sarony brought suit against the Burrow-Giles Lithographic Company, which had mass-reproduced for marketing purposes *Oscar Wilde No. 18*, one of the promotional photographs he took of the young author in 1882. Wilde's photographic likeness, mis-taken and unlawfully reproduced, became commercial currency to sell a variety of products. Central in the case, Sarony's *No. 18*, in particular, had been lithographically reprinted as an advertisement for the "tasteful styles" offered in the trimmed hat department of Ehrich Brothers' department store. In oral argument before the Supreme Court in December 1883, Sarony's counsel argued that the photographer acted as inventor, through the posing, costuming, and arrangement of Wilde within the photograph's (seemingly theatrical) staging. The defense countered that a "photograph was not such an original as could be copyrighted," and that Sarony should have instead sought out a patent if he wanted to invent.[28] The Court ruled in Sarony's favor, a legal decree that established a photograph as more than mere objective image capture and, instead, an "intellectual invention" authored by the photographer—a ruling that still stands as the basis of photographic copyright law in the United States today.

Wilde's very existence as an artist was etched by misrepresentation and its essential relation to re-presentation in performance, image, and text. Gilbert and Sullivan's projected image for Wilde was itself a misrecognition, his American lectures meant to coincide as if he were the real-life reproduction of the fictional Bunthorne in *Patience*. Understanding well the value of self-promotion, Wilde helped author a "complex cultural performance" that transformed him as an artist.[29] Though he was unwittingly made into a photographic model for aesthetically pleasing department store goods, he exploited the performative dimension of nineteenth-century aestheticism and "manipulated the press to achieve his aesthetic and pedagogical aims," capitalizing on the multifarious dimensions of lectures, articles, images, and interviews that would become crucial to posing as Wilde.[30] What the Supreme Court case inevitably affords is the ability to see the pose—like Alicia's posing as Tomorrow's Eve in Villiers's novel—as an artistic creation. Sarony may have invented the author's particular depictions in the series of thirty-two photographs he took, yet Wilde authored an infinity of poses, reflections, and aesthetic masquerades. Wilde understood the need for the dramatization of the material, or the material self, and its accomplishment as "a function of his pose (a 'static conception of motion,' like the *tableau vivant*)."[31]

Wilde avowed that *Salomé* was one of his most personal works, causing some to historically liken the artist to the depraved dancer, a comparison temporarily enforced by biographer Richard Ellmann's mistaken identification of Wilde cross-dressed as Salome in his 1969 biography of the author. Ellmann entitled this photograph *Wilde in Costume as Salome*, thinking he had chanced upon an objective photograph that exposed Wilde's secret life as a cross-dresser.[32] The error influenced some critical work that emerged in the decades following the biography's publication. In her book *Sexual Anarchy* (1990), Elaine Showalter argued that this unearthed photograph constituted one of the "play's buried and coded messages," suggesting a parallel between Wilde's self-identification with his Salome figure and that of Flaubert/Madame Bovary with her imagining of Wilde's pseudo proclamation, "Salomé, c'est moi"?[33] It turns out, rather fittingly, that these scholars misrecognized Wilde in the image—which actually captured Hungarian opera singer Alice Guszalewicz in a performance as Salome in 1906—by operating under the presumptive perception of a sameness between Wilde and his works of art. This very sameness between life and art became essentially fatal to the real Wilde. When he took the stand under cross-examination by Edward Carson during his 1895 Queensbury trial, one of the major threads of inquiry was over the immorality and possible perversion of his book *The Portrait of Dorian Gray* (1891), becoming one of the influences that advanced Wilde's guilty verdict and ruined life.

For Wilde, art "depends on the intensification of personality," and personality was not innate but always multiple, the very opportunity for a person to self-commodify based on their fancies.[34] In July 1896, during his imprisonment in Reading Gaol for gross indecency, Wilde proved himself the consummate actor by playing the part typecast for him by Nordau in order to improve his prison environment. In a 2,000-word document written to the home secretary, Wilde attempted to justify his need for additional reading materials, greater than the two books per week allowed. Joseph Bristow affirms that, "Hoping to persuade the authorities to take pity on his condition, Wilde claimed that his 'monstrous sexual perversion' could be explained through 'the works of eminent men of science such as [Cesare] Lombroso and Max Nordau' which had identified 'the intimate connection between madness and the literary and aesthetic temperament.'"[35] Bristow asks what seems to be an insoluble question, whether Wilde "honestly" believed Nordau's pseudoscientific theories, which will be expanded upon in the next section, or if he "truly" thought that Nordau's study "provided a plausible account of his literary success and his sexual behavior."[36] It seems quite reasonable that Bristow uses such perilous words as "honestly" and "truly" in order to reveal that a true and honest Wilde is an oxymoron of sorts. Instead, the author lived a "postmodernity yet to be born," standing "at the crossroads where ideas of a 'genuine self,' in Matthew Arnold's nostalgic phrase, began to be superseded by an unstable, performance-based subjectivity."[37] Of all the positions Wilde actually maintained it was his belief that art's good lies not with its didactic capacity but in its transformative potential, the good "what we become through it."[38] Wilde's "serial subjectivity" threatened the sanctity of a genuine self, or of a fixed aesthetic form, ultimately short-circuiting this logic, validating the idea of his cultural performance—from American tour to his trial for gross indecency in 1895—as "an important, perhaps foundational, text of aesthetic modernism."[39]

De-gene-ration

The images of degeneration familiar to the nineteenth century were indebted to theological interpretation, specifically regarding their inability to uphold the traditional gendered positions dictated by the book of Genesis and the father and mother of humanity therein, Adam and Eve. In a way, *Salomé* returns to a time before (like Villiers), or at least beyond, social mores restrictive of sex and gender; indeed, his play performs a sort of return to the Garden of Eros, a heterogeneric and genetic adaptation. In friend Robert Ross's "Note on 'Salome'" introducing the text, he defines Wilde through the author's own anecdote on the idea of literary borrowing and reproduction: "When I see a monstrous tulip with *four* wonderful petals in someone else's garden, I am impelled to grow a monstrous tulip with *five* wonderful petals" (xviii). Wilde's *Salomé*, which he called "the cardinal flower of the perverse garden," grows out of the soil of his particular genetic and aesthetic hybridity.[40]

Subjective desire on the part of Salome held no consequence within the biblical story of Herod's stepdaughter who danced for the head of John the Baptist; it was for her mother's vengeance that the biblically unnamed daughter dances in the Bible. Yet Wilde found the biblical story "dry and colourless; without lavishness, extravagance or sin."[41] Salome's original story possessed little in the realm of passions and pleasures, and Wilde found little inspiration in her original form, as a passive girl who obeys her mother. Instead, he wanted his heroine and her unbridled eroticism "to become the supreme incarnation of sexual love."[42] As Regenia Gagnier suggests, "Had it been performed, a play like *Salome* would have confronted Victorian audiences with a spectacle of purposeless, 'unnatural,' unproductive, and uncensored art and desire."[43] Unlike Villiers, Wilde was not searching for the daughter of obedient artificiality but one characterized by exquisite deviance, and an alarmingly labyrinthine lineage of contextuality—an inner network of intertextuality that also prefigures film adaptation.

Biological heredity was scrutinized as a source of contagion rather than a medium for progress, atavism becoming the paradoxical paradigm of modernity, an essential disturbance of its "eternal up-to-date-ness."[44] Modernity is at heart an atavism, Dana Seitler boldly claims in *Atavistic Tendencies*, a "'reproduction' and 'recurrence' of the past in the present" that erases immediate reproductive connections between parent and child, allowing for "dramatic reallocations of self, body, and subjectivity."[45] In terms of pathological atavism, Italian criminologist Cesare Lombroso believed in the notion of being "born criminal," and that women in particular displayed these traits, having been created as a "separate species," a partial foundation for early readings of "morbid activity" in Salomé's "psychic centres."[46]

A monogenist who believed that all human races evolved from the first couple in the Garden of Eden, Benedictin Augustin Morel opened the door for degeneration theory to become "a tool for measuring the moral health of society as well as the health of the individual" with his publication of *Traité des dégénérescences physiques, intellectuelles et morales de l'espèce humaine* in 1857.[47] By the end of the century, the concept was used to explore and explain the sense of human degradation emerging as an adverse effect of modernity, the city, and technology—a slipping of culture toward more primal and ultimately uncultured ways. Degenerationism came to denote "evolution reversed and compressed . . . a terrible regression, a downward spiral into madness, chaos, extinction."[48] Consequently, according to many leading physicians and social critics at the time, people were becoming corrupted into degenerates of type such as the hysteric, the homosexual, and the New Woman, to name a few. But most loathsome of these types within the art world was the Decadent, which an anonymous critic at the *National Observer* called an "invention as terrible as, and in some ways more shocking than, the New Woman."[49] While the previous chapter discussed the figure of the *andréïde* as a woman turned into a technological object, here we have a personality type turned into a modern invention.

Max Nordau, a Hungarian physician and author whose major work *Degeneration* (1895) enacted a moralist censure on degeneracy in the world of art and literature, leveled his reproach at a whole slew of artistic movements of the nineteenth century and those figures who spearheaded them, including the Pre-Raphaelites, Symbolists, Richard Wagner, Parnassians, Decadents, and

Aesthetes, and Ibsen and Nietzsche, whom he labels "ego-maniacs."[50] Because it banishes all that is natural in favor of the artificial, Nordau credits "decadentism"—which he traces through Gautier and Baudelaire—with artistic debauchery. Predictably, Oscar Wilde holds a notable place in Nordau's catalog as a "cultivator of the Ego" and the principal agent of the growth of the French-born *décadent* into the English Aesthete: "The ego-mania of decadentism, its love of the artificial, its aversion to nature, and to all forms of activity and movement, its megalomaniacal contempt for men and its exaggeration of the importance of art, have found their English representative among the 'Aesthetes,' the chief of whom is Oscar Wilde."[51] Maintaining that art should have a social and moral function, Nordau objected to the Aesthetes' conception of art as its own aim, as well as their belief that art need only be beautiful: "Beauty lies in the form. Hence the content is a matter of indifference."[52] One of the main premises of Nordau's evaluation of degeneracy is that homogeneity in art, or purity of word/form, had been overthrown, infected by aesthetic heterogeneity as a pathogenic agent, a disease. He laments that artistic language itself had become infected, that words could no longer be counted upon to house any stable, unique meaning. Nordau aspired for sameness and the stability of the referent, but Wilde's version of art offers solace in an instable identity, one constantly in flux according to style. Never reliant on a constant, linguistic referent, Wilde's artistic panorama expanded to account for meaning's (and desire's) inherently mechanical multiplicity.

In lieu of Nordau's siren call for artistic propriety, Wilde offers imagination and complex multiformity as the method of escaping what he identified as degenerative: Victorianism's propulsion toward "greater simplicity." Indeed, the decay of lying "means the social domination of the sincere: the single or homogeneous personality."[53] But Wilde's commitment to the disingenuous, as well as his lamentations on the decay of lying, equate to Wilde's own perverse, aesthetic Truth. Instead of the Arnoldian dictum that the artist must "see the object as in itself it really is," Wilde credited art's value in representing the object-as-it-can-be, always imaginatively transforming, the word or character continually rerendering all its artificial and visualized possibilities. Not only was Wilde "able to see the imagination as a principle of heterogeneity," but the "mythopoeic faculty now became for him the basis of an advanced and vital culture, not as before the sign of an infantile or unprogressive one."[54] Unlike figures like Nordau, Havelock Ellis determined that the decadent style "was really a refinement on the classic, an 'advance' on it, 'a further specialization, the homogeneous, in Spencer's phraseology, having become heterogeneous.'"[55] Wilde's ever-metamorphosing (art) object was constantly adaptive, somewhat emblematic of how cells and forms reproduce endlessly in their own constant advancements, and importantly antecedent to Jean Epstein's *photogénie*—the idea of a new sensory experience of the cinema reproduced from the same generational line of French Symbolism from Gautier to Wilde.

Queer Ekphrasis

Within literature, the Decadents' "supreme of artifice" reached a pinnacle in the book that British critic Arthur Symons referred to as "the breviary of the Decadence," Huysmans's *À Rebours*.[56] In particular, the novel marked a crowning point for the interchangeable representation of the decadent and the new femme fatale, who often acted as a substitute for society's New Woman and the fears she evoked in equivalent measure, all figures in this wellspring of counterpart stereotypes considered by the philistine English as disruptions of conventional standards of sex and gender. "Contradictory as these stereotypes may seem," as Franz Meier writes, "they all converge in a deviant, unproductive attitude towards sexuality that subverts gender boundaries and was thus considered a threat to the male-dominated symbolic order of Victorian culture."[57] All of these types were treated as unnatural complications.

In his biography, Richard Ellmann claims that the "principal engenderer" of Wilde's *Salomé* is the exceedingly synthetic "account in the fifth chapter of Huysmans' *À Rebours* of two paintings of Salome by Gustave Moreau, and in the fourteenth chapter of the same book a quotation from Mallarmé's poem 'Hérodiade.'"[58] In his notebooks, Moreau depicted Salome as "an emblem of sensuality, of unhealthy curiosity, and of that terrible fate reserved for searchers after a nameless ideal."[59] Accordingly, she became the most visible symbol for the French Symbolists' re-orient-ation of their modern, aesthetic ideal. Although it seems certain that Wilde's Salomé sprung from a far greater number of contextual sources, it is telling that the play's "principal engenderer," according to Ellmann, is such a self-conscious, artistic hybrid—a novel quoting a poem and performing ekphrases of paintings. In other words, it is an art form that must exploit other art forms, caught up in a constant and necessary circuit of deformation.

Though the decadent style finds itself subject to an ever-oscillating set of interpretations, Huysmans's novel and its protagonist, Des Esseintes, are oft considered paradigmatic of the movement. The product of biological devolution, Des Esseintes is depicted as a bloodless and frail china doll of sorts; a wasted copy of his forefathers, he retains no resemblance to the portraits of athletic soldiers and other forbidding fellows. Des Esseintes degenerates into something very unnatural—an unmanly man, subject to his own gender negation—because sex has become unnatural in the novel, at least by moral standards. He is a product of incest, normatively reproductive but an abominable version of the reproductive norm. Further, he revels specifically in the generation of artifice, that man can give art(ificial) life to inanimate objects like jewels, paintings, and locomotives. Des Esseintes finds a certain *puissance* in owning or admiring these products of male, creative ingenuity. Through both his biological ancestry and his literary lineage, Des Esseintes represents the apex of the artificial and the emergence of the decadent dandy.

Like Des Esseintes, with whom he admits to sharing the same sickness, Wilde defines his aesthetic subjectivity through this widely shared, haunting fascination with the strange and superhuman Salome of his dreams, who doubles as a reflective surface for the irresistible force of her cinematic future. Des Esseintes "experiences a kind of mimetic desire for the princess" as he stands in the same position as the "old king . . . crushed, annihilated, close to vertigo, before this dancer."[60] But the dancer transforms before his very eyes into "the accursed Beauty singled out from among all others by the cataleptic paroxysm that stiffens her flesh," an "unfeeling Beast" like "the Helen of antiquity" or "the royal harlot of the Apocalypse."[61] Equally paralyzed by the static painting, Des Esseintes finds himself suspended in a state of vertigo—an almost mechanically repetitive male response throughout these French texts that foretells my analysis of Hitchcock's *Vertigo* (1958) in chapter 5—impressed by the artist's powers of mimesis while at the same time dizzied by the impossible gulf that separates him, the seer, from the desired art object. This impossible divide also suggests that of the voyeuristic, cinematic spectator, always seeing and never seen. In essence, Des Esseintes looks for himself in a hedonistic masquerade that intimates the landscape of cinema. There is not a single natural detail "that human ingenuity cannot manufacture; no moonlit Forest of Fontainebleau that cannot be reproduced by stage scenery under floodlighting . . . no flower that carefully chosen taffeta and delicately coloured paper cannot match!" (23). As Françoise Meltzer writes, "Like the artificially induced flowers in Des Esseintes's hothouse, far more beautiful than those found in nature, the novel outdoes God at his own game, for writing produces 'life' where there is none, precisely by insisting upon the superiority of artifice."[62] Artifice usurps the real; in a horrifying reversal of expectations, this is a real that looks fake, an ekphrastic premonition of cinema itself.

While my analysis in this chapter offers Wilde's *Salomé* as an important traverse between ekphratic literature and film, Moreau's most sensational Salomé paintings unconsciously illustrate central protocinematic principles that emerged in chapter 1. Seduced by the paintings' "incantatory charm," Des Esseintes hints at their humanness, works that "breathed a strange magic" and "lived constantly before his eyes." In the first painting he describes, *Salomé dansant devant Hérode*, Des Esseintes likens the dancing figure to an "irresistible force" indifferent to "everything that sees her." Puzzling over the fact that Salomé holds in her hand the scepter of Isis, "the great lotus-blossom," he contemplates whether Moreau "had remembered the sepulchral rites of ancient Egypt, the solemn ceremonies of embalmment" during which the woman's body would be purified with that sacred flower's petals—preserved through the appearance of life.[63] But *L'Apparition* (figure 3.2) causes him more agitation, glittering and glowing "so warmly with exquisite fleshtints" it crosses over into the real. In the painting, John the Baptist's head floats, glowing eerily in a halo of light above the silver charger, as if an

FIG. 3.2 *L'Apparition*, painted by Gustave Moreau around 1875, depicting the biblical character Salome and her vision of John the Baptist's head, which resembles a hallucinatory, cinematic projection.

imagined hallucination, with no other figure in the painting reacting. Central to the composition, the prophet's head clearly resembles the cinematic projection of an image—or, possibly, that of a magic lantern—with Salomé's pointed finger and arm gesturing upward acting as the projector, as if she is casting off the glitter of her numerous jewels onto an imaginary screen. Despite the intricately woven web of begetting and begottenness, it has been suggested that seeing this painting in the Louvre museum in Paris in 1884—the same year as the publication of *À Rebours*—directly inspired Wilde to create his own adaptation.

Upon its publication a multitude of critics discerned that Wilde's Salomé had the same problems as Huysmans's Des Esseintes: deep-rooted corruption, amorality, ungodliness. And Wilde's play was so deeply enmeshed into this profusion of historical, artistic representations, into such a multitude of "first" authors, critics contended that not much of her was actually indebted to his artistic authority. "*Salomé* is a mosaic," writes an anonymous critic for the *Pall Mall Gazette* in 1893, "a library in itself."[64] Wilde's heroine is, he claims, "the daughter of too many fathers," naming Théophile Gautier, Gustave Flaubert, and Maurice Maeterlinck specifically as her most indispensable, literary forebears. The critic extends the metaphor, announcing tenaciously that, as the persistently reduplicated and thus disreputably degenerative female Symbol of the arts, Salomé functions as a symptom of a disease. He alleges that, like Des Esseintes, "she is the victim of heredity. Her bones want strength, her flesh wants vitality, her blood is polluted."[65] By the fin de siècle, Salome had become the polysemantic icon for the Victorian era's social woes, which stemmed from aggrandizing, sexualized blights on society: prostitution, syphilis, even the New Woman. But on the grounds of Salomé being the adulterated *fille* of far too many artistic progenitors, Wilde may have greeted the review with delight rather than offense. Wilde believed rather brazenly, even paradoxically, in the act of copying as an artist's developmental requirement. As he quipped to friend and contemporary literary critic Max Beerbohm, "Of course I plagiarise. . . . I never read Flaubert's *Tentation de Saint Antoine* without signing my name at the end of it. *Que voulez-vous*? All the best Hundred Books bear my signature in this manner."[66] So when the *Pall Mall Gazette* critic declares summarily that with *Salomé* Wilde proves, "not for the first time, that he can mimic, where he might have shown—for the first time—that he could create," he did not realize that Wilde's very intention for the piece was not creation, but perhaps instead, simulation—to produce a surface resemblance, or, most fundamentally, the tendency to assume the form of something else.

Wilde's play hinged itself upon notables, such as Sarah Bernhardt and the Symbolists, as well as other things, which caused his figuration of *Salomé* to be hybridized by its incessant heterogeneity, an endless reversibility of subjects and objects—ostensibly divergent from Gautier's artistic crusades toward *singularité* despite Wilde's adulation of *l'art pour l'art*. Others populated Wilde's text from the very start, his use of the French language serving to heighten the play's queerness, its impulse toward otherness. The text's hybrid form from the onset, in fact, may have been one of the reasons Wilde valued *Salomé* as one of his most subjective pieces, aligning with his own beliefs in aesthetic heterogeneity. Before he composed *Salomé* as a drama, Wilde played with an assortment of literary genres for its expression, including prose and poetry. Of course, Wilde's knowledge of the biblical story in its many generic transmutations was vast, which seemed to offer an equivalent array of models for his version. Yet the writing of the play was always secondary to its performance, whether real or mythological; Wilde seemingly first told the tale to a group of young men during his stay in Paris in 1891, writing the story down in a happenstance blank notebook upon returning to his chambers on the boulevard des Capucines that evening. These genre fluctuations gave way to a play, and a new Salome, marked by a growing and monstrous hybridity, one that paid little heed to demarcations of aesthetic form, temporality, or sexuality. In fact, Wilde's continuously turning reconceptions of Salome were somewhat virtual, temporarily simulated in and though any object or image of momentary, aesthetic force. In "How Oscar Wilde Dreamed of Salomé," Guatemalan writer Gómez Carrillo clarifies the essentially endless multiplicity of Wilde's distinctly subjective Salomania: "His 'Salomé' I say, and I am in error: for there were ten, no, a hundred Salomés that he imagined, that he began, that he abandoned. Each painting he saw in a museum suggested a new idea; each book he found in which the object of his interest was mentioned filled him with self-doubts."[67] Carrillo tells of the innumerable, almost mechanically repetitive Salomes saturating Wilde's artistic imaginings, each singularly rendering the Salome of his dreams, at least for that instant: those Salomes that filled the Museo del Prado, especially the one by Titian (1515), who Wilde proclaimed "paints with living flesh!"; the oil painting *Salome with the Head of John the Baptist* (1527) by Italian artist Bernardino Luini, a student and contemporary of Leonardo da Vinci's; and the most evident counterpoint to Wilde's version, Moreau's *Salomé dansant devant Hérode*, a painting Wilde believed to be "one of the wonders of the world."[68]

Using aestheticized language "to make us see," to give voice to the art object, represents what W. J. T. Mitchell calls "ekphrastic hope," empowering endless possibilities for overcoming the word/image dichotomy, and thus instead producing an "imagetext" or "synthetic form."[69] Generally considered a rhetorical device generated from Plato's concept of forms in the *Republic*, ekphrasis is a vivid, verbal description of a visual work of art (though the objectness of the subject matter may be increasingly abstract) that has infiltrated a large swath of literature in all categories—rhetoric, poetry, prose, drama—since Homer's description of Achilles's mighty shield in *The Iliad*, the first operative use in ancient Greek poetry. Aesthetically heterogeneous by definition, using one medium to describe the essence of another is a form of relational formalism that Wilde himself vindicates when he declares, "In a very ugly and sensible age, the arts borrow, not from life, but from each other."[70] Ekphrasis aspires, according to Mitchell, to overcome otherness; a text's encounter with its semiotic other reduces the threat of difference, creating instead a program of resemblance between text/image that encourages identification and, more important, imitation. This leads to what Mitchell designates as "ekphrastic fear," of what might become a dangerous promiscuity found in such free reciprocity.

Indeed, the necessary mating of multiple, aesthetic forms in the service of what I call artificial generation becomes an extremely poignant replication crisis at this particular period in the nineteenth century. Since ekphrasis seeks to create a "still moment" of plastic art in the narrative movement of literary language, it gets further ensnared in an increasingly elaborate network of adaptation at the onset of the moving picture. As Gotthold Ephraim Lessing expressed in "Laocoon" (1766), his essay on the limits of painting and poetry, ekphrasis invites idolatry, the reduction of beings into symbols, or even mere "feminine plaything." The Symbolists' concentration in and of Salomes offers a poignant and possibly meta-level exhibition of the ekphrastic mode, a constantly evolving adaptation of the unnamed biblical daughter into an exceedingly and dangerously promiscuous femme fatale. By the time Wilde copied her, his variegated figuration embodied how "ekphrasis could just as easily be seen as literature at its most mimetic, as a copy of a copy, an imitation with no original."[71]

Wilde exalted both the French and Greek languages as the most civilized and aesthetically necessary; Greek culture profoundly influenced both his artistic developments and his own "private codes of self-understanding," the discourse of Greek life and mythology allowing Wilde a "performative dimension" for his same-sex desires.[72] The word "ekphrasis" comes from the Greek *ek-* (out) and *phrasein* (speak), etymologically establishing the literary mode as a speaking out about, or as, something, in terms of an animation or a simulation. The root word also intimates the queerer possibilities of ekphrasis as a coming out. Whereas normative ekphrastic endeavors would seek to reify feminized objets d'art, shoring in heterosexual imperatives, queer forms of ekphrasis privileged the deformation of boundaries set between the visual and verbal, allowing for the revaluation of the queer subject's experience of being treated as "failed copies of the ideals of masculinity and femininity."[73] As Brian Glavey indicates, Wilde's *Dorian Gray* demarcates an important point in literary history wherein ekphrasis and queer theory become yoked, especially in regard to the "fetishistic tendency to treat people like pictures."[74] Glavey's remarkable work *The Wallflower Avant-Garde: Modernism, Sexuality, and Queer Ekphrasis* extends queer ekphrasis as a way of conceiving performance itself, specifically in relation to how theories of performance reconceive gender—which Judith Butler famously calls "*a kind of imitation for which there is no original.*"[75] One of the inaugural insights of queer theory is to conceive of gender and sexuality as themselves "ekphrastic illusions," and, according to Glavey, modernist aesthetic theory is much "queerer than imagined."[76] More queer, too, because of modernity's multiplication of mimesis to a higher power—mathematical, and in terms of its repetitive program of reoriginating divine subject matter—resulting in a hypermimetic aesthetic imperative of nearly mechanical effect.

Problems of Interpretation: The Dark Side of the Moon

Wilde's self-proclaimed enlargement of the "artistic horizon" with *Salomé* speaks primarily to the expansive spectrum of relationality offered through the play. Unsurprisingly, due to its constant recourse to otherness—textual, contextual, and sexual—and its hefty relationship to religious and artistic traditions, *Salomé* has generated a seemingly inexhaustible proliferation of readings. Elucidating any definite truths within the play becomes increasingly difficult when conflated with Wilde's perplexing, public provocations, most effective when "he actively participated in his own misrecognition, creating in advance," in Gregory Castle's exceptionally germane description, "the conditions of a future unveiling."[77] Historically, critics have interpreted the play's complex and pervasive topography of sadism, scopophilia, and castration anxiety through a homocentric and psychoanalytic perspective, as if in an attempt to pin down which fictional character Wilde meant for his own avatar. Many went to great lengths to create a static or fixed caricature for Wilde, "free of the recalcitrant and destabilizing dialectical image" the author himself perpetuated.[78]

However, the critical problem of *Salomé* is the very problem of the ever-mobile symbolic structures on which the play is built; the play operates as conduit for the inseparable relationship between desire and the image, "as if the two concepts were caught in a mutually generative circuit, desire generating images and images generating desire."[79] The most unsettling of these fluctuating signs, and the most powerful generator of meaning's endless reflectivity, is also the play's most all-powerful one—the moon, an importantly reflective surface that Wilde affirmed was its main protagonist. He animates it in order to invert and invest in its traditional, dramatic potential as the inconstant moon that Juliet warns Romeo against swearing by, "Lest that thy love prove likewise variable."[80] Throughout the play, characters use the interchangeable moon as a mirror, imparting their own subjective visions upon this vacillating and vacant signifier. Both the moon and Salomé start out as blank canvasses upon which he who gazes may inscribe whatever he so pleases, or whatever he may fear. The very beginning of *Salomé* reveals not only the primacy of its visual register but also, by association, the text's underlying conundrum of otherness, which translates symbolically into an impossible differentiation between persons and things, as well as forms of artistic expression.

This problematic and endless exchange arises, first and foremost, from the obvious lack of interlocution between characters. The one-act play unfolds on the moonlit terrace of Tetrarch Herod's palace, the cistern in which the prophet Iokanaan is imprisoned set in the background. On the balcony, secondary characters—including the first and second soldiers, the page of Herodias and the young Syrian, Narraboth—deliberate over a network of visuals: the beauty of Princess Salome, the somberness of Tetrarch Herod, the strangeness of the moon. Their brief dialogue illustrates this ekphrastically motivated, ontological dilemma:

THE YOUNG SYRIAN How beautiful is the Princess Salome to-night!

THE PAGE OF HERODIAS Look at the moon. How strange the moon seems! She is like a woman rising from a tomb. She is like a dead woman. One might fancy she was looking for dead things.

THE YOUNG SYRIAN She has a strange look. She is like a little princess who wears a yellow veil, and whose feet are of silver. She is like a princess who has little white doves for feet. One might fancy she was dancing.

THE PAGE OF HERODIAS She is like a woman who is dead. She moves very slowly. (1–2)

As readers we struggle to determine of who, or of what, these characters refer; a slippage materializes between the woman-subject, the princess who looks beautiful on this particular evening, and the moon-object, which ushers in the evening and itself resembles a princess. All at once, people and things are impossibly remote from one another and yet too close. So similar, it seems, that not only does the person become a thing in the immediate, abrupt directive for the young Syrian to "look at the moon" rather than Salomé, but the moon becomes a person, the page of Herodias perceiving it as a dead woman rising from the tomb, a liminal figure acting as portent of ensuing tragedy. Narraboth, however, sees the moon as Salomé in particular, and in a similarly prophetic way. It—now a she—resembles a princess dancing. Though the play ends with the climax of Salomé dancing for Iokanaan's death—his head on a silver charger—its very first visual gives the audience a projection of her danse macabre through her doppelgänger. Between Salomé and the moon there occurs an uneasy yet valuable sense of identification.

However, to define oneself symbolically through things might also, paradoxically, conduct the subject toward its own demise. Narraboth's suicide is the play's internal sacrifice to the traditional iconography of unrequited love and the perils of self-regard. Upon Salomé's entrance, Narraboth glimpses his own future by seeing Salomé, his beloved, as an object forewarning his destruction, "like a narcissus trembling in the wind. . . . She is like a silver flower" (10). By promising Narraboth that the next day she will look at him through her veils and let fall a little green flower for him—thus playing on his desire for her by offering to make *him* the object of her gaze—Salomé gains access to the prophet, Iokanaan. She soon finds herself amorous of Iokanaan's body and seduced by his melodious voice, which is like wine to her. But during her lustful valuation of Iokanaan's body, Narraboth kills himself, and his corpse falls between Salomé and Iokanaan. Straightaway, the page of Hérodias bewails his death, admitting that he had given Narraboth, his unwitting beloved, gifts, like a ring of agate he always wore, and that they would spend their evenings taking walks together during which Narraboth would have "much joy to gaze at himself in the river" (27). The page discovers that he would have never been seen by his beloved in any mutual exchange of affection because, like Narcissus, Narraboth was too busy looking only at himself. Hérode and Hérodias enter the scene then, Hérode looking not only for Salomé but also for signs, just like Narraboth and the page of Hérodias, in the moon and its reflections. He gets a clear signal of tragedy when he slips in the blood of Narraboth's corpse, as Hérodias continually warns him not to look at her daughter.

Wilde philosophized at length on the aesthetic value of the mask and the mirror as reflexive metaphors of artistic subjectivity, but in *Salomé* he uses the moon as the paradigm for such an identity surface, a self-referencing mirror and simultaneous simulacrum. Like the mirror and the mask, the moon embodies "both aspects of the paradox of reference in autonomy," referring "first to themselves . . . and at the same time to self-reference itself, as a problematic property of human desire."[81] It functions as a grotesque exaggeration of a symbol insomuch as it eradicates any singularity of meaning; if for Gautier the sun operated as the most prodigious of photosculptors, Wilde's moon metamorphoses the Symbolist system. Through "the jeweled, orientalist prose of the French decadents" Wilde so admired, using their language, "he told the story of the demise of their aesthetic, announcing the emergence of his own modern and unambiguously camp revision of it," exposing the dark side of the moon.[82]

Salomé is a tragedy not because it is a failed aesthetic quest, like *Dorian Gray*, but a successful one. If Wilde's play epitomizes Aesthetic pseudo-scripture, the most valuable lesson it imparts upon its audience is that looking (with desire) is dangerous. Because by looking I mean both the subject who looks (at the object) and the object that looks (like the subject, and vice versa), no one or no thing is exempt from this perilous relationship. Like a mirror, the play's moon catches everyone and everything in its glare, thus transmitting a bevy of dangerous resemblances indiscriminately. In defiance of expectations, Wilde ensures the play's prioritization of fate not through the death of the religious prophet but through the symbolic moon, which predicts and authorizes the play's ultimate tragedy: desire's fulfillment. Wilde's subversive strategy perversely challenges, perhaps even deconstructs, the pleasure found through the binary opposition between seer and seen. Although advocating for the ultimate value of the visual, the play demands its spectators to recognize the danger for those who look in lustful ways, offering a dialectical complexity of the relationship between theater and the cinema as a future aesthetic direction and dimension.

In turn, the protean reflections of the moon ensure that the "scandalous abandon" of visual, signifying structures causes a corresponding deformation of the value of the play's language. Wilde empties language of its merit in exactly the way Nordau feared, by breaking down concrete concepts in favor of their slippery, abstract potential; for Nordau, degenerate works "signify promiscuously," inducing anxiety by lacking language "'clear, homogeneous, and free from internal contradictions.'"[83] The disloyalty between words and their meanings is exploited within *Salomé* to parallel the dangerous resemblances perpetrated in the play: between subjects and objects, text and image, theatrical literature and future cinema. Early in the play, an exchange of views between secondary characters—the Cappadocian, the Nubian, and the first and second soldiers—actualizes Wilde's aesthetic belief in the transformative potential of things and the dangerous value of words. To these characters, the very thought of believing in something nonvisual is "altogether ridiculous" (6). Even more striking is their inability to hold any type of two-sided conversation, only understanding things if assimilated into their own subjective views. When the second soldier announces that one of the tetrarch's wines is purple like Caesar's cloak, the Cappadocian responds, "I have never seen Caesar" (4). When he says the other is "as yellow as gold," the Cappadocian responds that he loves gold, thus transforming the descriptive property of the wine into a blunt, tangible thing (4). The colored thinking of Wilde's characters seems inspired by French Symbolist poet Arthur Rimbaud, whose poem "Voyelles" was animated by his interest in sensory fusion and chromosthesia—colored sensation. Symbolism exalted synesthetic perception as art's future direction, to transmit a heightened, sensory experience. Though never realized, Wilde intended for *Salomé* to offer its audiences a full-spectrum sensory experience: "He envisioned a synaesthetic picture, appealing to the aural, visual, and olfactory faculties, and emphasizing Salome's effect on the audience. Salome's words were 'like music'; he first wanted her to be costumed in shades of yellow, then in gold or silver, then green like a lizard, then as unadorned as Victorian stages would permit; he wanted braziers of perfume wafting scented clouds before spectacular sets."[84] Wilde perpetuated Symbolist ideals of synesthetic experience and pushed them into rupturing the fourth wall of performance and conventional theatrical realism. He wished for his art to offer the illusion of life through the senses that define it.

On the whole, *Salomé* destabilizes both symbolism and the symbolic order, turning symbols into pseudo-symbols, emptied of any singular, traditional meaning. A tertiary character in Wilde's treatment of the story, only Hérodias refuses to believe in prophets, symbols, and maledictions, the only one reasonable enough to suggest "the moon is like the moon, that is all" (28). For every other character, the moon reflects, reveals, foreshadows, curses; it holds far more power than any of the play's language, although as a symbol the moon's authority corresponds to its seeming representational futility. All of the play's symbols, then, become as reflective as the moon, not meaningful in themselves but reproducing false appearances—making them into simulations. In fact, the play offers a somewhat cinematic structure: a beacon of cinema, the moon operates like a camera lens, lighting and capturing Salomé's performance of her dance of the seven veils, which will then produce the most indelible and inherently photographic image: the head of the prophet on a (reflective) silver platter—a metal canvas that parallels those used by Daguerre in capturing his first photographic images, which needed to be polished to a mirror finish. Less literature than perhaps lunagraph, Wilde's play is scattered with photographic and cinematic metaphors: Iokanaan is imprisoned inside the black hole of Hérode's cistern, which needs be penetrated by the moon's light, a possible likeness for a camera obscura; before giving her the head of Iokanaan, Hérode attempts to offer Salomé substitutive pleasures, such as "a great emerald" one can look through as if a lens pointed toward distant lands to "see that which passeth far off" (57). Above all, there is the dance of the moon's double, and object of its mechanistic gaze: a female screen "idol," Salomé is screened by veils and reflected in the light of the moon, compelling a possible reading of her as see-through. The dance of her photo-genic figure operates as a harbinger of her cinematic future and an important basis for the film medium, as I will continue to explore in chapter 4.

What is ultimately at stake in the play's fluctuating and interchangeable signs and symbols is the representation of desire, unfettered by any social or sexual edicts, instead "dedicated to the proliferation of an unpredictable spectrum of relationality, multiplying ways of desiring, identifying with, attaching to."[85] Intriguingly, Salomé's dance, the most pervasive and provocative feature of the story in its continual reinterpretation from biblical times, and that which traditionally reinforces heterosexual imperatives, is the weakest and most evasive of the visuals within Wilde's play, only made available through his simple stage direction: "*Salome dances the dance of the seven veils*" (54). Though he properly names the dance, Wilde offers no further elaboration on its visual qualities; in fact, as Rodney Shewan points out, Wilde only added this stage direction to the text after the play's London-based production was banned in 1893, previously relying on Sarah Bernhardt to manifest the text's visuals through performance. Although historically the dance had become strongly associated with a heterosexual imperative, its blankness in Wilde's text allows it to be visualized according to the whims of its audience. Or, to be more specific, the dance exists external to the printed text or any singular performance, its imagined torque and twirling operative in and as metasignifier of performance, as adaptation—and simulation.

Wilde's *Salomé* reigns over the world of the simulacrum; the dance's lacking description equates to a refusal of ekphrasis and its "still" moment, alternately amplifying the play's gesturing toward simulation, and specifically the interface between the cinematic and embodied simulation theory. The play's deformation of language is, more specifically, that of traditional literary language. Just as Epstein's nebulous concept of the *photogénie* thinks through our desirous relationship to the cinematic screen, *Salomé* instinctually theorizes the positions, performances, and desires relevant to a screened simulation that prefigures the cinematic. The dynamic scenes of visual perception, specifically the characters' subjective ways of seeing in the play, anticipate the way cinema imposes a shared identification and spatial connection between the spectator and the screened image(s). Based on his discovery of mirror neurons—which mimic the behavior of others and may form an important basis for learning new skills through simulation—Italian neuroscientist Vittorio Gallese pioneered a theory of social cognition called embodied simulation theory. Based in these mirroring mechanisms and the idea of vision being multimodal, some recent scholars have coupled elements of embodied simulation theory with film studies to explore how meaning-making in film may fit into a framework of this "second-generation" cognitive science that emphasizes embodiment as both sensory and cultural.

While Wilde seemingly enlarged the "artistic horizon" of *Salomé* through the play's prescience of the cinematic apparatus, he committed more consciously to freeing it artistically from the confines of corporeal form or specificity of language, deconstructing the specific meaning of words in favor of a molten style of musical expression, using recurrent phrases to "bind it together like a piece of music with recurring *motifs*" equal to the "refrains of old ballads."[86] The musicality of the French text—Wilde capitalizing on the rhyming capabilities of French words like *la mort* and *l'amour*, an important facet of the textual rhythms mostly lost in the English translation—absorbs the play's characters, visuals, and action. The play's ever-fluctuating associations between subjects and objects—as well as persons and things, words and meanings, real and artificial—are made dramatically musical through "its elaborately artificial, highly mannered patterning of dialogue."[87] Take, for example, the moment that Salomé persuades the young Syrian to allow her access to Iokanaan. She commands, "When I shall pass in my litter by the bridge of the idol-buyers, I will look at thee through the muslin veils, I will look at thee, Narraboth, it may be I will smile at thee. Look at me, Narraboth, look at me" (16). Salomé's continual reiteration of elementary phrases and repetition of the same linguistic structures in Wilde's original French—*je vous regarderai, je vous sourirai*—lend rhythmic power to her utterances, empowering her as a subject despite the fact that she often and unknowingly parrots the sentiments of others. The "strange music" of *Salomé*'s "studied dialogue is congruent with Western forms of musical exposition, wherein elementary patterns are proposed and developed through progressive elaborations on initial ur-patterns or motifs . . . interconnection and development."[88]

Wilde saw *Salomé* as a literary composition approaching musicality, which, first, makes it a major triumph of Aestheticism in the vein of Walter Pater's declaration in *The Renaissance* that "*all art aspires to the condition of music*"; second, the text uses music as a model for aesthetic transcendence as queer ekphrasis.[89] In *De Profundis*, Wilde reveals his belief that music was the one form "in which all subject is absorbed in expression and cannot be separated from it," thus eliciting a passionate symbiosis between the artist and their endless parade of changing forms.[90] The least discursive of the art forms, music allowed Wilde to psychically subjugate a patriarchal language that undermined the flexibility in both aesthetic and sexual form he so desired, socially and aesthetically constructing his own subjectivity within musicality, "an art that is essentially and actively other."[91]

Paradise Regained: The Palingenesis of the Play

In *L'Ève future*, Edison laments his inability to capture moments in history objectively, through technological mediums such as phonography and photography, in order to restore man's faith in humanity by being witness to those events that built our civilization and culture. But Wilde believed strongly that history is subjective, ripe to be recast; as he expresses in "The Critic as Artist" (1891), "The one duty we owe to history is to rewrite it."[92] Both authors rescript biblical stories in their very different Symbolist styles: Villiers tries to restore and repair the creation story from Genesis, but Wilde tries to enlarge the scope of Salome's story both aesthetically and subjectively. Wilde's project, then, compels itself toward the very radical otherness—or the inevitable reconciliation between history and modernity—from which Villiers sought refuge.

In the original story, dating back to the New Testament (Matthew 14:3–11; Mark 6:17–29), the unnamed girl dances for her stepfather, Herod, the tetrarch of Judea, at his birthday feast, pleasing him so much that he offers her anything she desires. Salome requests the beheading of John the Baptist under encouragement of her mother, Herodias—whose marriage has been condemned by John as incestuous—and thus is looked upon as the femme fatale responsible for the prophet's unfortunate demise.[93] The climax of Wilde's version resembles that of the biblical tale: Salomé dances for her stepfather, Hérode, to obtain the head of prophet Iokanaan on a silver charger. Most other facets of this particular biblical story, however, are mixed, magnified, or fictionalized in Wilde's version, especially on the level of character. Iokanaan, for instance, differs greatly from the figure of John the Baptist familiar through European iconography. As Katherine Brown Downey writes, he "does not have the appearance of the wild man dressed in animal skins and sustaining himself on locusts, as John the Baptist of tradition did—a tradition even the soldiers and others in the play maintain when they discuss what they had heard about Iokanaan. Rather, he is lovely to behold: thin, pale, and passionate."[94] Salomé, who Wilde emancipates from her mother's mandate, seems wholly unaware of the history of the prophet, taking him as a visual thing to behold and desire in the moment, unfettered by any historical prejudice. And notably, as Robert Ross remarks in his introductory note to the English edition of *Salome*, Wilde conflates Herod the Great, Herod Antipas, and Herod Agrippa intentionally into one Herod character, to make of him a type, a symbol, rather than a historical figure.[95] Other than Hérodias, the rest of Wilde's cast of characters is largely his own invention, though as Rodney Shewan acknowledges, one might be "glancing at times towards Maeterlinck, Flaubert, J. C. Heywood, or Wilde's earlier fables" to glean their origins.[96]

If Wilde's play can be considered a revisionist narrative akin to *L'Ève future*, it is because it attempts to recapture paradise insomuch as it allows for the possibility of eating the fruit and sexually possessing the other, not in the service of heteronormative reproduction but solely for pleasure. Fittingly, Wilde turned to another biblical intertext for *Salomé* that better suited his aesthetic aims: the Song of Songs, also known as Solomon's Song or the Song of Solomon, part of the Old Testament and best described as a collection of lyric love poems. As Marcia Falk asserts, "If we think of the lyric as sensual, the exquisitely rich imagery of the Song would certainly qualify the Song as lyric poetry . . . [fitting] the etymological definition, which proclaims the lyric to be musical or songlike."[97] Most likely, Wilde, uninterested in staying true to the biblical edicts of Salome's story, found himself drawn to its lyrical quality and plentitude of sensorial imagery, as well as its abundance of unfixed orientations. Falk outlines the variety of interpretations of the Song, including its characterization as a cycle of wedding poems and as an allegory of love between God and the people of Israel, only to conclude that her main objection to classical readings is "their imposition of fixed personae and either plot or contextual unity on a text that seems instead to present a variety of voices speaking in a range of settings and without narrative sequence."[98] What Falk calls "the variegated material of the Song" parallels the contextual chaos of Wilde's play and his hopes for a synesthetic, tangible experience in performance incited by *Salomé*'s tumult of images, "in the long catalogues of jewels and flowers, 'strange dyes, strange colors,' . . . the poet's language actually seeking to escape its traditional obligation to order, abstraction, and hierarchy and aspiring instead to the physicality and simultaneity of graphic art."[99]

The Song also pays thorough attention to the body, wholly uncharacteristic of biblical writings. We are told in the first chapter of Genesis that human beings are made in the (spiritual) "image" of a bodiless God and are offered no other visual clues except that these bodies are designated as two sexes, male and female. Yet physical beauty brings pleasure in the biblical world as well and the Song is one of the few, and the most graphic, accounts of this dimension. Here, these lovers detail each other's attributes seemingly as an expression of their own desire, using similes, metaphors, metonymy, and synecdoche. The biblical speakers look outside toward nature for linguistic resources for comparison, and "desire once awakened doubles back to these details, making them targets of lust-filled speech."[100]

Wilde also mimics the opulent carnality of the Song's erotic language by having Salomé praise her beloved through identical, metonymical images.[101] In *Salome and Judas in the Cave of Sex*, Ewa Kuryluk surveys the most obvious correspondences between Salomé's monologues and the ancient biblical poem, many of the images that she invokes to describe Iokanaan part by part slightly altered versions of the images in the Song.[102] Salomé focuses on three aspects of Iokanaan's physicality—his body, his hair, and his mouth—and expresses her captivation (and subsequent disgust) with each as if she were performing ekphrases of a triptych painting. She begins with his body, of which she is amorous, a body "white, like the lilies of a field that the mower hath never mowed," "white like the snows that lie on the mountains of Judea," the whitest of all things as she proclaims, "There is nothing in the world so white as thy body" (22). But when he bluntly rebuffs her advances by making clear that he obeys only the voice of the Lord God and not that of the daughter of Babylon, as he calls her, Salomé changes her tune, calling his body hideous, "like the body of a leper," "like a plastered wall where the scorpions have made their nest" (22). She proclaims, instead, that she is enamored of his hair, "like clusters of grapes," "like the great cedars of Lebanon" (22). Again after a subsequent repudiation, she calls his hair horrible, "like a knot of serpents," "like a crown of thorns," an obvious allusion to Jesus Christ's fate at the crucifixion (23). Ultimately, she quests passionately for Iokanaan's mouth, which, in some of the more blatantly Song-inspired images, she likens to "a pomegranate cut in twain," cooing that "pomegranate flowers that blossom in the gardens of Tyre, and are redder than roses, are not so red" as Iokanaan's mouth (23). The Song itself begins with a foundational desire that quite closely resembles Salomé's main yearning in Wilde's play: "Let him kiss me with the kisses of his mouth" (1:2). Wilde puts an imperative version of this desire into the mouth of Salomé, who, after Iokanaan spurns her advances a third time, reiterates no fewer than ten times at this point in the play some variation of "I will kiss thy mouth, Iokanaan." She takes to projecting, in a madwoman's quasi-mechanical repetition, her own prophecy.

Wilde's *Salomé* ventures toward the sensuous utopia of the Song of Songs, wherein love operates as supreme value and, more important, "the generative force through which society perpetuates itself."[103] Wilde deftly used a tightly circumscribed time and place—just like a garden—in order to induce an outbreak of desire, the likes of which were expelled after the Fall from Eden in favor of socialized commandments on the use of sex for reproduction, and within the confines of the husband-wife relationship. The Song invokes gender fluidity greatly divergent from these rigid sexual constructions. The Fall ushers in the doom of mortality, but it also dictates the unidirectionality of woman's desire to her husband. The Song, instead, offers a more pliable and equitable relation between lover and beloved. In progression, it reads: "My beloved *is* mine, and I *am* his" (2:16), "I *am* my beloved's, and my beloved *is* mine" (6:3), "I *am* my beloved's, and his desire *is* toward me" (7:10). It provides a fitting context considering that Wilde's independent magnification of the myth in terms of Salomé's proper desire for Iokanaan reverses traditional gender roles and "contributes to the play's insistence upon the fluid, communal nature of desire."[104] Some variant of sexual desire motivates most of the main characters; ironically, Hérodias, the most vilified character in historical and biblical accounts of the tale, is the only character fairly untainted by sexual desire in Wilde's version. As Norbert Kohl writes, "The lasciviousness of the virgin lusting after the chaste prophet, and the desires of the sterile old man lusting after his stepdaughter—this certainly represents a decadent variation on the old romantic theme of love."[105] Another variant, Salomé's eventual yearning for the male scopic position means that she encodes the desire of one man for another—a mirror image of the male couple, Narraboth and the page of Hérodias, represented at the play's onset.

The play ends with Salomé's lengthy address to the decapitated head of Iokanaan, in which she affirms, like Hérod, that people should not look so much at things—but for Salomé this is because her love is not just visual but beats to the strange music of a particular soundtrack. Seemingly in one-sided conversation with the prophet's lifeless head, she identifies his voice like a "censer that scattered strange perfumes, and when I looked on thee I heard a strange music. Ah! Wherefore didst thou not look at me, Iokanaan? If thou hadst seen me thou hadst loved me. . . . I love only thee . . . I am athirst for thy beauty; I am hungry for thy body; and neither wine nor apples can appease my desire" (65). Hearing Iokanaan's *musique étrange* causes Salomé to become a terrible, desiring machine. She equates the procurement of her object of affection, in the overly sexualized image of kissing a beheaded man's mouth, to consuming him like fruit. A carnivorous Eve, who in the Garden of Eden consumes the apple that was pleasing to the eye, Salomé hungers for Iokanaan's body as apple substitute.

In "The Song of Songs and the Garden of Eden," Francis Landy suggests the two stories share the same preoccupation, the Song presenting itself as Eden's "inversion, since it portrays Paradise in this world, rediscovered through love."[106] In it, the lover and beloved are allowed to reenter their sensual paradise: "Let my beloved come into his garden, and eat his pleasant fruits" (4:16). Salomé's use of the verb *voir* (to see) indicates that seeing Iokanaan means loving him so consumingly that she must, in turn, consume him, such power to internalize her beloved other-as-image rendered psychically possible in Wilde's perverse garden of a play. This consumption might also be read as an ekphrastic performance, adapting and adopting the language of the object of study and desire. The to-be-eatenness of Iokanaan clearly represents the "good taste" of French culture and aesthetics, which Wilde attempts to psychically assimilate by writing the play in the French language.[107] In a letter written around his composition of the play, Wilde describes "Art in France" as a "strange music"—repeating the same phrase Salomé uses in the play to describe her ineffable appetite for the prophet—as his clay for generating "a reflexive meditation on Symbolist image making."[108]

Rather than bear progeny painfully as God commanded, punishment for eating the fruit of the Tree of Knowledge, Wilde's Eve of artifice is empowered with a subjectivity that allows her to eat that which is pleasing to the eye—to consume graphic art in an equally graphic way—making Salomé a powerful figure for the very concept of the transformation of artistic mediums, and a harbinger for the transformative power of the camera in its quest for *photogénie*. The Tree of Knowledge in the Garden of Eden represents God inasmuch as eating its fruit means acquiring the divine traits that it represents. For Christianity, of which Iokanaan functions as prophet, eating such fruit would be inherently cannibalistic; in Catholic tradition, the Eucharist is foundational, the bread and wine transubstantiated from the Body and Blood of Jesus Christ. If death came into the world when Adam and Eve ate the fruit of mortality, consuming the Body and Blood of Christ restores life.[109] Iokanaan refuses to see Salomé, to love her, and for that he has to die, so that she can consume him in a perverse, eucharistic parody. Salomé fulfills her sensual destiny in one of the play's most repeated and most outrageous images: "Thou wouldst not suffer me to kiss thy mouth, Iokanaan. Well! I will kiss it now. I will bite it with my teeth as one bites a ripe fruit" (64). Instead of eating the fruit offered her by Hérod—who desired to see her oral imprint in it, "the mark of thy little teeth" (32)—Salome consumes her beloved Iokanaan like fruit. Horrified by her monstrousness, Hérode orders the lights to be turned out on her both literally and figuratively: "Hide the moon! Hide the stars! . . . [*The slaves put out the torches. The stars disappear.*]" (66). Metaphorically, the cameras are turned off.

Salomé's act of cannibalistic lust is primarily an act of love, a horrid yet harmonious union of subject and object, lover and beloved; it might also be looked upon as a monstrously inflated metaphor for the ekphrastic condition of consuming the aesthetic other. Indeed, cannibalism prominently emerged within the French tradition in the sixteenth century with the publication of Michel de Montaigne's essay "Des Cannibales." In observing the act within savage civilizations, which was usually constituted by the eating of one's ancestor and sometimes of one's enemy, Montaigne recognized cannibalism as an act of respect and a sign of love—the internalization of the desired object, whether it be adored or admired for its fearlessness. This most inhuman act then turns out to be quite human, foundational to subjectivity itself. As J. M. Blanchard writes, "It is perhaps instructive that the essay on the Cannibals is one of the few . . . where 'I' ('je') never means Montaigne's self, but rather serves to introduce what constitutes this 'je,' by delineating the field of knowledge, of its experience: of its culture. . . . *Des Cannibales* emblematizes . . . some sort of pre-Rimbaldian '*Je est un autre*.'"[110]

In James Joyce's *Ulysses*, Leopold Bloom confuses the concept of "metempsychosis" with that of Ovidian "metamorphosis"—"They believed you could be changed into a tree from grief"—yet eventually explains the former concept to his wife, Molly, as coming from the Greek meaning "transmigration of souls" or "reincarnation," to be made in/as flesh once again. Bloom believes that eating can lead to physical change, an acquisition of the other's body, and "regards Communion as the ceremony of 'eating bits of a corpse.'"[111] Varieties of metempsychosis, equivalent to models of queer ekphrasis, may even allow "the unlikely magic of seeing something as itself and something else at the same time."[112] However, to best depict this idea of continual re-creation, I suggest instead the reciprocal word "palingenesis," which signifies revival or rebirth. Akin to the archaeomodern turns taken by each of these artificial generation of writers—their resurrecting of ancient ideals and even mummies in times of modernity—palingenesis speaks of an equivalent ontogeny in biological terms, a tendency to recapitulate ancestral forms, or the "regeneration of living organisms from ashes" in increasingly philosophical dimensions.[113] Jesus uses palingenesis, the Greek word for regeneration (παλιγγενεσία), only once in the New Testament, in an eschatological context to refer to a futurity for the twelve disciples to inherit a newly re-created world. This usage occurs in the book of Matthew (19:28), the very same Gospel that tells the story of the nameless daughter of Herodias dancing for the head of John the Baptist—without whose death, Jesus may have been powerless to use such words.

Meta-morphosing the Illustrated Text

A conceptually threatening hybrid, *Salomé* becomes further enmeshed into its ever-expansive adaptation network when considering it, as one must, an illustrated text. Traditionally, illustrations accompanying a literary text would illuminate the most significant aspects of its narrative, the nineteenth century a particularly fruitful era for illustrated books, mass-market magazines, and other visually inspired media, including the emergence of the first modern cartoons and caricatures in the humorous British magazine *Punch*—also the first to facetiously "realize" Wilde. I would like to consider two major dimensions of *Salomé* as an illustrated text less from a traditional perspective and more in terms of transformative capacity, both replicating and reversing the ekphratic foundation for Salome's many meta-morphoses. First, in his signature style of transforming nature into ornament, Aubrey Beardsley's illustrations for the first English edition of *Salome* (1894) monumentally deviate from the play's language; rather than operating in harmony with the text, the illustrations' alterity produces their own singularity while, at the same time, ensuring Wilde's notions of aesthetic hybridity and continual transformation. Second, I must return to the crucial importance of the actress as primary, corporeal conduit for the realization of the text, paying special attention to Wilde's fictional Sibyl Vane, the Shakespearean stage actress in the pages of *The Portrait of Dorian Gray*, and returning to the Divine Sarah Bernhardt, who performed as an ekphrastic engine, generating art through her inimitable performance style. Wilde himself referred to Bernhardt's performances as her creations, plainly stating that it was "utterly impertinent" to talk solely of one man's textual creation (such as Shakespeare's Macbeth or Othello) without noting the absolute importance of an artiste to bring art to life "when the two combine"—Wilde's own aesthetically reproductive imperative.[114]

Aubrey Beardsley

Expectations might dictate that a book's illustrations represent the textual matter faithfully and appropriately, yet the sixteen plates drawn by Aubrey Beardsley that accompany *Salomé*'s text imported unwieldy otherness and sexual perversity to such a heightened degree, they risked emptying the play of any remnant of unified meaning. Though Beardsley was chosen specifically to illustrate the first Bodley Head edition of the play based on his drawing of Salome holding the head of John the Baptist in *The Studio*, from April 1893, Wilde also famously dismissed his final illustrations for being too Japanese, when he was hoping for something more Byzantine—like the work of Gustave Moreau.[115] Beardsley's illustrations extraordinarily defy the laws of descriptive drawing, foremost regarding their lack of color, so pertinent to the ekphrastic descriptions in Wilde's play. Wilde seemed to discern the alterity of Beardsley's images as threatening his own artistic design for the play, yet the internal caricatures mirrored Wilde's own irreverent, authorial posing. A drawing by Beardsley entitled *The Woman in the Moon* (figure 3.3) depicts two naked characters—the young Syrian and the Page of Hérodias—being gazed down upon by the moon. Originally titled *The Man in the Moon*, Beardsley's drawing depicts a likeness of Wilde's face in the moon alongside an emblematic rose, resembling a monocle or a camera's lens, given its proximity to Wilde's eyes. In *Enter Herodias*, Beardsley paints Wilde into the bottom right-hand corner in a curious costume that resembles a jester's. What is most striking about Wilde in this image is that he holds in his arm a copy of *Salome*, Beardsley's meta-level demonstration that Wilde's self and art are temporally confused and inextricably conflated. Though Wilde produced and perpetuated caricatures of himself and others throughout his artistic career,

FIG. 3.3 Aubrey Beardsley's illustration *The Woman in the Moon*, which depicts Wilde in/as a moon that gazes upon the characters it illuminates.

he disliked his obvious caricaturing in the illustrations for *Salome*.[116] Wilde claimed to have created Beardsley, but he might have misrecognized that his illustrations serve as another condition for his future "unveiling," of both author and text.[117]

Wilde's face-as-moon watches over the two male figures in *The Woman in the Moon*, a correlative to whatever homosexual liaisons are seemingly available within the play, this interpretation bolstered by the fact that Wilde dedicated a copy of *Salomé* to Beardsley with the following inscription: to "the only artist who, besides myself, knows what the dance of the seven veils is, and can see that invisible dance."[118] Other than a metaphor for the cinematic apparatus that, as we will see in the next chapter, becomes ever ready to render visible this dramatically "invisible dance," one might also suggest it as a substitutive allusion to the silent "love that dare not speak its name," a euphemism for homosexuality that was coined by Wilde's lover Bosie in his poem "Two Loves," published the same year as the English edition of *Salome*. Although it may have originally been meant to label a surreptitious kind of romance, the phrase came to signify gross indecency as well, the crime for which Wilde was convicted in 1895. The exchange of a love that cannot be heard for a dance that cannot be seen fits within the context of *Salomé*, a play in which the visual and the verbal become dangerous playmates. However, much like in the Song of Songs desire in *Salomé*

FIG. 3.4 Title page for *Salome*, illustrated by Aubrey Beardsley, populated with queer figures of indeterminate gender, form, or species.

flows indiscriminately, in complete disregard of social or sexual imperatives. The fatherlessness of *Salomé*—the legitimate father of Salomé and husband of Hérodias replaced with the licentious and illegitimate father/husband figure, Hérode—opens up a space for the play's insistence on overcoming sublimation and capitalizing on errant desire, reaching a crescendo within Beardsley's image of Salome orating her desire to the head of the dead prophet, as she succeeds in kissing his mouth.

Even though they diverge immensely from Wilde's intentions, Beardsley's drawings serve to emphasize the pervasive sexual ambiguity of Wilde's play, and thus their power lies in their very textual difference. Nicholas Frankel asserts that they "tease us with the prospect that they contain dangerous and perverse meanings, if only by the sheer profusion of undraped body parts and sex organs dispersed throughout."[119] In the image Beardsley created for the play's title page, for instance, a queer figure who rises out of a jungle of vines and roses is depicted with horns, Adam's apple, breasts with eyes for nipples, an eye where the navel should be, and a penis and testicles emerging from beads of hair that look more like the pubic region of a female (figure 3.4). This proliferation of body parts, traditionally considered signs of value regarding the figures' sex and/or gender, extends into many of the illustrations. In *Enter Herodias*, for example, Hérodias has breasts and the large stature of a man, while her page, despite his visible testicles, has the flowing hair, cheekbones, and delicate body of a woman. In

Beardsley's design for the book's "List of Pictures," the lines of the thighs of the impish, winged figure in the bottom right corner are not smooth but instead rippled in the shape of a string of breasts. To try to follow these figures' red thread of sexual orientation proves maddening; the sexual signifiers in Beardsley's indiscriminate proliferations have been drained of meaning so that "just when we think we glimpse the truths at which they hint, their 'signifieds' seem to collapse into their 'signifiers,' as if in a state of perpetual convertibility."[120] Even though Beardsley's panoply of sexual hybrids seemingly bear little resemblance to the characters within the play, and sometimes fail to resemble themselves from drawing to drawing, the illustrations succeed in indicating that in *Salome* there is no governing sense of sexual difference, little differentiation between persons and things.

Beardsley's *Salome* illustrations offer an extremely valuable context, too, for what guided Wilde, and later directly informed Epstein's notion of *photogénie*, the notion that "WE DO NOT LOOK AT OBJECTS AS THEY REALLY ARE."[121] Though singularly static, collectively Beardsley's series of drawings become theoretically coherent as re-producing the "something else" of the play's essence, in such way relating to the power of metamorphosis. Indeed, *photogénie* "hinges upon the existence of a gap between resemblance and difference" that relates to Eisenstein's theory of plasticity, an ostensible re-production of the continuous variability of form at heart in Wilde's aesthetic enterprise.

Miss Representation: Sibyl Vane and Sarah Bernhardt

The composition of the play, a patchwork at least on the unconscious level, pays homage to the notion of performance to such a degree that its frighteningly kaleidoscopic character, as well as that of Salomé and the moon, reflects its key personality: the actress. There are two vital, performative prototypes—one more fictive and the other more real, though such divisions have never been more exceedingly deceptive—necessary to examine in the context of the cult of the actress, each operating as "originals" of Wilde's "copy of a copy" of *Salomé*: Sibyl Vane and Sarah Bernhardt.

Published in the same year that he began his composition of *Salomé*, Wilde's most blatant manufacture of the poseuse occurs within the pages of *Dorian Gray*, through the figure of Sibyl Vane. While the influences at work in the tripartite relationship of Lord Henry, Basil Halliward, and Dorian Gray (both the personality and the magic portrait, a powerful ekphrastic metaphor) remain obscure and critically in flux, one of the clearest desires discernible in the story is Dorian's love for Sibyl Vane. He discovers her performing Shakespeare at a fairly dismal theater, "a tawdry affair," and reports to Lord Henry on her glorious ability to play an endless multiplicity of characters. Using language that echoes the sentiment of Pater's famously ekphratic description of the *Mona Lisa*, Dorian proclaims:

> She is everything to me in life. Night after night I go to see her play. One evening she is Rosalind, and the next evening she is Imogen. I have seen her die in the gloom of an Italian tomb, sucking the poison from her lover's lips. I have watched her wandering through the forest of Arden, disguised as a pretty boy in hose and doublet and dainty cap. She has been mad, and has come into the presence of a guilty king, and given him rue to wear, and bitter herbs to taste of. She has been innocent, and the black hands of jealousy have crushed her reed-like throat. I have seen her in every age and in every costume. (164)[122]

Here, Sibyl's timelessness is linked directly to the notion of performance; Dorian Gray finds himself overwrought with desire for an actress as the proprietor of infinite poses: a woman who, like Villiers's Hadaly, represents so many women "no harem could contain them all" (199). More than just a "recording," Sibyl functions as the performative embodiment of Shakespearean form, a mechanism for the recitation and vivification of his complete works.

The alliance between the performativity of the actress and the enactment of desire shows that Wilde's unique twist is not to define desire's ultimate aim but to find it within the process of becoming not one thing but any and every thing. Sibyl Vane, by the very etymology of her name, is a paradox, an unpredictable prophecy. A sibyl is "one or other of certain women of antiquity who were reputed to possess powers of prophecy and divination," a prophetess.[123] A vane, a common addition to the spires or other building pinnacles, is a plate of metal—like the daguerreotype's requisite metal sheet, or the silver platter for the head of the prophet—that will show which direction the wind is blowing, a weather-telling instrument. The word "vane" was used in the Elizabethan era (such as in Shakespeare's *Love's Labour's Lost*) and beyond to connote "an unstable or constantly changing person or thing."[124] Finally, we might suggest that the wordplay between "vane" and "vain" would be additionally provocative here, though ironically it is Dorian's vanity and not Sibyl's that leads to the novel's fated and tragic conclusions.

When Sibyl's own love for Dorian becomes too real and anchored to its fixed bearings, only then, in a reversal of expectations, does she become stagy and her acting "wrong in colour"—and so, Dorian's passion for her permanently dies. Her sincerity ensures that her gestures "became absurdly artificial." Dorian's only real passion is for the woman on the stage, the performativity of woman as a multitude of art's possibilities. By suggesting that she would leave it for a real life with him—hence, erasing her performative multiplicity in favor of a static persona as woman and wife—she enacts her own death sentence. As Regenia Gagnier suggests, "Sibyl Vane embodied Wilde's ideal—until she thought to give it all up for a part in a middle-class marriage. For that Wilde killed her."[125] Sibyl describes falling in love with Dorian through a dichotomous relation of art to life; she laments, "It was only in the theater that I lived. . . . The painted scenes were my world. I knew nothing but shadows, and I thought them real." Sibyl revels in the overthrow of these theatrical "shadows" in favor of what she calls "reality." She claims that Dorian, "brought [me] something higher, something of which all art is but a reflection." But Sibyl's reversal of sentiments shatters Dorian's illusions, as he tells her quite cruelly that his love for her has died because she now "simply produce[s] no effect."[126] Her "true" emotions get in the way of her acting, so that ultimately Sibyl represents a shift from good art to bad art by "assuming that most irritating pose of being natural."[127] As one of Vivian's doctrines of art in Wilde's "The Decay of Lying" reads, "All bad art comes from returning to Life and Nature, and elevating them into ideals."[128] In fact, it seems that giving in to her natural affections for Dorian in order to become his real-life beloved causes her to reach a contradictory state of nonbeing. Lord Henry advises Dorian, who is saddened by her eventual suicide, that he should not grieve for a woman who was never real:

> No, she will never come to life. She has played her last part. . . . The girl never really lived, and so she has never really died. To you at least she was always a dream, a phantom that flitted through Shakespeare's plays and left them lovelier for its presence, a reed through which Shakespeare's music sounded richer and more full of joy. . . . Mourn for Ophelia, if you like. Put ashes on your head because Cordelia was strangled. Cry out against Heaven because the daughter of Brabantio died. But don't waste your tears over Sibyl Vane. She was less real than they are.[129]

Thinking that art reflects a higher love, Sibyl gets it dead wrong. By renouncing art in favor of the real, she rescinds the life that art sustains—a failed ekphrasis that no longer "moves" Dorian.

The previous chapter cast light on Villiers's vituperation (and contemptuous mockery) of the actress in *L'Ève future*, reflecting some of the historical concerns over the cult of the stage actress at this particular period of the 1880s and 1890s. In contrast, the cult of the actress was Oscar Wilde's panacea, and Sarah Bernhardt—la Divine Sarah, as the French called her—one of his favorite theatrical muses. Overexaggerated gestures had become expected from the admirers of an actress as melodramatic and revered as Bernhardt was by the 1880s, and Wilde participated happily in her theater of admiration. According to Ellmann's biography, the author and the actress met in 1879; upon Bernhardt's arrival in Britain, "someone was heard to say, 'They will soon be making you a carpet of flowers,'" after which Wilde, "sensing his cue, said '*Voila!*' or its English equivalent, and cast an armful of lilies at her feet."[130] Bernhardt's facility to be both histrionic and historical onstage was her main claim to fame: she would prove herself masterful enough as a poseuse to flit effortlessly between life and death, male and female, good and evil, history and pure fiction. In *L'Art du théâtre*, Bernhardt warns her fellow actors, "Do not let us delude ourselves that we can wear the vesture of another's soul while preserving our own . . . that we can create an artificial exterior while maintaining our ordinary feelings intact." She avows that an actor "cannot divide his personality between himself and his part; he loses his *ego* during the time he remains on the stage, and thus his consciousness skips from age to age, from one people to another."[131] By the successful suppression of her own "I," Bernhardt made herself the figurehead of her own theatrical cult of personality. The ability to be more human than human onstage, to passionately play any and every character, demanded that Bernhardt exploit her very own otherness and endlessly self-objectify.

Indeed, Bernhardt already permeated the theatrical consciousness as the character of Salome before she was ever slated to play the role in Wilde's aborted 1892 production, and before the author actually composed any of the play. Bernhardt's cult of personality was so strong that she became emblematic of the catalog of femmes fatales that pervaded fin de siècle Decadent and Symbolist French literature. Three years earlier, theater critic A. B. Walkley had written that Bernhardt has "given us a new type (new, that is to the stage) which one would not willingly have missed" through "her embodiment of Oriental exotism: the strange, chimaeric, idol-woman: a compound of Baudelaire's Vierge du Mal, Swinburne's Our Lady of Pain, Gustave Moreau's Salome, Leonardo's enigmatic Mona Lisa. . . . But at what cost has she given us this! The essence of the type is a sort of nightmarish exaggeration, something not in nature, the supreme of artifice. To 'create' a stage-type that is nothing if not exaggerated, unnatural, artificial, what a danger for the artist!"[132] Bernhardt was able to typify the ensemble of French literature's ideal women, figures through which extremes like life and death, desire and disgust collide. Yet like Edison's Hadaly, the artificialized nature of Bernhardt's protean performances comes at a cost to mankind. Hadaly played the role of recorder, able to recite the catalog of man's written history, but Bernhardt functions as a bizarre recording, playing back the roles penned by the most famous artists, while somehow authenticating these roles in her own fashion. Villiers kept his Promethean figure Edison, and his *andréïde*, tucked away in the folds of fiction. Yet Walkley's review suggests that Bernhardt's acting allowed her to reach the acme of artificiality, as well as theatrical adaptation, and that her own Promethean endeavors of embodying this "supreme of artifice" were staged for all the world to see, thus coming at the cost of threatening nature in newly modernized and mechanized ways.

In Wilde's "*The Decay of Lying*," Vivian says of the "highest art" that it is "the ages that are her symbols," and Wilde lionized Sarah Bernhardt for being, like art, "not symbolic of any age" but, rather, capable of encapsulating all of them.[133] In *L'Ève future*, Villiers psychically repels progress by mummifying the future in terms of its quizzical prehistory, rewriting the actress Alicia as the *andréïde* Hadaly, a substitute Eve, and illustrating Edison as the adulterated copy of an ancient coin's human profile, bearing "a peaking likeness to those medals of Syracuse which show the features of Archimedes" (7). At the same time in history,

Wilde solicited the assistance of actress Lillie Langtry to search "among the Greek coins in the British Museum for Sarah Bernhardt's profile."[134] Here, Wilde takes Bernhardt as the prototype and original source, not looking for an ancient Greek coin that she resembles but one that resembles her. Bernhardt epitomized art's timelessness in such a way that her real age held little relevance for Wilde, particularly regarding her ability to re-present the myriad roles she came to define on the stages of late nineteenth-century Europe. In one of his last letters before his death in 1900, Wilde writes to Leonard Smithers, London publisher and cofounder of the literary and art criticism magazine the *Savoy*, that his most notorious female *rôle* could only be played by Bernhardt. "What has age to do with acting?" Wilde questions; the "only person in the world who could act Salomé is Sarah Bernhardt, that 'serpent of the old Nile,' older than the Pyramids."[135]

Incredibly striking and exceptionally relevant, then, is the fact that Sarah Bernhardt was characterized in remarkably analogous ways to both idealized icons of ancient Egypt, looking back, and the cinematically transformative notion of *photogénie*, looking forward. Describing her as a "priestess outside her temple," the writer Lucie Delarue-Mardrus called Bernhardt "the fantastic evocation of a modern poster, suddenly gifted with life, a breathing illustration of some very old Fairy Tale book, illuminated with gems and gold."[136] By 1905, Bernhardt, then in her sixties, was hailed as "any age or no age at all"—a reverberation of Wilde's own words evoking the irrelevance of the actress's true age—a "strange being" who had "ceased to be governed by the hampering laws of the flesh," becoming instead "something supernatural."[137] Louis Delluc—who, it bears repeating, was considered a film prophet in the Old Testament sense—proselytized in "La nue" (1920) that flesh had to be "eminently photogenic," achieved by the power of the camera's "living light."[138] Bernhardt seemed to possess an inherent ability to be cinema even before the medium officially arrived as the seventh art; in effect, Bernhardt operates as an important liminal figure between the Symbolists and film, and possibly the most powerful gateway between Wilde's play and the influence of Salome signifying systems in cinema's infancy.

The association between Bernhardt and a theatrical sense of mechanical reproduction began early in her career, perhaps even forming the substructure on which her version of theatrical modernism and its filmic future were based. Stage performers like Bernhardt were increasingly reproduced in cabinet cards, performance posters, sculptures, and other objets d'art, creating an external mobility and portability of their image paralleling their performative multiplicity. Yet the reverse was also true; Bernhardt played multitudes of the cast of Symbolist femmes fatales, and although these roles were modeled on icons of history, many of them were created for her. Playwright Victorien Sardou, for instance, wrote seven plays alone as vehicles for Bernhardt, including *Fédora*, *Théodora*, and *La Sorcière*. In his book *Daughters of Eve*, author Gamaliel Bradford suggests that although the prolific actress's pieces for the theater were as faithful as mechanism, Bernhardt, like the archetypal Eve, was "constantly and enormously human."[139] In reality, not only might she be the "original" from whence Wilde produces *Salomé*—the extension of her influence upon the piece's composition is unassailable, and thus she might pose here as the most authentic incarnation and dramatic textual embodiment—but Bernhardt's importantly coincidental presence lurks behind specific narrative occurrences in *L'Ève future*.

In that novel, Miss Alicia arrives in Menlo Park, New Jersey, via New York City in order to be convinced by Edison that she should be appropriately "recorded"—orally, sculpturally, and so forth—not only for her success on the stage but also to preserve her artistic personality for future generations. In 1880, years prior to the publication of *L'Ève future*, Sarah Bernhardt was staying in New York while starring in productions of *Adrienne Lecouvreur* and *La Dame aux camellias* during her inaugural American tour. One night after a performance, Bernhardt crossed the Hudson River to visit Edison at his laboratory in Menlo Park, choosing to engage in these newfound technologies by allowing Edison to record her reciting her most famous role, Phédre, thus allowing her gilded voice to become an ever-mobile commodity as well.[140] Villiers's choice for the means of Hadaly's nightly preservation, a coffin, is even more striking when considering the dubious history of the ever-enigmatic Bernhardt. Well known as a provocateur both on and off the stage, she was followed by a grandiose mythology that claimed that, like a vampire of sorts, she would renew herself nightly by sleeping in a coffin. The actress clearly had a hand in this self-fashioning because Bernhardt did, indeed, have herself photographed in her supposed coffin-bed, conveniently situated under a mantel on which one of her own artistic creations, a sculpted bust, rests (figure 3.5).

Bernhardt made herself legendary by re-producing herself as the embodiment of Symbolist principles that heralded cinematic modernity, most specifically through her use of spiraling movements, an essential element of her modernist theatrical performances, and then her early cinematic ones. An index for the numerous dead women revived through artificial generation, Bernhardt's early fame hinged upon her performance of death scenes, and specifically her use of a corporeal death spiral, a physical action that became her active structuring motif and "initiated her emerging association with the tendrilic curve that would later epitomize Art Nouveau."[141] By using herself as a pivot, an 1881 review of her performance in *La dame* suggests, Bernhardt was able to re–produce "the most elegant and poetic pose imaginable," causing "the movement imprinted" on the minds of spectators.[142] In essence, Bernhardt's embodiment of movement opens the theatrical to modernity's cinematic forms, themselves preconditioned in and through movement as primary engine of meaning. One of the first actresses to engage in cinematic reproductions, Bernhardt played Hamlet in a two-minute film—considered one of the first sound films ever made—presented as part of the Phono-Cinéma-Théâtre program at the Paris Exposition of 1900. Making

FIG. 3.5 Photograph by Melandri, one of a series that was used for a promotional cabinet card, *Sarah Bernhardt Posing in Her Coffin* (ca. 1880), meant to promote the actress's commitment to her tableaux of dying heroines onstage and in her own art. In the same year, Bernhardt sculpted *Death of Ophelia*, a bas-relief in which her Ophelia resembles herself in the coffin, which she frequently slept in for years.

moving picture productions out of her most famous theatrical roles, such as *La Tosca* (1908) and *Adrienne Lecouvreur* (1913), Bernhardt endured as a central figure in early cinema until her death in 1923; in 1915, she even starred in *Sarah Bernhardt at Home*, a film prognosticating our more contemporary examples of reality television, in which the actress recontextualizes famous paintings "at home." In recuperating Sarah Bernhardt as central to "imitation modernism," as Victoria Duckett suggests, her films can be considered "performative experimentations that can be reconceived as intermedial modernist experiments or 'ekphrastic machines.'"[143] Like the forged metal of Achilles's shield or Salomé's shimmering silver platter, Sarah Bernhardt proved herself "more enduring than brass," as modern as cinema and as equally enduring as the Egyptian Pyramids.[144]

Spectral Egypt

Wilde's posturing as French artist might be rivaled by his own aesthetic re-orient-ation in the queer legacies of ancient Greece and Egypt. Wilde employs a spectral Egypt as an "exotic prop" in many of his writings, affirmation of Edward Said's proposition of orientalism functioning as "an imaginative geography," the Orient as an other being "watched," allowed to serve as "a living tableau of queerness."[145] In *Dorian Gray*, the titular character—perilously worshipped by artist Basil Halliward—is described as "crowned with heavy lotus-blossoms" while he is caught "gazing across the green turbid Nile."[146] In "The Sphinx," Wilde adopted ancient Egyptian exoticism to address the theme of sexual transgression. In "The Truth of Masks," Wilde discusses the intersection of the aesthetic and the archaeological excavation of queer desire. In his essay "The Decay of Lying," Wilde delineates how, at the bidding of dramatic art, "the antique world rose from its tomb," enlisting life and its external forms to create "an entirely new race of beings."[147] In reconsideration of Plato's thoughts on mimesis, Wilde suggests in this essay that the whole history of the decorative arts traces a struggle between orientalism and the modern imitative spirit. A re-resurrection of Egypt provided a generative canvas for the film medium and its attendant magic, as I will discuss in the following chapter, and in many ways Wilde equally foretells early cinema here. For Wilde, all art is simulacral, his commitments to style in his work prophesying Gallese's current studies on the intersection of cinema and his embodied simulation theory: "Style is basically what strengthens our relationship with a work of art, what allows us to orient (or lose) ourselves within the imaginary worlds of fiction."[148] Wilde's contributions toward seeing things, and specifically seeing things as other things, liberates reality and opens literature into the realm of cinematic simulations, "the actual-virtual of the simulacrum."[149]

Or, being film.

Part 2

Cinematic Replications

4

Statuesque Cinema

Adapting Literature, Animating Film

> It is always pleasing to recognize again and again the fact that our cinema is not altogether without parents and without pedigree, without a past, without the traditions and rich cultural heritage of the past epochs. It is only very thoughtless and presumptuous people who can erect laws and an esthetic for cinema, proceeding from premises of some incredible virgin-birth of this art!
> —Sergei Eisenstein

The birth of cinema is anything but a new beginning.[1] In "Dickens, Griffith, and the Film Today," Soviet filmmaker and montage theorist Sergei Eisenstein posits that cinema's origins are not solely the product of Thomas Edison and fellow inventors but instead are based on "an enormous cultured past" that has been steadily moving in cinema's direction. In this way, literature may be the "first and most important place" to discern the earliest stages of development in this "art of viewing."[2] Eisenstein explores the development of montage structures, for instance, back to the "extraordinary optical faculty" in the literary works of Charles Dickens, like *The Cricket on the Hearth* (1845), thus suggesting how the films of D. W. Griffith have all of the "Dickens-esque sharpness and clarity as Dickens, on his part, had cinematic 'optical quality,' 'frame composition,' 'close-up,' and the alteration of emphasis by special lenses."[3]

As I continue to chart what metaphorically amounts to a shared DNA sequence of the artificial woman from the literary to the cinematic, I would like to note that Eisenstein calls the lineage between literature and film here organic, part of what he too calls "the 'genetic' line of descent."[4] In fact, Eisenstein believed the film shot operates like a "montage cell" or, in other words, the embryo of the film, proposing that "as cells in their division form a phenomenon of another order, the organism or embryo, so, on the other side of the dialectical leap from the shot, there is montage."[5] As in the creation of a human being, the conceptual product of Eisenstein's intellectual cinema is sexual; his filmic hieroglyphics copulating to reproduce something entirely new, the "combination of two 'representable' objects achieves the representation of something that cannot be graphically represented." Film images, like the different aesthetic and mechanical forms I have charted thus far, reproduce through an intimate violence to create a third term, a new descendant level of meaning. Although Eisenstein advocated early in his career for images in collision, a possibly violent and combative cinema, he later shifted "towards an interest in the protoplasmic forms of life, in the shapes and forms of things before identity is determined."[6] Indeed, some of the earliest historical applications in photography and the use of continuous motion picture technologies were made in the service of biological science. By the eighteenth century, biological motion was being microscopically probed and defined in organisms, whether plant or animal, in order to explore the very parameters of life as and through motion, a notion dating back to Aristotle's *Physics*.[7]

This association between embryology and form also meant a mating of the cinema and biological science. For both, movement defines, the formation of the embryo as well as the moving image. Along with Karl Ernst von Baer and Heinrich Rathke, Christian Pander transformed (chick) embryology into a proper branch of scientific inquiry, with the objective to render intelligible and virtually portray the gradual formation of the chick through a "succession of images that gave visibility to the formation happening in the egg."[8] From the start, this influential work was meant to be an illustrated text—he insisted on the participation of artist Joseph Wilhelm Eduard d'Alton to draw the images. Of the many hundreds of eggs examined, Pander "selected only those that lent themselves to being set in relationship to one another and lined up serially from picture to picture—quite independently of the incubation time."[9] Here one is struck by the communality between this scientific sense of serial illustration and the temporal elision afforded by Soviet montage theory, images cut and edited together to compress, or disobey, edicts of time in favor of simulated effect. In

Pander's embryological developments as in early film and the theory of montage—the term "montage" from the French word for mechanical assembly—"forms are in a state of continual change, the observer initially faces an undifferentiated mass of material, and as a result, development cannot be observed, but is constructed."[10] It was Pander and von Baer's adviser, Ignaz Döllinger, who insisted that an interdisciplinary team was necessary to accurately convey embryonic development; after Pander first attempted to publish his studies without pictures, von Baer and others found them "incomprehensible."[11] A gifted engraver—essential for the mass production of images at the time—d'Alton became most known for his work in biodiversity and comparative osteology. Along with Pander, d'Alton illustrated an extraordinary atlas of animal skeletal forms within shadowy silhouettes, ranging from fruit bats to wallabies to porcupines. At the basis of comparative osteology is the need to identify and differentiate human from nonhuman bones; indeed, they may bear striking similarities and can be easily confused. Similarly, the skeletal structure of film form around the turn of the twentieth century bore conspicuous resemblance to the archaeomodern complexities and literary figures I have examined thus far. More specifically, in acknowledging modernity's requisite hybridization of technological, literary, and aesthetic, we arrive at the equivalent and necessary recognition of the role science plays in the transition to the modern filmic text.

Animation Cells

Early film theorists ranging from Eisenstein to Siegfried Kracauer continuously acknowledged how lifelike film could be, and thus unsurprisingly the principle of life that biology investigates finds affinity in film's spectacle, insomuch that one might say film "functioned as the *materia operandi* of twentieth century cell biology and microphysics," a type of metaphysical machine.[12] The earliest motion picture films were shown by the Lumière brothers in Paris near the end of 1895, yet earlier that year German anatomist Friedrich Kopsch captured the first recorded images of moving cells in an embryo. Though Kopsch's images have not survived and are largely forgotten, he pioneered a connective relationship between the visualization of creation—more specifically, embryogenesis—and the life-giving and life-revealing properties offered by the cinematic apparatus. As the cells multiply and move within the embryo, so too does the filmic succession of images "animate" life artificially.[13]

Congruously lifegiving while asymmetrically coupling the natural with the artificial, the film medium helped biologists solve pressing scientific questions by rendering visual the literal secrets of cell replication, specifically helping probe the question of life as investigated through the generation and development of the embryo. Ludwig Graper's own investigations into the chick embryo also led him to employ time-lapse cinematography, as well as his own invention of stereocinematography. Based on the principles of the stereoscope, previously discussed at the beginning of chapter 2, Graper used a stereocinematographic apparatus to enhance the three-dimensionality of the visual representation of cell movement in relation to space, depth, and differentiation: movement alone, according to cultural historian of science Janina Wellmann, drives the formation of the embryo.[14] Graper's investigations ultimately determined a "double concurrent" in the development of the embryo; like couples doing the polonaise across a ballroom floor, the cells were actually dancing.[15]

Film not only offered advantages in observing cellular movement, but at the core of the medium—oft referred to, of course, as "motion pictures"—lies its ability to create the illusion of movement and the experience of motion. So far, this book has channeled modernity's vibrations as shifting sensibilities, between the solidity of the im-printed to the fleeting, virtual sensations of film movement with its basis in multiplicity and mechanical re-production—and the constant oscillation between the still and the moving. Though this generational through line remains fluid, a pause is necessary to examine the very moment of the century's turning, and the undeniable importance of the 1900 Paris Exposition.

The world expositions, which began with the Great Exhibition in London in 1851, were intended to offer, "in concentrated and spectacular form, the experience of modernity to masses of people."[16] The 1900 Paris Exposition, the first to present the invention of motion picture technology, fully demonstrated the newly evolved mobile gaze. The realistic experience offered by Hugo d'Alesi's Mareorama, for instance, was based in movement and simulation. The attraction consisted of two panoramas in motion, painted with continuous images of the sea and shoreline, which slowly unrolled as spectators stood on a platform that resembled a ship's deck, rocking back and forth aided by electric motors and hydraulic cylinders. The Mareorama, effectively the most sophisticated and last panoramic entertainment and installation, offered spectators voyage to Naples, Istanbul, and even the Suez Canal. Matching Wilde's designs for a synesthetic *Salomé* experience for theatergoers less than a decade earlier, the Mareoramic experience was complemented with symphonic strains from an unseen orchestra, winds from fans whistling in the rigging, and even wafting olfactory elements resembling seaweed and tar.

The Eiffel Tower was the star of the 1889 Exposition, but not until 1900 were sights from the static, vertically imposing tower offered through the dynamism of the moving, cinematic image. The Edison Company filmed ascending and descending views from the tower in the short film "Scene from the Elevator Ascending the Eiffel Tower," the elevator specifically improved and expanded for the 1900 exposition.[17] To this day, modern viewers, including my own graduate students, find themselves nauseously challenged by the camera's vertical climbs. Modernity met up with all manner of generationally appropriate and co-digestible model inventions, but another technology made a massive imprint on Paris during the 1900 exposition, *le trottoir roulant*. What is commonly known today as the moving walkway, a regular feature in modern airports that assists travelers with moving faster and more efficiently through the terminal, the version installed for the exposition was built on stilts more than twenty feet off the ground, had statuesque proportions, and looped more than two miles around the dozens of pavilions. This *rue de l'Avenir* (road of the future), as it was called, consisted of three separate platforms, fast, slower, and stationary. Back in 1871, New York inventor Alfred Speer invented the concept as an endless traveling sidewalk that would help transport Broadway theatergoers, his original plans including numerous cars that resembled those on a train, to be used for sitting and smoking. The initial scheme never came to fruition; after a faulty installation at the 1893 Chicago World's Exposition, the perfected and completed version installed in 1900 was acclaimed as both modern attraction and mode of transport.

Both the Lumière brothers and James Henry White, one of Thomas Edison's film producers, captured footage of the moving walkway and the numerous persons who would mount the platform and then disappear out of frame, right into a Parisian unknown. What is striking, too, is that the footage plays out like a mirror image of the Lumière brothers' famous early film *L'Arrivée d'un train à la Ciotat*, which shows a train pulling into the station from right background to left foreground, through and out of the frame; after a few seconds of footage, the passengers then disembark. The myth has been so oft and nearly mechanically repeated that it may not bear mentioning here, but to echo Tom Gunning and others, when the film was first projected for an audience at the Salon Indien in Paris in 1895, spectators supposedly "fled in terror, thinking an actual train was bearing down on them."[18] Although this may be an urban legend with little truth value, I retain the idea for its metaphoric significance, in sync with the Pygmalion effect, as regards the psychological implications of such spectacles in and of movement.

What gets created is life—or at least its likeness—through the movements rendered visible by cinematic technologies. Cinematic representations mirror the very creation fantasy of nineteenth-century France; as filmmaker Louis Lumière famously claimed, "Instead of holding to a reproduction of life (Lumière was adamant in later years: 'the film subjects I chose are the proof that I only wished to reproduce life'), it holds to a reproduction of the image of life"—a copy of life that turns out to be exceedingly real.[19] This notable quotation operates as a touchstone for the transposition of this persistent creation fantasy and mankind's unending obsession with its own art-ificial reproduction. Yet sometimes machine meets nature in unexpected ways, as light does shadow. A spectator at a later projection of *L'Arrivée* in 1896, Russian writer Maxim Gorky described the experience as fearful, a train barreling toward you sitting helpless in your seat, equal to the task of splintering your bones and "crushing into dust" the entire hall and its inhabitants—until he comes to realize it is only the movement of shadows.[20]

Cinema and the Cult of Egypt

The mobile gaze of film, like the fleeting quality of its medium, moored itself early and often in the familiar relics of this shared, ancient Egyptian past. In explaining "how cinema contracted Egyptomania," film and art historian Antonia Lant illustrates how this conceptual cohabitation persisted while cinema was still incubating as an aesthetic form—or was still developing as an embryo, I might suggest—and thus the life-giving properties of film were always already defined largely by this necessary, archaeomodern turn toward the stasis of ancient culture. As I have charted on our path through nineteenth-century French literature, Lant affirms that this alliance between ancient Egypt and illusory forms of representation is detectable since the French Revolution and persists through the century, specifically in prearchaic forms of film such as lantern shows, phantasmagoria, panoramas, dioramas, and photographs.[21] The popular touring panoramas exhibited in London starting in 1849, product of the opening of the overland trade route in India in the 1840s, offered the illusion of a journey to the East: the first "feature-length" panoramic river trip was exhibited, fittingly, at London's Egyptian Hall, built in the Egyptian Revival style in 1812 as a museum to exhibit artwork collections and Napoleon era relics.

Although the cinema offers mastery over death, it also demands the medium's perpetual encounter with mortality. The dark room from which the spectators have historically watched a film has long been associated with the darkened expanse of an Egyptian tomb: "The elaborate architecture of some of the early cinemas was even designed to suggest that the very activity of film spectatorship was defined by entry into a past world. Given that critical discourses of the silent film era commonly conceived 'of entering the cinema theatre as entering an Egyptian tomb' or a cave (be it of Ali Baba, of primitive humanity, or of the Platonic prisoners), it is not surprising that cinema architecture would seek through orientalism and classicism to give concrete shape to the visual seductiveness and aesthetic pedigree of the new medium."[22]

London's Egyptian Hall was first intended to showcase Egyptian curiosities of all kinds: colossal statues of Isis and Osiris flanked the entrance, welcoming its patrons into another world (or possibly, to borrow from Gautier, a second reality). The hall advertised itself from its front facade as the "home of mystery" specifically due to its display and projection of, as its front sign read, "improved animated photographs." By 1896, the hall was turned into a cinema, and "popularized Egyptology and the infant cinema were rubbing shoulders" under its roof, the vast array of meanings and understandings born of this Egyptomania now feeding into what would become the cinematic experience of the oncoming twentieth century.[23]

Yet a decade earlier, London's Egyptian Hall was home to the first exhibition of mummy portraits. In 1888, immediately after their excavation by Flinders Petri, who was anxious to sell them, these Fayum mummy portraits were displayed in a venue not only rendered in an architecturally appropriate style but known for its "overtones of mysticism and magic, where things and voices were conjured up out of the darkness," a fitting harbinger for its very near future as a cinema.[24] Not only was the exhibit provocative because it displayed a newly discovered genre of painting, but the nineteenth-century audience was enormously thrilled by "the vivid portrayals of the subjects, which seemed to bring the people of the past back to life, embodied in living, breathing flesh."[25] Circumstantial evidence suggests that Oscar Wilde himself was among the visitors, and that the Fayum portraits directly influenced *Dorian Gray*, which included other references to exhibits at the Egyptian Hall, thus advancing a possible reading of Dorian's picture—the novel's object of spectacle, entombed in the darkness of the attic—as itself a mummy portrait.[26]

Objectivity and Embalming in Bazin

While Wilde sought the truth in aesthetic fabrications and simulations, pioneering *Cahiers du cinéma* critic and film theorist André Bazin deemed the photographic image capable of a "quality of credibility" in its aesthetic objectivity. In the original French of his essay "The Ontology of the Photographic Image," his use of the word *objectif*, meaning "lens," provides the etymological undergirding of his theory that the camera reproduces the object in itself. In seeming affirmation that the photograph can capture the Platonic ideal of realism, Bazin's theory seems itself blindingly ideal, if only in consideration of the unwitting role Wilde played in photographic copyright law in the United States, and the case's intervention in considering the photograph a work of art. By virtue of its automatic nature, photography offered, according to Bazin, an image of the world formed "without the creative intervention of man."[27] In a sense, he commits a metaphoric murder of the human operator who, Bazin suggests, becomes unnecessary to the point of being an automaton, overtaken by photography's automation, photography the only art form that "derives an advantage" from man's absence. The film medium artificially preserves the "appearance" of life, thus practicing its own technical feats of embalming in rescuing the past from its "proper corruption." The photographic basis for film takes on a strange nonhuman quality in its automatic capture of the object "freed from the conditions of time and space that govern it."[28] Bazin's own fascinating, and extremely modern, twist on mimesis? That the photographic image, no matter how distorted, is the model, "by virtue of the very process of its becoming, the being of the model of which it is the reproduction."[29]

More famously, perhaps, in his essay on photographic ontology Bazin proposes a "mummy complex" that extends through the plastic arts, like painting and sculpture, into photography and then twentieth-century cinema. He draws a comparison between photography and the molding of death masks in their analogous quest toward this preservation, considering the photograph as itself a mold or the "taking of an impression, by the manipulation of light." A moment of time can be embalmed, and "change mummified" in the cinema, which he calls "objectivity in time."[30] Always timely and exceedingly timeless, the mummy has in many ways always told the story of an objectivity out of sync with time. As Lant suggests, Bazin's famous trope of the mummy complex is not unique to the cinematic medium or to the twentieth century because this alliance between "illusory forms of representation and ideas about Egypt" persisted throughout the nineteenth century and into the twentieth.[31] Object of spectacle, "mummified commodities are, on the one hand, the vestiges of a once-lived human body and, on the other, a cultural object" in an endless exchange where subject and object—or model and image—become interchangeable.[32] Bazin suggests that at the root of all the plastic arts "the practice of embalming the dead might turn out to be a fundamental factor in their creation. . . . The religion of ancient Egypt, aimed against death, saw survival as depending on the continued existence of the corporeal body. Thus, by providing a defense against the passage of time it satisfied a basic psychological need in man. . . . To preserve, artificially, his bodily appearance is to snatch it from the flow of time, to stow it away neatly, so to speak, in the hold of life."[33] He imparts upon cinema the same function as the Pygmalionesque literature that I have discussed thus far—animating, or artificially generating, the dead and inanimate bodies that have occupied humankind from the start. Film becomes the modern, artistic medium most agile at promoting an artificially generated, alternate reality fed by this Pygmalion effect—perpetuating humankind's unendingly obsessive and persistent creation fantasy. Yet although film can embalm time, the sense of history it conveys through its living scenes proves as illusory as real. Even Bazin, who treated the cinema as a phenomenological system, writes that the film screen hosted on a reality for which it planned to substitute, thus inscribing a necessary illusion into his reality scribing system.[34]

Mummy Movies

The vast trends of a century's Egyptomania—including the practice of embalming, the Spiritualist movement, and the fiction of Arthur Conan Doyle—influenced silent cinema's temporal rearrangements and spatial and temporal substitutions. But, to borrow Lant's fitting metaphor of reproductive assistance, Egypt played "midwife to film's birth" as subject matter as well.[35] Several major film companies, including the Lumière brothers and the Edison Company, sent crews to Egypt well before the First World War, many filming *actualités*, or documentaries—from the French word that can also refer to news or reality—such as Pathé's *Boats on the Nile* (1905) and *From Cairo to the Pyramids* (1905).[36] The persistently illusory quality of ancient Egypt met with film early on, when French film pioneer George Méliès, who started out as a magician, made one of the first and now lost horror films, *Robbing Cleopatra's Tomb* (1899), about the resurrection of the famous Egyptian princess. Cleopatra was a prime fetish object for the cinema, a charming imago deceased yet ever ready for her resurrection: five film versions of Cleopatra were filmed between 1908 and 1918, according to Lant, including *Cleopatra* (1917) starring Theda Bara, one of the most lavish and expensive Hollywood films at the time (a trend that would certainly continue with the Elizabeth Taylor starring vehicle of 1963). Bara was famously nicknamed "the Vamp," to emphasize the vampirish qualities of these femme fatale roles she faithfully played; as the reanimated ancient queen, never did the "fatal" make such literal meaning (*The Devil's Daughter*, *The Serpent*, and *The She-Devil* are all strikingly relevant titles and roles from Bara's other films).

After Méliès's filmic resurrection of Cleopatra's mummy in 1899, more than two dozen mummy films were made prior to the actual discovery of King Tutankhamen's tomb in 1922. Significantly, upon the tomb's excavation, the sex of the mummy within the realm of visual spectatorship seemingly shifted. From the beginning, as Basil Glynn points out in his expansive study *The Mummy on Screen*, mummies have cropped up in movies of boundless tonal variations. Many earlier silent, narrative films depicted the mummy as a figure of romance or comedy and oftentimes, despite the topos of the mummy's possibly duplicitous body and sex, along clearly demarcated gender lines: female mummies offered romantic stimulation, possibilities, or problems, whereas male mummies presented comedic ones.[37] Mummy films continued to proliferate at an intense rate, but upon British archaeologist Howard Carter's discovery of King Tut's tomb, the funny films were tempered a great deal with fearful ones, and most of the main mummy figures in the cinema became persistently male-coded. This turn might be partially emblematized through Boris Karloff's iconic performance in Karl Freund's art house horror film *The Mummy* (1932), which spurred Universal Studios to continue producing films through the 1940s prefaced on mummy hands (repetitious from those in Gautier's works), ghosts, and curses, during which time the mummy film became an early, relevant subgenre of American film. British Hammer films of midcentury and beyond began as remakes of the 1932 Universal horror icon, and exactly one hundred years after Méliès's *Robbing Cleopatra's Tomb*—quite probably the first official mummy movie—an action-oriented, hypermasculine strain of mummy films was born. *The Mummy* (1999), directed by Stephen Sommers and starring Brendan Fraser, even claims to be a remake of the 1932 version, though their surface resemblances—especially considering the computer-generated imagery used for the visual effects, created by Industrial Light & Magic—prove somewhat obscure.

Excavation, specifically of Tut's tomb, operates as surrogate for cinema spectatorship. Carter "invokes the onset of the cinema" when he writes of puncturing the entrance to Tut's tomb with "a hole large enough to insert an electric torch" so that its light could reveal "an astonishing sight."[38] As his eyes adjusted and "grew accustomed to the light, details of the room within emerged slowly from the mist, strange animals, statues, and gold." Indeed, much of the "proof" of this amazing discovery was recorded through photographs, every detail of the excavation cataloged photographically to the point where exact replicas of all the tomb's treasures were able to be reproduced.

From Dust to Cinema

In the simulation of life, film images seemingly satisfy what German art historian Wilhelm Worringer called "the urge to abstraction," which "finds its beauty in the life-denying inorganic."[39] In his book *Abstraction and Empathy* (1908), Worringer argued that the aesthetic sense is an objectified perception of self arising from a more primitive time and viewpoint. For him, the idea of art arises from psychic needs that may be traced back to ancient Egypt's own synchronous impulses, toward art and toward imitation.[40] In his later work *Egyptian Art* (1927), Worringer speaks of ancient Egyptian civilization as heterogeneous, "founded on land reclaimed, by means artificial and technological," therefore in some sense manufactured as much as organic.[41] In chapter 1, I identified a sense of the cinematically virtual mode of representation within Gautier's Egypt-inflected aesthetic of resurrection. Gautier used the discursive figure of the mummy in "La Morte amoureuse," as well as his more blatantly Egyptian stories like "Une nuit de Cléopâtre" and "Le pied de momie," to represent timelessness and the conquest of death—at least for his literary moment—in the *fantastique*. These are aptitudes that the cinema inherited in the evolution of the aesthetic modes of representation. Shots and sentiments of Gautier's fiction conspire with later screen history and help construct an image of how this strain of artificial generation in nineteenth-century France informs modern, cinematic forms, and the subjectivities and sexualities subsequently re-formed in the process. Cinema could bring the dead back to life, "set in motion what was thought to be immobile, and present in all its glory what was thought to be in ruins and decay."[42] As a medium, cinema offers a sensory experience that the prior arts and literatures could only dare dream of, bright lights and disorientating images, the hallucinatory effects of Gautier's fantastic fictions or the Salomé paintings by Moreau.

Interestingly, Gautier's name sometimes appears in recent literature on connections between cinema and either ancient Egypt or the statuary arts, but most mentions do not account for the fact that multiple early films actually adapt his stories as source texts. Indeed, French film manufacturer Pathé Frères adapted Gautier's novella of the same name to produce one of the earliest mummy films, *The Romance of the Mummy* (1911); once a canonical text of the French secondary school system, Gautier's *Le Roman de la momie* is now rarely read.[43] The story follows an English lord who, on an archaeological excavation, discovers a 5,000-year-old princess with a perfectly embalmed face (read: Clarimonde). She becomes an obsession—he dreams of her animation—to the point where he meets an American woman who resembles the mummy so completely she may just be its very animation (read: *Vertigo*). Beware that if one were to search the internet for the film, you might get pointed toward results for another American film it resembles called *The Mummy* (1911), one of many Egyptian-influenced short films done by Thanhauser Films. Equally interesting, its protagonist Jack purchases a mummy (he poses as an Egyptologist to impress his would-be father-in-law, who is one) and, once at home, accidentally exposes it to enough live electricity to animate it, and bring it to life—dancing, making love, and of course, complicating his relationship with his human sweetheart. Thanhauser Films would continue to make numerous films of Egyptian influence, including *Marble Heart* (1913), *Joseph in the Land of Egypt* (1914), and *Naidra, the Dream Woman* (1914). Yet *The Image Maker* (1917) might be the most interesting of the company's entries in this subgenre; it tells the story of Marion Bell, an actress with a penchant for sculpting, and her beau John Arden, who think they are reembodied spirits from a book telling the story of the *Royal Romance of Egypt*.

In furtherance of the cult of the ruin, the "ability of cinema to breathe life into the dust of Egypt" requires noting, as Antonia Lant does, these parallels between mummification as preservation of a life beyond and "the ghostliness of cinematic images." Gautier's "La Morte amoureuse" ended with his beloved, resurrected Mummy turning to dust; this "dust of Egypt" turns into a movie in 1915 when the Vitagraph Company of America (*vita* pointing etymologically to the cinema's life-giving prowess) released the fairly comedic *The Dust of Egypt*, based on a play written by Alan Campbell.[44] As early as the twelfth century, Europeans had employed *mumia*—which basically amounted to the powder made from the desiccated mummified bodies—as an apothecary prescription. The belief in the mummy's medically curative powers may have originated in the thought of Pliny the Elder, who wrote of the use of bitumen, the mineral used to embalm the dead in Egypt, in the treatment of a range of ailments from cataracts to dysentery.[45] The earliest existing photograph/heliograph created by Niépce around 1826, as mentioned in chapter 1, was actually produced by sensitizing a pewter plate (read: silver platter) with bitumen of Judea. A naturally occurring asphalt, the material is light-sensitive and allowed the reproduction of an image—or really, a negative—that was then etched using other acidic substances and printed on paper. However, using the word *mumia* to denote both the desiccated mummy and the mineral substance may, indeed, be due to a complicated history of transformation and substitution, the enforcement of a psychic resemblance through an etymological slippage. British librarian and Egyptologist Warren Royal Dawson contends that, after an extended study of the literature on mummification, the accounts of the Egyptian process of mummification abound in "errors and omissions."[46] Specifically, mummies were long and erroneously believed to have been treated with bitumen; however, it was instead resins that were actually used, which "are black and lustrous and simulate bitumen, but the resemblance is delusive."[47] Hence, a beginning for the oft-noted link between the chemistry of mummification and the science of photo and film printing born of the very notion of simulation. And at the turn of the century, this balm became electric.

The relevance of the mummy to all manner of performances, decorative arts, and even printing persevered, emboldening the utter heterogeneity of its symbolic and literal usage. Prior to the discovery of Tut's tomb, mummy unwrappings (or unrollings) became a spectacle popularized in large salons, and more specifically at private parties, becoming a fashionable pastime in 1820s and 1830s England. Once trips to Egypt became prevalent in the first half of the nineteenth century, using mummy parts and other curiosities of ancient Egyptian paraphernalia as decor became fashionable for the upper classes (Gustave Flaubert actually displayed a mummified foot on his desk). As far back as the sixteenth century, paint pigments and other art supplies were produced using mummy as material, specifically a color referred to as mummy brown that was available until the twentieth century. It is confirmed that mummy brown was even one of the pigments used by Delacroix in his 1854 painting of the Salon de la Paix in Paris.[48] A longstanding belief that mummy wrappings were used in printing, for imprinting, was also perpetuated from the 1850s, from records detailing cargo containing Egyptian rags coming over to America, which may have been processed into a pulp used to make paper for the printing of books and newspapers.[49]

Endless Re-turning: Of Statues and Salomes

> While the story of the relation between early film and other art forms is often told as one of slavish imitation or emancipatory rejection, the ancient world of early cinema suggests much more complex, diverse and dynamic forms of interaction between cinema and nineteenth-century arts, commercial entertainment and optical media. . . . early cinema sought to outperform and redefine other arts as well as other media and modes of popular entertainment (the ancient worlds of some of which are as under-researched as those of silent cinema). In cinema, neo-classical statues could be animated, famous paintings could be inhabited, the conventions of proscenium theatre could be violated, and opera could be rendered more accessible, while at the same time still photography could be set in motion.[50]
>
> —Vachel Lindsay

In what is widely considered the earliest work of film theory, *The Art of the Moving Picture*, poet Vachel Lindsay likens the cinema to sculpture in motion, admitting that he desires in moving pictures "not the stillness, but the majesty of sculpture," something like the "Venus de Milo, that comes directly to the soul through silence," requiring no further reference, or referent.[51] A poet who preached "the gospel of Beauty," Lindsay can be thought of as "re-enchanting modernity" through his ideas about the film medium, by his "seeing the innovations of technology from a fairytale perspective, so that electricity, locomotives, city lighting, and the new urban architecture of plate glass could be envisioned as what he calls 'a picture of fairy splendor.'"[52] Lindsay's project was the first to formally attempt to raise the value of film to the status of art, contrary to the 1915 ruling by the U.S. Supreme Court that movies were not suitable for the expression of ideas. He believed in the power of cinema to transform primitive energies, and accordingly posits the hieroglyph as film's central means of expression, quite before the idea became instrumental to the montage theories of Sergei Eisenstein in the 1920s; Lindsay also emphasized cinema's animation of the inanimate, specifically at the level of pictorial language, structured on this interrelationship between time period and art form. In regard to the Egyptian hierarchy of film, Lindsay attests that Americans were entering Egyptian caves to satisfy their ciné-spiritual hungers, since it is "sometimes out of the oldest dream [that] the youngest vision is born."[53] The animation of the mummy rivals the animation of the statue; statues of the dead were specifically produced as human substitutes, then placed along with the mummy in the tomb so that the *ka* (life force) of the Pharaoh might move safely into his sculptural double (*shabti*) necessary for its preservation. Indeed, on the first page of his essay "The Ontology of the Photographic Image" wherein he establishes the mummy complex, film theorist André Bazin asserts that the "first Egyptian statue, then, was a mummy, tanned and petrified in sodium."[54]

As I examined through the literary works of Gautier and Villiers, the metaphoric power of the animated statue becomes both source and subject of some of the earliest film experiments, especially by French filmmaker Georges Méliès. Possibly the first film auteur, Méliès pioneered the fantasy film from his early work in magic and stage illusion. In 1888, he purchased Paris's Théâtre Robert-Houdin, named after the father of modern magic, Jean-Eugène Robert-Houdin, who originally owned it, and for the following decade Méliès used its stage as a backdrop for his development of "special effects," utilizing the automata—mechanical figures that resemble human beings—that he gained with the theater's purchase as well. Prior to making any films, Méliès constructed his own automata in imitation of Robert-Houdin's, mechanical simulations of the body that would metaphorically translate into his cinematic projections of bodies, sometimes fragmented and always ephemeral, on-screen. Méliès's subsequent mastery of film served as evidence of his obsessive repetition of the same game, "playing, like the fetishist, upon the contradictory knowledge of presence and absence" and making it into the spectator's site of pleasure.[55] In reconstructing his own automata from those of Robert-Houdin, Méliès was actually producing "a simulation of a simulation," which he would repeat when he had to reinvent the *cinématographe* after Auguste Lumière refused to sell it to him. Thus, he was "fated to repeat the invention-construction of machines capable of ever more perfect and life-like Simulations of the human body."[56]

Fittingly, Méliès enacted such Pygmalionesque animations through his development and use of filmic tricks in his early films of the 1890s and 1900s. In 1898, he made *Pygmalion and Galatea*, considered the first actual film adaptation of the mythological story, which starred his wife, Eugénie, as a statue come to life that falls to pieces upon the sculptor's attempted embrace. In many of Méliès's works, "flashes of magnesium powder, or the technology of electricity, accompany the eruptions of life, or switches of form."[57] In one of his earliest films, *The Vanishing Lady* (also called *The Conjuring of a Woman chez Robert-Houdin*, filmed in that theater), he stars as a magician who quite expectedly makes his female assistant disappear, only to resurrect her as a skeleton. Méliès uses a substitution splice, a film editing technique, to create the illusion of appearance and disappearance, a trick usually achieved by a magician with the use of a trapdoor in the stage floor. The filmmaker claimed in his article "Les Vues cinématographiques" (1907) to have discovered this technique, also called a stop trick, by accident when an obstruction in his camera forced him to free the film and then restart filming at that point of interruption; he explicitly states that when he began filming again, men changed into women before his very eyes. The transformations made possible by use of this *trucage* became so emblematic of early fantasy films shot in France that the film manufacturer Pathé-Frères called them *scènes à transformations* in its catalogs.

In *The Animated Statue* (1903), a statue appears slowly, through a sequence of parts—the head, notably, emerging from the swirling machinery of a sunlike spiral—until its wholeness and its femaleness become fully displayed on a pedestal against the backdrop of a Grecian trompe l'oeil landscape, a bevy of white-wigged male artists arriving and proceeding to draw her beautiful, surprisingly animated, form. In *Extraordinary Illusions* (1903), Méliès submits the female body to dis-membering and reassembling akin to the movements in Villiers's *L'Ève*. The magician takes out of his magic (Pandora's) box several parts that he proceeds to assemble into a female mannequin, which turns into not only a living woman but a dancing one. Lucy Fischer emphasizes that one of Méliès's main tricks is to make the woman disappear or, more specifically, to offer the audience a cinematic substitution for/of/as woman.[58] In so doing, the filmmaker's magic conjures up the ghostly, feminine supplements of Gautier, Villiers, and Wilde, as well as the self-sameness of their aesthetic quests to give birth to, or artificially generate, new species of aesthetic organisms. Méliès's cine-magic allows him to "symbolically re-enact, and thus master through obsessive repetition, the problem of difference, the threat of disunity and dismemberment posed by the woman's body."[59] The statue has, since this book's introduction, represented the base figure of an artificially generated and not generative woman, and continues to present itself as the spiritual ground for film as a Pygmalion-esque enterprise. Able to bestow life on the ruins of antiquity through its mechanisms, early silent cinema became the esteemed medium for the statue-esque.

By the turn of the twentieth century, cinema was "the single most expansive discursive horizon in which the effects of modernity were reflected, rejected or denied, transmuted or negotiated."[60] In *Five Faces of Modernity*, Matei Calinescu discusses the evolution of cultural Decadence in the nineteenth century as movement itself, not as a structure but as a direction or tendency that flows outward from Romanticism and toward the dialectical complexity of its relationship to modernity.[61] The endlessly twirling Salome-as-signifiers at the end of nineteenth-century France instituted a most fertile province (and provenance) for charting this movement into cinema, specifically in addressing how this aesthetic of movement is inherently cinematic. As Alexander Bakshy asserts, the only real thing in the movies "is *movement* without which all its objects would appear as lifeless shadows."[62] This movement, or the kinetics of the dance—whether of cells or Salomes—corresponds to the infinite regress Jacques Rancière locates at the heart of Walter Benjamin's own conception of modernity. Benjamin determines the crisis of contemporary, mass-mediated modernity of the 1920s and 1930s proceeding from the nineteenth century's invention of modern life, inaugural moments of shock he traces back, for instance, to the poetry of Baudelaire. Benjamin's present is characterized by a premonitory past, a particular dialectics of temporality, of continual return, marked by an "explosive conjecture of modernity and prehistory" he sees created by capitalism.[63] Because it is not contemporaneous with itself, always looking forward or behind, the archaeomodern turn of modernity always "presupposes a new turn—one turn *more*. The deeper the dream, the further the awakening, the more consistent is the evidence of the modern cogito, of the collective subject of modernity. Just as sleep has become a dream, the dream becomes a phantasmagoria."[64] In the phantasmagoric realm of emerging cinematic means, the figure of the dancer—as if a figuration of such politics of modernity—turned and re-turned ad infinitum.

Salome and Her Cinematic Kin-esis

Films of dancing women cluttered the early cinematic landscape, the movement of the female body doubling for the movement of cinematic images. Felicia McCarren observes that doubleness lies at the heart of the enterprise of dance wherein the performer "occupies perpetually a liminal realm" that resembles the liminal life of film, its perpetuation of the illusion of both movement and three-dimensionality. Some of the earliest films produced by Thomas A. Edison used the figure of the dancing woman as the mesmerizing force of and for cinematic projection via kinetoscope, one of the first motion picture devices, invented by Edison and his employee William Kennedy Dickson between 1889 and 1892. In these first years of cinema production, films of dancing women proliferated. Several versions of Annabelle Whitford Moore, one of the first onymous women of early cinema, performing the Serpentine Dance and the Butterfly Dance—her transformative movements indicated through her named likeness to shape-shifting creatures—were recorded by Edison in his Black Maria studio by means of the Vitascope, his personally branded version of the kinetoscope.[65] But Moore was a disciple, or a copy if you will, of a far more importantly transformative woman in film.

I return to Eisenstein's affirmation that the cinema's creation owes a debt far surpassing its headlining male inventors, aimed at turning momentarily toward the importance of the women who invented in and through the cinema. Female stage performer Loie Fuller, who gained the cultlike devotion of the Symbolists for her serpentine and Salome-inspired dances, "created the cinema before cinematography by wedding movement to light," interlocking both aesthetic and scientific means in profound ways.[66] Fuller self-appropriated Salome as "the emblem of her destiny as a veil dancer" around the time she arrived in Paris in 1892, the very year Wilde published his literary version in one act.[67] By 1895, Fuller was performing her Salome at the Comédie Parisienne with sets painted by Georges-Antoine Rochegrosse, chosen mainly because of his earlier work illustrating Flaubert's "Hérodias" and his canvas *Salomé dansant devant Hérode* —the title directly copied from Gustave Moreau's painting discussed in chapter 3. Fuller also characterized her own art as a necessary resurrection of ancient dances and biblical figures (according to Rhonda Garelick, Fuller had interest in both Old and New Testament heroines), claiming to trace them "back to four thousand years ago: to the time when Miriam and the women of Israel filled with religious fervor and rapture, celebrated their release from Egyptian captivity with . . . dances."[68]

In *Electric Salome*, Garelick analyzes how Fuller evaded form and gender through the use of her own performative tricks, interwoven illusions created through fabrics and lights. However, Fuller was seemingly the absolute physical opposite of her lithe, seductively dancing figures. Untrained and with little grace offstage, she was an ill-dressed American Midwesterner who had found theatrical fame in Paris. Despite her ironic "shapelessness" in real life, she was able to vanish into an amalgam of her own making in performance, "replaced by her sequences of ephemeral sculptures," "transforming herself by turns into lilies, butterflies, raging fires, even the surface of the moon."[69] Garelick suggests that Fuller "invented an art form balanced delicately between the organic and the inorganic," a heterogeneously balanced combination of human and mechanical that produced exceedingly transformative visions.[70] Because much of Fuller's artistry was expressed largely through technologies of simulation, it proves consonant that she took her own turn at recasting Salome, one of the most simulated figures in the arts and letters of late nineteenth-century Paris; in her version, Salome moves closer to an innocent young child than a voraciously evil femme fatale.

In many senses, Fuller became a pioneer of cinema, the *fée électricité* considered "a female version of Thomas Edison."[71] Though she would make several films with the Lumière brothers and Georges Méliès, more significantly, she patented many of her cinematic inventions: she instituted the use of the first chemical mixes for gels and slides, and the first luminescent salts for lighting effects. Respected for her scientific knowledge, Fuller was friends with Marie Curie, making her acquaintance after writing to her and her husband, Pierre, to inquire if she could make an entire stage costume out of radium. But it was Fuller's quality of movement that benefited her becoming a true icon of cinematic

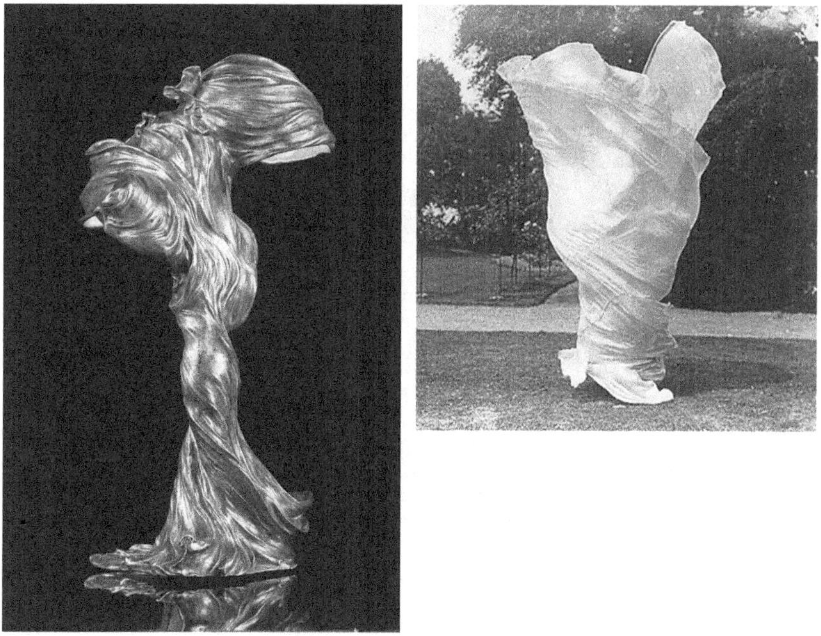

FIG. 4.1 French Art Nouveau gilt bronze sculptural lamp depicting Loie Fuller (left), sculpted by Raoul-François Larche; Photograph of Loie Fuller dancing by Samuel Joshua Beckett (right), gelatin silver print (ca. 1900), Metropolitan Museum of Art, Gilman Collection.

modernity. Significantly, the "effigy of Loie Fuller whirling under the projectors" was so truly modern that she should have crowned the entrance to the 1900 World's Fair, epitomizing the spirit of the exhibition itself. Tom Gunning suggests that the "frenzy of motion" Fuller offered might have been even greater than what cinema itself delivered, her dance operating as "a matrix from which form is born, a possibility of continuous transformation . . . a plasmatic energy that created forms."[72] The body's actual physique did not matter; as in her serpentine dance, "the body seems swallowed by a flux and reflux of motion, less solid matter than a materialization of energy and movement itself."[73] Stéphane Mallarmé, who considered her the apotheosis of Symbolist ideals, thought Fuller's dancing materialized the soul's vertigo, a dizziness made visible by sheer artifice. As much as she reformed cinema, Fuller was transformed into art objects too, most notably statues carved by numerous artists, such as Pierre Roche and Raoul-François Larche, who were captivated by the refashioning of her newfound shapes and movements created for the stage, through the screen (figure 4.1).

A defining trope of modernity, Fuller proved most exceptional for her increasingly complex portrayals of women in and as motion. Able to visually symbolize seeming polar opposites from fluidly natural butterflies to the metallicity of

Futurist dance, Fuller metamorphosed herself and her craft, blurring boundaries of performance that helped reshape the modern and the cinematic simultaneously.[74] Indeed, much of Fuller's theatrical artistry relied on a "screen" dynamic achieved through fabrics used as intermediaries to the cinema screen proper. For example, the electric lights cast upon the moving draperies during her famous Fire Dance (1890s) would give the appearance they, and she, were on fire. When made into a film, *Fire Dance* (1906) uses film edits and tricks to achieve these transformative qualities; Fuller twirls into a kinetic shape-shifter, the fabrics of her skirt lifting all the way until she is engulfed within the folds, as if consumed by fire. This ever-oscillating ideal of veiling and unveiling operates as the bedrock of woman-as-screen, one of the reasons too why Salome and her Dance of the Seven Veils became the meta-modern imperative for the medium of mechanized performances—and Fuller would become famous as the *Salome moderne*. Mary Ann Doane suggests that the veil "mimics the grain of the film, the material substrate of the medium, and becomes the screen as surface of division, separation, and hence solicited transgression."[75] Fuller transcended norms of performance, engineered uniquely scientific and cinematic spectacles, and made herself functionally a kaleidoscopic projection of form the Symbolists only dreamed of; Salome was an important figure for her transformative potential, and that of female entertainers to come.

Sex, Stardom, and Still Life: Salome Adaptations

Coupled with the provocation of Wilde's tragic and last role as homosexual martyr after his 1895 legal trials, *Salomé* helped precipitate a new direction and deployment of Salome re-presentations into early cinema. The play's sensorial flexibility and imperative liveness lent to shifts in modern theatrical expression upon the advent of new screen visibilities; in particular, Wilde's play rendered palpable a new, corporeal womanhood, an exciting role for female actresses, performers, and film pioneers to recuperate and replicate as means for their own performative expressions.[76] Whereas the craze to mimetically reproduce Salome commanded male-centric Symbolists through the latter half of the nineteenth century—for instance, Flaubert's early literary representation of the dancing girl as near-mechanical sex worker, inspired by a real woman—by the later 1890s, the sexually and aesthetically transgressive role spawned a whole new thriving entertainment industry. Wilde's play, in the words of Lois Cucullu "generating Salomania wherever it appeared," later adaptations centering emphatically around his imagined Dance of the Seven Veils as a metaphoric spinning top.[77]

Specifically and quite significantly, considering the indefatigable importance of Sarah Bernhardt as the possible "original" to Wilde's version, Salome became a staple of Jewish female entertainers after the turn of the twentieth century. Bernhardt's striking thinness—remarked upon incessantly by writers and critics, which led to her common caricatures as a skeleton or a birdlike figure—was bound directly to her Jewishness, both attributes further uniting her

Salome-ness. Indeed, according to Jonathan Freedman, Moreau's Salome paintings represented an eroticized Jewish body, "always already Jewish in the curious way that Jewishness was construed in France in the later years of the nineteenth century, as simultaneously a representative of an age-old Orient and an avatar of a problematic modernity."[78] Remarkably, Bernhardt reappropriated her thinness—a quality that inspired fellow actress Ellen Terry to describe her as "transparent," and "more a symbol, an ideal, an epitome, than a *woman*"—and made it fashionable, transforming the potential reading of her being afflicted with consumption or disease by re-presenting herself through death imagery, like the photographs she posed for in a coffin.[79]

In 1908, Fanny Brice manipulated a caricature of the Jewish princess as her own trademark act, her performance of Irving Berlin's "Sadie Salomé, Go Home" accelerating her stardom as a comedienne of the culture, of both Judaism and Salome, essentially interlinked. The most successful act of the Ziegfeld Follies in 1907, Salomes of the stage proliferated in full force for the following few years. Mlle Dazie (Daisy Peterkin, an American ballerina from Detroit) popularized her toe dance version for the Follies, with staging based on Aubrey Beardsley's illustrations. Once a student of Loie Fuller, Dazie capitalized on the craze by opening up a school for Salomes, which graduated upwards of 150 students a month to move on to numerous and growing vaudeville and burlesque shows. By autumn 1908, twenty-four Salomes performed on the circuit in New York (up from only four just two months prior), and by the next year every vaudeville or variety show in America was enchanting with its own Salome.[80]

"The most impressive personality of the screen," as decreed by the movie poster for *Out of the Fog* (1919), Jewish-Russian émigré Alla Nazimova found quick triumph as an actress in Hollywood by the end of the 1910s; in 1917, she was offered a five-year contract with Metro Studios that surpassed that of star American actress Mary Pickford, which afforded her freedom and control over casting, scriptwriting, and other major aspects of her films' production. An early female film auteur, screenwriting and directing films under male monikers, including that of her then partner Charles Bryant, Nazimova adapted Ibsen's *A Doll's House* and *Camille* from the work of Alexandre Dumas fils (a role Bernhardt made famous a few decades prior). However, her most important film was an adaptation of Wilde's *Salomé*, a film that offered an additional layer of filmic meaning, in consideration of the play as illustrated text. On a somewhat literal level, early silent films operated as illustrated texts, presenting moving image–based narratives sutured together with textual interludes offered on title cards. Though these were connected into one film, the experience of watching cuts back and forth between text and images can produce as disconnected an experience as a connected one, exceedingly relevant to the dissociative relationship between Wilde's words and Beardsley's illustrations. Yet because of its close depiction of both verbal and visual components, Nazimova's *Salome* (1922) thwarted Hollywood standards, pushing cinematic boundaries through her adaptation of

Wildean art as her own, a feminist and queer milestone in film history and a landmark in Art Nouveau. Petra Dierkes-Thrun suggests that Nazimova took Wilde's aesthetic vision quite seriously, identifying the filmic potentials of the play and thereafter "employing central cinematic techniques like camera work, mise-en-scène, and the process of visual narration through editing, to extend and interpret some of Wilde's main themes, such as fatality, synesthesia, veiling, and the dangerous gaze."[81] Accordingly, the film strongly extended this sense of modernity connected to the photo-genic woman and, in Nazimova's version, a female agency that railed against then common depictions of orientalized femmes fatales in Hollywood, such as in the 1919 film version in which Theda Bara plays the evil vamp role.[82]

Nazimova wanted to transform film into an aesthetic medium of serious importance, and with *Salome* she became one of the first female auteurs of Hollywood, overseeing virtually every aspect of its production and direction and even authoring the screenplay herself under the pseudonym Peter M. Winters.[83] One of the primary ways she imparted her artistic mark on the film was by virtually and visually conjoining the heterogeneous elements of the source texts, Beardsley's illustrations and Wilde's text. Nazimova and costume designer Natacha Rambova offered Art Nouveau–centered visuals based on Beardsley's style and his illustrations for the Bodley Head edition of the play. Additionally, she created a film adaptation that deepens the play's homoeroticism through its production. Seemingly a tribute to Wilde's biography as much as his art, Nazimova and Rambova exhibited as many men dressed in drag as they could, adorning them in elaborate wigs and other accoutrements; it was rumored that the film's entire cast and crew were actually gay and/or bisexual, as sort of an homage to Wilde himself too—a possible truth that nonetheless holds significant importance.[84] What distinctly emerges is a microcosmic network of Salome, as adapted by Wilde/Beardsley/Nazimova, that undermines gender difference and the very heterosexual significance of the early, biblically inflected tales. According to Dierkes-Thrun, this coupled with Nazimova's own gender ambiguity suggests a further doubled reading that equates to the doubleness of androgyny—women and men who pose in exchange; people like Ovid's Narcissus, who look like things; and even, in the real world of the 1920s, networks of women who loved other women. Rumors suggest Nazimova and Rambova were lovers, for instance, and this network of lesbian interrelations directly and biographically connects back with Oscar Wilde. In fact, Wilde's niece Dolly, herself a lesbian, was a frequent guest at Nazimova's home in Los Angeles and seemingly once played the role of Nazimova's lover as well. For Wilde, it was a love that dare not speak its name; Nazimova supposedly coined the phrase "sewing circle" as cipher for the lesbian and bisexual figures in Hollywood, and their interrelationships. Certainly, the decadent visions of both Wilde and Nazimova bestow exceedingly ornamental, moving images as means to artificially en-gender new, queer forms of art and identification.

FIG. 4.2 Lobby card for *Salome*, a mixed-media presentation of Alla Nazimova doing the Dance of the Seven Veils, the film image framed by a Beardsley-inspired illustration, including his signature roses, three candles, and the same dress patterning as found in Aubrey Beardsley's original illustration for Wilde's *Salomé* (bottom); Beardsley's *The Peacock Skirt* (left).

Arguing that illustrated texts function as networks, Kate Newell proposes that illustrations operate as a "gateway" to understanding a text and possibly resolving its ambiguities, depicting distinctive iconographies by distilling representative ideas and images, although the opposite could be said of Beardsley's drawings and their inherent unlikeness to Wilde's play. Yet in this network predicated on otherness and coupled with a constantly revolving hetero aesthetic, Nazimova's film adaptation operates in more harmonious resolution between word and image. Indeed, the film's lobby cards used still shots of her costumed as Salome from the film's production, these images set in a drawn border design reproduced in the exact style of Beardsley. Many of these lobby cards offered a reflective capacity between photograph and illustration; in the one showing Nazimova doing the Dance of the Seven Veils, her ivory bob mirrors that of the drawn Salome in the border illustration, whose skirt is directly replicated from Beardsley's *Salome* illustration *The Peacock Skirt* (figure 4.2). Beardsley's signature roses, which populate the upper left hand and bottom center of the illustrated border, echo graphically in the headdresses of her robed attendants. Nazimova's film functions as "an early illustration of the intermedial potency of Wilde's play: an extravagant mixture of written text, Beardsley's drawings, dance, a theatrical stage, and several overtly cinematic devices."[85] Her film version inherits this desire toward aesthetic simulation, association, and display, yet instead of further establishing Nazimova's success as an artist, the film ushered in her precipitous career decline.

Nazimova's auteurship and stardom were directly dismantled by her attempts to make film into true art—her film adaptation of *Salome* is oft considered one of the first American art films—making her a copy of Wilde, specifically in terms of real ruin at art's expense. Nazimova mainly self-funded the film's exorbitant production budget, which became too costly in trying to furnish particularly lavish or fastidious details, such as Rambova's insistence on creating all the costumes from fabrics shipped overseas from the Maison Lewis of Paris.[86] Once indicator of her success, Nazimova's mansion on Sunset Boulevard had to be converted into a residential hotel soon after the failure of *Salome*, and after less than three years was taken over by new management that rebranded it the "Garden of Allah" with a differentiating *h*. As a hotel complex, it housed some of Hollywood's most notable figures, from Orson Welles to Marlene Dietrich. Indeed, director Billy Wilder had been a frequent visitor, and it is in his 1950 film *Sunset Boulevard* that the mansion is reborn as a Hollywood Gothic castle, and Nazimova herself caricatured as the twentieth century's modern archetype of the aging, mad actress, Norma Desmond.

Like Wilde and Bernhardt, Norma Desmond's very existence is dominated by her image, which becomes in *Sunset Boulevard*'s mise-en-scène an endless refraction of her performative doubles. Early on in voice-over, the postmortem Joe Gillis tells the audience that Norma is a reproduction of Charles Dickens's Miss Havisham, "in her rotting wedding dress and her torn veil, taking it out on the world because she'd been giving the go-by." As well as resurrecting these literary images (remembering too that Eisenstein uses Dickens as exegetical of the cinema's precursory literary foundations), the film offers a self-reflexive illustration of Gillis's inevitable death in the film, and film as inevitable death, simulated through the "creeping paralysis" of Norma Desmond in her "grim Sunset mansion." Indeed, Desmond is part decadent vampire and part modern film actress, though these are not contradictory tropes. According to William Rothman, death is the very condition of all beings on film, and cinema's villains are specifically "the creation of the camera," which "fixes its human subjects, possesses their life," and creates of them liminal figures who are continually projected and thus "condemned to a condition of death-in-life from which they can never escape."[87]

Norma enacts "paralysis" through her state of suspended animation, having hermetically sealed herself into her own Gothic invisibility now that she is no

FIG. 4.3 One of many shots of Norma Desmond's pictures crowding most tabletops in her home, which are all real photographs and images from Gloria Swanson's personal collection.

longer the star of "moving" pictures. This is made all the more ironic and interesting when addressing the historical figure she hopes to portray as means for her comeback: Salome. Possibly practicing what Marie-Luise Kohlke calls neo-Victorian "sexsation," a new age Orientalism that located the exotic other in the Victorian past, Desmond seeks to overcome her own pastness, having once been a sexually appealing star of now defunct silent pictures, by reifying her own authority through a reanimation of culturally historic tropes.[88] The celluloid world and her phantom fans "in the dark" are what sustain Norma, who feeds off them to preserve her "still life" in that crumbling mansion, itself a fictional double for the Garden of Alla. In the film, the mansion reinforces the notion of maximum visibility, Norma sustaining a version of life rooted in illusory surfaces, mimicking her psychic need to be an actress, to perpetuate herself in/as illusion. Lounging on the divan in her sitting room, Norma suffocates herself with a multiplicity of her own still portraits cluttering the console—there is even an Art Nouveau drawing done of her in the style of Aubrey Beardsley propped up on an equally crowded table in her screening room, a clear nod to the Beardsley-inspired images of Nazimova's film—as Gillis questions in voice-over, "How could she breathe in that house so crowded with Norma Desmonds, and more Norma Desmonds, and still more Norma Desmonds?" (figure 4.3).[89]

Like Sarah Bernhardt's or Oscar Wilde's, Norma Desmond's subjectivity proves difficult if not entirely impossible to locate by the final scene; after she kills Gillis, whose body is floating in her famous pool, the police come to find a "sleepwalker" incognizant of any dividing line between reality and performance. She is convinced to leave her bedroom only by the promise of being consumed as an image by the rolling cameras, both internal to the scene and external for the filming. "Norma is like a dead star," Daniel Brown writes, "in that she gains her appearance of life from an external source, the projector that infuses her 'celluloid self' with light."[90] The last image of the film wherein Norma and the camera consume each other reciprocally only bolsters the film's metacinematic quality. They are conflated just like the princess Salomé and the moon in Wilde's play, gesturing back toward Wilde's unnatural order of things and the objectification of oneself through art. An earlier draft of the screenplay for *Sunset Boulevard* suggests that Norma's final descent down the staircase was based on the Dance of the Seven Veils from Wilde's play. And the shot of her head seemingly enwreathed in light bulbs is a clear re-production of Nazimova's styling from her 1922 film, specifically her pearl-covered headpiece (figure 4.4).

Wilde's play ends with a filmic meditation on the femme fatale's visual presence—"*A moonbeam falls on Salomé, covering her with light*"—followed by King Hérode's command that she be killed for her vile request of Iokanaan's head on a silver platter. In contrast, rather than offer inevitable death, *Sunset Boulevard* suggests Norma's perpetual reanimation. She directly addresses the audience, vowing that she will continue to live these celluloid lives: "And I promise you that I'll never desert you again because after *Salome* we'll make another picture and another picture. You see this is my life! It always will be! There's nothing else." Norma's face then gets consumed by the orb of the camera's lens operating as mechanical moon—the surface through which she renders her "self" and all her future iterations as legible, performative imprints. After 1950, Swanson was never able to escape what she called the "Gloria-Norma identification," sealed by her indelible performance as the cinema's new mad actress icon. She would receive endless numbers of scripts that were "'awful imitations' but admits that she did not want to spend the rest of her life playing Norma Desmond over and over again."[91] Gloria Swanson achieved a "return" to the Hollywood screen in *Sunset Boulevard* after the decline of her silent film stardom, but she was unable to escape the constant re-turning to the role that Hollywood desired.

In *The Stars*, Edgar Morin proposes that beauty is the real actress in the movies and should be as moving and magical as sacred masks, as "eloquent as the beauty of statues."[92] A star's beauty, according to Morin, develops under two important conditions: Hollywood stardom as the engine behind what he calls "an admirable industrial Pygmalionism," and by the camera's transformative power, able to turn doll into idol.[93] Unsurprisingly, early fan magazines and other media engines frequently equated twentieth-century female film stars with works of art, perpetuating the long-standing association between real women and their antique cultural antecedents. Michael Williams uses this hetero-negotiated aesthetic discourse to frame his discussion of "conferring imaginative form, and,

FIG. 4.4 Alla Nazimova in her pearl-covered headpiece for *Salomé* (top); the look's visual reproduction through Norma Desmond, wreathed by her backlighting that illuminates the round jewels in her hair, as she descends the staircase playing Salome in the final scene of *Sunset Boulevard* (bottom).

FIG. 4.5 Photograph of actress Gloria Swanson, wearing a gown adorned with Beardsley-inspired rose designs equivalent to one famously worn by Nazimova, posed next to a reproduction of the Venus de Milo; originally published in *Picture-Play*, September 1922.

above all, *presence* on the star."[94] He performs a detailed reading of a photo taken of Swanson in which she is framed as "grand and remote" by means of standing next to a reproduction of the Venus de Milo. In this picture, as in other publicity photographs of her where her statuesque pose is more implicitly constructed, "Swanson is as elusive a construct as the statue," he writes—"an image, a fragment," or, I hasten to add, an art object (figure 4.5).[95] The Venus de Milo persisted as a benchmark of female beauty, and the photo of Swanson and Venus side by side—a surrogate of their encounter that seems an almost exact replica of the scene in Villiers's novel when Alicia Clary meets Venus in the Louvre—points to the structuring influence of classical aesthetics on modern cinematic images. And, more specifically, on the actress's need to re-produce antique ideals, another value yielded through reference to the Venus de Milo, better known through copies, replicas of a lost Greek archetype.

Meet Me in Metropolis

The onset of industrial modernity further punctuated this incessant need for female-shaped simulations, the replication of the woman as symbolic projection of male anxieties, and the Weimar period—a time "when the sense of German nationhood was in an insecure, emasculated limbo" between world wars—yielded copious examples of the myth of the mechanized woman.[96] The female android reemerged as an ideal figure for a cinematic futurism that also necessitated its corresponding, literary past and an acknowledgment of the android's statuesqueness. The substructure of the female robot undoubtedly originates in the notion of sculptural form and reproduction.

In search of a synthesis of art forms akin to the Gesamtkunstwerk—a core aesthetic value equating to an ideal, total, or all-embracing art form early defined by German composer Richard Wagner in "The Artwork of the Future" (1849)—German sculptor Rudolf Belling commanded all styles of classical modernism in his sculptural ventures. Yet his work broke away from classic principles too, Belling's sculptures becoming climactically modern, and possibly cinematic, through their "powerful tectonic form" and strongly three-dimensional creation of "effective spatial bodies."[97] He built his multiperspectival sculptures, which pioneered the manipulation of negative and positive space, by organizing the forms, according to the sculptor himself, and making them "grow like a tree or a human being."[98] Belling designed and patented the *Moden-Plastiken*, or fashion sculptures, his most commercial achievement, in 1921; heavily promoted and popularly used in avant-garde shop window displays, his creations serve as the foundation for modern store mannequins, still unceasingly produced. Done in varnished papier-mâché, the *Moden-Plastiken* operated as sculptural embodiments of the *mannequin vivant*, or "living" fashion model, of 1870s Paris. Supposedly dubbed as goddesses of aluminum, the fashion sculptures also function as prognostications for the lineage of female androids and automatons cinema would likewise reproduce in striking, near three-dimensionality. Indeed, Belling's *Kopf in Messing* (*Head in Brass,* 1925), a masterpiece of modernist sculpture, exhibits machine age aesthetics through the head of a technoid woman. Putting these parts together, brass head atop mannequin, strikes me as an original design from which the robot-woman of Fritz Lang's *Metropolis* (1927) is copied.

Indeed, both Belling's head in brass and his fashion sculptures, representations of the modernization and transformation of sculptural forms, become psycho-cinematically incorporated and animated through the *Maschinenmensch* (machine-human) of *Metropolis*. Tom Gunning argues that the film stages man's confrontation with the (female) machine directly, but *Metropolis* hinges equally upon the history of the statue as human re-presentation, and the dream of its animation. Fundamentally, the statue, like the robot, represents the desire to change (human) form. In *The Haunted Screen*, Lotte Eisner charts some central elements of German Expressionist cinema, echoes from the prior century's artificial generation of artists, including overpowering obsessiveness, visual instability and disorientation, object and scenic distortion, and the sense of being haunted—sometimes even by animated objects, like statues.[99] *Metropolis*'s robot of manifold names—*Machinenmensch*, new Hel, robot Maria, Futura, Ultima—was actually created by German sculptor Walter Schulze-Mittendorff, who built numerous other art pieces material to the film, including Hel's memorial bust and the sepulchral *Death and the Seven Deadly Sins.* In 2014, conceptual design and prop workshop Kropserkel accomplished what it calls the "resurrection of a cultural icon" by "faithfully recreating in loving detail" an exact replica of the original robot Maria used on set in 1927.[100] In its marketing materials, Kropserkel asserts that the contemporaneous discovery of Tut's tomb profoundly impacted Schulze-Mittendorff's robot design, Tut's nemes headdress, coal-lined eyes, and golden facial features direct influences on the sculptor's own *Maschinenmensch.*[101]

Even more definitively, *Metropolis* reproduces essential aspects of Villiers's *L'Ève future*: on a theoretical level, the novel's important, literary prefiguration of the cinema as a medium for animating the feminine ideal, signal of Pygmalionism shifting from literature to film;[102] on a factual one, Theo von Harbou, Lang's wife and collaborator, adapts the book when writing her own novel and the screenplay for *Metropolis.*[103] In Villiers's novel, the very function of cinema gets mapped onto the female body, artificially re-produced and reanimated on-screen in a quest for what Stephen Heath calls "the satisfying projection of a basic oneness," both psychological, in relation to gender, and aesthetic: the novel's *andréïde* operating as a metaphor for the synesthetic possibilities of modern arts, a Gesamtkunstwerk in itself.[104]

In the famous creation-transformation scene of *Metropolis,* Lang painstakingly shows mad scientist Rotwang's process of turning metal-clad Futura—the robot already inscribed visually as female—into the very human likeness of Maria as meta-level projection, a photographic superimposition that produces a simulacrum. In Villiers's novel, Edison transmits Alicia's likeness onto Hadaly by means of a similarly described process, transferring image onto photochromatic skin the same way the process is transferred on and in film. Edison employs his "cylinder of movements" to transplant her gestures, a photographic cylinder to record words for recitation. In Lang's film, as *L'Ève future,* we get a chance to watch the transfer of identity and "the illusory power of false appearance."[105] But Rotwang's underlying pain is very real, fixated on the memory of a dead woman he loved. Hel, her name a palpable allusion to the bad place, first lives on through a stone memorial, an essential material image in this unmistakable assembly line: dead woman to statue to female android to human be-ing. Hel died in natural childbirth, giving life to Freder, son of Joh Fredersen who now controls the city; thus, the mechanical woman is the incarnation of the dead and absent mother, as well as the re-animation of the lost love object, represented through the film's large statuary bust of her head. In von Harbou's original story, Freder's Christic tale of heroism is increasingly Oedipal as well; when he first sees Maria in the Garden, Freder recognizes the "sweet countenance of the mother," for instance, ethereally reanimated. Likewise, *Metropolis* repeats and reframes foundational biblical allusions, the film's Eternal Gardens representing the Garden of Eden with the angelic Maria, who first appears to Freder there, preaching a gospel of goodness.

Yet futures projected by such techno-feminine figures often prove to be dystopic ones, congenerous with the fall of empires brought about by the Whore of Babylon in the book of Revelations (17:1–18), a figure through which "evil" Maria is coded. Lang's film replicates the association between the city and the seductively sinful woman from biblical tradition, the Whore historically used to personify the city and its indulgence of pride, vanity, and alluring wealth. At the Yoshiwara nightclub, in the film's futuristic red-light district, robot Maria dances in the style of Salome—judged an equally scarlet woman and "daughter of Babylon" as by Iokanaan in Wilde's play—a frenzied, bewitching dance of gauzy fabrics and bared midriff. Earlier, while awaiting Maria in the cathedral, Freder had overheard a sermon about the coming apocalypse; in that scene, Lang splices in a page from Revelations, an intertext illustrated with an image of the Whore of Babylon sitting atop a multiheaded monster. When the robot Maria emerges from an enormous urn to dance at Yoshiwara, it equates to a striptease based on death and subsequent re-animation, of both the robot body and the illustrated text—an ekphratic machine in every respect. Indeed, in medieval art and literature, the figure of the Whore exemplified the space between the text and its visualization, a figure emblematic of representational strategies of the medieval artist.[106]

Formal acts in *Metropolis* adhere to create structural meaning in relation to reproduction and animation. The crosscutting between the android Maria dancing and the ill, bedridden Freder—reminiscent of that between Count Orlok and Ellen in F. W. Murnau's *Nosferatu* (1922), the first and unauthorized adaptation of Bram Stoker's *Dracula*—reinforces her vampirically hypnotic power, of animated dead and mechanized woman alike. When the figures of *Death and the Seven Deadly Sins* in the cathedral come to life, these moving statues—the dead re-animated—further signify the android's infrastructure, the mechanical human recalling "the metal robot that moves beneath the synthetically reproduced flesh of the false Maria."[107] The sculptures' dance of death, no doubt, is cut to the same measure as the danse macabre that formed the filmic centerpiece of Villiers's novel. The fake Maria dances at Yoshiwara as an imitation game, challenging our recognition—both the male spectators at the club and the film's audience—of the real versus fake Maria; a powerful mise en abyme that represents the illusion of reality advanced by the cinematic medium. On one hand, *Metropolis* signals abject fear of technology, the film seeming to desire a reaffirmation of "the humanitarian anti-technological ethos of expressionism"; yet, as Andreas Huyssen points out, Lang ironically relies on novel cinematic techniques that reinforce the very concept of artificial reproduction in and through multiplicity and projection.[108] A mirror technique, *Spiegeltechnik* uses a camera with two lenses to record two separate images, or actors, on one single strip of film. In this way, the film's form creates its content, a meta-level interrelationship emerging in *Metropolis* between cinematic technologies of reproduction and the psychic underpinnings of the narrative.

Beneath the Whore of Babylon imagery darts the mechanism of modernity, a relevant intermediation of Henry Adams's proclamation that the Gallery of Machines in the 1900 Paris Exhibition runs on "The Dynamo and the Virgin." The rays of faith interchangeable with and as powerful as electric ones, they equally share "the force of modernity," eternal entanglements with sexual energy—specifically the Virgin, in *Metropolis* signified by Maria—representing the force behind the architectural feats of the Gothic cathedrals.[109] The climax of the film corresponds to a crisis of replication and parallels the aesthetically engineered woman with the architecturally engineered edifice as mirrored images. Thinking that the real Maria is actually Hel, the maniacal Rotwang ascends the cathedral's vertical climb in pursuit of her. On one hand, to be statuesque, from the Venus de Milo to robot Maria, means to exhibit qualities of a statue, or visually attractive ones, such as graceful shape or posture. On the other, to be statuesque can describe that which is imposing, high in stature or great in vertical dimension, like the climbs of the modern city in *Metropolis*.

Alfred Hitchcock—who began his filmmaking career in Germany's UFA Studios and was heavily influenced by Lang's and other German filmmakers' Expressionist landscapes[110]—seemingly reproduces the climactic climb in *Metropolis* as an inverted mirror image at the end of *Vertigo*, the central film text in the next chapter. Whereas Lang found inventive ways to convey the immense height of buildings in his cinematic city, its vertical structure a representation of social hierarchies and "a multitude of discontents," Hitchcock designed novel means to depict nearly falling from them.[111] I might look to Patrick McGilligan, biographer of both directors, who asserts that Lang believed Hitchcock "borrowed shamelessly" from him, copying his work. By the 1940s, Lang's seeming frustrations intensified when Hitchcock reached new vertical climbs and "usurped his title as king of suspense."[112]

And the copy possibly superseded the original.

5

See-Through Woman

Reproductive Delusions in Alfred Hitchcock's *Vertigo*

> Two spirals entangled and confounded the one with the other, yet never touching, would afford a fair representation of this bicephalic life.
> —Théophile Gautier, "La Morte amoureuse"

Henri Agel, founder of the Parisian film journal *Études cinématographiques*, argued that Alfred Hitchcock's films were all marked by *l'emprise du mal* (the grip of evil), his villains beautifully modernized equivalents to Satan in Milton's *Paradise Lost*. His construction of films, Agel suggested, was comparable to that of the "great Christian works portraying the relativity of all human notions in light of divine justice and grace."[1] In the very first issue of *Cahiers du cinéma* published in April 1951, Alexandre Astruc wrote two articles on Hitchcock, who, in his estimation, "proved himself capable of writing cinema with the camera, with style, grace, and internal unity worthy of Milton."[2] French critical interest in "le cas de Hitchcock" began initially around 1950, due in large part to the emergence of the "politique des auteurs"—later deemed auteur theory—from the annals of *Cahiers*; one of its founding elements was Astruc's notion of the *caméra-stylo* (1948), granting film directors the right to employ their cameras as authors wield their pens. The repeated connections between Hitchcock and Milton were not random but were designed to gesture toward the Catholicism at the bedrock of Hitchcock's upbringing and, consequently, his filmic authorship, an essential component of his signature style according to *Cahiers* critics and filmmakers François Truffaut and Claude Chabrol. In his essay "Une certaine tendance du cinéma français" (1954), Truffaut would first apply the term "auteur" in its newfound, cinematic sense, and the *Cahiers* scholarship that followed accordingly would impact the direction of film criticism by considering film directing as a form of creation, and directors less as technicians than as authors engaged in creating a corpus of works that cohesively testify to a singular, artistic vision. *Cahiers* critics Eric Rohmer and Chabrol pointed toward Hitchcock's ever-present Platonism, calling the auteur "one of the greatest inventors of form in the history of cinema"—indeed, with *Vertigo* (1958), as I will examine in this chapter, "form does not merely embellish content, but actually creates it."[3]

The French Hitchcock: *Vertigo* and Auteurism

If Hitchcock was the modern, filmmaking equivalent of John Milton—famous for recasting man's fall from the graces of the Father—then he was also a prime example of the rebellion against past forms and the regeneration of a new aesthetic order. The ascendant cinematic license *Cahiers* critics ascribed to American film directors like Hitchcock, Orson Welles, and Howard Hawks represented a generational divide from the historical tendency—soon to be washed away by France's New Wave—of typically script-heavy, literary cinema branded "le cinema de papa" (Daddy's cinema), or the "tradition de qualité." The films of post-war France were often literary adaptations—like that of Balzac's great novel *Colonel Chabert* (1943, dir. René le Hénaff)—predicated on a level of prestige enacted primarily through the preexisting source text and its traditional over-valuation rather than, as the *Cahiers* writers proposed, a glorification of the possibilities of visual storytelling the cinematic medium alone provided. The meaning of these *qualité* films was buried in the literary a priori, the scriptwriter equivalent to the director, or *metteur en scène* who, according to André Bazin, merely adapts the material rather than making it their own. Conversely, the film work of an auteur would carry the personal signature of the artist, its value pushing past the boundaries of formal and technical properties (though the technical skill of a director was of the utmost, foundational importance) and into a deeper semantic dimension wherein a film's interior meaning could be discovered somewhere between the directorial style and the film material—a tension, according to the earliest auteur critics, that is embedded in the substance of cinema.

Though Alfred Hitchcock and his cinematic oeuvre were praised and largely adopted by the French critical tradition, his filmmaking career traversed Germany, England, and America. In London in 1919, he started out as the illustrator of title cards for silent films; through the early 1920s, he acted as assistant director at London's Players-Lasky studio as well as at Germany's UFA Studios, experiences that help account for the Expressionistic character that would come to characterize many of his later films. Hitchcock's earliest directed picture was *The Pleasure Garden* (1925), an Anglo-German production, and from *The Lodger* (1926) to *Jamaica Inn* (1939), Hitchcock built his own prototype of suspense films in Great Britain. Never returning to the British film system, he made more than thirty films in Hollywood, his first being *Rebecca* (1940) and his last, *Family Plot* (1976). His most inspired period of filmmaking, however, occurred from the 1950s to early 1960s, a period during which he created the ultimate in sophisticated thrillers, like the Grace Kelly vehicles *Dial M for Murder* (1954) and *To Catch a Thief* (1955), metacinematic masterpieces like *Rear Window* (1954), and his masterwork of horror, *Psycho* (1960).

In a piece entitled "Le chef-d'œuvre inconnu," named after the famous short story by Honoré de Balzac and published in *Cahiers* in 1954, French film critic Jean Domarchi discusses how Hitchcock combines classical narrative techniques with a modernist emphasis on the subconscious. This particular issue of *Cahiers* was dedicated to advancing the concept of Hitchcock as a creator in the world of cinema and also explicitly linked him to important French literary forebears. As a matter of fact, Hitchcock had an ostensible fascination with French language and culture from a young age, excelling at French in school and able to offer sustained French narration and conversation by adulthood. He used Paris as the setting for his first published story, "Gas," and for many of his early British films such as *Downhill* (1927) and *Easy Virtue* (1928). Many of his American films through the 1940s continued to include notable allusions to French heritage or setting; and personally Hitchcock and wife, Alma Reville—whom he referred to as "Madame"—imported all manner of French culture to Los Angeles with them, from decor to cuisine.[4]

In February 1955, *Cahiers* published its second issue devoted to Hitchcock, which revolved around the director's recent interview with Truffaut and Chabrol. The interviewers asked Hitchcock about a nascent project that promised to be his most French-influenced film. At the time, it bore the name *From Amongst the Dead*, an English translation of *D'entre les morts* (1954), the title of the French novel written by Pierre Boileau and Thomas Narcejac used as the film's substructure. It is well known that Hitchcock wanted to purchase the rights to Boileau and Narcejac's earlier novel, *Celle qui n'était plus* (1951) (in English, *She Who Was No More*) but was beaten out by Henri-Georges Clouzot, who adapted the story into the immensely successful film *Les Diaboliques* (1955). Hitchcock's admiration for *Les Diaboliques* was unsurprising considering his own desire to have told that particular story on film, and the fact that Clouzot, often referred to as "the French Hitchcock," had many of the same directorial attitudes to themes such as obsession, paranoia, and morbidity.[5] In his interview of Hitchcock—which would later form the basis for the seminal text *Hitchcock*, first published in

1967—Truffaut hinted quite strongly that the story line of *D'entre les morts*, which would later become *Vertigo*, seemed so perfectly tailored to Hitchcock's cinematic concerns that it could have been written for him. In fact, in a letter by Truffaut to Jacques Rivette, which was appended to the end of the interview, Truffaut states that there was reason to believe that the French novelists had concocted the story, with its thematic debts to Hitchcock films such as *Rebecca* and *Strangers on a Train* (1955), explicitly for the director himself. James M. Vest maintains that in doing this, Truffaut gives indirect credit to the *Cahiers* writers for the film's origins by "suggesting that specific themes—themes identified and promoted by *Cahiers* writers—were purposely introduced into the novel on which *Vertigo* is based."[6]

This strange permutation implies that the auteur system of interpretation was already inscribed into the original French text, which would then be turned into the film many critics would consider Hitchcock's most masterful and most personal.[7] It also offers an externally powerful mise en abyme that represents *Vertigo*'s internal narrative: a man falls for a woman/story/script that is seemingly produced for his eyes only, a subjective piece of theater. Hitchcock seemingly plays along in his responses preserved in *Hitchcock*; he first thwarts the suggestion that Boileau and Narcejac wrote the book for him, but at Truffaut's insistence he responds, "Do you really think so? What if I hadn't bought it?"[8] Just a few exchanges later in the interview, Hitchcock redoubles a connection between the plausibility of his purchasing the rights to a book written specifically for him by scratching at his own *Vertigo* itch, admitting to being bothered by the premise of the film's murder plot: "But how could he know that James Stewart wouldn't make it up those stairs? . . . How could he be sure of that?"[9] Despite the resemblance that percolates here between the director and the male protagonist of *Vertigo*, by the time the film's screenplay was finished in 1957, its resemblance to the original novel had become increasingly remote, by then stamped indelibly with Hitchcock's signature style. It bears mentioning that Narcejac also maintains the book was not intentionally written for Hitchcock, though he admits to shared interests between them. Rather, and even more strikingly, he reveals that the idea for the story was actually born from his experience in a French cinema. Thinking he recognized someone from his past while watching the newsreel—it being common to have "lost" friends and family displaced by the war—Narcejac found himself provoked explicitly by the concept of bringing back something, or someone, either lost or dead, a story suited for the regenerative quality of the cinema.[10]

In particular, *Vertigo* reenacts with striking similarity the cinematic embodiment of woman as the site for the conversion of absence into presence, of "lack into a form of representational plentitude," and of death into life.[11] Dead women have haunted the cinema since its birth, but Hitchcock's Orphic romance of the 1950s was one of the most perverse and self-aware examples of a film that revolves around the notion of a dead woman. And as Hitchcock's only film adapted directly from a French work, *Vertigo* stands as the most French of his films, most distinctly in consideration of its visual reproduction of the same Pygmalionesque delusions that largely overwhelmed nineteenth-century Aestheticism and Symbolism, as studied in this book's prior chapters. Hitchcock's films invoked the woman as narrative locus as well as the node of impossible narration, thus inscribing textual meaning and tension through visual paradigms founded upon feminized objects of visual fascination. Many of his films re-produce yet another copy of the story that kept repeating throughout the nineteenth century, what in regard to *Vertigo* Robert Samuels calls "a constant alternation between the attempt to control and shape the feminine form on the one hand, and on the other hand, a deep awareness of masculine loss and lack."[12]

Vertigo's main protagonist, John "Scottie" Fergusson, is haunted from the very beginning of the film. The film opens with a chase scene across the rooftops of San Francisco: a criminal being pursued by two law enforcement officials, an unnamed policeman and Scottie, following quickly behind. Though the criminal and the policeman manage to leap from one roof to the next, Scottie's jump falls short, and he slides down the roof's slope and hangs from the gutter, which bends under the force of his weight. Dangling from such a height, Scottie is seized by an attack of vertigo when he looks downward, illustrated by Hitchcock's famous, signature forward zoom/reverse tracking shot, which I will discuss in depth later in the chapter.

Turning back to help Scottie, his fellow policeman tumbles off the roof to his death on the city street below. Cut to Scottie in the apartment of friend Midge, his college sweetheart and ex-fiancée; he has mainly recovered except that he wears a "darn corset" that binds—a fitting metaphor for the frailty, and early feminization, of the male protagonist. Having quit the police force because of his perceived inability to perform such duties, now that he suffers from acrophobia, he has no plans for getting past the past or planning for the future. A man of "independent means," Scottie does not have to do anything, thus giving the audience a clear indication that he is still, despite his miraculous and mysterious escape from the roof after his near-death fall, in a state of suspension.

After surviving the fall, Scottie is hired by an old school chum, Gavin Elster, to follow his wife, Madeleine; Elster believes that "someone out of the past" takes possession of his wife from time to time, and that this "someone dead" will cause her harm. During her fits, Elster tells Scottie, Madeleine is "somewhere else, away from me, someone I don't know," and when she returns to her self again, she "doesn't even know she's been away." Though reluctant about reentering detective work, Scottie finds himself easily lured into the mystery behind Madeleine's strange behavior after seeing her for the first time dining at Ernie's restaurant; he follows her as she wanders, unconsciously we would assume, to a variety of spots across San Francisco: the florist shop; the graveyard at Mission Dolores, where Madeleine pays her respects at the grave site of Carlotta Valdes (1831–1857); the art gallery in the Palace of the Legion of Honor, where Madeleine gazes at a particular portrait, enraptured by it. The museum guard tells Scottie what he had already suspected: that the woman in the portrait is Carlotta Valdes, the same woman resting in the grave Madeleine visited earlier. Pop Liebl, the owner of the Argosy Book Shop and an "authority on San Francisco history," tells Midge and Scottie the story of Carlotta Valdes, the beautiful mistress of a wealthy man, who built the McKittrick Hotel originally as a home for her—one of the latter stops Madeleine makes while Scottie follows. Carlotta bore the man's child, but he still "threw her away," which led her to become "the sad Carlotta" and then "the mad Carlotta," before she eventually committed suicide—a fate Madeleine seems possessed by and attempts in the San Francisco Bay, seeing as she is the same age, twenty-six, at which her great-grandmother took her own life.

Soon, Scottie and Madeleine go out "wandering" together, and Scottie learns that Madeleine has hallucinations of death and does indeed identify (unconsciously, it seems) as the long-dead Carlotta. She believes that the only explanation is that she is "mad." She tells him of a recurrent dream she has, set in a Spanish mission, and Scottie, desperate to unravel the mystery and free Madeleine from her "possession," unveils that her dream setting is real. The next day he takes her to the site of these dreams, San Juan Bautista, blissfully optimistic that he has solved the mystery and can free the woman he now loves from her possession, in order to possess her himself. But she becomes distraught and runs up the stairs of the bell tower; because Scottie's vertigo impedes him from reaching the summit, he cannot keep her from throwing herself from the tower to her death.

Though freed from any legal blame in Madeleine's death, Scottie spends a year in an asylum, where Midge, unsuccessfully, plays him Mozart to "sweep the cobwebs away." But even after his release, Scottie's obsession perseveres, and he experiences a dream (sequence) that suggests his own madness forcing his return to the same settings in which he had seen Madeleine while she was alive. He soon spots a woman, Judy Barton from Salina, Kansas, who bears an uncanny resemblance to Madeleine. Obviously enamored with her based on her resemblance to Madeleine (though Judy is more unrefined), Scottie molds her into the image of Madeleine, dressing her in the same clothes, making her hair the same blond, pinned in the same way.

But once successfully remodeled into the image of Madeleine, Judy makes the fatal mistake of putting on the same necklace from the portrait of Carlotta, a sentimental keepsake from Elster. The audience has already discovered that she was in on the "trick"; Judy writes a letter earlier, the contents of which are narrated for the audience and accompanied by a flashback, explaining that she played the role of Elster's wife, Madeleine, all along as part of his plan to murder her. Elster staged an artificialized mystery through the figure of Carlotta Valdes, hiring Scottie specifically because of his vertigo, so that Elster could throw his wife's dead body from the top of the tower at Mission San Juan Bautista while Scottie would fail to ascend, forced to "witness" Madeleine's body fall to its presumed death. A witting player in Elster's deception, Judy yields to a second charade directed by Scottie in the hopes he will return her love. The symbol of the necklace unlocks the mystery, spurring Scottie to bring Judy back to the Mission in order to "be free of the past." He forces her up the stairs of the bell tower, staging the scene of Madeleine's death. He berates Judy for having been "the copy, the counterfeit," and tells her, "It's too late, there's no bringing her back." Suddenly, a nun appears in the shadows, and Judy, in fright, throws herself from the tower.

Although Hitchcock was regarded as "the master of suspense," *Vertigo*—of all the films in his canon—undermines the traditional formula of the genre in which the director had become marvelously proficient. Consequently, the film presents itself as a somewhat perplexing, cinematic hybrid. Exceedingly heterogeneous, the film's resistance to a fixed genre ironically defines its singularity.[13] Indeed, *Vertigo* strays from the formula for romance in 1950s Hollywood, instead offering the audience a frighteningly bleak love story—the first Hitchcock romance to end in "abject failure."[14] As Lesley Brill defends, "Hitchcock's romantic films are organized around quests that lead . . . to the creation (or recovery) through love of the protagonists' personal and social identities," and that, conversely, the "miscarrying of that search constitutes the central frustration of *Vertigo*."[15] Theatrically released in May 1958, the film failed to achieve the commercial success expected from a Hitchcock film largely, it seemed at the time, due to its deviation from the traditional romantic-thriller formula (as well as what the audience deemed to be its unnecessary length). Certainly, it qualifies as a "suspense" film inasmuch as Hitchcock considered the development of his distinctive formula to derive from the literary talents of nineteenth-century author Edgar Allan Poe. In "Why I Am Afraid of the Dark," Hitchcock admits that "very probably, it's because I liked Edgar Allan Poe stories so much that I began to make suspense films," contending that he and Poe were both "prisoners" of the genre.[16] In an analysis in *Cahiers* soon after the release of *Vertigo*, Eric Rohmer calls attention to parallels between Hitchcock's work and Poe's tales like "Morella," remarking on the director's innovative reproductions of classic themes. But while the film's esoteric nature made it possibly more attractive to French audiences than American ones, its seeming "Frenchness" requires us to acknowledge the concurrent development of these same, repeated themes: like Gautier, Poe found himself prisoner of his own literary women operating as both *fascinante* and *revenante*. While the film exhumes and perpetuates the animated dreams of nineteenth-century French literature as I have examined, and internally seeks to resurrect the dead (woman) on a visual and symbolic level, *Vertigo* itself had to undergo numerous self-resurrections on its way to gaining its more current, and possibly obsessive, admirations.

Film theorist Robin Wood reclaimed some attention for the film when he published *Hitchcock's Films* in 1968, in which he esteems *Vertigo* as "Hitchcock's masterpiece to date and one of the four or five most profound and beautiful films the cinema has yet given us."[17] Wood called *Vertigo* "a perfect organism of a film"—a living, breathing "thing" the likes of which the American theatergoer had never seen before—a newly invented species. And yet the film might be the most unreal ever made, invading the spectator's consciousness with a new order, a film that "completely creates a decadent, artificial world unrelated in any way to the real one."[18] As an organism, it needed to re-generate itself before reaching the zenith it has today; in 2010, the British Film Institute's *Sight and Sound* magazine declared *Vertigo* the greatest film of all time, dethroning *Citizen Kane* (1940), which had held the top spot since 1962. As one of five films owned by Hitchcock himself, *Vertigo*—which Hitchcock reluctantly told Truffaut was one of his favorites—was removed from circulation between 1973 and 1983, curbing theoretical discussion of the film and making it a lost but desired object.

During the last year that *Vertigo* was available to the public (1973), film theorist Laura Mulvey wrote "Visual Pleasure and Narrative Cinema," an essay that analyzed how classical Hollywood cinema reflected the patriarchal order by which it was dominated. Mulvey's essay uses feminist-inflected "psychoanalysis to discover where and how the fascination of film is reinforced by *pre-existing patterns of fascination* already at work within the individual subject and the social formations that have moulded him."[19] She uses *Vertigo* as an example exegetical of her premise that the cinema develops scopophilia, or desire in looking phallocentrically, "in a world ordered by sexual imbalance" wherein "pleasure in looking has been split between active/male and passive/female."[20] Indeed, Mulvey interprets film as a signifying system determined by a gender dichotomy that, at its foundation, recalls the traditional, Pygmalionesque structure. She writes that "the determining male gaze projects its phantasy on to the female figure which is styled accordingly" so that the woman "displayed as sexual object is the leitmotif of erotic spectacle"; by holding the look, woman plays to and thus signifies male desire.[21] But her analysis of Scottie's fetishistic investments is somewhat overly simplified, and her reading deceives itself into promoting the same patriarchal symbolism of the cinema that, simultaneously, it decries. Mulvey suggests that Scottie, a policeman with "all the attributes of the patriarchal superego," sadistically "follows, watches, and falls in love with a perfect image of female beauty and mystery," consequently "break[ing] her down" and "exposing her guilt."[22] Though Mulvey's claim that Hitchcock uses the process of identification to show "its perverted side," she somehow doubly perverts the psychoanalytic complexity of the film's narrative.

Rather than empowered and sadistic, Scottie is instead characterized as a man afflicted by myriad delusions—all of which may be gathered under the blanket term "vertigo"—from the film's beginning to its end. In her book *The Woman Who Knew Too Much* on Hitchcock and feminist film theory, Tania Modleski offers the compelling mirror image to Mulvey's principal argument, instead contending that the film's fascination with femininity actually "throws masculine identity into question and crisis," and that the film's offering of femininity as "largely a male construct, a male 'design,'" is evoked either humorously or with horror therein.[23] Indeed, Scottie does not break woman down; rather, she shatters him, through both the supposed death fall of "Madeleine" and Judy's fall to her very real death at the film's end. Though one of Scottie's main preoccupations, especially after losing Madeleine when she falls from the tower, is to be "free of the past," the film itself obsesses over man's history as an idealized past, a time during which man had "the freedom and the power." But, aside from Gavin Elster's ability to carry out the murder of his wife and never get caught, man's "freedom and power" is neither palpable nor present within the film's narrative. The past is just that: a long-departed concept to be mourned, an impossibly missed connection. Although we may find ourselves interpreting Scottie's fetishistic refashioning of Judy into Madeleine as an attempt to regenerate his subjective power and control, by the film's end, we cannot but consider it a failed endeavor.

The narrative of *Vertigo*, a film dominated by the past to such a degree, represents a hollowing out. Rather than demarcating the presence of the present here and now, the narrative conjures mainly absences, voids, and missed encounters. Scottie embodies the very sentiments that predominate over the story: lack, guilt, and repression. Before Scottie falls in love with a dead woman—or one who is as good as dead, at least, in her supposed desire to commit suicide like her great-grandmother, Carlotta Valdes—he is marked by the death of the policeman that will effectively end his law enforcement career, a career that the audience only knows about by witnessing the fall that marks its demise and consequent absence from the story. But Scottie, dangling from the roof after the policeman falls to his death, is as good as fallen himself, as if the story begins at the very moment he is ejected from an Eden-like environment. That first scene ends on the shot of Scottie still dangling from the rooftop's gutter, and since the explanation of how he got off the rooftop is not part of the film's diegesis, Scottie remains throughout the film, at least in a metaphoric sense, dangling over the abyss of death.[24]

Symbolist Dreams and Vanishing Ladies

> Very early, I was immensely struck by the Symbolists. For a time, I had Symbolist dreams.
>
> —Alfred Hitchcock

Hitchcock's films are largely reliant on symbolic codes constructed purposefully by the director himself, and on the one hand, *Vertigo* confronts us with powerful symbols that codify meanings within the film. Yet, on the other hand, the narrative relies ultimately on the misrecognition of these very symbols and the consequent undermining of the film's interpretative system. In order to illustrate this juxtaposition, we should consider that failure, or visual mis-representation and the necessary deconstruction of fantasy, is built into the film's narrative. The internal story pits paternal forces, signified through the protective husband (Gavin Elster) against maternal ones, signified through the diseased, matrilineal lineage (Carlotta Valdes), supposedly passing suicidal tendencies from mother to daughter like a particularly feminine, degenerative disease. Scottie tries to read and interpret these images, not knowing they are synthetic, false, and that they are being projected upon him by way of performance for his eyes only: a subjective piece of theater. As Deborah Linderman argues in "The Mise-en-Abîme in Hitchcock's Vertigo," the determination of the textual system to misrepresent becomes most conspicuous when Judy writes the letter to Scottie, which tells the truth of Elster's murder scheme and her involvement, only to destroy it.[25] But the film's reliance on the audience's (and Scottie's) stupendous misrecognition performs an important function: it gives us, identifying with Scottie's point of view, our own sense of vertigo. As Vest contends, "Hitchcock's strength lay in the fact that his keys opened the door of a mystery that led to another mystery that connected to a third and left viewers wondering whether the first key truly unlocked the initial door, resulting in a very real sense of vertigo. The resulting impression of dislocation, of the uncanny, invoked in the viewer a vertiginous disequilibrium."[26] After being hired by Elster to follow his wife, Scottie amasses clues to this woman's mystery, left for him like bread crumbs, up until she falls to her death off the bell tower. And although these projected images seemingly lead to an "elsewhere"—the mystery of her female lineage—they actually precipitate Scottie's identification, forcing him to look inside himself on an uncanny cinematic return home. Yet he will never reach his destination because "the spiral of pursuit remains initially, nonetheless, in a state of unstable equilibrium."[27]

The most idiosyncratic feature of the film was Hitchcock's insistence on giving away the secret—that Judy really is Madeleine—just a bit over halfway through its running time. This ensured that the film differed markedly from the traditional suspense formula, with a sustained building of tension, as in the source novel, where Boileau and Narcejac did not reveal Judy's true identity until the very end, so that both reader and male protagonist discover the secret simultaneously. Yet Hitchcock insisted on the reveal being situated midfilm, causing the discontent of everyone involved in the production, including the screenplay writer, Samuel Taylor. In his 1962 interview with Truffaut, Hitchcock explains how his desire to unveil the mystery to the entire narrative prematurely proved quite unpopular with most of the film crew:

> Everyone around me was against this change; they all felt that the revelation should be saved for the end of the picture. I put myself in the place of a child whose mother is telling him a story. When there's a pause in the narration, the child always says, "What comes next, Mommy?" Well, I felt that the second part of the novel was written as if nothing came next, whereas in my formula, the little boy, knowing that Madeleine and Judy are the same person, would

> then ask, "And Stewart doesn't know, does he? What will he do when he finds out about it?"[28]

Effectively splitting the film into two main parts, unveiling the secret prematurely ensured that the second half of the diegesis allows the audience to forgo the mystery of the woman's identity; switching the audience identification then toward sharing the buildup of anxiety in the male protagonist makes *Vertigo* one of Hitchcock's most introspectively psychological films. In his interview with Truffaut, Hitchcock confirmed that his interest was to have the audience in on the secret, so that "suspense will hinge around the question of how Stewart is going to react when he discovers that Judy and Madeleine are actually the same person."[29] Hitchcock's formula seems suspiciously interchangeable with Edison's unveiling of his *andréïde* to Ewald in *L'Ève future*. Ewald converses with Alicia Clary, not discovering until well later that he is instead engaged with Hadaly, Alicia's mechanical copy "performing" the role of the actress. Though Villiers's book is not invested so much in the horror but the beauty of Ewald's realization, the structural trick predicated through these feminine substitutes functions by similar design.

Just as auteur theory "reveals authors where none had been seen before," this sudden actualization of male cinematic authorship necessitates the disappearance of woman; or, to borrow the title of Hitchcock's film, *The Lady Vanishes* (1938).[30] Though adapted from Ethel Lina White's novel *The Wheel Spins* (1936), Hitchcock acknowledges that the source is actually an older folklorish story that takes place in Paris during the 1889 Exposition—the one that featured the Eiffel Tower—wherein a daughter and mother arrive to visit and the mother suddenly disappears; as the story goes, she succumbs to the bubonic plague and is "erased" by officials, who negate the daughter's story that there even was a mother, in order to keep the city clean and functional for the exposition.[31] The film's title obviously alludes to Méliès's *The Vanishing Lady*, discussed in chapter 4, which was a prime example of his ushering in the birth of cinematic magic as an obsessive substitute to maternity. Lucy Fischer posits that "Méliès may also have to stand as the inadvertent patriarch of a particular cinematic vision of women" in conversation with our particular trajectory of artificial generation as appropriation of the woman's procreative function, his work important to this complex drama of gender relations.[32] In many of these early trick films, women would appear as products of the male imagination, in artificially rendered tableaux, or directly linked to the dead. Méliès uses his substitution trick in *The Vanishing Lady* to replace the woman with a skeleton, which, it is worth noting, seems like a direct antecedent to the "trick" Hitchcock plays at the end of *Psycho* when Lila finally meets Mrs. Bates. With *Vertigo*, Hitchcock reinvents the substitution "trick" in multiple ways: Gavin Elster uses Judy to play Madeline to substitute for his wife's dead body, which he throws off the tower; Scottie tries to substitute Judy for the

FIG. 5.1 Shot of Madeleine at Ernie's restaurant in *Vertigo*, which represents her as a carefully composed portrait in fixed profile.

seemingly deceased Madeleine in his remaking of her; and, most notably, the trick is on Scottie, as Hitchcock's earlier words affirm, since the mystery at the heart of the film is our waiting anxiously to see his reaction when he discovers he has been deceived. Slavoj Žižek maintains that the persistent critical misrepresentations in Hitchcock studies demand their own theoretical resonance, and that one of the outstanding cases of misrepresentation in *Vertigo* involves the scene in Ernie's restaurant, when Scottie sees Madeleine for the first time. Scottie sits at the bar in the front room of the restaurant, and a long panning shot scans the restaurant from front room to back room, the camera finally resting on the "*fascinum* which fixes our gaze," the exposed back of a beautiful woman, who the audience concludes is Madeleine.[33] This tracking shot seems to permit us access to Scottie's subjective point of view as he surveys the restaurant for the target of his investigation; because he is seated at the bar, however, Scottie's back is turned, his only visual access possible in the form of glances backward, not head-on. Elster and Madeleine rise from the table and walk toward the exit, causing them to pass directly behind Scottie. In the scene's most famous shot, Madeleine pauses immediately behind Scottie and the camera captures her, for a moment, in fixed profile. This framing of her face against the rich background of the restaurant's red wallpaper approximates a carefully composed painting (figure 5.1). Given Scottie's Pygmalionesque fixations on Madeleine, illustrated in his re-producing Judy in her aesthetic image in the last third of the film, many presume this shot to be from Scottie's subjective point of view; he represents a lover of Madeleine-as-art, captivated by her at the specific moment he captures her image, aestheticized and idealized, in profile. But Scottie does not turn around in his seat at the bar, the realistic requirement to have actually seen

Madeleine in this composition; however, the image's directionality gets complicated because the back of the bar he faces is mirrored, thus extending the metaphoric property of her portrait as a mirror image to his own. The camera captures Madeleine's portrait-like profile in "still life" and projects the sentiment onto Scottie, who becomes "mysteriously captivated by it." As Žižek suggests, in this shot we encounter the "kino-eye," a shot that is subjectivized without the subject, the eye functioning "as the 'organ-without-body,' directly registering the passion of an intensity that cannot be assumed by the (diegetic) subject."[34] The film's objectification of subjective perception undermines Scottie's control, which, in turn, emphasizes the importance of seeing things psychically, a strange but telling inversion of the unconscious optics of nineteenth-century literature as in the *fantastique*.

Whereas Gautier started out as a painter, Hitchcock compared himself to one when interviewed by Truffaut and Chabrol, yet with "a message too deep to convey on canvas."[35] Entire monographs, like Dominique Paini and Guy Cogeval's *Hitchcock and Art: Fatal Coincidences* and Christine Sprengler's *Hitchcock and Contemporary Art*, are dedicated to the necessary intersection between aesthetic modes in the works of Hitchcock, and how his films result from this specific aesthetic heterogeneity. The Hitchcocks were famously art lovers, collectors, and supporters: after the London premiere of *The Lady Vanishes*, Alfred stopped at an art exhibition and purchased *Mask and Scythe* (1938), a piece by Bauhaus modernist Paul Klee that set the foundation for a future, museum-worthy family art collection. Kindred spirits in the play of light and shadow, comedy and suspense, Hitchcock remarked to his biographer Charlotte Chandler that Klee would have been gifted at making storyboards for films. In turn, she proceeded to claim that many of Hitchcock's own storyboards bore a "certain resemblance" to Klee's work. One can see an homage to Klee's *Highways and Byways*, inspired by his trip to Egypt, in the crosshatched furrows of Hitchcock's farmland setting for the famous scene in *North by Northwest*. Klee even spoke in a Wildean fashion of the parallels between music and the fine arts, which Hitchcock echoes in his own numerous comments about the director acting as a composer, or that endeavoring toward pure cinema required constructing the pieces of film like notes in a melody.[36] Yet all sorts of paintings, real or artificially created, seemingly influenced Hitchcock and his cinematic art directly. Paintings of internal characters preside over the mise-en-scène in films like *Rebecca* and *Suspicion* (1941); the peephole in Norman's parlor at the Bates Motel is covered over by a framed reproduction of *Susannah and the Elders* (1732, Willem van Mieris), but right above it hangs the possibly more provocative *Venus with a Mirror* (1555, Titian); production designer Robert Boyle admits that the visual production of *The Birds* (1963) is largely modeled on Edvard Munch's *The Scream* (1893). Ken Mogg confirms that Hitchcock kept many art books at his Universal Studios office, and he would use them regularly to show a particular work, painting, or illustration to demonstrate the type of film shot he desired.

FIG. 5.2 Madeleine gazes at the portrait of Carlotta, a prop painted by John Ferren, in the art gallery of San Francisco's Palace of the Legion of Honor, which was built as a three-quarter scale replica of the Palais de le Légion d'Honneur in Paris.

To be "seized by representation" functions as the bedrock of the determining impulses in Hitchcock's films, and in *Vertigo* that impulse reaches its apex.[37] "Madeleine" offers a canvas for the film's self-aware meditations on the concept of an artificially generated woman in ways prefigured yet (visually) inaccessible in the prior century's literary repetitions. Scottie pursues "her," equally an object of investigation and an object of his own fascination, to settings that define her as an art object and suggest the irrevocable connection between her living body and the ideas of death she solicits. At the graveyard at Mission Dolores, Scottie lurks behind the hedges watching her from a distance, the color of her suit reflecting the grayness of the row of gray tombstones among which she stands. Brigitte Peucker suggests that in this scene "her unmoving body [is] positioned as though it were a funerary sculpture next to the grave and headstone of Carlotta Valdes."[38] Madeleine thus mirrors the death of Carlotta through her costuming and her posing, a visual indicator of the death that has already taken her over psychologically—her psychic drive (however feigned) toward killing herself as her great-grandmother Carlotta did at the same age. But it is at the art gallery in the Palace of the Legion of Honor, yet another site of memorialization, where Scottie and the audience identify Madeleine most strongly with a work of art. Madeleine sits on a bench in front of a portrait, and the camera, standing in for Scottie's gaze, watches her from behind (figure 5.2). Although Madeleine sits in front of the painting, gazing at it, the shot from behind suggests her continuity with the portrait, encouraging our awareness of a direct connection between

Scottie and the portrait, with Madeleine in the position of a go-between, or screen, between the two.[39] Scottie's glances between the real (the bouquet lying next to Madeleine on the bench, and her hair fashioned into a bun) and the artificialized (the same bouquet held by the woman in the portrait [Carlotta], with her hair fashioned into an identical twist) allows for the collapse between Madeleine and the painting and the expansion of her figure as representative of the ever-permeable thresholds between real and artificial, subject and object, life and death.

The French twist of Madeleine's hair further implicates the French aesthetic and Symbolist heritage of *Vertigo*, and how such vertiginously swirling, twirling, dancing figures have been in constant rotation since Gautier's fantastic renderings of the art-ificial woman in the 1830s. The hair's swirling shape represents Scottie's vertigo: on a metaphoric level, directly linked to this failure to discern between these very dimensions, while literally representing the (cinematic) delusion of three-dimensionality. As Victor Stoichita maintains, this painting within the film "implies a complex play of nesting images, since it places a fixed image within a mobile image," and symbolically, the mobile image represents "action, movement, life" while the fixed represents death.[40] The complication of vertigo is that it symbolizes, both theoretically and metacritically, a crisis in perception between life and death; thus the delusion of movement it stimulates is also the inability to rely on such symbolic connotations. Gautier speaks of Romuald's delusional relationship with Clarimonde as a life split in two, and he visualized it through "two spirals entangled and confounded the one with the other, yet never touching" (61). Likewise in *L'Ève future*, Lord Ewald succumbs to an attack of vertigo at the Louvre with Alicia Clary (a scene with possible connections to the one wherein Scottie follows Madeleine to the museum at the Legion of Honor), with Villiers using the exactness of the French word *vertige* to characterize the effect of this impossible incongruity between real and artificial women.

If Žižek's "kino-eye" functions as an organ without a body, as with any good Hitchcock film we have to acknowledge the absolute necessity of the reverse: a body without organs and, with that, the importance of sculptural art to our reading of *Vertigo* as symbolist dreamwork. Hitchcock confessed to Chandler that if he had gone into the art world, he would have liked to have been a sculptor, and specifically like French sculptor Auguste Rodin. Oft considered one of the forefathers of modern art, Rodin freed the form from traditional constraints, especially by using the movement of his models as essential to capturing the interplay of light and shadow so integral to his exceedingly human forms. He used "sequential construction" in his works as early as *Man with the Broken Nose* (1862–1864), taking into account the various poses and postures of the model (possibly while moving) so as to create his work out of a "multiplicity of profiles."[41] Rodin's methods of capturing naturalistic bodies seemed to emerge from some of François Willème's methods for photosculpture of the 1860s, as discussed in chapter 1, specifically the idea that the sum of a model's profiles would "yield the volumetric whole."[42]

Two scenes in *Vertigo*—one that focuses on moments of stillness, and the other that predicates itself on movement—suggest a direct connection to Rodin's sculptural techniques and themes: first, his use of relief, specifically in *The Gates of Hell* (*La Porte d'Enfer*, 1880–1917), and second, his in-the-round design of *The Kiss* (*Le Baiser*, 1882).

In our first sighting of Madeleine in Ernie's restaurant, her face is framed in profile and thrown into relief against a sumptuous red backdrop, suggesting that at the very moment she becomes real (or comes on reel), she is also rendered static and deadened into art. When the camera follows her as she exits the restaurant with Elster, it "lingers on her motionless body, surrounded by the draperies of stole and dress, and focuses on the marmoreal whiteness of her naked back and neck."[43] When the shot returns to representing Scottie's actual, subjective point of view, she is centered again, now within the frame of the restaurant's doorway, a threshold space, evoking my earlier discussion of Gradiva-like figures from Gautier to Dali, who open up new portals to second realities and surrealistic fantasies. Gradiva, after all, blurs the distinctions between animate and inanimate as the one "who advances." But for a moment in this moving image medium, Hitchcock catches "Madeleine" in stillness in the doorway; and then she begins to move, according to Peucker, "creating the effect of a sculpture not quite fully brought to life, her movements interspersed with static shots that present her face in profile, in cameo-like relief."[44] A metonymical representation of Scottie's own future movement into the metaphoric realm of the dead, these scenic details suggest a lineage born of Rodin's lifelong project *The Gates of Hell*, a monumental sculptural work depicting scenes from Dante's *Inferno*. Intended as the entrance to a planned decorative arts museum in Paris (which was never built), Rodin's design includes more than 180 figures done in relief, meaning they project out from a supporting background. Reliefs on walls of stone buildings were common in ancient Egypt, and relief sculptures featured prominently in the sarcophagi of Roman art from the second century—fitting death-related uses of the form considering the word "relief" comes from the Italian, meaning to raise, as if from the dead.

Rodin lifts one figure of *The Gates* out of relief and into full three-dimensionality in his sculpture *The Kiss*, a trajectory Hitchcock himself follows, from the still moments in Ernie's restaurant to the full animation of his own (filmed) kiss, shared by Scottie and Judy-as-Madeleine. Later in the film, after the full transformation of Judy into the feminine Ideal of Madeleine (a re-reproduction, of course), she emerges from the bathroom of her apartment fully swathed in the unearthly green light that Hitchcock specifically chooses to symbolize the ghostly character of his muse. It bears noting here that *Vertigo* can be considered his green film; the French word for green is *vert*, so the title of the film can be considered a play on the children's heuristic "green means go," vert-I-go.[45] Hitchcock films the embrace of Scottie and Judy in full 360 degrees—a seeming cinematic repetition of Rodin's design of sculpture in the round for his composition of *The Kiss*—as if the actors were placed on an animation stand spinning in rotation. Hitchcock's use of the spiraling camera here achieves the "mirror effect of the vertigo shot," wherein Scottie "is magically united with his object of desire."[46]

In his review of "*Hitchcock and Art: Fatal Coincidences*" (Montreal Museum of Fine Arts, and later at Paris's Centre Pompidou), David M. Lubin notes the exhibit's suggestion that such scenes, found in *Vertigo* as well as in *Notorious* (1946), echoed Hitchcock's own "phenomenological experience of walking up to and around his favorite works of modern sculpture, such as Rodin's *The Kiss*."[47] Inasmuch as sculpture is the most notable art of reproduction emulated in and through early cinema, so too is it an art "that invites movement as shifting positions of the viewer in space are necessary to see and experience it in the round."[48] As far back as 1778 in his treatise on sculpture, Johann Gottfried Herder noted that observing sculpture was a visual perception that involved this kind of mobility that could never "be assimilated in a single fixed image," instead emphasizing the necessary "kinesthetic apprehension of sculpture."[49] A pioneer of modernist art, Hungarian sculptor and Rodin disciple Constantin Brâncuși believed every sculpture a form of motion, and in photography's capacity to formulate "optical manifestoes" in representing sculptural forms across time and space.[50] Modernist poet Ezra Pound saw an entire universe of form in Brâncuși's work, just as Hitchcock, operating as a modernist artist through his offerings of layered, graphic triangles (*The Lodger*), Cartesian grids (*North by Northwest*), or dizzying heliocoids (*Vertigo*), proved himself capable of reinventing the dynamism of form in the American cinema.[51]

See-Through Women

We might suggest that, contrary to expectations, *Vertigo* bears the possibility that it is fixedly "real" women, not artificial ones, who incite Scottie's malady. The extremely unartificial and all too realistic Midge character serves to amplify the film's encoding of feminine artifice. Writer Samuel Taylor added Midge's character, not part of the original novel on which the film was based, as a foil for Madeleine to the first draft of his 1957 screenplay, which was characterized by its whimsical title *From the Dead or There'll Never Be Another You*.[52] Madeleine represents a riddle to investigate and solve, whereas, conversely, Midge seems to have all the answers. Knowledgeable about a bra that offers "revolutionary uplift" based on the principles of the cantilever bridge—bridges, of course, also prime models of modern engineering—she reminds Scottie, who is a "big boy" now, that he should understand such things. (This is the last day that he must also wear his "darn corset" after his in-duty injury; he asks Midge whether she thinks many men wear them, to which she responds, "More than you think.") When Scottie asks for an expert on San Francisco history, Midge delivers him to Pop Liebl's bookshop. She even has the formula—a preemptory cocktail and dinner—for getting Scottie to take her to a movie. In the mental ward, she juggles all sorts of musical balms for whatever ailment, "music for dipsomaniacs, and music for melancholiacs." Everything about Midge is matter-of-fact, of flesh and blood reality: see-through in the sense of our being able to detect the true nature of, or "to see clearly," just as she does. The very idea of Midge resists the notion of femininity as mysterious or chimerical.

Yet none of her real-life solutions succeed in curing Scottie, not even a little. In fact, Scottie manifests signs of being unwell most perceptibly during scenes with him and Midge. For instance, early in Midge's apartment when the two chat about Scottie's plans for after retirement, she fetches a yellow step stool for him to climb in an effort to prove he can "lick" his vertigo. But when he gets to the top, he experiences another attack and collapses limply in Midge's motherly arms. And during the scene in the mental facility, after Madeleine's supposed death causes him to go mad, Scottie sits unmoving and unresponsive, plunged into psychosis, as Midge plays him music in an attempt to break him free of his mental illness. But the music fails to reach him, and Midge, bankrupted of any more solutions, tells the doctor in the last scene in which she appears, "I don't think Mozart is going to help at all!" She is reasonable enough to recognize that neither playing mother nor playing Mozart will help save Scottie from his romantic delusions.

Despite her exceptional independence and her dexterity in the real world, Midge proves irreconcilable within a film that derives its dominant image structure from a constant interplay of doubles and doppelgängers, subjects and objects. Midge fails miserably when she returns to her first love, painting, seemingly in order to make her other first love, Scottie, accept her visually as a love object. In one of the film's most tragicomic scenes, Midge decides to reproduce the painting of Carlotta Valdes from the art gallery, except with one major revision: she paints her head onto Carlotta's body (figure 5.3). While in her apartment, she invites Scottie to look at the painting; in the shot, we see through Scottie's eyes as they pan up the woman's painted dress and quickly land on the face of Midge where the face of Carlotta should be. Indeed, Scottie's expectations are thwarted; this female figure is chimerical, but in all the wrong ways. The shot quickly cuts to Scottie, who shows his vexation quite clearly as he shakes his head disapprovingly at Midge. The next shot, however, truly signifies what is at stake here. The film cutting quickly to what he sees behind the canvas, as the camera pans out farther, the shot gives the effect of a split screen, with the painting in the right foreground and Midge sitting in the background on the left. In effect, this perspective shows Midge doubled; quite literally, she sits at the very angle at which Carlotta's body is posed in the painting. But this shot differs markedly from the one of Madeleine and the original portrait in the museum. In

FIG. 5.3 Midge and her chimeric self-portrait as Carlotta, an image that gives the deceptive effect of a split screen.

that scene, we watch Madeleine absorbed in the painting as she looks at it as if looking in a mirror, and we too are absorbed, like Scottie, into her mystery. Her own self-reflection is erased from the film, preconditioned by a painting of someone else, a dead woman. Theoretically, the doubling effect between Madeleine and the portrait of Carlotta serves to provide the complete profile, falsely filling the gap in Scottie's (visual) knowledge of the woman. But the side-by-side view of Midge and her counterfeit portrait gives us too many faces—a startlingly, unnatural excess.[53]

Vertigo illustrates the magnetism of the artificial woman, Madeleine, by showing her obliquely, in profile, or from behind, and specifically as the "vanishing point" in central perspective. Peucker explains that Scottie's angled vision in this scene actually deviates from central perspective, not just as a surrogate modernist but, more important, as someone "who displays a 'bordering subjectivity,' someone who transgresses the boundary between fantasy and reality, art and life."[54] Midge, in contrast, is always seen squarely, the roundness of her glasses serving to magnify the fullness of her face. Rather than evoking fantasy, Midge's lighthearted attempt to double herself in her self-painted portrait destroys it entirely. Not amused, Scottie vacates her apartment abruptly, leaving her to face her dreadful mistake somewhat literally. Clearly upset, Midge slashes at the canvas with the brush a few times and then throws the brush against the window; the scene ends with her fleeting yet uncomplicated self-reflection in the glass. We are left to see what Midge sees when she looks in the mirror: her own face.

During his second pursuit of Madeleine, the day after fishing her out of San Francisco Bay, Scottie follows her trajectory toward an imperative "somewhere else" only to end up uncannily at his point of origin, his own home.[55] By this point in the film, we become aware that Scottie attempts to elude his own trauma by mastering Madeleine's mystery, and when the two join each other in their "wandering," among the ancient redwoods and along the rocky shores of the Pacific Ocean, their dialogue reveals his compulsive, displaced need to be "free of the past" by freeing her from her "possession" by Carlotta. Mulvey contends that Scottie may be striving for a somewhat sadistic possession of Madeleine, but careful attention paid to the visual clues within the film suggests that he never captures her optically but, instead, is captured by her. Modleski maintains that during the scene when Scottie peers at Madeleine in the florist shop from the door's tiny opening, we watch as "Madeleine turns around and comes toward the camera, and with the cut we expect the reverse shot to show that . . . the man is in visual possession of the woman."[56] Modleski recognizes that "by implication he (and we) may be seen as her reflection," but she suggests further that this shot prophesies the film's repetition of Scottie's mirroring relationship with Madeleine and her desire, "as if he were continually confronted with the fact that woman's uncanny otherness has some relation to himself."[57]

What we actually witness in the first half of the film is this dilemma: What happens when a man falls in love with an actress, playing a role solely for him, and he does not recognize that she is acting? Objectified and already double, a copy, Madeleine operates as Scottie's reflection because she is purely reflexive, with him falling in love with "Madeleine" the same way that Lord Ewald fell in love with Hadaly, or Narcissus with his own image. As Scottie pursues her and falls deeper into his obsession, "she is transfixed by images that will reconstitute her as pure scopic object" so that "her look . . . tautologically vehiculates his—to herself as an image."[58] The relationship between Scottie and "Madeleine" thus echoes that of Lord Ewald and Hadaly the *andréïde*; she is see-through, metaphorically translucent, or simply the outline of a shadowy figure, as she is literally depicted on the film's famous poster. Judy casts herself as a voyeuristic object willfully in these repeated self-exhibitions and blatant poses, artificial reproductions both for man and "of man." In the end, "Madeleine" is purely "filmy," nothing more than a role played willingly by Judy—a celluloid ghost. This is only confirmed by the fact that the film never acknowledges or recognizes the true Mrs. Madeleine Elster. The actual Madeleine, in fact, only shows up onscreen once, during the flashback sequence accompanying Judy's letter writing, when we see Elster holding her dead body in his arms about to throw it off the bell tower.[59] In the only filmic moment that renders the real Madeleine present to the audience, she is already departed, dead and gone. Like Hadaly, she turns out to be an artificial Eurydice.[60] And this constant interplay of doubles, most notably the doubling of Scottie as Madeleine in his dream of falling/being buried, also marks the film's direct engagement with its own objectivity and what it means to be a film. A screen replica of life and therefore the phantom of life, film's determining impulse is death.

In this way, the film represents Scottie's journey beyond the pleasure principle. In Freudian terms, his instinctual desire for death manifests itself in his drive—tailing Madeleine in pursuit through the streets of San Francisco, and psychologically, his irresistible urge toward her—to be (with) her. In "Beyond the Pleasure Principle," Freud uses the "fort-da" game his grandson plays as evidence of the child's own invention of symbolism, his re-presentation of the absent object, his mother, in a present object, a wooden reel he would play with by throwing it over the edge of his bed to have it disappear (*fort*, German for "gone"), only to pull it back to himself to have it once again (*da*, German for "here").[61] *Vertigo* is the filmic equivalent of the fort-da game played by Freud's grandson, except the subject has turned into the object. As R. Barton Palmer asserts, Scottie's "self-canceling movement away and toward the object of desire becomes the film's central figure, as expressed in the famous zoom in/track out that characterizes the main character's perceptual malady, his disorienting and paralyzing vertigo."[62] As if the wooden reel was suspended in midair and came alive, clear metaphor for animation, Scottie experiences both the "fort" and the "da" in his vertiginous sensation of falling while stationary.

We are conducted to read Midge as a mother figure explicitly in the here and now, and Madeleine as an evocation of the absent, dead mother through her (however feigned) drive toward repeating her great-grandmother's death. *Vertigo* plays with the theoretical notion of the mother figure in many ways, but perhaps the film's most maternal figure is, somewhat predictably, its most mysterious. Symbolically, the film positions the dis-figured woman in its opening credit sequence as its archaic and abjected mother, key to the narrative yet exiled from it, an Eve imperiled by the cinematic apparatus. Perhaps this woman functions as the "source" from which the vertigo proceeds, as suggested through shots of the vertiginous swirls emanating from her eyes, her face the proper canvas for this sense of delusional imbalance. She is also the ultimate construction of both man and the camera's voyeuristic eye, which fragments her into pieces, derealizing her into objecthood. The text of the credits is stamped over shots of parts—lips, nose, eyes—visually fractured from this anonymous female face. On his designing of the opening sequence, Saul Bass explained, "Here is a woman made into what a man wants her to be. She is put together piece by piece. I tried to suggest something of this . . . by my shifting images."[63] On the flip side, if Kim Novak plays the role of this paratextual female figure we *do not recognize her* specifically because she is broken down into parts rather than being "made up." Her eyebrows are not penciled in, her face unadorned by colorations from blush or lipstick, she bears little resemblance to the Kim-Novak-as-Madeleine we will meet early in the film, and thus to the aesthetic Ideal. In fact, it remains unclear who plays this role because she remains uncredited: not Kim Novak, some claim it to be Hitchcock's own daughter, Patricia, though that theory has been disproved, and it seems more likely that actress Audrey Lowell played the part. But the fact that the mystery over who plays the role remains unresolved—and, more important, that this results in a face that is unrecognizable—only deepens the efficacy of the sequence and gives us license to suggest that the woman functions as the MacGuffin from the verti-get-go. Coined by screenwriter Angus McPhail as a particularly Hitchcockian device, the MacGuffin is a motif, object, or event that motivates plot or narrative but is irrelevant or insignificant itself. Or, to re-cite Hitchcock's words, a MacGuffin is actually "nothing at all."

Keep It Moving

Primarily a balance disorder wherein one experiences the sensation that the environment moves when in fact no movement occurs, vertigo operates metaphorically for Pygmalionism, as it doubles for the cinema itself, predicated on the "illusion of movement" and embodying in form the long-standing human desire for the animation of the inanimate.[64] Scottie experiences vertigo as false sensations of movement, a condition that may emblematize the fact that all of cinema's perceptions, according to Christian Metz, are fake too:

> Or rather, the activity of perception which it involves is real (the cinema is not phantasy), but the perceived is not really the object, it is its shade, its phantom, its double, its *replica* in a new kind of mirror. . . . The unique position of the cinema lies in this dual character of its signifier: unaccustomed perceptual wealth, but at the same time stamped with unreality to an unusual degree, and from the very onset. More than the other arts, or in a more unique way, the cinema involves us in the imaginary: it drums up all perception, but to switch it immediately over into its absence, which is nonetheless the only signifier present.[65]

Many seminal texts in film theory, as an academic discipline, have been written first as organic examinations of Hitchcock films: Mulvey's "Narrative Pleasure" utilizes Hitchcockian films to solidify the notion of the "male gaze," for instance, and Stephen Heath does a close reading of a sequence in *Suspicion* (1941) to argue that narrative space both takes place and makes meaning in the cinematic mise-en-scène, to name just two. Metz's "The Imaginary Signifier" has nothing directly to do with Hitchcock's *Vertigo*, but one could just as easily input Scottie into the cited passage and see it as a reading of his exact dilemma, wherein he operates as a functional surrogate of the spectator who, from the onset, is offered an imaginary, perceptual wealth, drumming up perception (of a real woman, Madeleine) but only to switch immediately into its/her absence—nothingness functioning as the "only signifier present." The constitution of the cinematic signifier is dependent, according to Metz, on a chain of "mirror-effects," but *Vertigo*, as Marilyn Fabe suggests, "performs another turn of the Metzian screw" because Madeleine is really an "*imaginary* imaginary signifier"—never more than fantasy imago or fiction.[66]

While *Vertigo* appears to echo the myth of Pygmalion on a narrative level, the camera's equal objectification of the male artist-subject (Scottie) suggests that it, rather than he, plays the role of creator. Hitchcock trusted the camera as the ultimate master of pure cinema, his films reliant on meaning's conveyance through cinematography and the image above all else. To restate the issue, Hitchcock seems to replace his subjective directorship in many ways with the all-perceiving object, the camera able to propagate a more subjective point of view for the audience as a whole—indicative of a collective consciousness born from the prior century's dreams of artificial generation. Many of his collaborators, such as *Vertigo* script supervisor Peggy Robertson, reveal that Hitchcock never even looked through the camera's viewfinder. His films were so meticulously scripted visually and storyboarded by the director beforehand, it was as if he imagined them through his mind as the camera, and therefore had no need to step behind the actual lens.[67]

Scottie's dream sequence presents a visual tableau of his identification with the feminine and death, and consequently demarcates the moment he goes mad, just like the "mad Carlotta." Indeed, *Vertigo* presents identity as a construction of visual projection and Madeleine is like Oscar Wilde's moon, not so much an image as an endless refraction of images in an intricately executed danse macabre of portraits, masks, and false memorials. But we must remember that here Scottie's mirroring relationship with Madeleine is, more specifically, a relationship to a woman objectified, therefore a woman without desire. That is to say, "Madeleine" is never real. Thus, it seems incredibly consequential that Hitchcock chose for this sequence to be animated, providing a stark yet technicolored contrast to the mostly realistic images in the rest of the film's composition. The sequence was created by artist John Ferren, an active member of the New York School of art and one of its strongest links to midcentury European modernism, having lived in Paris through the 1930s. Gertrude Stein wrote of Ferren that he was the only American painter in Paris at the time whose work Parisian artists found acceptably interesting.[68]

The vertiginously swirling spiral in Hitchcock's film operates as a metaphor for the machinery of cinematic history, linked to technologies of rotation like the zoopraxiscope (1879), a revolving mechanism that projected a sequence of stills rapidly enough they were then processed in viewers' brains as "continuous movement."[69] Invented by Eadweard Muybridge, the zoopraxiscope built on nineteenth-century modernity's interest in this phenomenon of vision and its vicissitudes of temporality, and itself was an extremely heterogeneous technology, combining three—photography, the magic lantern, and the zoetrope—together into one. His most famous moving images in animal locomotion, specifically of a galloping horse, were famously disbelieved by many in the 1870s;

spectators thought the images fake because it was too unbelievable that all four of a horse's hooves would leave the ground simultaneously.

Motion picture technologies negotiated the chasm between still and moving and became indicative of a "new kinaesthetic" that developed in and through what Hillel Schwartz deems "kinestructs," like the "seductive spirals of vamps" or the "menacing torque" of villains, and vertigo.[70] These vertigo motifs evoke not just these machineries of movement but also mathematics; *Vertigo*'s title sequence is considered the first use of computer-generated imagery (CGI) in American film history. American graphic artist Saul Bass, who was also a modernist working in the Bauhaus and the Eastern Modern movement style, hoped to portray the sense of disequilibrium at the heart of the film's narrative and the film-watching experience by, somewhat ironically, reproducing shapes based on mathematical equations. Lissajous curves, named after nineteenth-century French physicist Jules Antoine Lissajous, were created by an apparatus that allowed light to bounce off a mirror attached to a tuning fork, reflected off a second mirror and tuning fork, then onto a flat surface. Because these images could not be hand-drawn, John Whitney Sr.—one of the early pioneers in computer animation who first adopted these machineries for artistic purposes—helped Bass and Hitchcock create these curves, based on parametric equations, with the use of a World War II M5 gun director rigged to a platform, synchronized with a pendulum. Of course, CGI refers to a tool that can capture static images in dynamic, moving ways, or stillness and movement simultaneously.

The mathematical equation for this simultaneity bears similarity to the proof compiled by Villiers's Edison, both algebraic equation and prearchaic cinematic formula, necessary to create an artificial woman who mirrors man's desires in these moments of modernity. Indeed, in his assessment of *Vertigo*, French filmmaker Chris Marker makes claims that sound familiar to ones I have presented in previous chapters, specifically that the film is "about reliving a moment lost in the past," and that in his madness, Scottie "looks for proof in her life." The classical dialectic that arises out of Freudian psychoanalysis, which has been a determining impulse of the readings in this book, also equates to an approach toward a seemingly calculated balance impossible to achieve except through these artificially generated, and symbolically female, supplements: "Between man and woman, through woman's look as appropriated by the camera, this mirror—or doubling—effect . . . serves to structure the male subject as the subject of the scopic drive, that is to say, a subject who imaginarily attributes to woman the lack he himself has been assigned."[71] The opening credits first illustrate a stealing of woman's life by rendering "woman" the object of a fetishistic, cinematic investigation, her face (and identity) sacrificed to the vampiric mirror of man's camera and the superimposition of masculine, mathematical formulas.

The geometry of modern, vertical architectures incite a new level of mortality anxiety by the early twentieth century, which plays out directly in the cinematic infrastructure of *Vertigo*, deepening this relationship between woman and the machinery of mathematics. Yet the "vertiginous experience" of Hitchcock's film traces back to the 1900 Paris Exposition, at which one attraction promised to satisfy this fear and desire, using those very words, through a simulated free fall from the Eiffel Tower of 325 yards, in order to delight the "lovers of sensational emotions."[72] Gunning asserts that at the heart of the energy and experience of modernity is this desire to experience the "shock of extreme motion" from a safe position—simply put, to experience the illusion of movement. The devastating shock experienced by postwar patients of Freud led them, according to the psychoanalyst, to self-protect through anxiety as a defense mechanism. Hitchcock's films are created in this very realm of defenses: as the director famously claimed, the only way to get rid of his own fears was to make films about them.

To dig deeper, the bedrock of this project is not just modern but also necessarily ancient (Egypt). I might momentarily note the thoughts of Flaubert after his visit to the East with Maxime du Camp in 1849. Tremendously affected by the Egyptian pyramids, and the sheer human engineering behind such enormous marvels, Flaubert famously remarked that the sight of the Sphinx gave him "one of the most vertiginous pleasures of his life."[73] It is worth noting, too, that on the trip du Camp, who had studied photography, took photographs with his Calotype camera that would later serve as the basis for an album sold as "Egypte, Nubie, Palestine, Syrie," which may be considered the first travel photo journal—transporting viewers to other lands via the use of photographic images—and the birth of what we now refer to as travel photography.

Skyscraper landscapes produce a psycho-reality of falling and vertigo, which Catherine James refers to as "that dizzy preparation for the fall," was consequently "rehearsed in the wider cultural imagination," thereafter becoming "a valve through which to mediate a darker malaise at the heart of modernity."[74] Increasing architectural elevations, based in complex geometric equations and units of mathematics, further provoked man's vulnerability, specifically of the human body. Indeed, though architecture is all about math, the scale of skyscraper to human is "off," imbalanced, thus logically producing a sense of disorientation and disequilibrium born distinctly and directly from the use of technology in urban development. The horrifically heterogeneous proportions between man and environment—being endlessly not to scale both psychologically and architecturally—cause a crisis in perception that equates to the cinema's illusion of movement, further redefining the doubleness between the challenges, of the statuesque woman and the tower Scottie must climb.

Seeing and Being Double

Although Scottie's vertigo ties to concerns of altitude, due both to urban architecture and to the geographic climbs San Francisco is known for, it remains most strongly bonded to his seeing double. The issue of doubling becomes most

FIG. 5.4 Scottie and Judy in her apartment upon first meeting, Scottie's missing reflection in the mirror foreboding his impossibility to see through her as reflection of his desires.

problematic to interpret regarding the last sequence of the film, during which Scottie meets Judy and tries to re-form her image into that of the dead Madeleine, whom she already resembles so uncannily. While in the first half of the film Scottie misrecognizes that Judy has been "cast" to play his love interest, in the second half he is unmistaken about and unwavering in his desire to repeat this very gesture. Molding Judy's outward appearance so that she may perform the role of his lost love, Scottie invites a new level of virtual reality, not re-creating a human being but instead provoking a counterfeit spectacle. Scottie's direction over her performance as Madeleine necessarily repeats—is itself a copy—causing Judy to re-resemble the woman she has *already* played under the direction of Gavin Elster. Both men "try to transform the Real Judy into a Symbolic substitute."[75] Yet, despite the fact that she plays the role of his original Madeleine, Scottie can never truly love the real Judy. In her apartment on the day she and Scottie meet, Judy goes to her dresser to retrieve her license to prove her identity. She looks up from her purse on the dresser and into the mirror, where her face is directly reflected. Although Scottie stands immediately behind her on the left, Hitchcock takes the shot from such an angle that Scottie, like a mythological vampire, has no reflection in the mirror—a visual that suggests the impossibility for Judy, who reflects herself in the mirror, to ever be the mirror of Scottie's desire (figure 5.4).

The film's chain of performances, or the linked substitution of one personality for another, lends to the audience what Victor Stoichita calls a sense of "intoxication caused by the successive nesting of simulacra."[76] First, we have the actress, Kim Novak, playing Judy playing Madeleine playing Carlotta. And the fact that Scottie's role for Judy to play is simply a re-production from "Elster's script" should make his love for Madeleine, in every sense, counterfeit as well.

Indeed, it seems bizarre that so much scholarship historically insisted on treating Madeleine as a person Scottie loves and ends up reflecting, when as concerns the film, she is not human. As Bronfen asserts, "The brilliant twist introduced by Hitchcock is that the desired beloved is not merely an image and a revenant but in fact a masquerade, a false image, the dissimulation of a revenant."[77] In the literal sense, Madeleine is not a person but a projection, and Scottie has not been "in love with a woman so much as with—almost in the platonic sense—an Idea."[78] Scottie represents another reproduction, too, of the male protagonists who have occupied us from the beginning of this project—Gautier's Romuald, Villiers's Lord Ewald—a man who suffers from the ailment of "this rejection of life for an unattainable Idea," set into an ever-paradoxical, artistic production of "the triumph of illusion, the perfect re-creation of the dream," which, at its core, represents something fundamental to humanity.[79]

Scottie's ability to reach the top of the bell tower suggests his health has been restored, but the film's perplexing final scene might also demonstrate that he has fallen fully into the chasm of delusion. He drives Judy out to Mission San Juan Bautista in order to finally be "free of the past." But, now that he knows Judy is Madeleine, whatever does this mean? What we do know is that when they reach the bell tower, Scottie reproduces the scene of the crime step-by-step, a theatrically reproduced mise-en-scène of the mysterious murder. He berates Judy for having been "the copy, the counterfeit," betraying his rage over the fact that Elster made her over just like he made her over, "only better," "not only the clothes and the hair, but the looks, and the manner, and the words." There is no greater disappointment than falling in love with someone else's Galatea, another's beloved; as Žižek contends, Scottie plays the role of the "deceived Platonist" shocked not so much by the traditional deception, when "the original turns out to be merely a copy—but that (what we took to be) *the copy turns out to be the original*."[80] Once they make it to the top of the tower, in what should be a triumphant moment, he tells Judy, "It's too late, there's no bringing her back." We have no choice but to be left a bit stunned by Scottie's lament, for who, indeed, is the "her" he wants to return? If he has truly recognized that Madeleine never existed, and that all along Judy had been playing the role of the Madeleine he fell in love with, then who is the woman it is "too late" for? Even more striking is the fact that Scottie tells Judy, "I loved you so, *Madeleine*" (emphasis mine). His fear of heights may be cured, but Scottie has failed to access any healthy "real," and his eventual, repetitive loss of the female Ideal "should in fact be the recognition of a loss of something that has never existed."[81]

As he stands on the ledge of the tower and looks down, Scottie's body is posed as if it were the one sprawled on the ground, his limbs positioned in the exact same way as when he envisioned his shadowy body falling from the tower in his mad dream. If we read Scottie's vertigo metaphorically as an illness that causes him to teeter between the limits of real and illusion, then we must accept that Scottie plunges irrevocably into the abyss he spent the film dangling over; the film leaves us, as Scottie was at the beginning, hanging off the edge. Much commentary, conversation, and scholarship on *Vertigo* obsessively returns to the concept of endless returns and the general sense that the film's capitulation of reproductive delusion has equated to spectators' own compulsions toward repetitious viewings. Film scholar Charles Barr is one of many to admit his own propensities toward re-viewing, and this impulse's relationship to an end that seems like a story "about to replay itself" with Scottie perhaps "ready to go through it all again."[82] These revolutions in and of watching equate to what Robert J. Belton calls the "hermeneutic spiral" incited by the film, the endless proliferation of interpretations, a specific semiotic plurality that emerges in *Vertigo*.[83] In the language of the Lissajous curve, no matter how circuitous the path of/to the figure, one always comes back to the beginning of reinterpretation.

Fall from Grace

Raymond Durgnat long established the idea that if the story is Pygmalionesque—which he asserts by comparing Scottie's plotline to that of Ovid's Pygmalion in his book *The Strange Case of Alfred Hitchcock* (1974)—the sense of "creation" metaphorically usurped is that of God, and that the entire enterprise is Scottie's rivaling the Father.[84] Despite being heralded by *Cahiers* critics of the midcentury for his unique filmmaking in the face of the stilted traditions of Daddy's cinema, Hitchcock reintroduces the importance of God the Father upon woman's second fall at the end of *Vertigo*. Indeed, Judy's fall seems the result of the sudden reemergence of an almost literal deus ex machina, a metacinematic God in the machinery. The somewhat spectral nun materializes out of the darkness of the bell tower, frightening Judy to the point that she pushes away from Scottie and plummets to her death. When the nun proclaims, "God have mercy," the film directly manifests Judy's fall as a distorted replication of Adam and Eve's from Genesis.

And the lady vanishes, with Scottie left stunned and stuck atop the towering turret, all alone.[85]

Epilogue

Still Mother–Adapting to Life in *Blade Runner 2049*

> A system of cells interlinked within
> Cells interlinked within cells interlinked
> —Vladimir Nabokov

"I can't tell you how / I knew—but I know that I had crossed / The border," reveals fictional poet John Shade, who—spurred on by the recent death of his daughter, Hazel, and a sudden heart attack—becomes engulfed in a "blood-black nothingness [that] began to spin" into the contemplation of a "system of cells interlinked."[1] Divided into four cantos, Shade's 999-line poem functions as the basis of Vladimir Nabokov's novel *Pale Fire* (1962). The book's lengthy foreword—along with extensive commentary and final index—is penned by erstwhile editor and unreliable narrator Charles Kinbote, who concludes his introductory comments by confiding to the reader that without his notes, "Shade's text simply has no human reality at all."[2] The moon, "an arrant thief" in Shakespeare's *Timon of Athens*, snatches its "pale fire" from the sun's reflected light, just as Nabokov poaches the term for his novel's title: "But *this* transparent thingum does require / Some moondrop title. Help me, Will! *Pale Fire*."[3] Further, Kinbote seizes the poem's authority—or, its lifelikeness—from its professed author, the posthumous Shade, who himself becomes the adumbral figure behind the text from the poem's opening line: "I was the shadow of the waxwing slain / By the false azure in the windowpane." This first image that Shade/Kinbote/Nabokov offers is, indeed, nothing but a reflection, about death; the waxwing flies into the window, causing its own demise, because it sees reflected in the clear glass an illusory paradise, not knowing that it is not real. Common, real-life occurrences called glass collisions, which kill up to a billion birds a year in the United States, are caused because birds often see their natural habitats or outside vegetation cruelly doubled in the see-through glass (and Shade equating himself to a bird befits his own heritage, since his predeceased parents were both ornithologists).

Essentially, *Pale Fire* reflects on how art mirrors life through its many manifestations of doubles, in so doing striking toward the very mirror identification Christian Metz saw developed in and by the cinema, wherein "the perceived is not really the object, it is its shade, its phantom, its *replica* in a new kind of mirror."[4] A literary phantom himself, John Shade becomes undeniably interlinked with a new kind of replica in our cinema-of-the-future, too: the replicant K in *Blade Runner 2049* (2017).

Cells and Cinematic Offspring

As a blade runner in the world of *2049*, K (Ryan Gosling) must constantly submit to post-traumatic baseline tests at the LAPD headquarters meant to detect any anomalous emotional developments; his diagnostic recitation begins with lines repeated verbatim from Shade's poem in *Pale Fire*: "And blood-black nothingness began to spin / A system of cells interlinked within / Cells interlinked within cells interlinked / Within one stem. And dreadfully distinct / Against the dark, a tall white fountain played." After the poetic recital, a disembodied voice asks K—who is likely nicknamed "Constant K" as in the mathematical constant *k*, a mathematically "fixed" value—a series of questions wherein the value of words may fluctuate but K's responses are locked into just two possibilities, cells and interlinked: "Have you ever been in an institution? *Cells*. . . . What's it like to hold your child in your arms? *Interlinked*." Nabokov's novel can be considered a forerunner of the invention of hypertext—a nonlinear, digital presentation of a text that includes links to other connections and references, creating a larger interactive structure that serves as the basis for the "web" today—a term coined by author and IT pioneer Ted Nelson in 1963, one year after the publication of *Pale Fire*.[5] Exceedingly clever, then, is the way that *2049* engages inter- and extratextually with the concept of hypertext through the replicant as programmed information system (the shadow of which might already exist in Nabokov/Shade's use of "automaton" in the novel). The newest link in a flexible and formidable network of films, books, comics, architectural movements, and information networks, *2049* can also be considered a cell generated from the same pattern of replication that *Artificial Generation* has, in some sense, been investigating and interconnecting within its own hypertextual system.[6] I will try to briefly assess how our literary replication crisis, starting with the works of Gautier, ends most fittingly with an investigation of the newest lineage of replicants created in *2049*.

In the "original" *Blade Runner* (1982) film, as adapted from Philip K. Dick's novel *Do Androids Dream of Electric Sheep?*, the Voight-Kampff test measures physiological responses of test subjects, primarily focused on the dilation of the eye; it is also conspicuously predicated on the replicants' lack of an origin story, as manifested through the question replicant Leon (Brion James) is asked early in the film for which he has no answer, except that of violence: "Tell me about your mother."[7] Indeed, the film takes a mythopoetic approach to the Christian origin story in the book of Genesis, thus specifically linking itself into the intertextual framework that includes *Paradise Lost* and *Frankenstein*—one of the most compelling science fiction myths in existence—as well as *L'Ève future*. A fitting update to past literary insurrections against humankind's post-Edenic mortality, Roy Batty (Rutger Hauer) leads a replicant sedition motivated by their collective quest for "more life," beyond their programmed four-year "life" spans. Prodigal son and fallen angel, Batty is positioned as Milton's Lucifer, descending to the off-world and falling out of the creator Tyrell's good graces, until he finally kills his creator by brutally and fittingly gouging out his eyes. Forced out of retirement and summoned to contain the replicant rebellion, blade runner Rick Deckard (Harrison Ford) visits Tyrell Corporation, where he uses the Voight-Kampff test on Tyrell's assistant, Rachael (Sean Young). Deckard's discovery that she is indeed a replicant manufactured by Tyrell causes Rachael's own (self-?) discovery that she has been duped into believing herself human, primarily via manufactured memories implanted and ensured through photographs—most specifically, one photograph in particular that seemingly shows young Rachael and her mother. Due to his feelings, Deckard refuses to "retire" her; instead, they embark on a socially forbidden, romantic relationship that leads them to run off together at the film's end. Though modern film scholars (myself included) tend to favor "The Final Cut" of *Blade Runner*, with its restoration of key elements like Deckard's mysterious vision of the unicorn, the theatrical release's additional end scene casts Deckard and Rachael as a neoteric Adam and Eve. As they drive off through the countryside as metaphoric Eden—the only naturally lit shots in the entire film—the lovers' escape symbolically positions them as the new "first" couple, and additionally implies a fresh generation of species, thus creating a fascinating bridge to the film's own descendant, *Blade Runner 2049*.

The world of *Blade Runner 2049*, as "Madame" Lieutenant Joshi (Robin Wright) warns, is "built on a wall that separates kind," thus demarcating humans and replicants, the manufactured species introduced in the original film that continues to dominate the narrative in the sequel. The crux of differentiating who is on either side of this wall reaffirms this very question—of woman born? About halfway into the film, Officer K finds himself seeking the source of a wooden and quite literal Trojan horse that, he has been told, originates from a hotbed of radioactivity. K sends his drone-like camera into the vaporous twilight to find the locus of contamination. Constantly moving and recentering simultaneously, the viewfinder reveals the first of numerous, gigantic sculpted women littering the Vegas wasteland like mod Egyptian sphinxes. A "heat analysis" reveals "life" collecting in a tangerine puddle at the fingertips of one's delicately carved hand. The digital equivalent of these deserted Galateas, K's holographic companion Joi (Ana de Armas) asks, "What is it?" to which K retorts, "Guess we're about to find out." Like life itself, both this question and the film's very quest are of woman (figure) born.

Directed by Denis Villeneuve, *Blade Runner 2049* is a direct sequel to the original *Blade Runner* (directed by Ridley Scott, who served as an executive producer on the sequel), written by David Webb Peoples and Hampton Fancher, who also wrote the screenplay for the original. Thirty years after the events of the first film, Officer K finds himself commissioned to kill replicant Sapper Morton (Dave Bautista), and at Morton's farm he stumbles upon a discovery: an ossuary. The bones, found buried at the roots of a dead tree, belong to replicant Rachael (Sean Young) from the original film, and so the sequel first predicates itself upon the infiltration of a woman's tomb. More than the mystery of the body's identity is the riddle of its procreative powers. An autopsy reveals "she" died while giving birth to a child, a point that further complicates the concept of being "of woman born" while powerfully amplifying the Tyrell Corporation's motto from the original film, which boasted that the company manufactured beings "more human than human"—mechanical copies that surpass the originals. The remainder of the film largely focuses on K's quest to find this "miracle" child born of Rachael and Rick Deckard in the space between the original film and its "sequel," a word that fittingly comes from late Middle English, meaning "offspring" or "descendant."

In 2049, there is power in being "of woman born," and in this way the replicants' defiance, spurred by the film's miracle birth, equates to the resistance Adrienne Rich says is bound to emerge when patriarchy is unmasked as the true illusion, as "a pervasive recognition is developing that the patriarchal system cannot answer for itself; that it is not inevitable; that it is transitory."[8] Indeed, Freysa (Hiam Abbass), the leader of the replicant resistance, almost literally quotes from the sentiments found in Rich's *Of Woman Born: Motherhood as Experience and Institution* when she explains their cause to K near the film's end. In *2049*, replicants can finally affirm being "more human than human," specifically because a child has been born to one of them—an equal affirmation of maternity and humanity, and an opportunity to become one's own procreative master. Many of the female characters in *2049* do mother, or at least protect their charges, whether it be Freysa, who helped deliver Rachael's baby and thus plays maternal midwife, or Lieutenant Joshi, one of the film's only seemingly real, biological women, who displays enough warmth to offer K safe passage from the building once he is designated rebelliously off baseline. What flows through the veins of both films is still mother, as well as the necessity for the mother to be dead, rendered "still."

In "*Blade Runner*'s Moving Still," Elissa Marder asserts that "the photograph is the true 'subject'" of the original film as well as its "site of humanity and the locus of the film's quest for origins."[9] The "still" photograph Marder analyzes is the one Rachael has of her mother, false evidence that she is a "real girl," since the mother in the photo is "no more Rachel's mother than she is anyone else's."[10] *Blade Runner 2049* repeats a similar photographic gesture when K unearths a photo of a mystery woman holding the baby he now pursues. Since we know the baby's mother, Rachael, has died in childbirth, we also can decipher that this woman (who we later learn is Freysa) only operates as mother symbolically, just like in Rachael's mother-picture in the original film.

Beginning with a literal unearthing of the bones of the miraculously procreative Rachael, buried in Sapper Morton's army-issued box as makeshift coffin, *2049* affirms even more powerfully than the original that "mother is not easily buried."[11] Cracking the code lies in the fluctuation of just a few sequential letters: replicant Rachael represents Rachel from the book of Genesis, whose name in Hebrew means "ewe," or sheep, just one middle letter shifted down the alphabet from Eve, whose name means "living one." If the title of Philip K. Dick's source novel questions, *Do Androids Dream of Electric Sheep?*, in *2049*—wherein any determination on either Deckard's or Rachael's state of "being" remains willfully ambiguous—I might recast this titular sentiment as, do androids (like Deckard?) dream of electric Rachaels? (why, yes, they do).

One of the four major matriarchs of the tribes of Israel, Rachel descends directly from Eve, one of her most important descendants in terms of the post-Edenic sins that womankind acquires. By dying in childbirth, Rachel—fruitful in spite of her prior infertility—represents both death and reproduction, interlinked. It might also be why Jacob buries her in such a cursory manner on the side of the road en route to Bethlehem; death in childbirth often necessitated the suspension of the normative Jewish funeral rites of burying family members together. Rachel's tomb represents one of the holiest sites still in existence today, one of the cornerstones of Jewish-Israeli identity and Rachel herself—symbolic of both fertility and resurrection—extensively worshipped in three major monotheistic religions: Christianity, Judaism, and Islam.

The grave site of the cinematic Rachael in *2049* operates as a reproduction of the holy site of Rachel's tomb, marked by the dead tree as funeral pillar, whose roots metaphorically symbolize the religious roots of these textual cells, interlinked from the starting point of biblical genesis. In ancient Israel, sacred trees were considered necessary adjuncts of an altar, standing tall near the tombs of the righteous; Rachel's tomb is marked by an ancient olive tree, seen in common nineteenth-century illustrations, during which time the tomb acquired its ultimately cultlike status (today it is behind heavily guarded walls to separate kind,

Israel from Palestine). To visually reproduce it in the film, VFX supervisor Peter Eszenyi actually used pictures of a lonely tree that also acts as a funerary pillar and marker of the dead, growing in London's Mortlake Cemetery.

Despite science fiction's emergence at the expense and usurpation of the female body and its procreative powers in the tradition of *Frankenstein*, *2049* exalts the miraculously reproductive Rachael to goddess-like status. Breaking the code of Rach(a)el's tomb as replication of a major, biblical matriarch coheres with Niander Wallace's suggestion that he "could storm Eden and retake her." Wallace (Jared Leto), *2049*'s savior industrialist and CEO of replicant manufacturing, not only embraces but hopes for his own scientific reinstitution of that which has been cast out: a procreative female. He aims for his "new model" to be tomorrow's Eve, if we may—original of a next generation of replicants who can actually reproduce children, as we are told Rachael has done with Deckard (not to put aside that this act of procreation equates to her death). But the door to such mysteries remains closed to him—a point brutally actualized when Wallace slits open the "barren" midsection of a failed new model, an aborted attempt at giving life that begets life. Just as the myth of Eve manifests the prospect of reconquering paradise in the afterlife, Wallace comes to realize that he needs a she, since no birth, even biblical, can be singular.[12] Once his highest-powered "angel" Luv (Sylvia Hoeks) steals Rachael's bones from the LAPD, he finally discovers that the answer of artificial generation is found in the very repetition of the words and figures of our collective, ancient past—and specifically finds the secret of life in a dead "woman." Indeed, Wallace speaks in largely unabashed and undisguised biblical metaphors throughout the film, and explicitly uses Abrahamic stories to reveal the quandaries of life-giving in *2049*. Unveiling Rachael's skull as the "key" to the lock he had been looking for all along, Wallace directly recites the words of Genesis 29:31: "And God remembered Rachael. And heeded her. And opened her womb."[13] The lock-and-key metaphor Wallace uses here takes on increased significance because a key to the tomb of Rachel has been historically considered a *segula*—a charm or treasure that supersedes logic—that symbolizes fertility: women in childbirth or difficult labor were said to have been given the key to the tomb, which was oft visited by those experiencing, like Wallace, fertility troubles.[14]

By revivifying the technology, Wallace resurrects Rachael the replicant, duplicate of the biblical figure of redemption and resurrection, in order to regain a postmodern paradise. To do so, he hopes to allow Deckard to access "the first hours of love, immobilized, the hour of the Ideal made prisoner" once again.[15] In an undoubtedly meta-moment, *Blade Runner 2049* uncannily reproduces the original film's Rachael in the digital flesh, part of Wallace's attempt to dupe a love-starved Deckard into revealing the whereabouts of the replicant resistance. Watching the emergence of the revivified Rachael from the watery shadows of Wallace's lair, I could not help but realize I had seen this before, on first watch, finding myself just as stunned by the resemblance between this scene and

Vertigo as Deckard is meant to be lovingly thunderstruck by Rachael's diegetic reanimation. Wallace confides to Deckard that perhaps he was specifically created to play a role in this world of postmodern procreation, one that was predicated on his loving Rachael all along: "Did it never occur to you that was why you were summoned in the first place? Designed to do nothing short of fall for her right then and there. All to make that single, perfect . . . specimen." Specifically recalling the realization that *Vertigo*'s Scottie was cast as the dupe of a husband's plan to murder his wife because of his fear of heights, the woman he was originally assigned to follow and with whom he ends up falling in love was never real but instead was "the copy, the counterfeit"—a replica in a new kind of mirror. A repetitive ol' switcheroo, the scene replicates the concept of masculinity by design through the figure of Deckard-as-Adam, possible parallel for the first man "designed" to fall in love and multiply. Yet Deckard actively resists being deceived here, coldly revealing the seeming incongruity between Wallace's model and the "original" Rachael ("Her eyes were green").

Taking over the role of mechanical mother, the conditions of the film's making mirror its narrative. To depict the resurrected Rachael, London-based effects establishment the Moving Picture Company (MPC) digitally de-aged images of 1982 Sean Young and combined them with current photographs of her taken with a capture rig and kit, essentially reproducing her from "stills" along with the assistance of many computer programs, some of which—like 3D animation software Maya and painting program Mari—are named as if they were women themselves. MPC's reproductive work within the film—similar to the early digital re-creations of the predeceased Peter Cushing in *Rogue One: A Star Wars Story* (2016)—and the ethical ramifications of reanimating the dead (what Victor Frankenstein quite literally does in Shelley's novel) reinforce the boundless ethical and philosophical quandaries born of *Blade Runner* and continued here in the sequel. "Leading the race to digital humans with a photoreal character" made specifically for *2049*, as self-marketed on its website, MPC re-created actress Young as a fully digital, entirely animated double, and did so mainly with focus paid to her bones, and in particular her skull.[16] Since 2001, University of Southern California's Institute for Creative Technologies (ICT), through its Vision and Graphics Laboratory, has been virtually creating "digitally generated humans" using an ICT Light Stage, which MPC used early in the process to get a digital capture of Young's head to begin the re-creation of Rachael. In 2008, ICT's "Digital Emily" project successfully animated a digital face that was the first to cross the "uncanny valley" that historically divides real, human expressions and synthetically generated ones. The Light Stage system—which originates from Paul Debevec's foundational experiments in light reflection and, specifically, his methods using the light that travels under the skin—consists of a movable camera, a fully rotational light, dual optical filters, and a computer.

Flashing back to the beginning (of this book), or at least to the end of chapter 1, Alexander Galloway's "Cybernetic Hypothesis" advanced the importance of François Willème's landmark invention of photosculpture as the basis for the full realization of three-dimensional scanning we have today; we can clearly chart the route from Willème's work rotunda to the Light Stage used to artificially generate Rachael in *2049*. Combining the Light Stage scan along with videogrammatical references from scenes in the original film, MPC artists were able to hand model a three-dimensional, computer-generated replica of the actress's skull; fittingly, MPC named the secret studio for developing these digital humans the "Shadow Lab." As the animators approached the final product, they needed to test the likeness, recreating three scenes from the original movie with the digitally rendered character, and showed them to the filmmakers and director Denis Villeneuve. As it turns out, according to VFX supervisor Richard Clegg, discerning between the original cinematic replicant and the re-animated, digitally rendered one proved increasingly difficult.

By 2020, we arrive at another new frontier in the quest to create an aesthetic supplement better than the real thing: in June, announcements were made that an artificial woman had been cast as lead actress in a $70 million sci-fi film currently titled "b," which would make her Hollywood's first fully autonomous, artificially intelligent actor. Hiroshi Ishiguro, roboticist at Osaka University, designed Erica to be "the most beautiful woman in the world" based on his dream for a world "filled with Ericas"; first created in 2015, Erica is considered the most humanlike android in existence.[17] The filmmakers of "b" intend for her to perform in the same manner that a human actress would in real time, rather than being moved or motivated by any programming sequence. And how do we know this robot, deemed an actress, is "female"? Because her maker says so.

Seeing Through Women (Once Again)

Indeed, *2049* presents a kaleidoscopic bevy of womankind, almost none of the women real in any traditional sense, but offers its most distinct pleasures through the figure of Joi. Not unlike Samantha in Spike Jonze's *Her* (2013), Joi is an operating system created by the Wallace Corporation, a program projected as a dimensional hologrammatic woman designed to serve as, yet again, man's projection: a companion that offers anything one's heart desires. In the scene in K's apartment when we are introduced to Joi, she literally manifests on-screen, a projected figure suddenly thrown into relief. Translucent enough that we can see background buildings and landscapes right through her, Joi ventures into the living room like a marionette on invisible strings, her pathways charted by the metal framework on the ceiling that allows her to move. K's first digital projection of Joi as 1960s housewife corroborates traditional stereotypes—wearing an apron, having dinner on the table—though I would suggest only to ultimately reveal how they are as unreal as "she," and film itself, might be. And yet, Joi becomes possibly the most important character as cellular unit in the film, precisely because she evolves and takes on new forms and freedoms, by developing as a cell might in replication. The etymological resemblance here is not accidental; while cowriting the screenplay for the original *Blade Runner*, David Peoples consulted his daughter, who, based on her interest in microbiology, suggested the idea of "replicating," the biological process of cells making copies of themselves. Granted a newfound freedom after K buys her an "emanator," which allows her to break away from the confines of her hardware and traverse anywhere she wants, Joi begins to more autonomously develop a different and more human kind of "attachment" to K, ultimately becoming "totally real."[18]

Of all the roles Joi plays, the most powerful is that of mother figure, guiding K on a path to self-discovery. Ultimately she sacrifices herself for him, who she believes to be the mysterious miracle child of Rachael and Deckard. Joi fittingly borrows the words of the Nicene Creed, itself intended as a symbol of faith in Christian liturgy, to portray her conviction that K was "born not made."[19] Believing in his singularity, Joi decides K needs "a real boy" name, as his mother would have given him, and settles on one analogous to her own—Jo, aptly taking away her "I." The precariousness between gender and identity here compels us into acknowledging that the film takes the misdirection of both as central to its story, *2049* reflecting upon gender disparities—like the erasure of sexual difference in postmodern science fiction films that Vivian Sobchak deems "*andro(oid)*-ogyny"—more deeply than its predecessor.[20] In order to seek out an anomaly in the computerized birth records of 6-10-21, Jo and Joi (who wears a see-through plastic raincoat, a nod to the clear raincoat worn by replicant Zhora [Joanna Cassidy] in the original film) join forces by literally syncing bodies, only to unearth the aberration: two children, one male and one female, with the same DNA. Because this would be impossible, Jo concludes that one is a copy, and since the records indicate the boy survived, we are led to believe the girl has perished.

This interpretation is aided later in the film by the fact that actors Harrison Ford and Ryan Gosling appear as if they come from the same family line themselves, therefore "syncing" in both looks and performance, and suggesting a neobiological connection through appropriate film casting. Following the code of the biblical source text, naming him Jo advances the theory he is the miraculous firstborn of replicant Rachael, just as the infertile Rachel and Jacob beget a first, favored son named Joseph. But the film plays up these literal resemblances—here specifically causing our expectation that it will affirm the historically masculine perspective and make K the prodigal son—only to thwart them. The film participates in traditional gender stereotypes and iconographies not to confirm but at least to contaminate them—to render them as intensely radioactive as the wood used to make K's Trojan horse.

In Sync: Re-sembling the Real

Postmodernism often signals a necessary re-representation of modern signifiers, and *Blade Runner* is oft and best considered a metaphor for the postmodern condition. For instance, Giuliana Bruno suggests a reading of the film's invocation of Fredric Jameson's notion of schizophrenia, a breakdown of the relationship between signifiers, and its classification as pastiche, indicative of an aesthetic built on the imitation of "dead styles" pushed to the limit.[21] Indeed, the film—often classified as both noir, a style historically centered in postwar American films from roughly 1941 to 1958, and sci-fi, of necessity future-reaching—operates most interestingly as a nostalgic return, most notably "to the city as a cinematic environment, an industrial space poeticized and narrated by the camera."[22] Always already artificialized in some sense, the mise-en-scène of *Blade Runner* presents hybridized quotations from the structure of Egyptian pyramids (Tyrell Corporation building), turn-of-the-century landmarks of modern architecture, by now made famous for their usage in Hollywood films (the Bradbury building, the Ennis House), and the modern fluorescent signage common of our capitalistic present. Doubled into another reflection in the mirror of pastiche, the film also quotes directly from other filmic environments, already of importance to this book, to reproduce its own unique one: effects supervisor David Dryer used stills from Fritz Lang's *Metropolis* in order to (re-?) create many of the (miniature) building in *Blade Runner.* Not only does postmodern theory stress the utter heterogeneity of text, a fragmented and hybrid, deformed sense of social and cultural identities, but Jean-François Lyotard also locates its very definition within a necessary asynchronicity, a point of time's rupture: to begin something new, "we have to re-set the hands of the clock at zero."[23]

How, then, can a film's sequel released thirty-five years later possibly ever sync with a film predicated on its out-of-sync-ness? In essence, the sheer making of *2049* becomes a replication crisis; in science, this would connote the inability to reproduce scientifically experimental work, an ongoing methodological crisis today that spans from social sciences to water resource management. It also seems to be Wallace's exact problem in the film; unable to discover the method by which Tyrell was able to manufacture reproductive replicants positions him as a possible projection of Villeneuve's anxieties to direct a sequel on a par with the magical world of the original.[24] Of note too, on a literary level the idea of a replication crisis finds root in Jorge Luis Borges's short story "The Garden of Forking Paths" (1941), considered one of the earliest examples of hypertextual fiction and cited as a major influence for new media scholars (cells interlinked). Stop here, and we might find that one of the keys to unlocking the mystery of *2049* is to reverse the postmodern foundations of the original, fractured universe of *Blade Runner*: in *2049*, many things are, instead, deceptively in sync.

On a technological level, the film offers numerous scenes of characters "syncing" their bodies together, most times to unlock a mystery that can only be accomplished through such corporeal harmony. Joi synchronizes with K to aid his fast-paced perusal of the DNA records in the search for the child. She later syncs her projected form with Mariette's (Mackenzie Davis's) body in order to satisfy K sexually, in what might be the most unique presentation of a ménage à trois as a play on the union of body and spirit. Even on the level of form, the film makes rather interesting choices to synchronize its presentation of doubles, such as in the scene where the resurrected Rachael is revealed to Deckard in Wallace's aqueous, underground lair, a fitting space for the representation of the film's own primordial birth. Villeneuve first splices in the original scene from *Blade Runner* where Rachael walks toward Deckard upon their first meeting; minutes later, the resurrected Rachael of *2049* emerges from the shadows and reveals herself to Deckard as a repetition of the original, on then multiple levels. A cinematic Turing test of sorts, this structure suggests that the film is requiring us to recognize the synchronicity between the two Rachaels, despite Deckard's seeming affirmation of the aberration between them.

A creed, like the Nicene one Joi imitates when she tells K he's been "born not made," comes from the Greek word *symbolon*, which originally meant half of a broken object that, when reunited with its other half, could act as verification of the bearers' identities. The word later morphs through Latin and then English to become "symbol," as in an outward manifestation or sign. In either case, one of *2049*'s most potent symbols is the small, wooden Trojan horse in K's possession. Regarding the horse, the film conjoins a series of pieces that ostensibly fit together to verify the identity of K as the sought-after child: the date at the bottom of the horse (6-10-21) matches the same date carved at the bottom of the tree under which Rachael is buried; K has a tangible memory of hiding the horse as a young child at the Morrill Cole Orphanage (which we see in flashback) and finds it in the exact same spot (which we see play out in the film's present). But lest we forget, the Trojan horse is historically a symbol of subterfuge, the oversized version used to hide men inside and transport them behind the gates of the ancient city of Troy. In more modern terms of computation, a Trojan horse refers to any type of malware that misleads users as to its true intent.

Accordingly, there are many synchronicities that the film seemingly hides in plain sight, a few that specifically create a connection between K and Dr. Ana Stelline (Carla Juri), the sovereign maker of replicant memories who works from inside a glass dome. Upon their meeting, shots of the two are taken from such a precise angle that K's translucent reflection lays directly on top of Ana's body image, creating a shadowy, visual effect, possibly unconscious but nearly identical to the explicit moments of characters syncing in the film's diegesis. Their connection becomes even more colorful if we recognize that the deep emerald green of Ana's lanyard matches that of K's coat (Jo and the Amazing Techniverdant Dreamcoat?), the one flowing into the other within the image. The film text tells us, through just these few congruencies, that these characters are interlinked.

Whereas the prominent green palette in *Vertigo* indicates sickness, haunting, and the sense of cinematic malady, *2049* uses green to represent filmic fecundity and the possibility of regeneration. It also somehow grasps a singularity, oft repeated as Gautier's aesthetic goal, and the same singularity that completely evades Scottie in *Vertigo*. The two films' connection may run even deeper than textual collisions and coincidences. Though Villeneuve uses mathematical equations to specifically design all of his films, it is the moment that exceeds such calculations he always looks for in his own filmmaking: "He describes it as a sense of vertigo. Not in the traditional sense, but more that nothing is what it seemed, so everything is now possible."[25] A deep, dreamlike anxiety, Villeneuve remembers when he first felt it—watching the opening scene of *Blade Runner*.

In the 1920s, Swiss psychiatrist Carl Jung first introduced the concept of synchronicity as meaningful coincidence in time, or between events; in his published work *Synchronicity: An Acausal Connecting Principle* (1960), he relates the story of how, at the very moment a young patient tells him about a dream she had about a golden scarab, an actual scarabaeid beetle tapped at the window, caught by Jung as it flew inside, who suggests that it "evidently felt an urge" to get in at that particular moment. Is it meaningful coincidence, then, that the images that effectively introduce Stelline, indicative of memories she herself is producing, show a verdant forest, a Garden of Eden wherein we see a beetle climbing on a leaf, shimmering in the sunlight? The screenplay indicates a "scarab," a direct parallel to the insect that helps form the foundation for Jung's concept of synchronicity, and the same scarab beetle that the ancient Egyptians exalted as the embodiment of the sun god Ra and a symbol of life itself. The Trojan horse, appropriately, functions as artifice; alternatively, it is the beetle that becomes the film's silent symbol of the source of life—Stelline, the true child of Deckard and Rachael. In fact, on first watch it is easy to miss the clear resemblance shared by the child, who we see in flashback hiding the horse, and the grown Ana; but once the film actually syncs the young and adult Ana together, editing the shots together in quick succession and thus recontextualizing them through montage, we cannot deny the kinship. And the woman is also the solution to the riddle, for (mother) nature finds a way. It is the boy child who was fake, and in some strangely satisfying reversal of all expectations for a film predicated on artificially generated humans, *2049* offers us a real girl.

Traditional projections become empowered prophecies, and in the end we realize that it will be woman who leads the promised resistance, both of the replicants in *2049* and, perhaps, of cinematic re-presentation.[26]

Acknowledgments

Many books take a while to write, I imagine, but this one has taken long enough to qualify as a regeneration, possibly equivalent to the reanimated mummies that are the subject of discussion in the first chapter and beyond. Many, many things, forces, and people have helped me create this work—more than I can possibly mention—so I can only hope to give thanks to some of the most relevant here.

I owe my gratitude to a number of people who helped guide and inspire my undergraduate studies at Hamilton College, especially Austin Briggs, Cheryl Morgan, and Margaret Thickstun. The pages of this book bear major traces of what I learned from them all, in classes on Joyce, Milton, Gothic literature, and French language and literature, and, even more important, from their intellectual generosity. Special thanks to my honors thesis director at Hamilton, Dana Luciano (now at Rutgers), who was incredibly generous in mentoring my project on the maternal Gothic. I would not be publishing this book, or likely be in academia, if it were not for her confidence in my scholarship and her early, unwavering support.

I have benefited enormously from my graduate mentors at Emory University who shared their expertise and provided models of intellectual inquiry I can only hope to one day live up to, especially Shoshana Felman, Nina K. Martin (now at Connecticut College), Claire Nouvet, Karla Oeler (now at Stanford), and Deborah Elise White. To Elissa Marder, in many ways the "mother" of this project, words of appreciation can never fully express how much I have valued your inspiration and wise counsel; I can only aspire to be a mere copy, and do so with respect and gratitude. Considerable love and thanks to my friends from Emory who I continue to cherish, including Naomi Beeman (whose company made copyediting duties a near delight), Scott Branson, Jacob Hovind, Lauren Rule Maxwell, and Brent Young.

Many thanks to my colleagues in the English Department at Florida State University for their encouragement and assistance, including Leigh Edwards, Barry Faulk, Robin Truth Goodman, Aaron Jaffe, David Johnson, Gary Taylor, and numerous others for their words of support, group writing sessions, and more. I want to especially thank Robert Olen Butler for his generous support of our department's visiting editor program, which enabled my meeting Nicole Solano of Rutgers University Press. An enthusiastic advocate of the project, I owe her special thanks for being such a kind guide through this publication journey. Thanks as well to Kathleen A. Kelly for her keen editorial suggestions and much-appreciated encouragement.

I am incredibly grateful for the financial and research support from Emory University, the Andrew W. Mellon Foundation, and Florida State University that has contributed to early stages of research as well as more recent writing. Particular thanks to UCLA's Williams Andrews Clark Memorial Library Center for Seventeenth- and Eighteenth-Century Studies Fellowship for Postdoctoral Research, which allowed me to do archival work on Oscar Wilde that serves as the foundation for this book's third chapter.

My deepest and most heartfelt appreciation goes out to all the friends and family who have supported me along the way, with very special thanks to my father, Michael, for being the one to get it all started, and to Marlowe and Elvin, my cherished-before-book babies, who bring me boundless love and joy—and to whom I dedicate this work.

The last one yet really the first, though, is my husband, James—loving match, outstanding father, sometime editor, all-the-time dishwasher, fellow em dash enthusiast and lima bean hater—without whom this book would simply not exist. *His like is positively not to be found anywhere under the sun.* All my love, for everything.

Notes

Introduction

1 Though Delluc was posthumously recognized as one of the founding creators of film criticism by the French association of film critics, his life and career were marked by a remarkable intertextuality of art and literature; within his brief life span, he acted as poet, literary critic, writer of comedies, journalist, editor, and early Impressionist film director.

2 Claims made by Eugene McCreary, "Louis Delluc, Film Theorist, Critic, and Prophet," *Cinema Journal* 16, no. 1 (Autumn 1976): 15.

3 Jean Epstein, "On Certain Characteristics of Photogénie," in *Film Theory: Critical Concepts in Media and Cultural Studies*, ed. Philip Simpson (New York: Routledge, 2004), 52, 53.

4 Epstein, 54.

5 Epstein, "*Photogénie* and the Imponderable," in *Critical Visions in Film Theory: Classic and Contemporary Readings*, ed. Timothy Corrigan, Patricia White, and Meta Mazaj (New York: Bedford St. Martin's, 2011), 254.

6 Max Campbell, "Looking at William Henry Fox Talbot's Pioneering Photographs—Without Causing Them to Disappear," *New Yorker*, November 26, 2017, https://www.newyorker.com/culture/photo-booth/looking-at-william-henry-fox-talbots-pioneering-photographswithout-causing-them-to-disappear.

7 *Oxford English Dictionary Online*, s.v. "photogenic (adj.)," accessed May 24, 2021, https://www-oed-com.proxy.lib.fsu.edu/view/Entry/142812?redirectedFrom=photogenic#eid.

8 Michael North, *Camera Works: Photography and the Twentieth-Century Word* (Oxford: Oxford University Press, 2005), 11.

9 Steve Choe, "The One in Photogénie: Plotinus and Jean Epstein," in *Plotinus and the Moving Image*, ed. Thorsten Botz-Bornstein and Giannis Stamatellos (Amsterdam: Brill, 2017), 31.

10 André Bazin, "The Myth of Total Cinema," in *What Is Cinema? Volume 1* (Berkeley: University of California Press, 1967), 22.

11 Bazin, 20.

12 Bazin, 18–19.

13 Bazin, 19.
14 Epstein, "*Photogénie* and the Imponderable," 254.
15 I am using the notion of the "supplement" in a Derridean sense; Jacques Derrida's category of the supplement, as in the way writing supplements speech, comes primarily from the French root of *le supplement*, a word derived from *supplémenter*, "to add on to," and *suppléer*, "to substitute." Accordingly, this book will examine how artificial women, who often derive from reproductions of Eve as man's first companion-as-supplement, operate as substitutes of real women as much as of men themselves.
16 Leon Battista Alberti, *On Painting* (New York: Penguin, 1991), 61.
17 Paul Barolsky, "A Very Brief History of Art from Narcissus to Picasso," *Classical Journal* 90, no. 3 (1995): 256.
18 J. Hillis Miller, *Versions of Pygmalion* (Cambridge, MA: Harvard University Press, 1990), 5.
19 Hillel Schwartz, *The Culture of the Copy* (New York: Zone Books, 2014), 59.
20 Epstein, "*Photogénie* and the Imponderable," 254.
21 Paula James, *Ovid's Myth of Pygmalion on Screen* (London: Continuum, 2001).
22 Martin Winkler, *Ovid on Screen: A Montage of Attractions* (Cambridge: Cambridge University Press, 2020).
23 Roxana Marcoci, "The Original Copy: Photography of Sculpture, 1839 to Today," in *The Original Copy: Photography of Sculpture, 1839 to Today* (New York: Museum of Modern Art, 2010), 16.
24 Victor Stoichita, *The Pygmalion Effect: From Ovid to Hitchcock* (Chicago: University of Chicago Press, 2008).
25 Elisabeth Bronfen, *Over Her Dead Body: Death, Femininity and the Aesthetic* (New York: Routledge, 1992), 6–7.
26 Mary Ann Doane, "The Close-Up: Scale and Detail in the Cinema," *differences* 14, no. 3 (December 1, 2003), 89.
27 See Andreas Huyssen, "Authentic Ruins: Products of Modernity," in *Ruins of Modernity*, ed. Julia Hell and Andreas Schönle (Durham, NC: Duke University Press, 2010), 17–28.
28 Bakshy in Laura Marcus and David Bradshaw, "Introduction: Modernism as 'a space that is filled with moving,'" in *Moving Modernisms: Motion, Technology, and Modernity*, ed. David Bradshaw, Laura Marcus, and Rebecca Roach (Oxford: Oxford University Press, 2016), 2.
29 Malcolm Turvey, *The Filming of Modern Life: European Avant-Garde Film of the 1920s* (Cambridge, MA: MIT Press, 2011), 163.
30 Raymond Bellour, "Ideal Hadaly," *Camera Obscura* 5, no. 3 (Fall 1986): 111–134.
31 Annette Michelson, "On the Eve of the Future: The Reasonable Facsimile and the Philosophical Toy," *October* 29 (Summer 1984): 19.
32 Oscar Wilde, "De Profundis," in *The Annotated Oscar Wilde: Poems, Fictions, Plays, Lectures, Essays, and Letters*, ed. H. Montgomery Hyde (New York: Clarkson N. Potter, 1982), 462.
33 Martin Winkler, "Ovid and the Cinema: An Introduction," in *A Handbook to the Reception of Ovid*, ed. John F. Miller and Carol E. Newlands (West Sussex: Wiley Blackwell, 2014), 471.
34 Tom Gunning, "The Birth of Film Out of the Spirit of Modernity," in *Masterpieces of Modernist Cinema*, ed. Ted Perry (Bloomington: Indiana University Press, 2006), 27.
35 Olga Taxidou, "'Do Not Call Me a Dancer' (Isadora Duncan, 1929): Dance and Modernist Experimentation," in *Moving Modernisms*, 111.

36 Robert Samuels, *Hitchcock's Bi-textuality: Lacan, Feminisms and Queer Theory* (Albany: State University of New York Press, 1998), 77.
37 See Slavoj Žižek, "The Hitchcockian Blot," in *Hitchcock Centenary Essays*, ed. Richard Allen and S. Ishii-Gonzalès (London: BFI Publishing, 1999), 122–139.
38 Hillel Schwartz, "Torque: The New Kinaesthetic of the Twentieth Century," in *Incorporations*, ed. Jonathan Crary and Sanford Kwinter (New York: Zone Books, 1992), 70–127.

1. The Literary Afterlife

1 Charles Baudelaire, "Théophile Gautier," in *Curiosités esthétiques, l'Art Romantique et autres œuvres critiques* (Paris: Éditions Garnier Frères, 1962), 682. Baudelaire's dedication of *Les Fleurs du mal* to Gautier reads, "Au poète impeccable, au parfait magicien ès lettres françaises" (Paris: Larousse, 2001), 38.
2 Baudelaire, "Théophile Gautier," 678 (English translation mine).
3 Marcoci, "Original Copy," 12.
4 Marcoci, 12.
5 Marcoci, 12 (emphasis mine).
6 Sabine T. Kriebel, "Theories of Photography: A Short History," in *Photography Theory*, ed. James Elkins (New York: Routledge, 2007), 7.
7 See Marcoci, *The Original Copy*, 51.
8 Geoffrey Batchen, "An Almost Unlimited Variety: Photography and Sculpture in the Nineteenth Century," in *The Original Copy*, 20.
9 Stephen C. Pinson, *Speculating Daguerre* (Chicago: University of Chicago Press, 2012), 146.
10 Eric Downing, *After Images: Photography, Archaeology, and Psychoanalysis and the Tradition of Bildung* (Detroit: Wayne State University Press, 2006), 3.
11 Downing, 7.
12 Downing, 11.
13 James Kearns, "On His Knees to the Past? Gautier, Ingres, and Forms of Modern Art," in *Impressions of French Modernity: Art and Literature in France 1850–1900*, ed. Richard Hobbs (Manchester: Manchester University Press, 1998), 68.
14 See William G. Allen, "Gautier's *Albertus*: The Fantastic and the Fashionable," in *Correspondences: Studies in Literature, History, and the Arts in Nineteenth-Century France*, ed. Keith Busby (New York: Rodopi, 1992), 9. The red waistcoat deserves mention also because Oscar Wilde, a disciple of Gautier's *l'art pour l'art* movement and the focus in chapter 3, dressed himself quite specifically alike. As English painter William Rothenstein recollects, Wilde sat "for his portrait, in a red waistcoat, which he wore, doubtless, in imitation of Théophile Gautier"; Rothenstein, *Men and Memories: Recollections of William Rothenstein, 1872–1900* (London: Faber & Faber, 1931), https://archive.org/details/in.ernet.dli.2015.44702/page/n9/mode/2up.
15 Andrea Goulet, *Optiques: The Science of the Eye and the Birth of Modern French Fiction* (Philadelphia: University of Pennsylvania Press, 2006), 4.
16 Jonathan Crary, "Modernizing Vision," in *Vision and Visuality*, ed. Hal Foster (Seattle: Bay Press, 1988), 35.
17 Baudelaire, "Théophile Gautier," 679.
18 Baudelaire, 679.
19 Amy J. Ransom, *The Feminine as Fantastic in the Conte Fantastique: Visions of the Other* (New York: Peter Lang, 1995), 90.

20 Baudelaire, "Théophile Gautier," 680.
21 See Marie Lathers, *The Aesthetics of Artifice: Villiers's L'Eve Future* (Chapel Hill: University of North Carolina Press, 1996), 58.
22 Théophile Gautier, "Portrait de Théophile Gautier par lui-même," in *Portrait de Balzac précédé de Portrait de Théophile Gautier par lui-même* (Montpellier: L'Anabase, 1994), 14 (English translation mine).
23 Albert B. Smith, *Théophile Gautier and the Fantastic* (University, MS: Romance Monographs, 1977), 55.
24 This painting, and Delacroix himself, also had the privilege of being the object of dedication for Balzac's *La Fille aux yeux d'or* (1835), written at the same time period as "La Morte amoureuse."
25 Sigmund Freud, *The Uncanny* (New York: Penguin, 2003), 226. Freud's theory of the uncanny expands upon the work of Ernest Jentsch in his essay "On the Psychology of the Uncanny" (1906).
26 *Oxford English Dictionary Online*, s.v. "fantastic (adj. and n.)," accessed May 24, 2021, https://www-oed-com.proxy.lib.fsu.edu/view/Entry/68107?redirectedFrom=fantastic#eid.
27 In Baudelaire, according to Elissa Marder, "'good' and 'evil' are terms that only acquire significance to the extent that they determine temporal possibilities or failures"; Marder, *Dead Time: Temporal Disorders in the Wake of Modernity (Baudelaire and Flaubert)* (Stanford, CA: Stanford University Press, 2001), 20. This idea applies to the figure of Clarimonde, especially in relation to her first appearance in the church and the depiction of time going haywire in response.
28 See North, *Camera Works*.
29 Sigmund Freud, "Delusions and Dreams in Jensen's *Gradiva*," in *Writings on Art and Literature* (Stanford, CA: Stanford University Press, 1997), 6. Gautier went a step further in linking these literary fantasies and the excavation of identity formation by calling his *Arria Marcella* "Souvenir de Pompeii," suggesting that the protagonist's fantasy of Pompeii is actually *real* in some sense, a memory trace.
30 Surrealists like Salvador Dali adopted Freud's Gradiva as muse, revealing an inherent impulse toward psychoanalytical, unconscious premiums set upon artistic subjectivity; Dali referred to his wife, Gala, his "real" muse, as Galatea as well as Gradiva.
31 Whitney Chadwick, "Masson's Gradiva: The Metamorphosis of a Surrealist Myth," *Art Bulletin* 52, no. 4 (December 1970): 419.
32 Marder, *Dead Time* 44. Marder invokes this image in her discussion of Baudelaire's "La Chevelure," where she writes, "Bersani implies that the reason the poet desires the woman's absence is so that she can become an object of 'memory.'"
33 John Frederick Logan, "The Age of Intoxication," *Yale French Studies* 50 (1974): 89.
34 Théophile Gautier, "The Mummy's Foot" (Whitefish, MT: Kessinger Publishing, 2010), 10.
35 Gautier, 10.
36 Walter Benjamin, "On Some Motifs in Baudelaire," in *Illuminations* (New York: Schocken Books, 1969), 169.
37 Benjamin, 184.
38 Claire Nouvet, "An Impossible Response: The Disaster of Narcissus," *Yale French Studies* 79 (1991): 108.
39 Hilda Nelson, "Théophile Gautier: The Invisible and Impalpable World: A Demi-Conviction," *French Review* 45, no. 4 (1972): 820.

40 Jean Bellemin-Noël, *Plaisirs de vampire* (Paris: Presses universitaires de France, 2001), 43, 47. On occasion, the story's title has been translated into English, somewhat unsuitably, as *The Beautiful Vampire.*

41 Sabine Jarrot, *Le Vampire dans la littérature du XIXe et XXe siècle* (Paris: L'Harmattan, 1999), 149.

42 Bellemin-Noël, *Plaisirs de vampire*, 51.

43 Melanie C. Hawthorne, "Dis-Covering the Female: Gautier's Roman de la Momie," *French Review* 66, no. 5 (1993): 723.

44 Aby Warburg's comparative work, *Mnemosyne Atlas*, is devoted to highlighting what he calls "the afterlife of antiquity," and his larger project of art historical research centers around this concept of the recurrence of the past in the works of the present, to an extent that it becomes an extremely detachable phrase oft reproduced to signal his contribution.

45 See Natalie David-Weill, *Rêve de Pierre: La Quête de la femme chez Théophile Gautier* (Geneva: Droz, 1989), 41–42.

46 According to Barbara Walker, the Arabic words for snake and life are related to the name of Eve: *The Woman's Dictionary of Symbols and Sacred Objects* (Edison, NJ: Castle Books, 1988), 207.

47 A 2018 issue of *Nineteenth Century Contexts* was devoted to the topic "Ancient Egypt in Nineteenth Century Culture," and recent books like Maria Fleischhack's *Narrating Ancient Egypt* (New York: Peter Lang, 2015) and Scott Trafton's *Egypt Land: Race and Nineteenth-Century Egyptomania* (Durham, NC: Duke University Press, 2004) have helped lay the foundation for the newly emerging field of studies in the reception and representation of ancient Egyptian culture specific to the century.

48 Fleischhack, *Narrating Ancient Egypt*, 213.

49 After "La Morte amoureuse," Gautier wrote "Une Nuit de Cléopâtre" (1838), in which he describes the Priestess's eyes very much in the same way he describes the power of Clarimonde's in the church, her every look equaling a Homerian poem. And Cleopatra accepts the lethal sting of an asp as her preferred means of suicide, clasping the reptile to her breast in a scene made famous and morbidly erotic in William Shakespeare's *The Tragedy of Antony and Cleopatra*. The bite of an asp causes an intense burn at the site of the wound; when the burn disappears, in its place the victim experiences a state of giddiness that borders on delirium.

50 Baudelaire, "Théophile Gautier," 675.

51 Christian Metz, *Film Language: A Semiotics of the Cinema* (Chicago: University of Chicago Press, 1974), 4.

52 See Christian Metz, "Photography and Fetish," *October* 34 (Autumn 1985): 81–90.

53 Nicholas Daly, "The Obscure Object of Desire: Victorian Commodity Culture and Fictions of the Mummy," *Novel: A Forum on Fiction* 28, no. 1 (Autumn 1994): 46.

54 See also Baudelaire, "Hymne à la Beauté," in *Les Fleurs du mal* (Paris: Larousse, 2001), 74.

55 Chasseguet-Smirgel in Charles Bernheimer, "Fetishism and Decadence: Salome's severed heads," in *Fetishism as Cultural Discourse*, ed. Emily Apter and William Pietz (Ithaca, NY: Cornell University Press, 1993), 69.

56 Bronfen, *Over Her Dead Body*, 33.

57 Sigmund Freud, "Fetishism," in *Sexuality and the Psychology of Love* (New York: Simon and Schuster, 1963), 216.

58 See Sigmund Freud's *Leonardo da Vinci and a Memory of His Childhood* (New York: W. W. Norton, 1964).
59 Naomi Segal, *Narcissus and Echo: Women in the French Récit* (Manchester: Manchester University Press, 1988), 85.
60 Segal, 94.
61 Bernheimer, "Fetishism and Decadence," 68.
62 David-Weill, *Rêve de Pierre*, 75.
63 Gautier chose Venice as a beloved site because it loved him back; as Baudelaire writes in his essay "L'Art philosophique," "Venise a pratiqué l'amour de l'art pour l'art," in *Curiosités Esthetiques, l'Art Romantique et autres œuvres critiques* (Paris: Éditions Garnier Frères, 1962), 508.
64 Freud, *The Uncanny*, 210.
65 Freud, *Leonardo da Vinci*, 44.
66 Freud, 44.
67 Pierre-Georges Castex, *Le Conte fantastiques en France: De Nodier à Maupassant* (Paris: J. Corti, 1951), 219.
68 *Oxford English Dictionary Online*, s.v. "fantastic (adj. and n.)," accessed May 24, 2021, https://www-oed-com.proxy.lib.fsu.edu/view/Entry/68107?redirectedFrom=fantastic#eid.
69 Marder, *Dead Time*, 45.
70 Laurent Guido, "Dancing Dolls and Mechanical Eyes," in *Cinema beyond Film: Media Epistemology in the Modern Era*, ed. François Albera and Maria Tortajada (Amsterdam: Amsterdam University Press, 2010), 176.
71 M. C. Schapira, *Le Regard de Narcisse: Romans et nouvelles de Théophile Gautier* (Lyon: Presses universitaires de Lyon, 1984), 20.
72 Donald Kuspit, "A Mighty Metaphor: The Analogy of Archaeology and Psychoanalysis," in *Sigmund Freud and Art: His Personal Collection of Antiquities*, ed. Lynn Gamwell and Richard Wells (New York: Harry N Abrams, 1989), 134.
73 Metz, "Photography and Fetish," 139.
74 Kenneth Reinhard, "The Freudian Things: Construction and the Archeological Metaphor," in *Excavations and Their Objects: Freud's Collection of Antiquity*, ed. Stephen Barker (Albany: State University of New York Press, 1996), 74.
75 Literary allusion, the name Sérapion directly suggests the work of E.T.A. Hoffmann, *The Serapion Brotherhood*. Later taken as the name for a group of Soviet literati who hoped to maintain artistic independence under the new regime after World War I, Hoffmann's brotherhood institutes secret societies and magical orders in the world of a hermit, wherein natural and supernatural powers are equal. Serapionism, named for Saint Serapion and founded on his feast day, is dedicated to presenting paranormal phenomena convincingly. Gautier intentionally alludes to Hoffmann's literary edicts as recourse to the idea of a secret society—the illuminati—within the literary world. Hoffmann led a famously double life—as Prussian civil servant by day, writer of fantastic tales by night. Serapionism, then, takes on the character of an "inner world" that must be fed by the necessary relation between the "light" used to produce images in nineteenth-century dioramas, daguerreotypes, and the like that are unconsciously emerging in the optical models and arrangements in "La Morte."
76 Karl H. Dannenfeldt, "Egyptian Mumia: The Sixteenth Century Experience," *Sixteenth Century Journal* 16, no. 2 (Summer 1985): 167.
77 Dannenfeldt, 165.
78 Schwartz, *Culture of the Copy*, 79.

79 Lathers, *Aesthetics of Artifice*, 51.
80 Théophile Gautier, *Photosculpture* (Paris: Paul Dupont, 1864), 5.
81 Gautier, 4 (English translation mine).
82 Gautier, 9.
83 Galloway gives this talk for the Winchester Centre for Global Futures in Art Design & Media in 2012, and later publishes "The Cybernetic Hypothesis" in *differences* 25, no. 1 (May 2014): 107–131. The titular phrase is reproduced directly from the title of the second issue of French collective and leftist journal publication *Tiqqun* (2001), which extended an epistemological regime that combines both human and non-human agents, and was later turned into a book. See *The Cybernetic Hypothesis* (Cambridge, MA: MIT Press, 2020).
84 Sean Cubitt, *The Practice of Light: A Genealogy of Visual Technologies from Prints to Pixels* (Cambridge, MA: MIT Press, 2014), 240.
85 Friedrich Kittler, *Literature, Media, Information Systems* (London: Routledge, 1997), 96.

2. Book of Genesis

1 Colleen Ramos, *Deviant Modernism* (Cambridge: Cambridge University Press, 1998), 97.
2 Auguste Villiers de l'Isle-Adam, *L'Ève future; Édition établie par Nadine Satiat* (Paris: GF Flammarion, 1992), 99.
3 Is it significant that Reverend Fletcher's "Christ's Victory and Triumph" influenced John Milton, who is said to have borrowed liberally from it in regard to his writing of *Paradise Lost*, discussed later in this chapter as an essential intertext, and *Paradise Regained*.
4 One for each chapter—except chapter 14, which curiously has two epigraphs—plus the epigraph on the title page, for a total of seventy-six. For more information on specific epigraphs, see Gwenhaël Ponnau's "Sur les épigraphes de *L'Eve future*," in *Société des études romantiques: Villiers de l'Isle-Adam (1838–1889)* (Paris: Sedes, 1990).
5 A. W. Raitt writes a footnote for this epigraph in his edition of *L'Ève future* claiming the original quote had not been found (Paris: Gallimard, 1993), 405.
6 A. W. Raitt, *The Life of Villiers de l'Isle-Adam* (Oxford: Clarendon Press, 1981), 189.
7 Some of the authors Villiers cites from include Ovid, Milton, Goethe, Balzac, and Poe; some epigraphs offer ventriloquized versions of women's sentiments: "Guess, or I devour you."—The Sphinx (a female-coded monster of Egyptian and Greek origin). The epigraph he uses from Gautier's *Le Roman de la momie* ("I was mummified with astonishment") clearly bridges the two authors, and their like reanimations of artificial(ly preserved) women.
8 Raitt, *Life of Villiers*, 198.
9 Genesis 2:7 in *The Old Testament: The Authorized or King James Version of 1611* (London: Everyman's Library, 1996).
10 Genesis 2:18.
11 Genesis 2:22.
12 Genesis 2:23.
13 Raitt in *L'Ève future*, 26.
14 The use of this word, "Adieu," as the title of the last chapter further proves Villiers's somewhat playful use of language. While it means goodbye, if you parsed the word into two words—*À Dieu*—it would refer to everything being up to God in the end.
15 Raitt in *L'Ève future*, 9–10.

16 The quote in the original French reads: "A vingt-cinq lieues de New York, au centre d'un réseau de *fils électriques*, apparaît une habitation qu'entourent de profonds jardins solitaires" (139).

17 An inherent and purposeful paradox because these daughters of Eve, emblematic of human life, are all made by male artists, women deadened in art, as in Poe's "Ligeia" or "The Oval Portrait."

18 This sentiment about Doré, originated in the *Art Journal*, gets oft repeated and reproduced in numerous biographies and encyclopedic resources on the artist.

19 Oliver Wendell Holmes, "The Stereoscope and the Stereograph," *The Atlantic*, June 1859, https://www.theatlantic.com/magazine/archive/1859/06/the-stereoscope-and-the-stereograph/303361/.

20 Holmes invented the stereoscope viewer but did not patent the idea, instead just giving it away.

21 Holmes, "The Stereoscope."

22 Similar to Ovid's Pygmalion in the *Metamorphoses*, which is the only tale in that collection that tells the story of a thing becoming a person, rather than the reverse.

23 Gaby Wood, *Edison's Eve: A Magical History of the Quest for Mechanical Life* (New York: Alfred A. Knopf, 2002), 55.

24 Holmes, "The Stereoscope."

25 The line verbatim from the Norton Critical Edition of *Paradise Lost* reads "Hail, holy Light, offspring of Heav'n, first-born" (3:1). As both A. W. Raitt and Nadine Satiat point out in their respective editions of *L'Ève future*, Villiers misquotes Milton so that the "offspring" becomes specifically a "daughter."

26 For more information, see Eleanor Gertrude Brown, *Milton's Blindness* (New York: Columbia University Press, 1934).

27 Remy de Gourmont, who was then on staff at the Bibliothèque Nationale, assisted Villiers in his research and became his close friend and admirer.

28 *Paradise Lost* (4.635); see T. Ross Leasure, "Yesterday's Eve and Her Electric Avatar: Villiers's Debt to Milton's *Paradise Lost*," *Latch: A Journal for the Study of the Literary Artifact in Theory, Culture or History* 1 (2008): 134, for further discussion.

29 Genesis 3:16.

30 Raitt, *Life of Villiers*, 326.

31 Modris Eksteins, "History and Degeneration: Of Birds and Cages," in *Degeneration: The Dark Side of Progress*, ed. J. Edward Chamberlin and Sander Gilman (New York: Columbia University Press, 1985), 3.

32 For more information, see Raitt, *Life of Villiers*, 82, 160.

33 There are no epigraphs or direct evidence that Villiers directly engages with *Frankenstein*. Nonetheless, it would be hard to ignore all the ways that *L'Ève future* either mimics or extends the *Frankenstein* narrative. For further reading, see Marie Lathers's *The Aesthetics of Artifice*.

34 Sandra M. Gilbert and Susan Gubar, "Horror's Twin: Mary Shelley's Monstrous Eve," in *The Madwoman in the Attic: The Woman Writer and the Nineteenth-Century Literary Imagination* (New Haven, CT: Yale University Press, 2020), 225.

35 Modern scholars tend to view Victor Frankenstein as more the antihero of the story, illustrating the shifting, critical reception of these Pygmalionesque madmen from the nineteenth to twentieth century. Wood, *Edison's Eve*, 129–130.

36 Alain Corbin, *Women for Hire: Prostitution and Sexuality in France after 1850* (Boston: Harvard University Press, 1990), 30.

37 Jules Michelet, *Love* (New York: Rudd and Carleton, 1859), 68. In mythology, Pandora figures as the first mortal woman; therefore, she may be compared to Eve as

an archetype for woman. She was created out of clay by the Gods (Hephaestus at the behest of Zeus), in retaliation for the stealing of fire by Prometheus. After being delivered to Prometheus's brother Epimetheus, Pandora opens the jar Zeus had given her, thus unleashing the evil spirits contained within. She was named Pandora, meaning "all-gifted" or "the gift."

38 Jules Michelet, *Woman* (New York: Rudd and Carleton, 1860), 52.

39 Michelet, *Love*, 68.

40 Anne Geisler-Szmulewicz, *Le Mythe de Pygmalion au XIXe siècle: Pour une approche de la coalescence des mythes* (Paris: Honoré Champion Éditeur, 1999), 361. Geisler-Szmulewicz likens Ewald to an avatar of Pygmalion, Hadaly as a product of the Pygmalion-Prometheus legends combined. By considering Edison and Ewald as avatars of these mythical legends, Geisler-Szmulewicz implicitly suggests that Villiers proffers his male protagonists as human incarnations (or copies) of the mythical. Ironically perhaps, the word "avatar" has come to currently signify a graphical representation of a person, usually in a computer-generated environment. An avatar connotes the technological replication of the real thing and is also the title of another Gautier tale, "Avatar."

41 Marie Lathers, *The Aesthetics of Artifice: Villiers's L'Ève future* (Chapel Hill: University of North Carolina Press, 1996).

42 Given that much emphasis has been placed on Villiers's strategic and subversive use of epigraphs, note that Jean Baudrillard uses a "citation" from Ecclesiastes for the epigraph to *Simulacra and Simulation* that seems to be completely fictionalized. It reads, "The simulacra is never what hides the truth–it is truth that hides the fact that there is none. The simulacrum is true"; Baudrillard, *Simulacra and Simulation* (Ann Arbor: University of Michigan Press, 1995), 1.

43 See Marie Lathers, "The Decadent Goddess: L'Ève future and the Venus de Milo," in *Jeering Dreamers: Villiers de l'Isle Adam's L'Eve future at our fin de siècle: A collection of essays*, ed. John Anzalone (Amsterdam: Rodopi, 1996), 50.

44 Lathers, 50.

45 Art historians Caroline Arscott and Katie Scott extend the symbolic significance of the Venus de Milo's installment in the Louvre, which "secured for her, in her dual capacity of ancient object and modern icon, a place which worked simultaneously for the elevation of beauty and the erasure of the sexual. As Ian Jenkins has made clear, nineteenth-century arrangements of antique sculpture tended initially to follow the conventions of an earlier era, conventions he characterises by a phrase taken from political discourse, 'the chain of being'" (7). See Arscott and Scott's "Introducing Venus," in *Manifestations of Venus: Art and Sexuality*, ed. Caroline Arscott and Katie Scott (Manchester: Manchester University Press, 2000).

46 Jennifer Shaw, "The Figure of Venus: Rhetoric of the Ideal and the Salon of 1863," in *Manifestations of Venus: Art and Sexuality*, ed. Caroline Arscott and Katie Scott (Manchester: Manchester University Press, 2000), 90.

47 Shaw, 91.

48 Shaw, 92.

49 Ewald's early description of his predicament with Alicia ("Mais cette femme! . . . Ah! c'est l'Irrémédiable") alludes to the Baudelaire poem "L'Irrémédiable," in *Les Fleurs du mal* (1857). The term also encapsulates the idea of evil by including the word *diable* (devil) within it. Miss Alicia is likened as the irrefutable devil of the novel, a monstrous representation of female nature and vanity.

50 Arscott and Scott contend, "The passage from Venus as a figure for artistic creativity to Venus as a sign for art itself is easily made. Since Venus is pre-eminent in beauty,

as well as in sexual love, her presence in art triggers a meditation on the domain of the aesthetic"; "Introducing Venus," 5.

51 Villiers adopts the disequilibrium problem he discerns in Alicia, between body and soul, as his own disordered physiological condition—vertigo. This physiological condition and its relationship to the disparity between "real" and the ideal will be discussed in chapter 5, on Hitchcock's *Vertigo*.

52 In an article for the *Moniteur de le photographie* in May 1861, the inventor Willème gave this description of photosculpture as producing "de la sculpture exactement semblable au modèle."

53 See Geisler-Szmulewicz, *Le Mythe de Pygmalion*, 365.

54 Raitt, *Life of Villiers*, 10.

55 Gustave Guiches in Raitt, 188.

56 Raitt, 296.

57 Raitt, 139.

58 Raitt, 141. The Eyre Powell country house was in Staffordshire, also the seat of Alicia Clary's family in *L'Ève future*.

59 Raitt, *Life of Villiers*, 141 (emphasis mine). I have placed emphasis on the sections of this quotation that directly replicate the words of the book of Ecclesiastes.

60 Raitt, 143.

61 As Raitt footnotes in the 1993 Gallimard edition of *L'Ève future*: "Villiers avait mis en épigraphe à L'Annonciateur dans les Contes cruels en 1883 la phrase: 'Habal habalim, vêk'hôl habal,' c'est-à-dire la 'vanité des vanités' de l'Ecclésiaste. Le nom signifie donc 'Vanité'" (420).

62 Sylvie Jouanny, *L'Actrice et ses doubles: Figures et représentations de la femme de spectacle à la fin du XIXe siècle* (Geneva: Droz, 2002), 310.

63 Edison claims that "the name HADALY in the identical letters" to those on the silver plaque that adorns the android's coffin "in Iranian signify the IDEAL" (76). In the original French text, Villiers adjoins his own footnote as "proof" of the usage: "Selon Gilbert Lazard, orientaliste consulté par Pierre Citron, le mot n'existe pas sous cette forme en iranien, mais 'had-é-ali' (en iranien: limité supérieure) peut être pris métaphoriquement au sens d' 'être suprême'" (Villiers 1992, 209). This footnote gets completely edited out of the novel's English edition.

64 In terms of photography, according to the *Oxford English Dictionary Online*, a proof is usually taken to mean a "trial print from a particular negative" or "a test print made for the purpose of evaluating subject composition: density, color, balance, etc."

65 The title of this chapter is a direct allusion to Baudelaire's poem of the same name from *Les Fleurs du mal*. The chapter's focus on the protocinematic female ideal can be regarded as double-edged. It speaks to a desire from within the narrative (Edison's) but also from Villiers's real detestation of industrialization. For more on the literary relevance of Villiers's friendship with and admiration for Baudelaire, see A. W. Raitt's *Villiers de l'Isle-Adam et le mouvement Symboliste* (Paris: Jose Corti, 1965).

66 Rhonda Garelick, *Rising Star: Dandyism, Gender, and Performance in the Fin de Siècle* (Princeton, NJ: Princeton University Press, 1998), 90.

67 Andre Bazin takes this scene as a primary instance of the development of cinematic technology catching up with the mythology of representation of the woman in "The Myth of Total Cinema," in *What Is Cinema? Volume 1* (Berkeley: University of California Press, 1967).

68 Michelson, "On the Eve of the Future," 19–20.

69 Raymond Bellour, "Ideal Hadaly," *Camera Obscura* 5, no. 3 (Fall 1986): 115.

70 Bellour, 115.

71 From the Latin for "darkened chamber," the camera obscura is an optical device consisting of a box with a pinhole in one side, which projects an image when light from the external scene passes through the hole. It was invented in eleventh-century Egypt and was consistently developed until the eighteenth century, forming the basis for more modern camera inventions and photographic processes developed by Joseph Niépce, Louis Daguerre, and William Fox Talbot in the early nineteenth century.

72 Crary, "Modernizing Vision," 42.

73 Bellour, "Ideal Hadaly," 113.

74 Lathers, "Decadent Goddess," 61. She claims, in relation to her discussion of the statue of the Venus de Milo, that "the greatest paradox of *L'Eve future* is perhaps just this: from a copy, an original is produced. And this is indeed the newly discovered reproductive power of technology."

75 In *Edison's Eve*, Gaby Wood finds appealing evidence that Edison in reality believed that women were perfectible creatures. Wood offers the following excerpt from Edison's journal of 1885: "Thought of Mina, Daisy, Mamma G [the wife of one of his colleagues]. Put all 3 in my mental kaleidoscope to obtain a new combination à la Galton. Took Mina as basis, and tried to improve her beauty by discarding and adding certain features borrowed from Daisy and Mamma G" (146).

76 I am appropriating the understanding of the navel of women in Freud's dream of Irma's injection as discussed by Shoshana Felman in "The Dream from Which Psychoanalysis Proceeds." Hadaly functions as the navel by representing this "knot" of women—Miss Alicia, Evelyn Habal, Sowana—from within the narrative as well as symbolizing the very notion of a technological navel, that is to say, a modern, prosthetic point of origin. For further discussion, see Felman, *What Does a Woman Want? Reading and Sexual Difference* (Baltimore: Johns Hopkins University Press, 1981).

77 Lathers, "Decadent Goddess," 65.

78 The epigraph of this last chapter ("Fate") is the only one from the Bible's book of Genesis.

79 Villiers uses the Latin version of this citation for the actual epigraph of the chapter "Fatum"; this is the footnote by Satiat of the French translation, 409.

80 Felicia Miller Frank, *The Mechanical Song: Women, Voice, and the Artificial in Nineteenth-Century French Narrative* (Stanford, CA: Stanford University Press, 1995), 159.

81 Kaja Silverman, "Liberty, Maternity, Commodification," *New Formations*, no. 5 (Summer 1988): 79.

82 Shelley Wood Cordulack, "A Franco-American Battle of Beams: Electricity and the Selling of Modernity," *Journal of Design History* 18, no. 2 (Summer 2005): 149.

83 Cordulack, 150.

84 Cordulack, 151.

85 See Elizabeth Mitchell, *Liberty's Torch: The Great Adventure to Build the Statue of Liberty* (New York: Grove Press, 2015).

86 Leon Bloy wrote novels, essays, poems and pamphlets; in the foreword to his "Artifices," Jorge Luis Borges references Bloy as one on his "heterogeneous list of authors" whom he continually reread. "Artifices" was paired with "The Garden of Forking Paths," which will be mentioned in relation to hypertext in my epilogue, to create the larger volume of Borges's *Ficciones*.

3. Salomania

1 I will be using the original French title of Wilde's play, *Salomé*, and the equivalent French name for the title character, Salomé, for the majority of references throughout the chapter. Although citations from the play will be offered mainly in English translation, it is important to the project of assessing Wilde's text as necessarily French—linguistically, culturally, and even more broadly—to retain the original French title for the play and its main character. However, Wilde's text and/or character name will be referred to as *Salome*/Salome when directly appropriate, such as when I discuss the English Bodley Head edition (for which Aubrey Beardsley does his illustrations), and otherwise.

2 Robert Stam, *Literature through Film: Realism, Magic and the Art of Adaptation* (London: Wiley-Blackwell, 2004), 65.

3 Stam, 5.

4 Richard Ellmann, *Oscar Wilde* (New York: Vintage Books, 1988), 372.

5 William A. Cohen, "Wilde's French," in *Wilde Discoveries: Traditions, Histories, Archives*, ed. Joseph Bristow (Toronto: University of Toronto Press, 2013), 236.

6 Cohen, 235, 240.

7 "Oscar Wilde Repudiates England for France," *New York Times*, July 18, 1892, 2.

8 Wilde, in Joseph Donohue, "Distance, Death and Desire in Salome," in *The Cambridge Companion to Oscar Wilde*, ed. Peter Raby (Cambridge: Cambridge University Press, 1997), 118. Nicholas Frankel writes that the 1894 text of *Salomé* could also be "the physical embodiment of what Vivian, in 'The Decay of Lying,' would call a 'beautiful, untrue thing'"; Frankel, *Oscar Wilde's Decorated Books* (Ann Arbor: University of Michigan Press, 2000), 72.

9 Merlin Holland, *Oscar Wilde: A Life in Letters* (London: Fourth Estate, 2003), 161.

10 See Cohen, "Wilde's French," 248.

11 William Tydeman and Steven Price, *Wilde: Salome* (Cambridge: Cambridge University Press, 1996), 12.

12 Kerry Powell, *Oscar Wilde and the Theatre of the 1890s* (Cambridge: Cambridge University Press, 2009), 40.

13 Ellmann, *Oscar Wilde*, 371.

14 Sarah Bernhardt, *The Art of the Theatre* (New York: Books for Libraries Press, 1969), 50.

15 Ellmann, *Oscar Wilde*, 118.

16 Powell, *Theatre of the 1890s*, 42.

17 Holland, *Oscar Wilde*, 164.

18 Frankel, *Oscar Wilde's Decorated Books*, 49.

19 Powell, *Theatre of the 1890s*, 41.

20 Oscar Wilde, *De Profundis* (New York: Modern Library, 2000), 115.

21 Françoise Meltzer, *Salome and the Dance of Writing: Portraits of Mimesis in Literature* (Chicago: University of Chicago Press, 1987), 19.

22 Frankel, *Oscar Wilde's Decorated Books*, 51. Perhaps part of an attempt by Douglas to revise his fin de siècle reputation as Wilde's boy toy and to solidify a more respectable reputation for himself after becoming a husband and father.

23 Frankel, 51.

24 Some of the original targets of the satire included Dante Gabriel Rossetti and James McNeill Whistler.

25 Ellmann, *Oscar Wilde*, 151.

26 John Stokes, *The French Actress and Her English Audience* (Cambridge: Cambridge University Press, 2005), 138.

27 Roy Morris Jr., *Declaring His Genius: Oscar Wilde in North America* (Cambridge, MA: Belknap Press, 2013), 95.
28 "Did Sarony Invent Oscar Wilde?," *New York Times*, December 14, 1883, 4, https://timesmachine.nytimes.com/timesmachine/1883/12/14/106266967.html?pageNumber=4.
29 Gregory Castle, "Misrecognizing Wilde: Media and Performance on the American Tour of 1882," in *Wilde Discoveries*, ed. Joseph Bristow (Toronto: University of Toronto Press, 2013), 87.
30 Castle, 91, 93.
31 Castle, 103.
32 Ellmann, *Oscar Wilde*, 428–429.
33 Elaine Showalter, *Sexual Anarchy: Gender and Culture at the Fin de Siècle* (New York: Penguin, 1990), 156.
34 Wilde, *De Profundis*.
35 Joseph Bristow, "Biographies," in *Palgrave Advances in Oscar Wilde Studies*, ed. Frederick S. Roden (London: Palgrave, 2004), 28.
36 Bristow, 28.
37 Kerry Powell, *Acting Wilde: Victorian Sexuality, Theater, and Oscar Wilde* (Cambridge: Cambridge University Press, 2009), 4.
38 Allison Pease, "Aestheticism and Aesthetic Theory," in *Palgrave Advances in Oscar Wilde Studies*, ed. Frederick S. Rosen (New York: Palgrave, 2005), 111.
39 Castle, "Misrecognizing Wilde," 93.
40 Ellmann, *Oscar Wilde*, 344.
41 Enrique Gómez Carrillo, "How Oscar Wilde Dreamed of Salomé," in *Oscar Wilde: Interviews and Recollections*, ed. E. H. Mikhail (New York: Barnes and Noble, 1979), 194.
42 Gómez Carrillo, 194.
43 Regenia Gagnier, *Idylls of the Marketplace: Oscar Wilde and the Victorian Public* (Stanford, CA: Stanford University Press, 1986), 141, 165.
44 Dana Seitler, *Atavistic Tendencies: The Culture of Science in American Modernity* (Minneapolis: University of Minnesota Press, 2008), 1.
45 Seitler, 1.
46 See Gulru Cakmak, "'For the Strong-Minded Alone': Evolution, Female Atavism, and Degeneration in Aubrey Beardsley's *Salomé*," in *Decadence, Degeneration, and the End*, ed. Marja Härmänmaa and Christopher Nissen (New York: Palgrave Macmillan, 2014), 183–200.
47 Kelly Hurley, *The Gothic Body: Sexuality, Materialism, and Degeneration at the Fin de Siècle* (Cambridge: Cambridge University Press, 1996), 71.
48 Hurley, 66.
49 Sandra Siegel, "Literature and Degeneration: The Representation of 'Decadence,'" in *Degeneration: The Dark Side of Progress*, ed. J. Edward Chamberlin and Sander L. Gilman (New York: Columbia University Press, 1985), 209.
50 Originally published in German in 1892 under the title *Entartung*.
51 Max Nordau, *Degeneration* (London: Heinemann, 1895), 317, 319.
52 Nordau, 327.
53 Bruce Haley, "Wilde's 'Decadence' and the Positivist Tradition," *Victorian Studies* 28, no. 2 (Winter 1985): 223.
54 Haley, 221.
55 Ellis in Haley, 228.
56 Meltzer, *Salome and the Dance of Writing*, 13.

57 Franz Meier, "Oscar Wilde and the Myth of the *Femme Fatale* in *Fin-de-Siècle* Culture," in *The Importance of Reinventing Oscar: Versions of Wilde during the Last 100 Years*, ed. Uwe Boker, Richard Corballis, and Julie Hibbard (Amsterdam: Rodopi, 2002), 119.
58 Ellmann, *Oscar Wilde*, 340.
59 Donohue, "Distance, Death and Desire," 128.
60 Garelick, *Rising Star*, 131.
61 J. K. Huysmans, *Against Nature* (Oxford: Oxford University Press, 2009), 42.
62 Meltzer, *Salome and the Dance of Writing*, 28.
63 Huysmans, *Against Nature*, 50.
64 Powell, *Theater of the 1890s*, 45.
65 Powell, 45.
66 Ellmann, *Oscar Wilde*, 376.
67 Carrillo, "How Oscar Wilde Dreamed of Salomé," 194.
68 Carrillo, 192, 195.
69 W. J. T. Mitchell, *Picture Theory* (Chicago: University of Chicago Press, 1994), 152.
70 Oscar Wilde, *The Decay of Lying and Other Essays* (New York: Penguin Classic, 2010), 288.
71 Brian Glavey, "Dazzling Estrangement: Modernism, Queer Ekphrasis, and the Spatial Form of 'Nightwood,'" *PMLA* 124, no. 3 (May 2009): 751.
72 See "The Greek Life of Oscar Wilde" in Stefano Evangelista, *British Aestheticism and Ancient Greece: Hellenism, Reception, Gods in Exile* (London: Palgrave Macmillan, 2009), 125–126.
73 Brian Glavey, *The Wallflower Avant-Garde: Modernism, Sexuality, and Queer Ekphrasis* (Oxford: Oxford University Press, 2016), 7.
74 Glavey, "Dazzling Estrangement," 757.
75 Butler quoted in Glavey, *Wallflower Avant-Garde*, 8. For more regarding gender identity as performance, "performatively constituted by the very 'expressions' that are said to be its results," see Judith Butler's seminal work *Gender Trouble: Feminism and the Subversion of Identity* (New York: Routledge, 1999), 33.
76 Glavey, 8, 7.
77 Castle, "Misrecognizing Wilde," 93.
78 Castle, 100.
79 W. J. T. Mitchell, *What Do Pictures Want? The Lives and Loves of Images* (Chicago: University of Chicago Press, 2005), 58.
80 William Shakespeare, *Romeo and Juliet*, in *The Norton Shakespeare* (New York: W. W. Norton, 1997), 2.2.111.
81 James Winchell, "Wilde and Huysmans: Autonomy, Reference, and the Myth of Expiation," in *Critical Essays on Oscar Wilde*, ed. Regenia Gagnier (New York: G. K. Hall, 1991), 226.
82 Garelick, *Rising Star*, 128.
83 Stephen Arata, *Fictions of Loss in the Victorian Fin de Siècle* (Cambridge: Cambridge University Press, 1996), 91.
84 Gagnier, *Idylls of the Marketplace*, 165.
85 Glavey, *Wallflower Avant-Garde*, 6.
86 Letter written to Lord Alfred Douglas [June 2, 1897?] from the Hôtel de la Plage, Berneval-sur-Mer, in Holland, *Oscar Wilde*, 254.
87 David Wayne Thomas, "The 'Strange Music' of Salome: Oscar Wilde's Rhetoric of Verbal Musicality," *Mosaic* 33, no. 1 (2000): 21.
88 Thomas, 21.

89 See Brad Bucknell, "Re-reading Pater: The Musical Aesthetics of Temporality," *Modern Fiction Studies* 38, no. 3 (Autumn 1992): 597–614.
90 Wilde, *De Profundis*, 67.
91 Thomas, "The 'Strange Music' of Salome," 27.
92 Spoken by Gilbert, in dialogue with Ernest, who insists that Gilbert treats "the world as if it were a crystal ball," reversing it "to please a wilful fancy." Oscar Wilde, "The Critic as Artist," in *The Artist as Critic: Critical Writings of Oscar Wilde*, ed. Richard Ellmann (New York: Random House, 1969), 359.
93 According to Matthew, when he heard of the fame of Jesus after John's death, he thought that it was John the Baptist risen, "and therefore mighty works do shew forth themselves in him."
94 Katherine Brown Downey, *Perverse Midrash: Oscar Wilde, André Gide, and the Censorship of Biblical Drama* (New York: Continuum, 2004), 101.
95 Robert Ross in *Salome* (New York: Dover Publications, 1967), xvii–xviii.
96 Rodney Shewan, *Oscar Wilde: Art and Egotism* (New York: Barnes and Noble, 1977), 134.
97 Marcia Falk, *The Song of Songs: A New Translation and Interpretation* (San Francisco: HarperCollins, 1990), 113.
98 Falk, 103.
99 Elliott L. Gilbert, "'Tumult of Images': Wilde, Beardsley, 'Salome,'" *Victorian Studies* 26, no. 2 (Winter 1983): 133–159.
100 Carey Walsh, *Exquisite Desire: Religion, the Erotic and the Song of Songs* (Minneapolis: Fortress Press, 2000), 58.
101 Garelick, *Rising Star*, 138.
102 Ewa Kuryluk, *Salome and Judas in the Cave of Sex* (Evanston, IL: Northwestern University Press, 1987).
103 Francis Landy, "The Song of Songs and the Garden of Eden," *Journal of Biblical Literature* 98, no. 4 (December 1979): 522.
104 Garelick, *Rising Star*, 138.
105 Norbert Kohl, *Oscar Wilde: The Works of a Conformist Rebel* (Cambridge: Cambridge University Press, 1980), 182.
106 Landy, "Song of Songs," 513.
107 The word "aesthetically" comes from the German root of the word, meaning "in good taste."
108 Cohen, "Wilde's French," 240–241.
109 In the King James Bible, John 6:51 recounts the promise made by Jesus to his people: "I am the living bread which came down from heaven: if any man eat of this bread, he shall live forever: and the bread that I will give is my flesh, which I will give for the life of the world."
110 J. M. Blanchard, "Of Cannibalism and Autobiography," *MLN* 93, no. 4 (May 1978): 667.
111 Motohiro Kojima, "Leopold Bloom's 'metempsychosis' and 'parallax' in *Ulysses*," *Journal of Irish Studies* 20 (2005): 24.
112 Glavey, *Wallflower Avant-Garde*, 4.
113 *Oxford English Dictionary Online*, s.v. "palingenesis (n.)," accessed May 27, 2021, https://www-oed-com.proxy.lib.fsu.edu/view/Entry/136328?redirectedFrom=palingenesis#eid.
114 Ellmann, *Oscar Wilde*, 250.
115 The Beardsley drawing from *The Studio*, April 1893, was originally titled *J'ai baisé ta bouche Iokanaan* and led Bodley Head publisher John Lane to commission him to

execute a series of illustrations for the first English edition of the play, in which the reproduction of this image was named *The Climax*. According to Sir Kenneth Clark, *The Studio* drawing "aroused more horror and indignation than any graphic work hitherto produced in England"; *The Annotated Oscar Wilde*, 313. Also see Ellmann, *Oscar Wilde*, 376.

116 Donohue, "Distance, Death and Desire," 122. Beardsley drew Wilde within four of his illustrations for *Salomé*.

117 Ellmann, *Oscar Wilde*, 307.

118 See Michael Bennett, ed., *Refiguring Oscar Wilde's Salome* (Amsterdam: Rodopi, 2011), 125.

119 Frankel, *Oscar Wilde's Decorated Books*, 73.

120 Frankel, 73.

121 Choe, "The One," 33.

122 Wilde, *Annotated Oscar Wilde*, 164. We recognize that Sibyl Vane only plays Shakespearean heroines: Rosalind from *As You Like It*, Imogen the daughter of the king in *Cymbeline*, and Juliet from *Romeo and Juliet*. Jaques's famous monologue from *As You Like It* offers an apt sentiment for Wilde's theory of theatrical performance as, in itself, a representation of human growth and existence: "All the world's a stage / And all the men and women merely players; / They have their exits and their entrances, / And one man in his time plays many parts, / His acts being seven ages" (2.7.139–143).

123 *Oxford English Dictionary Online*, s.v. "sibyl (n.)," accessed August 21, 2020, https://www-oed-com.proxy.lib.fsu.edu/view/Entry/179151?redirectedFrom=sibyl#eid.

124 *Oxford English Dictionary Online*, s.v. "vane (n.)," accessed August 21, 2020, https://www-oed-com.proxy.lib.fsu.edu/view/Entry/221362?redirectedFrom=vane#eid.

125 Gagnier, *Idylls of the Marketplace*, 99.

126 Wilde, *Annotated Oscar Wilde*, 182.

127 Wilde, 141. Cf. Patrice Hannon, "Theatre and Theory in the Language of 'Dorian Gray,'" *Victorian Literature and Culture* 19 (1991): 158.

128 Wilde, *Decay of Lying*, 52.

129 Wilde, *Annotated Oscar Wilde*, 189. Sibyl as a "reed through which Shakespeare's music sounded richer" seems like a sentiment directly borrowed from Sarah Bernhardt, who, in describing the occupation of the actor-artist, notes, "The artist must be like one of those sounding discs which vibrate to every wind, and are agitated by the slightest breeze" (*Art of the Theatre*, 104). It is also important to note that the extremely thin Bernhardt was oft caricatured as "a slender reed." See Jonathan Freedman, "Transformations of a Jewish Princess: Salomé and the Remaking of the Jewish Female Body from Sarah Bernhardt to Betty Boop," *Philological Quarterly* 92, no. 1 (2013): 89–114.

130 Ellmann, *Oscar Wilde*, 117.

131 Bernhardt, *Art of the Theatre*, 105.

132 A. B. Walkley, *Playhouse Impressions* (New York: Garland, 1984), 241.

133 Wilde, *Decay of Lying*, 43.

134 Ellmann, *Oscar Wilde*, 118.

135 Merlin Holland and Rupert Hart-Davis, eds. *The Complete Letters of Oscar Wilde* (New York: Henry Holt, 2000), 834. That "serpent of the old Nile," as Wilde refers to Bernhardt, is the moniker for Cleopatra in Shakespeare's *Antony and Cleopatra*, act 1, scene 5.

136 In Mary Louise Roberts, *Disruptive Acts: The New Woman in Fin-de-Siècle France* (Chicago: University of Chicago Press, 2002), 166–167.
137 Calling her a "strange being" seems a repetition of what Sigmund Freud wrote in 1884 upon seeing Bernhardt's enchanted performance of *Theodora*: "Strange Creature!"
138 McCreary, "Louis Delluc," 28.
139 Gamaliel Bradford, *Daughters of Eve* (New York: New Impressions, 1969), 271.
140 Bernhardt was brought to Edison's home by her agent, Edward Jarrett, who, like Bernhardt herself, was always eager for headlines. The following day's headlines read "THE MOST FAMOUS MAN IN THE UNITED STATES MEETS THE MOST FAMOUS WOMAN IN FRANCE." For more information, see Arthur Gold and Robert Fizdale, *The Divine Sarah: A Life of Sarah Bernhardt* (New York: Alfred A. Knopf, 1991), 174. The recording of her recitation of some lines from Phédre that Edison made on that evening in 1880 can be heard today. The audio file has been preserved by the Cylinder Preservation and Digitization Project at the Donald C. Davidson Library, University of California, Santa Barbara.
141 Victoria Duckett, "Performing Art Nouveau: Sarah Bernhardt and the Development of Industrial Modernism," *Modernism/Modernity* 4, cycle 3 (2019), https://modernismmodernity.org/forums/posts/performing-art-nouveau.
142 Duckett.
143 Duckett.
144 Stephen W. Bush, "Bernhardt and Rejane in Pictures," *Moving Picture World*, March 1912, 760.
145 Edward Said, *Orientalism* (New York: Vintage Books, 1979), 103
146 Dominic Montserrat, ed., *Changing Bodies, Changing Meanings: Studies on the Human Body in Antiquity* (London: Routledge, 1998), 178.
147 Wilde, *Decay of Lying*, 16.
148 Vittorio Gallese, "Naturalizing Aesthetic Experience: The Role of (Liberated) Embodied Simulation," *Projections* 12, no. 2 (December 2018): 50–59.
149 For more discussion of the relationship of the thoughts of Plato, Wilde, and Deleuze's notion of the "actual-virtual," see Giles Whiteley's *Oscar Wilde and the Simulacrum: The Truth of Masks* (London: Legenda, 2015), 20.

4. Statuesque Cinema

1 Considering my opening analysis in chapter 2, it bears mentioning this quote of Eisenstein's has already been used as an epigraph, specifically in Edward L. Ruhe, "Film: The 'Literary' Approach," *Literature/Film Quarterly* 1, no. 1 (Winter 1973): 76–83.
2 Sergei Eisenstein, "Dickens, Griffith, and the Film Today," in *Film Form: Essays in Film Theory* (San Diego: Harcourt, 1977), 233.
3 Eisenstein, 210, 213. Eisenstein does make the important note that D. W. Griffith actually directed a film adaptation of *The Cricket on the Hearth* in 1909.
4 Eisenstein, 195.
5 Sergei Eisenstein, "The Cinematographic Principle and the Ideogram," in *Film Form*, 37.
6 Anne Nesbet, *Savage Junctures: Sergei Eisenstein and the Shape of Thinking* (London: Tauris, 2007), 142.
7 Aristotle defines motion as and through change of any kind (metamorphosis, so we might say), and the very actuality of being movable—thus a conjunction of two concepts that seem inherently contradictory.

8 Janina Wellmann, *The Form of Becoming: Embryology and the Epistemology of Rhythm, 1760–1830* (New York: Zone Books, 2017), 267.
9 Wellmann, 283.
10 Wellmann, 282. She calls one of her chapter sections "An 'Assemblage of Embryos': Pander's Plates." For more information on the relationship between embryology and aestheticism, or the specific organicism they argue is an essential part of Eisenstein's film criticism, see Gilbert and Faber, "Looking at Embryos: The Visual and Conceptual Aesthetics of Emerging Form," in *The Elusive Synthesis: Aesthetics and Science*, ed. Alfred Tauber (Dordrecht, The Netherlands: Kluwer, 1997), 125–152.
11 John B. Wallingford, "The 200 Year Effort to See the Embryo," *Science* 365, no. 6455 (August 23, 2019): 758–759.
12 Jimena Canales, "Dead and Alive: Micro-cinematography between Physics and Biology," *Configurations* 23, no. 2 (Spring 2015): 251.
13 Tom Gunning differentiates "animation" as those cinematic images that are artificially made to move, as opposed to the movement captured by continuous motion picture cinematography.
14 Janina Wellmann, "Biological Motion," Fellows' Presentation Series at the Radcliffe Institute for Advanced Study, May 9, 2018, https://www.youtube.com/watch?v=feFAs3GDbMo.
15 For a full discussion of the use of film in the study of cell development, see Janina Wellmann's "Model and Movement: Studying Cell Movement in Early Morphogenesis, 1900 to the Present," *History and Philosophy of the Life Sciences* 40 (2018): 59, https://pubmed.ncbi.nlm.nih.gov/30206717/.
16 Gunning, "Birth of Film," 14.
17 See Gunning. Footage available to view online at the Library of Congress: https://www.loc.gov/item/00694299/.
18 Gunning, 19.
19 Lumière in Stephen Heath, *Questions of Cinema* (Bloomington: Indiana University Press, 1981), 4.
20 Gunning, "Birth of Film," 36. Gorky famously described his first film-watching experience as a visit to "the Kingdom of Shadows."
21 Antonia Lant, "The Curse of the Pharaoh, or How Cinema Contracted Egyptomania," *Visions of the East: Orientalism in Film*, ed. Matthew Bernstein and Gaylyn Studlar (New Brunswick, NJ: Rutgers University Press, 1997), 71.
22 Pantelis Michelakis and Maria Wyke, "Introduction: Silent Cinema, Antiquity, and 'the Exhaustless Urn of Time,'" in *The Ancient World in Silent Cinema*, ed. Pantelis Michelakis and Maria Wyke (Cambridge: Cambridge University Press, 2013), 8.
23 Lant, "Curse of the Pharaoh," 80–81.
24 Dominic Montserrat, "Unidentified Human Remains: Mummies and the Erotics of Biography," in Montserrat, *Changing Bodies, Changing Meanings*, 173.
25 Montserrat, 173.
26 In *Sexual Personae*, Camille Paglia originally suggests it as mummy portrait (New Haven, CT: Yale University Press, 1990); for fuller discussion, also see Montserrat, "Unidentified Human Remains," 178–180.
27 André Bazin, "The Ontology of the Photographic Image," in *What Is Cinema?*, 13.
28 Bazin, 14.
29 Bazin, 14.
30 Bazin, 15, 14.
31 Lant, "Curse of the Pharaoh," 71.

32 Lynn Meskell, "Consuming Bodies: Cultural Fantasies of Ancient Egypt," *Body and Society* 4, no. 1 (1998): 66.
33 Bazin, "Ontology of the Photographic Image," 9.
34 Philip Rosen, *Change Mummified: Cinema, Historicity, Theory* (Minneapolis: University of Minnesota Press, 2001), 13.
35 Lant, "Curse of the Pharaoh," 101.
36 Lant, 101.
37 Basil Glynn, *The Mummy on Screen: Orientalism and Monstrosity in Horror Cinema* (London: Bloomsbury, 2019).
38 Glynn, 72.
39 Wilhelm Worringer, *Abstraction and Empathy* (Chicago: Elephant, 1997), 4.
40 Worringer, 12.
41 Worringer in Laura Marcus, "'Hieroglyphics in motion': representing ancient Egypt and the Middle East in film theory and criticism of the silent period," in *Ancient World in Silent Cinema*, 80.
42 Michelakis and Wyke, *Ancient World in Silent Cinema*, 10.
43 Hawthorne, "Dis-covering the Female," 718.
44 Vitagraph also released a film called *The Egyptian Mummy* the year before, in 1914.
45 Dannenfelt, "Egyptian Mumia," 164.
46 Warren R. Dawson, "Making a Mummy," *Journal of Egyptian Archaeology* 13, no. ½ (April 1927): 40.
47 Dawson, "Mummy as Drug," *Proceedings of the Royal Society of Medicine* 21, no. 1 (1927): 34–35.
48 Philip McCouat, "The Life and Death of Mummy Brown," *Journal of Art in Society* (2013), accessed May 27, 2021, http://www.artinsociety.com/the-life-and-death-of-mummy-brown.html.
49 For instance, the July 31, 1856, edition of the *Syracuse Standard* noted for its readers that it was printed on paper made from these Egyptian rags. For more information, see Nicholson Baker's book *Double Fold: Libraries and the Assault on Paper* (New York: Random House, 2001).
50 Michelakis and Wyke, *Ancient World in Silent Cinema*, 5.
51 Vachel Lindsay, *The Art of the Moving Picture* (New York: Modern Library, 2000), 74.
52 Tom Gunning, "Vachel Lindsay: Theory of Movie Hieroglyphics," in *Thinking in the Dark*, ed. R. Barton Palmer and Murray Pomerance (New Brunswick, NJ: Rutgers University Press, 2015), 21.
53 Lindsay, *Art of the Moving Picture*, 170.
54 Bazin, "Ontology of the Photographic Image," 9.
55 Linda Williams, "Film Body: An Implantation of Perversions," *Cinetracts* 3, no. 4 (Winter 1981): 28.
56 Williams, 28.
57 Antonia Lant, "Cinema in the time of the pharaohs," in Michelakis and Wyke, *Ancient World in Silent Cinema*, 60.
58 See Lucy Fischer, *Cinematernity: Film, Motherhood, Genre* (Princeton, NJ: Princeton University Press, 2014).
59 Williams, "Film Body," 31.
60 Miriam Bratu Hansen, "America, Paris, the Alps: Kracauer (and Benjamin) on Cinema and Modernity," in *Cinema and the Invention of Modern Life*, eds. Leo Charney and Vanessa R. Schwartz (Berkeley: University of California Press, 1995), 365.
61 See Matei Calinescu, *Five Faces of Modernity: Modernism, Avant-Garde, Decadence, Kitsch, Postmodernism* (Durham: Duke University Press, 1987).

62 In Bradshaw, Marcus, and Roach, *Moving Modernisms*, 2.
63 Hansen, "America, Paris, the Alps," 380.
64 Jacques Rancière, "The Archaeomodern Turn," in *Walter Benjamin and the Demands of History*, ed. Michael P. Steinberg (Ithaca, NY: Cornell University Press, 1996), 28.
65 The kinetoscope was renamed the Vitascope in order for the Edison Manufacturing Company to agree to market the invention, under a new name associated only with Edison. Upon its premiere in 1896, the *New York Times* proclaimed, "The views were all wonderfully real and singularly exhilarating." For more information, see Martin V. Melosi, *Thomas A. Edison and the Modernization of America* (New York: Harper Collins, 1990), 131. For more information on the cinematic projection of the Butterfly Dance, see Charles Musser, *The Emergence of Cinema: The American Screen to 1907* (Berkeley: University of California Press, 1994).
66 Tom Gunning, "Loie Fuller and the Art of Motion: Body, Light, Electricity, and the Origins of Cinema," in *Camera Obscura, Camera Lucida: Essays in Honor of Annette Michelson*, ed. Richard Allen and Malcolm Turvey (Amsterdam: Amsterdam University Press, 2003), 85.
67 Rhonda Garelick, *Electric Salome: Loie Fuller's Performance of Modernism* (Princeton, NJ: Princeton University Press, 2009), 92.
68 Garelick, 109.
69 Garelick, 4.
70 Garelick, 5.
71 Garelick, 6.
72 Gunning, "Birth of Film," 27.
73 Tom Gunning, "The Attraction of Motion: Modern Representation and the Image of Movement," in *Film 1900: Technology, Perception, Culture*, ed. Annemone Ligensa and Klaus Kreimeier (Bloomington: Indiana University Press, 2009), 166–167.
74 See Elizabeth Coffman, "Women in Motion: Loie Fuller and the 'Interpenetration' of Art and Science," *Camera Obscura* 17, no. 1 (2002).
75 Mary Ann Doane, *Femmes Fatales: Feminism, Film Theory, Psychoanalysis* (New York: Routledge, 1991), 72.
76 See Lois Cucullu's "Modern Women's Sexual Turn from *Salomé* to *Ulysses*," in *Wilde Discoveries: Traditions, Histories, Archives* (Toronto: University of Toronto Press, 2013), 274.
77 Lois Cucullu, "Wilde and Wilder Salomés: Modernizing the Nubile Princess," *Modernism/Modernity* 18, no. 3 (September 2011): 506.
78 Freedman, "Transformations of a Jewish Princess," 97.
79 Freedman, 99.
80 Toni Bentley, *Sisters of Salome* (New Haven, CT: Yale University Press, 2002), 40.
81 Petra Dierkes-Thrun, *Salome's Modernity: Oscar Wilde and the Aesthetics of Transgression* (Ann Arbor: University of Michigan Press, 2011), 140.
82 Dierkes-Thrun notes that the "cultural vogue" (141) of Orientalism in America at this time may have influenced Nazimova's choice of subject. For more information, also see Gaylyn Studlar's "Out-Salomeing Salome," in Bernstein and Studlar, *Visions of the East*.
83 Dierkes-Thrun, *Salome's Modernity*, 139.
84 Dierkes-Thrun, 146.
85 Steven Price, "Salome on Sunset Boulevard," in Bennett, *Refiguring Oscar Wilde's Salome*, 258.
86 Price, 258.

87 William Rothman, "Virtue and Villainy in the Face of the Camera," in *The "I" of the Camera: Essays in Film Criticism, History, and Aesthetics* (New York: Cambridge University Press, 2004), 81.
88 See Marie-Luise Kohlke, "Sexsation and the Neo-Victorian Novel: Orientalising the Nineteenth Century in Contemporary Fiction," in *Negotiating Sexual Idioms: Image, Text, Performance*, ed. Kohlke and Luisa Orza (Amsterdam: Brill, 2008), 53–77.
89 In a further conflation of art and reality, all the photos in the film's mise-en-scène are actually from the personal collection of Gloria Swanson.
90 Daniel Brown, "Wilde and Wilder," *PMLA* 119, no. 5 (October 2004): 1221.
91 Gloria Swanson, *Swanson on Swanson* (New York: Random House, 1980), 489.
92 Edgar Morin, *The Stars* (Minneapolis: University of Minnesota Press, 2005), 131.
93 Morin, 42, 131.
94 Michael Williams, "Gloria Swanson as Venus," in Michelakis and Wyke, *Ancient World in Silent Cinema*, 133.
95 Williams, 136.
96 See Matthew Brio's *The Dada Cyborg: Visions of the New Human in Weimar Berlin* (Minneapolis: University of Minnesota Press, 2009).
97 Paul Monty Paret, "Forget Rudolf Belling: Getting the Carl Einstein We Deserve," in *Carl Einstein and the European Avant-Garde*, ed. Nicola Creighton and Andreas Kramer (Berlin: De Gruyter, 2012), 107.
98 "Rudolf Belling," Thomas Michel Contemporary Art, http://thomas-michel-contemporary-art.de/rudolf-belling/?lang=en.
99 See Lotte Eisner, *The Haunted Screen: Expressionism in the German Cinema and the Influence of Max Reinhardt* (Berkeley: University of California Press, 1969).
100 Notably, it was Schulze-Mittendorff's daughter Bertina who commissioned the work.
101 "Metropolis Robot," Kropserkel, www.kropserkel.com/robot.html.
102 For more information, see Michelle E. Bloom, "Pygmalionesque Delusions and Illusions of Movement: Animation from Hoffmann to Truffaut," *Comparative Literature* 52, no. 4 (Autumn 2000): 300.
103 Von Harbou authored the science fiction novel in 1925, and then somewhat simultaneously the screenplay for the 1927 film. The novel was serialized in 1926 in *Illustriertes Blatt* accompanied by still shots from the film adaptation's production.
104 Heath, *Questions of Cinema*, 58.
105 Tom Gunning, *The Films of Fritz Lang: Allegories of Vision and Modernity* (London: BFI Publishing, 2000), 68.
106 Rosemary Muir Wright, "The Great Whore in the Illustrated Apocalypse Cycles," *Journal of Medieval History* 23, no. 3 (1997): 200.
107 Gunning, *Films of Fritz Lang*, 74.
108 Andreas Huyssen, "The Vamp and the Machine," in *Fritz Lang's Metropolis: Cinematic Visions of Technology and Fear*, ed. Michael Minder and Holger Bachmann (Rochester, NY: Camden House, 2000), 201.
109 Gunning, *Films of Fritz Lang*, 71, 81.
110 Robert Kolker, *The Extraordinary Image: Orson Welles, Alfred Hitchcock, Stanley Kubrick and the Reimagining of Cinema* (New Brunswick, NJ: Rutgers University Press, 2017), 130.
111 Ludmilla Jordanova, "Science, Machines, and Gender," in Minder and Bachmann, *Fritz Lang's Metropolis*, 189.
112 Patrick McGilligan, *Fritz Lang: The Nature of the Beast* (New York: St. Martin's, 1997), 122, 353.

5. See-through Woman

1 James M. Vest, *Hitchcock and France: The Forging of an Auteur* (Westport, CT: Praeger, 2003), 183.
2 Vest, 22.
3 Quoted in François Truffaut, Alfred Hitchcock, and Helen G. Scott, *Hitchcock* (New York: Simon and Schuster, 1967), 17. Discussion of *Vertigo* by the *Cahiers* contributors proved minimal, and the first book-length critical examination of Hitchcock—*Hitchcock: Classiques du Cinéma*—was published in 1957, the year during which Hitchcock filmed *Vertigo*. The book, written by Claude Chabrol and Eric Rohmer, ends on an analysis of Hitchcock's forty-fourth film, *The Wrong Man*; *Vertigo* is his forty-fifth.
4 Vest, *Hitchcock and France*, 2–3.
5 Remi Fournier Lanzoni maintains that "one associates Henri-Georges Clouzot, known as the "French Hitchcock," with the development of psychological thrillers in France during the postwar era"; Lanzoni, *French Cinema: From Its Beginnings to the Present*, 2nd ed. (New York: Bloomsbury, 2015), 167. However, the nickname was also periodically used for French film directors Claude Chabrol and Louis Malle. See footnote 11 in Joan Hawkins, "'See It from the Beginning': Hitchcock's Reconstruction of Film History," in *Framing Hitchcock: Selected Essays from the Hitchcock Annual*, ed. Sidney Gottlieb and Christopher Brookhouse (Detroit: Wayne State University Press, 2002), 384.
6 Vest, *Hitchcock and France*, 98.
7 See Vest, 168.
8 Truffaut, *Hitchcock*, 243.
9 Truffaut, 243, 247.
10 Dan Auiler, *Vertigo: The Making of a Hitchcock Classic* (New York: St. Martin's, 1998), 28.
11 Samuels, *Hitchcock's Bi-textuality*, 77.
12 Samuels, 77.
13 Lesley Brill *The Hitchcock Romance: Love and Irony in Hitchcock's Films* (Princeton, NJ: Princeton University Press, 1988), 207.
14 Patrick McGilligan, *Alfred Hitchcock: A Life in Darkness and Light* (New York: Harper, 2003), 548.
15 Brill, *The Hitchcock Romance*, 207.
16 Alfred Hitchcock, "Why I Am Afraid of the Dark," in *Hitchcock on Hitchcock*, ed. Sidney Gottlieb (Berkeley: University of California Press, 1995), 143, 145.
17 Robin Wood, *Hitchcock's Films Revisited*, rev. ed. (New York: Columbia University Press, 2002).
18 Charles Higham, "Hitchcock's World," *Film Quarterly* 16, no. 2 (Winter 1962–1963): 3–16.
19 Laura Mulvey, "Visual Pleasure and Narrative Cinema," in *Film Theory and Criticism*, 7th ed., ed. Baudry and Cohen (New York: Oxford University Press, 2009), 711 (emphasis mine).
20 Mulvey, 715.
21 Mulvey, 715.
22 Mulvey, 720.
23 Tania Modleski, *The Women Who Knew Too Much: Hitchcock and Feminist Theory* (New York: Routledge, 1988), 91.

24 See Wood, *Hitchcock's Films Revisited*, 111. Wood claims that when the opening scene ends, "We do not see, and are never told, how he got down from the gutter: there seems no possible way he *could* have got down. The effect is of having him, throughout the film, metaphorically suspended over a great abyss."
25 Deborah Linderman, "The Mise-en-Abîme in Hitchcock's *Vertigo*," *Cinema Journal* 30, no. 4 (Summer 1991): 51–74.
26 Vest, *Hitchcock and France*, 180.
27 Richard Allen, *Hitchcock's Romantic Irony* (New York: Columbia University Press, 2007), 204.
28 Truffaut, *Hitchcock*, 184–185.
29 Truffaut, 185.
30 Peter Wollen, *Signs and Meaning in the Cinema* (Bloomington: Indiana University Press, 1972), 77.
31 Alfred Hitchcock, "Highly Informative Interview with Alfred Hitchcock," in *Alfred Hitchcock Interviews* (Newark, NJ: Audible, 2016), https://books.apple.com/us/audiobook/alfred-hitchcock-interviews/id1086727144.
32 Lucy Fischer, "The Trick Film: The Lady Vanishes: Women, Magic, and the Movies," in *Cinematernity: Film, Motherhood, Genre* (Princeton, NJ: Princeton University Press, 2014), 39.
33 Slavoj Žižek, "*Vertigo*: The Drama of a Deceived Platonist," in *Hitchcock Annual* (2003–2004), 69.
34 Žižek, 70.
35 Vest, *Hitchcock and France*, 96.
36 Joel Gunz, "Alfred Hitchcock and Paul Klee at the Intersection of Artistic Invention," October 2 2015, https://medium.com/@joelgunz/alfred-hitchcock-and-paul-klee-at-the-intersection-of-artistic-invention-a9713f1e03d8.
37 Brigitte Peucker, "Aesthetic Space in Hitchcock," in *A Companion to Alfred Hitchcock*, ed. Thomas Leitch and Leland Poague (London: Wiley-Blackwell, 2011), 216.
38 Peucker, 216.
39 Julia Tanski affirms that "Hitchcock's women are screens on which infinite metamorphoses are played out"; Tanski, "The Symbolist Woman in Alfred Hitchcock's Films," in *Hitchcock and Art: Fatal Coincidences*, ed. Dominique Paini and Guy Cogeval (Milan: Mazzotta, 2000), 150. Tanski also references Mallarmé's description of *Hérodiade*, inspired by "that divine name . . . red, as a pomegranate," as a parallel to how from word/clay grew the "ripe fruit" of Hitchcock's women: "Hitchcock started with an actress and she became a flower, a statue, a bird" (153).
40 Victor I. Stoichita, *The Pygmalion Effect: From Ovid to Hitchcock* (Chicago: University of Chicago Press, 2008), 184.
41 Robert A. Sobieszek, "Sculpture as the Sum of Its Profiles: François Willème and Photosculpture in France, 1859–1868," *Art Bulletin* 62, no. 4 (1980): 617.
42 Sobieszek, 618.
43 Brigitte Peucker, "The Cut of Representation: Painting and Sculpture in Hitchcock," in *Alfred Hitchcock: Centenary Essays*, ed. Richard Allen and S. Ishii-Gonzalès (London: BFI Publishing, 1999), 150.
44 Peucker, 150.
45 See Vest, *Hitchcock and France*, 168.
46 Allen, *Hitchcock's Romantic Irony*, 204.
47 David M. Lubin, "Hitchcock and Art: Fatal Coincidences," *Artforum* 40, no. 3 (November 2001): 140.

48 Steven Jacobs, "Introduction: The Marble Camera," in *Screening Statues: Sculpture in Film*, ed. Stephen Jacobs, Susan Felleman, Vitio Adriaensens, and Lisa Colpaert (Edinburgh: Edinburgh University Press, 2018).
49 Jacobs, 1–3.
50 See Marcoci, *Original Copy*, 16.
51 See Peter J. Hutchings, "Modernity: A Film by Alfred Hitchcock," *Senses of Cinema*, no. 6 (May 2000), https://www.sensesofcinema.com/2000/conference-for-the-love-of-fear/modernity/.
52 Auiler, *Vertigo*, 51. Taylor had the very actress who played the role of Midge, well-renowned Broadway actress Barbara Bel Geddes, specifically in mind when creating the character she would play on-screen.
53 Hitchcock was sent laundry lists of possible titles for the film, even after he came up with *Vertigo*, which was not so popular with the studio's advertising executives. They sent a message from the New York office that reads: "No execs like *Vertigo* and believe it handicap to selling and advertising picture whether potential customers know what word Vertigo means or not—believe decidedly better title would be 'Face in the Shadow.'" Other suggested titles included "The Face Variations" and "The Mask and the Face." See also, Auiler, *Vertigo*, 113.
54 Peucker, "Aesthetic Space in Hitchcock," 212.
55 Madeleine gives the quasi explanation of how she found Scottie's apartment in order to return to deliver him a thank-you note for rescuing her. She tells him that she remembered Coit Tower as a landmark, which leads her straight back to his apartment. Scottie responds, "That's the first time I've been grateful for Coit Tower." The tower proves to be an unconsciously symbolic choice on the part of Hitchcock (who claimed he used it simply as a "phallic symbol"), because it was built in 1933 at the behest of a woman who bore the same name as the director, Lillie Hitchcock Coit. She was one of the more eccentric female figures in San Francisco history, earning a reputation as a very "unladylike lady" for smoking cigars and often dressing in men's clothes. She was also a firefighting enthusiast from childhood until her death, and today she is considered the patron saint of the city's firefighters. For more information, see the Virtual Museum of the City of San Francisco at www.sfmuseum.org.
56 Modleski, *Women Who Knew Too Much*, 92.
57 Modleski, 92.
58 Linderman, "Mise-en-Abîme in Hitchcock's *Vertigo*," 62.
59 Though Kim Novak is credited as playing the dual roles of Madeleine and Judy, she did not play the "real" Madeleine. The role of "Mrs. Elster" was played by Jean Corbett.
60 Royal S. Brown does an entire reading of *Vertigo* as an Orphic Tragedy and highlights that the authors of *D'entre les morts* specifically allude to the Orpheus myth, having the heroine called "my little Eurydice" several times in the book; Brown, "*Vertigo* As Orphic Tragedy," *Literature/Film Quarterly* 14, no. 1 (1986): 32–43.
61 Sigmund Freud, *Beyond the Pleasure Principle* (New York: W. W. Norton, 1989), 14.
62 R. Barton Palmer, "The Hitchcock Romance and the 70s Paranoid Thriller," in *Alfred Hitchcock: Influence, Imitation and Intertextuality*, ed. David Boyd and R. Barton Palmer (Austin: University of Texas Press, 2006), 86.
63 Pat Kirkham, "Reassessing the Saul Bass and Alfred Hitchcock Collaboration," *West 86th* 18, no. 1 (Spring–Summer 2011), https://www.west86th.bgc.bard.edu/articles/reassessing-the-saul-bass-and-alfred-hitchcock-collaboration/.

64 Bloom, "Pygmalionesque Delusions," 292.
65 Christian Metz, "The Imaginary Signifier," in *Film Theory and Criticism*, 7th ed., ed. Leo Baudry and Marshall Cohen (New York: Oxford University Press, 2009), 696.
66 Marilyn Fabe, "Mourning *Vertigo*," *American Imago* 66, no. 3 (Fall 2009): 347.
67 For more information, see *Vertigo* documentary *Obsessed with "Vertigo,"* narrated by Roddy McDowall (1997).
68 Susan Felleman, *Real Objects in Unreal Situations: Modern Art in Fiction Films* (Bristol: Intellect, 2014), 96.
69 Robert J. Belton, *Alfred Hitchcock's Vertigo and the Hermeneutic Spiral* (Cham, Switzerland: Palgrave Macmillan, 2017), 54.
70 Schwartz, "Torque: The New Kinaesthetic," 101.
71 Raymond Bellour, "Psychosis, Neurosis, Perversion (on *Psycho*)," in *The Analysis of Film* (Bloomington: Indiana University Press, 2000), 249.
72 Gunning, "Birth of Film," 22.
73 Lewis Piaget Shanks, "Gustave Flaubert," *Open Court* 36, no. 3 (March 1922): 136.
74 Catherine James, "*Vertigo:* Redeeming the fall" in *Performance Research* 18, no. 4 (2013): 91.
75 Samuels, *Hitchcock's Bi-textuality*, 78.
76 Stoichita, *Pygmalion Effect*, 184.
77 Bronfen, *Over Her Dead Body*, 340.
78 Wood, *Hitchcock's Films Revisited*, 126.
79 Wood, 127.
80 Žižek, "*Vertigo*," 215.
81 Vlad Dima, "A Fantasy of One's Own: Rooms in Hitchcock's 'Vertigo' and Baudelaire's Prose Texts," *Mosaic: An Interdisciplinary Critical Journal* 45, no. 4 (December 2012): 82.
82 Charles Barr, *Vertigo* (London: BFI Publishing, 2002), 80.
83 See Belton's *Alfred Hitchcock's Vertigo and the Hermeneutic Spiral.*
84 Durgnat in Belton, 29–30.
85 *Vertigo*'s Pygmalionesque reformation of the blond beauty within the narrative echoes Hitchcock's own proclivity for fashioning his leading ladies according to his aesthetic template. Biographer of both, Donald Spoto calls Grace Kelly Hitchcock's "willing and winsome Galatea." The director meticulously constructed her screen image, exceptionally precise about every color and style choice in her film wardrobe. By making her "appear like a piece of Dresden china, something slightly untouchable"—equivalent to the blue china decorating his room at Oxford that Wilde quipped he was unable to live up to—Hitchcock put "his dream together in the studio" (Edith Head in Donald Spoto, *Spellbound by Beauty: Alfred Hitchcock and His Leading Ladies* [London: Hutchinson, 2008], 210). After Kelly's departure from Hollywood, Hitchcock tried to fashion other actresses into copies of her, supposedly telling them something like, "I will make you into the next Grace Kelly." The title of this last section in the chapter suggests that *Vertigo* reflects Hitchcock's own anxieties over the loss of his filmic ideal—his fall from Grace (Kelly).

Epilogue

1 Vladimir Nabokov, *Pale Fire* (New York: Vintage Books, 1989), 33.
2 Nabokov, 28.
3 Nabokov, 68.

4 Metz, "Imaginary Signifier," 732.

5 Nelson, who also coined the word "virtuality," used *Pale Fire* explicitly at a 1969 hypertext conference hosted at Brown University. The "Orson Welles of software," Nelson saw himself as a literary romantic, the son of a film director father, Ralph Nelson, and actress mother, Celeste Holm. See "Ted Nelson," *Forbes*, August 25, 1997, https://www.forbes.com/asap/1997/0825/134.html.

6 Though I am linking *Blade Runner 2049* into a particular lineage of French texts on which this book focuses, simply by focusing on this reading here in the epilogue, I would not make any claim to its utter "Frenchness," but instead that by this point the literary and cinematic cells of the replication crisis I have been charting since the 1830s has now *become something else*. However, it bears mentioning that the original *Blade Runner* was largely influenced by the French comic anthology *Métal hurlant* (1974), and specifically "The Long Tomorrow," by French artist and illustrator Moebius (Jean Giraud). Considered one of the most influential cartoonists in modern times, his work has created a long line of cinematic descendants done in spirited style, including Alejandro Jodorowsky's *Dune* (Moebius was working simultaneously with the filmmaker at the time), Ridley Scott's *Alien* (1979), and Luc Besson's *The Fifth Element* (1997). Denis Villeneuve, a French-Canadian who grew up in Quebec, claims that the two largest influences on him as a child, in developing his cinematic sensibilities as a director, were watching *Blade Runner* and reading through a box of sci-fi comic books by French artists—including Moebius and Philippe Druillet, who created a comic book trilogy based on Flaubert's *Salammbô* in 1980—that was sent to him by his aunt, who strongly believed in extraterrestrials. For more, see https://www.wired.co.uk/article/blade-runner-2049-denis-villeneuve.

7 Donna Haraway's critical essay "A Cyborg Manifesto," originally written in 1985, suggests the cyborg being de-gendered and having no origin story. See Haraway, "A Cyborg Manifesto," in *Simians, Cyborgs, and Women: The Reinvention of Nature* (New York: Routledge, 1991), 149–181.

8 Adrienne Rich, *Of Woman Born: Motherhood as Experience and Institution* (New York: W. W. Norton, 1995).

9 Elissa Marder, "*Blade Runner*'s Moving Still," in *The Mother in the Age of Mechanical Reproduction: Psychoanalysis, Photography, Deconstruction* (New York: Fordham University Press, 2012), 139.

10 Marder, 143.

11 Marder, 140.

12 In Genesis 4:1, Eve proclaims "I have produced a man with the help of the LORD," just as God has to aid in opening Rachel's womb to give her a child.

13 Hampton Fancher and Michael Green, *Blade Runner 2049*, film script (2017), 93.

14 The significance of the site of Rachel's tomb and its role according to midrash evolves over the centuries. Some suggest that its cultlike status did not develop until the nineteenth century. For more information, see Susan Starr Sered, "Rachel's Tomb: The Development of a Cult," *Jewish Studies Quarterly* 2, no. 2 (1995): 103–148.

15 The quote is from Villiers's *L'Ève future* (135), repeated here from its first use in chapter 2.

16 "Blade Runner 2049," MPC Film, https://www.mpcfilm.com/filmography/film/blade-runner-2049.

17 Sarah Bahr, "The Star of This $70 Million Sci-Fi Film Is a Robot," *New York Times*, July 24, 2020, https://www.nytimes.com/2020/07/24/movies/humanoid-robot-actor.html.

18 Hampton Fancher, who cowrote the screenplay to both *Blade Runner* films, says that Joi becomes "totally real to herself" despite her programming in the DVD extra on "Joi."

19 "I believe in one God, the Father Almighty, Maker of heaven and earth, and of all things visible and invisible . . . begotten, not made, being of one substance with the Father . . . and I look for the resurrection of the dead, and the life of the world to come. Amen."

20 See Vivian Sobchack, *Screening Space: The American Science Fiction Film* (New Brunswick, NJ: Rutgers University Press, 1999), 297.

21 See Giuliana Bruno, "Ramble City: Postmodernism and 'Blade Runner,'" *October* 41 (Summer 1987): 61–74.

22 Scott Bukatman, *Blade Runner* (London: BFI Film Classics, 2012), 74.

23 Jean-François Lyotard, "Defining the Postmodern," in *The Cultural Studies Reader*, ed. Simon During (New York: Routledge, 1993), 171.

24 It seems Villeneuve relaxed after making peace with the idea that his cinematic sequel would never measure up, although, in fitting with the dynamics of modernity, I find the second film (read: the copy) more inspired than the original. See Stuart McGurk, "Blade Runner 2049 Director Denis Villeneuve Is Science-Fiction's Brave New Hope," *Wired*, September 15, 2017, https://www.wired.co.uk/article/blade-runner-2049-denis-villeneuve.

25 McGurk.

26 Cara Buckley at the *New York Times* points to a strong pattern of female protagonists in many of Villeneuve's films and suggests his feminist leanings are "ingrained in Mr. Villeneuve's DNA," as if he were programmed like one of the film's replicants. Cara Buckley, "Denis Villeneuve of 'Arrival' Leans In to Strong Heroines," *New York Times*, November 10, 2016, https://www.nytimes.com/2016/11/13/movies/denis-villeneuve-interview-arrival.html.

Bibliography

Albera, François, and Maria Tortajada, eds. *Cinema Beyond Film: Media Epistemology in the Modern Era*. Amsterdam: Amsterdam University Press, 2010.

Alberti, Leon Battista. *On Painting*. New York: Penguin, 1991.

Allen, Richard. *Hitchcock's Romantic Irony*. New York: Columbia University Press, 2007.

Allen, Richard, and S. Ishii-Gonzalès, eds. *Hitchcock Centenary Essays*. London: BFI Publishing, 1999.

Allen, Richard, and Malcolm Turvey, eds. *Camera Obscura, Camera Lucida: Essays in Honor of Annette Michelson*. Amsterdam: Amsterdam University Press, 2003.

Allen, William G. "Gautier's *Albertus*: The Fantastic and the Fashionable." In *Correspondences: Studies in Literature, History, and the Arts in Nineteenth-Century France*, edited by Keith Busby, 9–19. New York: Rodopi, 1992.

Anzalone, John, ed. *Jeering Dreamers: Villiers de l'Isle Adam's L'Eve future at our fin de siècle: A collection of essays*. Amsterdam: Rodopi, 1996.

Apter, Emily S. *Feminizing the Fetish: Psychoanalysis and Narrative Obsession in Turn-of-the-Century France*. Ithaca, NY: Cornell University Press, 1991.

Apter, Emily S., and William Pietz. *Fetishism as Cultural Discourse*. Ithaca, NY: Cornell University Press, 1993.

Arata, Stephen. *Fictions of Loss in the Victorian Fin de Siècle*. Cambridge: Cambridge University Press, 1996.

Arscott, Caroline, and Katie Scott. "Introducing Venus." In *Manifestations of Venus: Art and Sexuality*, edited by Caroline Arscott and Katie Scott, 1–23. Manchester: Manchester University Press, 2000.

Auiler, Dan. *Vertigo: The Making of a Hitchcock Classic*. New York: St. Martin's, 1998.

Bahr, Sarah. "The Star of This $70 Million Sci-Fi Film Is a Robot." *New York Times*, July 24, 2020. https://www.nytimes.com/2020/07/24/movies/humanoid-robot-actor.html.

Baker, Nicholson. *Double Fold: Libraries and the Assault on Paper*. New York: Random House, 2001.

Barker, Stephen, ed. *Excavations and Their Objects: Freud's Collection of Antiquity*. Albany: State University of New York Press, 1996.

Barolsky, Paul. "A Very Brief History of Art from Narcissus to Plato." *Classical Journal* 90, no. 3 (1995): 255–259.
Barr, Charles. *Vertigo*. London: BFI Publishing, 2002.
Baudelaire, Charles. *Curiosités esthétiques, l'Art Romantique et autres œuvres critiques*. Paris: Éditions Garnier Frères, 1962.
———. *Les Fleurs du mal*. Paris: Larousse, 2001.
Baudry, Jean Louis. "Ideological Effects of the Basic Cinematic Apparatus." *Film Quarterly* 28, no. 2 (Winter 1974–1975): 39–47.
Bauer, Douglas F. "The Function of Pygmalion in the Metamorphoses of Ovid." *Transactions and Proceedings of the American Philological Association* 93 (1962): 1–21.
Bazin, Andre. *What Is Cinema? Volume 1*. Berkeley: University of California Press, 1967.
Beardsley, Aubrey, and Oscar Wilde. *Salomé*. Mineola, NY: Dover, 1967.
Bellemin-Noël, Jean. *Plaisirs de vampire*. Paris: Presses universitaires de France, 2001.
Bellour, Raymond. *The Analysis of Film*. Bloomington: Indiana University Press, 2000.
———. "Ideal Hadaly." *Camera Obscura*, 5, no. 3 (Fall 1986): 111–134.
Belton, Robert J. *Alfred Hitchcock's Vertigo and the Hermeneutic Spiral*. Cham, Switzerland: Palgrave Macmillan, 2017.
Benjamin, Walter. *Illuminations*. New York: Schocken Books, 1969.
Bennett, Michael, ed. *Refiguring Oscar Wilde's Salome*. Amsterdam: Rodopi, 2011.
Bentley, Toni. *Sisters of Salome*. New Haven, CT: Yale University Press, 2002.
Bergstrom, Janet. "Androids and Androgyny." *Camera Obscura* 5, no. 3 (Fall 1986): 37–66.
Bernhardt, Sarah. *The Art of the Theatre*. New York: Books for Libraries Press, 1969.
Bernheimer, Charles. "Fetishism and Decadence: Salome's severed heads." In *Fetishism as Cultural Discourse*, edited by Emily Apter and William Pietz, 62–83. Ithaca, NY: Cornell University Press, 1993.
———. "Huysmans: Writing against (Female) Nature." *Poetics Today* 6, no. ½ (1985): 311–324.
Bernstein, Matthew, and Gaylyn Studlar, eds. *Visions of the East: Orientalism in Film*. New Brunswick, NJ: Rutgers University Press, 1997.
Blanchard, J. M. "Of Cannibalism and Autobiography." *MLN* 93, no. 4 (May 1978): 654–676.
Bloom, Michelle. "Pygmalionesque Delusions and Illusions of Movement: Animation from Hoffmann to Truffaut." *Comparative Literature* 52, no. 4 (Autumn 2000): 291–320.
Bloy, Léon. *La Résurrection de Villiers de l'Isle-Adam*. Paris: Lecampion, 1906.
Bornecque, Jacques-Henry. *Villiers de l'Isle-Adam: Créateur et visionnaire*. Paris, Nizet, 1974.
Boyd, David, and R. Barton Palmer, eds. *Alfred Hitchcock: Influence, Imitation and Intertextuality*. Austin: University of Texas Press, 2006.
Bradford, Gamaliel. *Daughters of Eve*. New York: New Impressions, 1969.
Bradshaw, David, Laura Marcus, and Rebecca Roach, eds. *Moving Modernisms: Motion, Technology, and Modernity*. Oxford: Oxford University Press, 2016.
Braudy, Leo, and Marshall Cohen, eds. *Film Theory and Criticism*. 7th ed. New York: Oxford University Press, 2009.
Brent, Jessica. "Beyond the Gaze: Visual Fascination and the Feminine Image in Silent Hitchcock." *Camera Obscura* 19, no. 1 (2004): 77–111.
Brill, Lesley. *The Hitchcock Romance: Love and Irony in Hitchcock's Films*. Princeton, NJ: Princeton University Press, 1988.

Bristow, Joseph. *Wilde Discoveries: Traditions, Histories, Archives*. Toronto: University of Toronto Press, 2013.

Bronfen, Elisabeth. *Over Her Dead Body: Death, Femininity and the Aesthetic*. New York: Routledge, 1992.

Brown, Daniel. "Wilde and Wilder." *PMLA* 119, no. 5 (October 2004): 1216–1230.

Brown, Julia Prewitt. *Oscar Wilde's Philosophy of Art*. Charlottesville: University Press of Virginia, 1997.

Brown, Royal S. "*Vertigo* As Orphic Tragedy." *Literature/Film Quarterly* 14, no. 1 (1986): 32–43.

Bruno, Giuliana. "Ramble City: Postmodernism and 'Blade Runner,'" *October* 41 (Summer 1987): 61–74.

Bryson, Norman. *Vision and Painting: The Logic of the Gaze*. New Haven, CT: Yale University Press, 1983.

Buci-Glucksmann, Christine. "Catastrophic Utopia: The Feminine as Allegory of the Modern." *Representations* 14 (Spring 1986): 220–229.

———. *La Raison Baroque de Baudelaire à Benjamin*. Paris: Galilée, 1984.

Buckley, Cara. "Denis Villeneuve of 'Arrival' Leans In to Strong Heroines." *New York Times*, November 10, 2016. https://www.nytimes.com/2016/11/13/movies/denis-villeneuve-interview-arrival.html.

Bucknell, Brad. "On 'Seeing' Salome." *English Literary History* 60, no. 2 (1993): 503–526.

———. "Re-reading Pater: The Musical Aesthetics of Temporality." *Modern Fiction Studies* 38, no. 3 (Autumn 1992): 597–614.

Bukatman, Scott. *Blade Runner*. London: BFI Film Classics, 2012.

Butler, Judith. *Gender Trouble: Feminism and the Subversion of Identity*. New York: Routledge, 1999.

Cakmak, Gulru. "'For the Strong-Minded Alone': Evolution, Female Atavism, and Degeneration in Aubrey Beardsley's *Salomé*." In *Decadence, Degeneration, and the End*, edited by Marja Härmänmaa and Christopher Nissen, 183–200. New York: Palgrave Macmillan, 2014.

Calinescu, Matei. *Five Faces of Modernity: Modernism, Avant-Garde, Decadence, Kitsch, Postmodernism*. Durham, NC: Duke University Press, 1987.

Calo, Jeanne. *La Création de la femme chez Michelet*. Paris: Nizet, 1975.

Canales, Jimena. "Dead and Alive: Micro-cinematography between Physics and Biology." *Configurations* 23, no. 2 (Spring 2015): 235–251.

Carr, J. L. "Pygmalion and the Philosophes: The Animated Statue in Eighteenth-Century France." *Journal of the Warburg and Courtauld Institutes* 23, no. 3/4 (July–December 1960): 239–255.

Carroll, Noël. "Vertigo and the Pathologies of Romantic Love." In *Hitchcock and Philosophy: Dial M for Metaphysics*, edited by David Baggett and William A. Drumin, 101–127. La Salle, IL: Open Court, 2007.

Castex, Pierre-Georges. *Le Conte fantastiques en France: De Nodier à Maupassant*. Paris: J. Corti, 1951.

Chadwick, Whitney. "Masson's Gradiva: The Metamorphosis of a Surrealist Myth." *Art Bulletin* 52, no. 4 (December 1970): 415–422.

Chamberlin, J. Edward, and Sander Gilman, eds. *Degeneration: The Dark Side of Progress*. New York: Columbia University Press, 1985.

Charney, Leo, and Vanessa R. Schwartz, eds. *Cinema and the Invention of Modern Life*. Berkeley: University of California Press, 1995.

Choe, Steve. "The One in Photogénie: Plotinus and Jean Epstein." In *Plotinus and the Moving Image*, edited by Thorsten Botz-Bornstein and Giannis Stamatellos. Amsterdam: Brill, 2017.

Cipriani, Fernando. "Le Mythe de l'Artificiel dans l'œuvre de Villiers." In *Société des études romantiques: Villiers de l'Isle-Adam (1838–1889)*, 133–148. Paris: Sedes, 1990.

Cockerham, Harry. "Gautier: From Hallucination to Supernatural Vision." *Yale French Studies* 50 (1974): 41–53.

Coffman, Elizabeth. "Women in Motion: Loie Fuller and the 'Interpenetration' of Art and Science" *Camera Obscura* 17, no. 1 (2002): 1–104.

Conley, Katharine. *Automatic Woman: The Representation of Woman in Surrealism*. Lincoln: University of Nebraska Press, 1996.

Constable, E. L. "Critical Departures: Salammbô's Orientalism." *MLN* 111, no. 4 (September 1996): 625–646.

Corbin, Alain. *Women for Hire: Prostitution and Sexuality in France after 1850*. Boston: Harvard University Press, 1990.

Cordulack, Shelley Wood. "A Franco-American Battle of Beams: Electricity and the Selling of Modernity." *Journal of Design History* 18, no. 2 (Summer 2005): 147–166.

Craft, Christopher. "Come See about Me: Enchantment of the Double in *The Picture of Dorian Gray*." *Representations* 91, no. 1 (Summer 2005): 109–136.

Crary, Jonathan. "Modernizing Vision." In *Vision and Visuality*, edited by Hal Foster, 29–49. Seattle: Bay Press, 1988.

Cubitt, Sean. *The Practice of Light: A Genealogy of Visual Technologies from Prints to Pixels*. Cambridge, MA: MIT Press, 2014.

Cucullu, Lois. "Wilde and Wilder Salomés: Modernizing the Nubile Princess." *Modernism/Modernity* 18, no. 3 (September 2011): 495–524.

Daly, Nicholas. "The Obscure Object of Desire: Victorian Commodity Culture and Fictions of the Mummy." *Novel: A Forum on Fiction* 28, no. 1 (Autumn 1994): 24–51.

Dannenfeldt, Karl H. "Egyptian Mumia: The Sixteenth Century Experience." *Sixteenth Century Journal* 16, no. 2 (Summer 1985): 163–180.

David-Weill, Natalie. *Rêve de Pierre: La Quête de la femme chez Théophile Gautier*. Geneva: Droz, 1989.

Dawson, Warren R. "Making a Mummy." *Journal of Egyptian Archaeology* 13, no. ½ (April 1927): 40–49.

———. "Mummy as Drug." *Proceedings of the Royal Society of Medicine* 21, no. 1 (1927): 34–39.

Detmers, Ines. "Oscar's Fashion: Constructing a Rhetoric of Androgyny." In *Importance of Reinventing Oscar: Versions of Wilde during the Last 100 Years*, edited by Uwe Boker, Richard Corballis, and Julie Hibbard, 111–116. Amsterdam: Rodopi, 2002.

Dierkes-Thrun, Petra. *Salome's Modernity: Oscar Wilde and the Aesthetics of Transgression*. Ann Arbor: University of Michigan Press, 2011.

Dima, Vlad. "A Fantasy of One's Own: Rooms in Hitchcock's 'Vertigo' and Baudelaire's Prose Texts." *Mosaic: An Interdisciplinary Critical Journal* 45, no. 4 (December 2012): 69–84.

Doane, Mary Ann. *Femmes Fatales: Feminism, Film Theory, and Psychoanalysis*. New York: Routledge, 1991.

———. "The Close-Up: Scale and Detail in the Cinema," *differences* 14, no. 3 (December 1, 2003): 89–111.

Domarchi, Jean. "Le Chef-d'oeuvre inconnu." *Cahiers du cinéma* 39 (October 1954): 33–39.

Downey, Katherine Brown. *Perverse Midrash: Oscar Wilde, André Gide, and Censorship of Biblical Drama*. New York: Continuum, 2004.

Downing, Eric. *After Images: Photography, Archaeology, and Psychoanalysis and the Tradition of Bildung*. Detroit: Wayne State University Press, 2006.

Duckett, Victoria. "Performing Art Nouveau: Sarah Bernhardt and the Development of Industrial Modernism." *Modernism/Modernity* 4, cycle 3 (2019). https://modernismmodernity.org/forums/posts/performing-art-nouveau.

Eisenstein, Sergei. *Film Form: Essays in Film Theory*. San Diego: Harcourt, 1977.

Eisner, Lotte. *The Haunted Screen: Expressionism in the German Cinema and the Influence of Max Reinhardt*. Berkeley: University of California Press, 1969.

Eksteins, Modris. "History and Degeneration: Of Birds and Cages." In *Degeneration: The Dark Side of Progress*, edited by J. Edward Chamberlin and Sander Gilman, 1–23. New York: Columbia University Press, 1985.

Elkins, James, ed. *Photography Theory*. New York: Routledge, 2007.

Ellmann, Richard. *Oscar Wilde*. New York: Vintage Books, 1988.

Epstein, Jean. "On Certain Characteristics of Photogénie." In *Film Theory: Critical Concepts in Media and Cultural Studies*, edited by Philip Simpson, 52–56. New York: Routledge, 2004.

———. "*Photogénie* and the Imponderable." In *Critical Visions in Film Theory: Classic and Contemporary Readings*, edited by Timothy Corrigan, Patricia White, and Meta Mazaj, 252–257. New York: Bedford St. Martin's, 2011.

Fabe, Marilyn. "Mourning *Vertigo*." *American Imago* 66, no. 3 (Fall 2009): 343–367.

Falk, Marcia. *The Song of Songs: A New Translation and Interpretation*. San Francisco: HarperCollins, 1990.

Felleman, Susan. *Real Objects in Unreal Situations: Modern Art in Fiction Films*. Bristol: Intellect, 2014.

Felman, Shoshana. *What Does a Woman Want? Reading and Sexual Difference*. Baltimore: Johns Hopkins University Press, 1981.

Fernbach, Amanda. "Wilde's 'Salomé' and the Ambiguous Fetish." *Victorian Literature and Culture* 29, no. 1 (2001): 195–218.

Ferris, David S., ed. *The Cambridge Companion to Walter Benjamin*. Cambridge: Cambridge University Press, 2004.

Fischer, Lucy. *Cinematernity: Film, Motherhood, Genre*. Princeton, NJ: Princeton University Press, 2014.

Fleischhack, Maria. *Narrating Ancient Egypt*. New York: Peter Lang, 2015.

Forrest, Jennifer. "The Lord of Hadaly's Rings: Regulating the Female Body in Villiers de l'Isle Adam's *l'Eve Future*." *South Central Review* 13, no. 4 (1996): 5–17.

Fortin, Jutta. "Brides of the Fantastic: Gautier's *Le Pied de Momie* and Hoffmann's *Der Sandmann*." *Comparative Literature Studies* 41, no. 2 (2004): 257–275.

Frank, Felicia Miller. *The Mechanical Song: Women, Voice, and the Artificial in Nineteenth-Century French Narrative*. Stanford, CA: Stanford University Press, 1995.

Frankel, Nicholas. *Oscar Wilde's Decorated Books*. Ann Arbor: University of Michigan Press, 2000.

Freedman, Jonathan. "Transformations of a Jewish Princess: Salomé and the Remaking of the Jewish Female Body from Sarah Bernhardt to Betty Boop." *Philological Quarterly* 92, no. 1 (2013): 89–114.

Freud, Sigmund. *Beyond the Pleasure Principle*. New York: W. W. Norton, 1989.

———. *General Psychological Theory*. New York: Touchstone, 1997.

———. *Leonardo da Vinci and a Memory of His Childhood*. New York: W. W. Norton, 1964.

———. *Sexuality and the Psychology of Love*. New York: Simon and Schuster, 1963.

———. *The Uncanny*. New York: Penguin, 2003.

———. *Writings on Art and Literature*. Stanford, CA: Stanford University Press, 1997.

Gagnier, Regenia. *Idylls of the Marketplace: Oscar Wilde and the Victorian Public.* Stanford, CA: Stanford University Press, 1986.

———. "Sexuality, the Public, and the Art World." In *Critical Essays on Oscar Wilde*, edited by Regenia Gagnier, 23–45. New York: G. K. Hall, 1991.

Gallese, Vittorio. "Naturalizing Aesthetic Experience: The Role of (Liberated) Embodied Simulation." *Projections* 12, no. 2 (December 2018): 50–59.

Gamwell, Lynn, and Richard Wells, eds. *Sigmund Freud and Art: His Personal Collection of Antiquities*. New York: Harry N Abrams, 1989.

Garelick, Rhonda. *Electric Salome: Loie Fuller's Performance of Modernism*. Princeton, NJ: Princeton University Press, 2009.

———. *Rising Star: Dandyism, Gender, and Performance in the Fin de Siècle*. Princeton, NJ: Princeton University Press, 1998.

Gasché, Rodolphe. "The Falls of History: Huysmans's À Rebours." *Yale French Studies* no. 74 (1988): 183–204.

Gautier, Théophile. *Clarimonde*. Los Angeles: Aegypan, 2011.

———. *La Morte amoureuse: Avatar et autre récits fantastiques*. Paris: Gallimard, 1981.

———. *Photosculpture*. Paris: Paul Dupont, 1864.

———. *Portrait de Balzac précédé de Portrait de Théophile Gautier par lui-même*. Montpellier: L'Anabase, 1994.

———. *Le Roman de la Momie*. Paris: Sogemo, 1988.

———. *Tous les contes fantastiques*. Paris: Néo, 1990.

Geisler-Szmulewicz, Anne. *Le Mythe de Pygmalion au XIXe siècle: Pour une approche de la coalescence des mythes*. Paris: Honoré Champion Éditeur, 1999.

Gilbert, Elliott L. "'Tumult of Images': Wilde, Beardsley, 'Salome.'" *Victorian Studies* 26, no. 2 (Winter 1983): 133–159.

Gilbert, Sandra M., and Susan Gubar. *The Madwoman in the Attic: The Woman Writer and the Nineteenth-Century Literary Imagination*. New Haven, CT: Yale University Press, 2020.

Gilbert, Scott F., and Marion Faber. "Looking at Embryos: The Visual and Conceptual Aesthetics of Emerging Form." In *The Elusive Synthesis: Aesthetics and Science*, edited by Alfred Tauber, 125–152. Dordrecht, The Netherlands: Kluwer, 1997.

Glancy, Jennifer A. "Unveiling Masculinity: The Construction of Gender in Mark 6:17–29." *Biblical Interpretation* 2, no. 1 (1994): 34–50.

Glavey, Brian. "Dazzling Estrangement: Modernism, Queer Ekphrasis, and the Spatial Form of 'Nightwood.'" *PMLA* 124, no. 3 (May 2009).

———. *The Wallflower Avant-Garde: Modernism, Sexuality, and Queer Ekphrasis*. Oxford: Oxford University Press, 2016.

Glick, Elisa. "The Dialectics of Dandyism." *Cultural Critique* 48 (Spring 2001): 129–162.

Glynn, Basil. *The Mummy on Screen: Orientalism and Monstrosity in Horror Cinema*. London: Bloomsbury, 2019.

Gold, Arthur, and Robert Fizdale. *The Divine Sarah: A Life of Sarah Bernhardt*. New York: Alfred A. Knopf, 1991.

Gómez Carrillo, Enrique. "How Oscar Wilde Dreamed of Salomé." In *Oscar Wilde: Interviews and Recollections*, edited by E. H. Mikhail, 192–195. New York: Barnes and Noble, 1979.

Gottlieb, Sidney, ed. *Hitchcock on Hitchcock*. Berkeley: University of California Press, 1995.

Goulet, Andrea. *Optiques: The Science of the Eye and the Birth of Modern French Fiction*. Philadelphia: University of Pennsylvania Press, 2006.

Gross, Kenneth. *The Dream of the Moving Statue*. Ithaca, NY: Cornell University Press, 1992.

Gunning, Tom. "The Birth of Film Out of the Spirit of Modernity." In *Masterpieces of Modernist Cinema*, edited by Ted Perry, 13–38. Bloomington: Indiana University Press, 2006.

———. *The Films of Fritz Lang: Allegories of Vision and Modernity*. London: BFI Publishing, 2000.

Gunz, Joel. "Alfred Hitchcock and Paul Klee at the Intersection of Artistic Invention." October 2 2015. https://medium.com/@joelgunz/alfred-hitchcock-and-paul-klee-at-the-intersection-of-artistic-invention-a9713f1e03d8.

Hadlock, Philip G. "(Per)Versions of Masculinity in Maupassant's *La Mère aux Monstres*." *French Forum* 27, no. 1 (Winter 2002): 59–79.

Haley, Bruce. "Wilde's 'Decadence' and the Positivist Tradition." *Victorian Studies* 28, no. 2 (Winter 1985): 215–229.

Hannon, Patrice. "Theatre and Theory in the Language of 'Dorian Gray.'" *Victorian Literature and Culture* 19 (1991): 143–166.

Haraway, Donna. "A Cyborg Manifesto." In *Simians, Cyborgs, and Women: The Reinvention of Nature*, 149–181. New York: Routledge, 1991.

Harris, Wendell V. "Arnold, Pater, Wilde, and the Object as in Themselves They See It." *Studies in English Literature, 1500–1900* 11, no. 4 (Autumn 1971): 733–747.

Hawkins, Joan. "'See It from the Beginning': Hitchcock's Reconstruction of Film History." In *Framing Hitchcock: Selected Essays from the Hitchcock Annual*, ed. Sidney Gottlieb and Christopher Brookhouse, 373–386. Detroit, MI: Wayne State University Press, 2002.

Hawthorne, Melanie C. "Dis-covering the Female: Gautier's Roman de la Momie." *French Review* 66, no. 5 (1993): 718–729.

Heath, Stephen. *Questions of Cinema*. Bloomington: Indiana University Press, 1981.

Higham, Charles. "Hitchcock's World." *Film Quarterly* 16, no. 2 (Winter 1962–1963): 3–16.

Hitchcock, Alfred. *Alfred Hitchcock Interviews*. Narrated by John Dunning. Newark, NJ: Audible, 2016. https://books.apple.com/us/audiobook/alfred-hitchcock-interviews/id1086727144.

Hobbs, Richard, ed. *Impressions of French Modernity: Art and Literature in France 1850–1900*. Manchester: Manchester University Press, 1998.

Holland, Merlin, ed. *Oscar Wilde: A Life in Letters*. London: Fourth Estate, 2003.

———. *The Wilde Album*. New York: Henry Holt, 1997.

Holland, Merlin, and Rupert Hart-Davis, eds. *The Complete Letters of Oscar Wilde*. New York: Henry Holt, 2000.

Holmes, Oliver Wendell. "The Stereoscope and the Stereograph." *The Atlantic*, June 1859. https://www.theatlantic.com/magazine/archive/1859/06/the-stereoscope-and-the-stereograph/303361/.

Huet, Mary-Hélène. "Living Images: Monstrosity and Representation." *Representations* 4 (Autumn 1983): 73–87.

Hurley, Kelly. *The Gothic Body: Sexuality, Materialism, and Degeneration at the Fin de Siècle*. Cambridge: Cambridge University Press, 1996.

Hutchings, Peter J. "Modernity: A Film by Alfred Hitchcock." *Senses of Cinema*, no. 6 (May 2000). https://www.sensesofcinema.com/2000/conference-for-the-love-of-fear/modernity/.

Huysmans, J. K. *Against Nature*. Oxford: Oxford University Press, 2009.

Huyssen, Andreas. "Authentic Ruins: Products of Modernity." In *Ruins of Modernity*, edited by Julia Hell and Andreas Schönle, 17–28. Durham, NC: Duke University Press, 2010.

Jacobs, Stephen, Susan Felleman, Vito Adriaensens, and Lisa Colpaert, eds. *Screening Statues: Sculpture in Film*. Edinburgh: Edinburgh University Press, 2018.

James, Catherine. "*Vertigo:* Redeeming the fall." *Performance Research* 18, no. 4 (2013): 91–97.

James, Heather. "Milton's Eve, the Romance Genre, and Ovid." *Comparative Literature* 45, no. 2 (1993): 121–145.

James, Paula. *Ovid's Myth of Pygmalion on Screen*. London: Continuum, 2001.

Jarrot, Sabine. *Le Vampire dans la littérature du XIXe et XXe siècle*. Paris: L'Harmattan, 1999.

Johnson, Barbara. *Persons and Things*. Cambridge, MA: Harvard University Press, 2008.

Jordanova, Ludmilla. *Sexual Visions: Images of Gender in Science and Medicine between the Eighteenth and Twentieth Centuries*. Madison: University of Wisconsin Press, 1989.

Jouanny, Sylvie. *L'Actrice et ses doubles: Figures et représentations de la femme de spectacle à la fin du XIXe siècle*. Geneva: Droz, 2002.

Katz, Jack. "The Social Psychology of Adam and Eve." *Theory and Society* 25, no. 4 (August 1996): 545–582.

Kirkham, Pat. "Reassessing the Saul Bass and Alfred Hitchcock Collaboration." *West 86th* 18, no. 1 (Spring–Summer 2011). http://www.west86th.bgc.bard.edu/articles/reassessing-the-saul-bass-and-alfred-hitchcock-collaboration/.

Kirkup, Gill, ed. *The Gendered Cyborg: A Reader*. London: Routledge, 2000.

Kittler, Friedrich. *Literature, Media, Information Systems*. London: Routledge, 1997.

Kofman, Sarah. *The Enigma of Woman: Woman in Freud's Writings*. Ithaca, NY: Cornell University Press, 1985.

Kohl, Norbert. *Oscar Wilde: The Works of a Conformist Rebel*. Cambridge: Cambridge University Press, 1980.

Kohlke, Marie-Luise. "Sexsation and the Neo-Victorian Novel: Orientalising the Nineteenth Century in Contemporary Fiction." In *Negotiating Sexual Idioms: Image, Text, Performance*, edited by Kohlke and Luisa Orza, 53–77. Amsterdam: Brill, 2008.

Kojima, Motohiro. "Leopold Bloom's 'metempsychosis' and 'parallax' in *Ulysses*," *Journal of Irish Studies* 20 (2005): 21–30.

Kolker, Robert. *The Extraordinary Image: Orson Welles, Alfred Hitchcock, Stanley Kubrick and the Reimagining of Cinema*. New Brunswick, NJ: Rutgers University Press, 2017.

Kriebel, Sabine T. "Theories of Photography: A Short History." In *Photography Theory*, edited by James Elkins, 3–50. New York: Routledge, 2007.

Kuryluk, Ewa. *Salome and Judas in the Cave of Sex*. Evanston, IL: Northwestern University Press, 1987.

Lacan, Jacques. *Écrits I*. Nouvelle ed. Paris: Éditions du Seuil, 1999.

Landy, Francis. "The Song of Songs and the Garden of Eden." *Journal of Biblical Literature* 98, no. 4 (December 1979): 513–528.

Lanzoni, Remi Fournier. *French Cinema: From Its Beginnings to the Present*. 2nd ed. New York: Bloomsbury, 2015.

Lathers, Marie. *The Aesthetics of Artifice: Villiers's l'Ève Future*. Chapel Hill, NC: University of North Carolina Press, 1996.

Lauretis, Teresa de. *Technologies of Gender: Essays on Theory, Film, and Fiction*. Bloomington: Indiana University Press, 1987.

Leasure, T. Ross. "Yesterday's Eve and Her Electric Avatar: Villiers's Debt to Milton's *Paradise Lost*." *Latch: A Journal for the Study of the Literary Artifact in Theory, Culture or History* 1 (2008): 129–144.

Leitch, Thomas, and Leland Poague, eds. *A Companion to Alfred Hitchcock*. London: Wiley-Blackwell, 2011.
Ligensa, Annemone, and Klaus Kreimeier, eds. *Film 1900: Technology, Perception, Culture*. Bloomington: Indiana University Press, 2009.
Linderman, Deborah. "The Mise-en-Abîme in Hitchcock's *Vertigo*." *Cinema Journal* 30, no. 4 (Summer 1991): 51–74.
Lindsay, Vachel. *The Art of the Moving Picture*. New York: Modern Library, 2000.
Logan, John Frederick. "The Age of Intoxication." *Yale French Studies* 50 (1974): 81–94.
Lubin, David. "Hitchcock and Art: Fatal Coincidences." *Artforum* 40, no. 3 (November 2001): 140.
Lyotard, Jean-François. "Defining the Postmodern." In *The Cultural Studies Reader*, edited by Simon During, 170–175. New York: Routledge, 1993.
Maier, Sarah E. "Symbolist Salomés and the Dance of Dionysus." *Nineteenth-Century Contexts* 28, no. 3 (September 2006): 211–223.
Marcoci, Roxana. *The Original Copy: Photography of Sculpture, 1839 to Today*. New York: Museum of Modern Art, 2010.
Marder, Elissa. "*Blade Runner*'s Moving Still." In *The Mother in the Age of Mechanical Reproduction: Psychoanalysis, Photography, Deconstruction*, 130–148. New York: Fordham University Press, 2012.
———. *Dead Time: Temporal Disorders in the Wake of Modernity (Baudelaire and Flaubert)*. Stanford, CA: Stanford University Press, 2001.
McCouat, Philip. "The Life and Death of Mummy Brown." *Journal of Art in Society* (2013). http://www.artinsociety.com/the-life-and-death-of-mummy-brown.html.
McCreary, Eugene. "Louis Delluc, Film Theorist, Critic, and Prophet." *Cinema Journal* 16, no. 1 (Autumn 1976): 14–35.
McGilligan, Patrick. *Alfred Hitchcock: A Life in Darkness and Light*. New York: Harper, 2003.
———. *Fritz Lang: The Nature of the Beast*. New York: St. Martin's, 1997.
McGurk, Stuart. "Blade Runner 2049 Director Denis Villeneuve Is Science-Fiction's Brave New Hope." *Wired*, September 15, 2017. https://www.wired.co.uk/article/blade-runner-2049-denis-villeneuve.
Meier, Franz. "Oscar Wilde and the Myth of the *Femme Fatale* in *Fin-de-Siècle* Culture." In *The Importance of Reinventing Oscar: Versions of Wilde during the Last 100 Years*, edited by Uwe Boker, Richard Corballis, and Julie Hibbard, 117–134. Amsterdam: Rodopi, 2002.
Melosi, Martin V. *Thomas A. Edison and the Modernization of America*. New York: HarperCollins, 1990.
Meltzer, Françoise. *Salome and the Dance of Writing: Portraits of Mimesis in Literature*. Chicago: University of Chicago Press, 1987.
Meskell, Lynn. "Consuming Bodies: Cultural Fantasies of Ancient Egypt." *Body and Society* 4, no. 1 (1998): 63–76.
Metz, Christian. *Film Language: A Semiotics of the Cinema*. Chicago: University of Chicago Press, 1974.
———. *Langage et cinéma*. Paris: Librairie Larousse, 1971.
———."Photography and Fetish." *October* 34 (Autumn 1985): 81–90.
Meyer, Michael. "Wilde's Lectures and Trials: The Imitation, Reproduction, and Simulation of Pose." In *Importance of Reinventing Oscar: Versions of Wilde during the Last 100 Years*, edited by Uwe Boker, Richard Corballis, and Julie Hibbard, 103–109. Amsterdam: Rodopi, 2002.

Michelakis, Pantelis, and Maria Wyke, eds. *The Ancient World in Silent Cinema*. Cambridge: Cambridge University Press, 2013.
Michelet, Jules. *Love*. New York: Rudd and Carleton, 1859.
———. *Woman*. New York: Rudd and Carleton, 1860.
Michelson, Annette. "On the Eve of the Future: The Reasonable Facsimile and the Philosophical Toy." *October* 29 (Summer 1984): 3–20.
Mikhail, E. H, ed. *Oscar Wilde: Interviews and Recollections*. Vol. 1. New York: Barnes and Noble, 1979.
Mikkonen, Kai. *The Plot Machine: The French Novel and the Bachelor Machines in the Electric Years (1880–1914)*. Amsterdam: Rodopi, 2001.
Miller, J. Hillis. *Versions of Pygmalion*. Cambridge, MA: Harvard University Press, 1990.
Milton, John. *Paradise Lost: Norton Critical Edition*. Edited by Gordon Teskey. New York: W. W. Norton, 2005.
Minder, Michael, and Holger Bachmann, eds. *Fritz Lang's Metropolis: Cinematic Visions of Technology and Fear*. Rochester, NY: Camden House, 2000.
Mitchell, Elizabeth. *Liberty's Torch: The Great Adventure to Build the Statue of Liberty*. New York: Grove Press, 2015.
Mitchell, W.J.T. *Picture Theory*. Chicago: University of Chicago Press, 1994.
Modleski, Tania. *The Women Who Knew Too Much: Hitchcock and Feminist Theory*. New York: Routledge, 1988.
Montserrat, Dominic, ed. *Changing Bodies, Changing Meanings: Studies on the Human Body in Antiquity*. London: Routledge, 1998.
Morin, Edgar. *The Stars*. Minneapolis: University of Minnesota Press, 2005.
Musser, Charles. *The Emergence of Cinema: The American Screen to 1907*. Berkeley: University of California Press, 1994.
Nabokov, Vladimir. *Pale Fire*. New York: Vintage Books, 1989.
Nassaar, Christopher. *Into the Demon Universe: A Literary Exploration of Oscar Wilde*. New Haven, CT: Yale University Press, 1974.
Nelson, Hilda. "Théophile Gautier: The Invisible and Impalpable World: A Demi-Conviction." *French Review* 45, no. 4 (1972): 819–830.
Nesbet, Anne. *Savage Junctures: Sergei Eisenstein and the Shape of Thinking*. London: Tauris, 2007.
Nordau, Max. *Degeneration*. London: Heinemann, 1895.
North, Michael. *Camera Works: Photography and the Twentieth-Century Word*. Oxford: Oxford University Press, 2005.
Nouvet, Claire. "An Impossible Response: The Disaster of Narcissus." *Yale French Studies* 79 (1991): 103–134.
Novak, Daniel A. *Realism, Photography, and Nineteenth-Century Fiction*. New York: Cambridge University Press, 2008.
The Old Testament: The Authorized or King James Version of 1611. London: Everyman's Library, 1996.
Ovid. *Metamorphoses*. Translated by A. D. Melville. Oxford: Oxford University Press, 1986.
Paini, Dominique, and Guy Cogeval, eds. *Hitchcock and Art: Fatal Coincidences*. Milan: Mazzotta, 2000.
Palmer, R. Barton, and Murray Pomerance, eds. *Thinking in the Dark: Cinema, Theory, Practice*. New Brunswick, NJ: Rutgers University Press, 2015.
Paret, Paul Monty. "Forget Rudolf Belling: Getting the Carl Einstein We Deserve." In *Carl Einstein and the European Avant-Garde*, edited by Nicola Creighton and Andreas Kramer, 104–121. Berlin: De Gruyter, 2012.

Pater, Walter. *The Renaissance: Studies in Art and Poetry*. Berkeley: University of California Press, 1980.
Perala, Tiffany. "'Oscar Wilde and Music': A Lecture by Merlin Holland at the William Andrews Clark Memorial Library, 14th October 2007." *The OScholars*, no. 42, October/November 2007. http://www.oscholarship.com/TO/Archive/Forty-two/And_I/AND%20I.2.htm.
Pinson, Stephen. *Speculating Daguerre*. Chicago: University of Chicago Press, 2012.
Pomerance, Murray. *An Eye for Hitchcock*. New Brunswick, NJ: Rutgers University Press, 2004.
Ponnau, Gwenhaël. *L'Eve Future, ou l'œuvre en question*. Paris: Presses universitaires de France, 2000.
———. "Sur les épigraphes de L'Ève future." In *Société des études romantiques: Villiers de l'Isle-Adam (1838–1889)*, 149–156. Paris: Sedes, 1990.
Powell, Kerry. *Acting Wilde: Victorian Sexuality, Theater, and Oscar Wilde*. Cambridge: Cambridge University Press, 2009.
———. *Oscar Wilde and the Theater of the 1890s*. Cambridge: Cambridge University Press, 2009.
Psomiades, Kathy Alexis. *Beauty's Body: Femininity and Representation in British Aestheticism*. Stanford, CA: Stanford University Press, 1997.
Rabaté, Jean-Michel, ed. *Writing the Image after Roland Barthes*. Philadelphia: University of Pennsylvania Press, 1997.
Raby, Peter, ed. *The Cambridge Companion to Oscar Wilde*. Cambridge: Cambridge University Press, 1997.
Raitt, A. W. *The Life of Villiers de l'Isle-Adam*. Oxford: Clarendon Press, 1981.
———. *Villiers de l'Isle-Adam et le mouvement Symboliste*. Paris: Jose Corti, 1965.
Ramos, Colleen. *Deviant Modernism*. Cambridge: Cambridge University Press, 1998.
Rancière, Jacques. "The Archaeomodern Turn." In *Walter Benjamin and the Demands of History*, edited by Michael P. Steinberg, 24–40. Ithaca, NY: Cornell University Press, 1996.
Ransom, Amy J. *The Feminine as Fantastic in the Conte Fantastique: Visions of the Other*. New York: Peter Lang, 1995.
Rich, Adrienne. *Of Woman Born: Motherhood as Experience and Institution*. New York: W. W. Norton, 1995.
Roberts, Jeanne Addison. "Anxiety and Influence: Milton, Ovid, and Shakespeare." *South Atlantic Review* 53, no. 2 (1988): 59–75.
Roberts, Mary Louise. *Disruptive Acts: The New Woman in Fin-de-Siècle France*. Chicago: University of Chicago Press, 2002.
Roden, Frederick S., ed. *Palgrave Advances in Oscar Wilde Studies*. London: Palgrave, 2004.
Rose, Louis. *The Survival of Images: Art Historians, Psychoanalysts, and the Ancients*. Detroit: Wayne State University Press, 2001.
Rosen, Philip. *Change Mummified: Cinema, Historicity, Theory*. Minneapolis: University of Minnesota Press, 2001.
———. *Narrative, Apparatus, Ideology: A Film Theory Reader*. New York: Columbia University Press, 1986.
Rothman, William. *The "I" of the Camera: Essays in Film Criticism, History, and Aesthetics*. New York: Cambridge University Press, 2004.
Rothenstein, William. *Men and Memories: Recollections of William Rothenstein, 1872–1900*. London: Faber & Faber, 1931.
Ruhe, Edward L. "Film: The 'Literary' Approach," *Literature/Film Quarterly* 1, no. 1 (Winter 1973): 76–83.

Said, Edward. *Orientalism*. New York: Vintage Books, 1979.
Samuels, Robert. *Hitchcock's Bi-textuality: Lacan, Feminisms and Queer Theory*. Albany: State University of New York Press, 1998.
Schapira, M. C. *Le Regard de Narcisse: Romans et nouvelles de Théophile Gautier*. Lyon: Presses universitaires de Lyon, 1984.
Schulz, David. "Redressing Oscar: Performance and the Trials of Oscar Wilde." *TDR* 40, no. 2 (Summer 1996): 37–59.
Schwartz, Hillel. *The Culture of the Copy*. New York: Zone Books, 2014.
———. "Torque: The New Kinaesthetic of the Twentieth Century." In *Incorporations*, edited by Jonathan Crary and Sanford Kwinter, 70–127. New York: Zone Books, 1992.
Segal, Naomi. *Narcissus and Echo: Women in the French Récit*. Manchester: Manchester University Press, 1988.
Seitler, Dana. *Atavistic Tendencies: The Culture of Science in American Modernity*. Minneapolis: University of Minnesota Press, 2008.
Shanks, Lewis Piaget. "Gustave Flaubert." *Open Court* 36, no. 3 (March 1922): 129–145.
Sharrock, A. R. "Womanufacture." *Journal of Roman Studies* 81 (1991): 36–49.
Shaw, Jennifer. "The Figure of Venus: Rhetoric of the Ideal and the Salon of 1863." In *Manifestations of Venus: Art and Sexuality*, edited by Caroline Arscott and Katie Scott, 90–108. Manchester: Manchester University Press, 2000.
Shewan, Rodney. *Oscar Wilde: Art and Egotism*. New York: Barnes and Noble, 1977.
Showalter, Elaine. *Sexual Anarchy: Gender and Culture at the Fin de Siècle*. New York: Penguin, 1990.
Silverman, Kaja. "Liberty, Maternity, Commodification." *New Formations*, no. 5 (Summer 1988): 69–89.
Sinfield, Alan. *The Wilde Century: Effeminacy, Oscar Wilde and the Queer Moment*. London: Cassell, 1994.
Smith, Albert B. *Théophile Gautier and the Fantastic*. University, MS: Romance Monographs, 1977.
Sobchack, Vivian. *Screening Space: The American Science Fiction Film*. New Brunswick, NJ: Rutgers University Press, 1999.
Sobieszek, Robert A. "Sculpture as the Sum of Its Profiles: François Willème and Photosculpture in France, 1859–1868." *Art Bulletin* 62, no. 4 (1980): 617–630.
Spoto, Donald. *Spellbound by Beauty: Alfred Hitchcock and His Leading Ladies*. London: Hutchinson, 2008.
Stam, Robert. *Literature Through Film: Realism, Magic, and the Art of Adaptation*. London: Wiley-Blackwell, 2004.
Stoichita, Victor I. *The Pygmalion Effect: From Ovid to Hitchcock*. Chicago: University of Chicago Press, 2008.
Stokes, John. *The French Actress and Her English Audience*. Cambridge: Cambridge University Press, 2005.
Stross, Randall. *The Wizard of Menlo Park: How Thomas Alva Edison Invented the Modern World*. New York: Crown, 2007.
Swanson, Gloria. *Swanson on Swanson*. New York: Random House, 1980.
Thomas, David Wayne. "The 'Strange Music' of Salome: Oscar Wilde's Rhetoric of Verbal Musicality." *Mosaic* 33, no. 1 (2000): 15–38.
Truffaut, François, Alfred Hitchcock, and Helen G. Scott. *Hitchcock*. New York: Simon and Schuster, 1967.
Turvey, Malcolm. *The Filming of Modern Life: European Avant-Garde Film of the 1920s*. Cambridge, MA: MIT Press, 2011.

Tydeman, William, and Steven Price. *Wilde: Salome*. Cambridge: Cambridge University Press, 1996.
Vest, James M. *Hitchcock and France: The Forging of an Auteur*. Westport, CT: Praeger, 2003.
Villiers de l'Isle-Adam, Auguste. "Les Filles de Milton." *Nouveau Contes Cruels et propos d'au dela (Deuxième Édition)*. Paris: Calmann Levy, 1893.
———. *L'Ève future (Édition établie par Nadine Satiat)*. Paris: GF Flammarion, 1992.
———. *L'Ève future (Édition présentée établie et annotée par Alan Raitt)*. Paris: Gallimard, 1993.
Waldrep, Shelton. *The Aesthetics of Self-Invention: Oscar Wilde to David Bowie*. Minneapolis: University of Minnesota Press, 2004.
Walker, Julia M. "The Poetics of Antitext and the Politics of Milton's Allusions." *Studies in English Literature, 1500–1900* 37, no. 1 (1997): 151–171.
Walkley, A. B. *Playhouse Impressions*. New York: Garland, 1984.
Wallingford, John B. "The 200 Year Effort to See the Embryo." *Science* 365, no. 6455 (August 23, 2019): 758–759.
Walsh, Carey. *Exquisite Desire: Religion, the Erotic and the Song of Songs*. Minneapolis: Fortress Press, 2000.
Wellmann, Janina. "Biological Motion." Fellows' Presentation Series at the Radcliffe Institute for Advanced Study, May 9, 2018. https://www.youtube.com/watch?v=feFAs3GDbMo.
———. *The Form of Becoming: Embryology and the Epistemology of Rhythm, 1760–1830*. New York: Zone Books, 2017.
———. "Model and Movement: Studying Cell Movement in Early Morphogenesis, 1900 to the Present." *History and Philosophy of the Life Sciences* 40 (2018): 59. https://pubmed.ncbi.nlm.nih.gov/30206717/.
Wettlaufer, Alexandra K. *Pen vs. Paintbrush: Girodet, Balzac and the Myth of Pygmalion in Postrevolutionary France*. New York: Palgrave, 2001.
White, Susan. "*Vertigo* and Problems of Knowledge in Feminist Film Theory." In *Alfred Hitchcock: Centenary Essays*, edited by Richard Allen and S. Ishii-Gonzalès, 141–158. London: BFI Publishing, 1999.
Whiteley, Giles. *Oscar Wilde and the Simulacrum: The Truth of Masks*. London: Legenda, 2015.
Wilde, Oscar. *The Annotated Oscar Wilde: Poems, Fictions, Plays, Lectures, Essays, and Letters*. Edited by H. Montgomery Hyde. New York: Clarkson N. Potter, 1982.
———. *The Artist as Critic: Critical Writings of Oscar Wilde*. Edited by Richard Ellmann. New York: Random House, 1969.
———. *The Decay of Lying and Other Essays*. New York: Penguin Classic, 2010.
———. *De Profundis*. New York: Modern Library, 2000.
———. *Salome*. New York: Dover Publications, 1967.
———. *Salomé, drame en un acte: Illustré par Aubrey Beardsley*. Toulouse: Éditions Ombres, 1992.
Williams, Linda. "Film Body: An Implantation of Perversions." *Cinetracts* 33, no. 4 (Winter 1981): 19–35.
Winchell, James. "Wilde and Huysmans: Autonomy, Reference, and the Myth of Expiation." In *Critical Essays on Oscar Wilde*, edited by Regenia Gagnier, 223–240. New York: G. K. Hall, 1991.
Winkler, Martin. *Ovid on Screen: A Montage of Attractions*. Cambridge: Cambridge University Press, 2020.
Wollen, Peter. *Signs and Meaning in the Cinema*. Bloomington: Indiana University Press, 1972.

Wood, Gaby. *Edison's Eve: A Magical History of the Quest for Mechanical Life*. New York: Alfred A. Knopf, 2002.
Wood, Robin. *Hitchcock's Films Revisited*. Rev. ed. New York: Columbia University Press, 2002.
Worringer, Wilhelm. *Abstraction and Empathy*. Chicago: Elephant, 1997.
Wright, Rosemary Muir. "The Great Whore in the Illustrated Apocalypse Cycles." *Journal of Medieval History* 23, no. 3 (1997): 191–210.
Zagona, Helen Grace. *The Legend of Salome and the Principle of Art for Art's Sake*. Geneva: Droz, 1960.
Žižek, Slavoj. "*Vertigo*: The Drama of a Deceived Platonist." In *Hitchcock Annual* (2003–2004): 67–82.

Films

Bryant, Charles, dir. *Salome*. 1923; Los Angeles, CA, Nazimova Productions, 2012. DVD
Hitchcock, Alfred, dir. *Vertigo*. 1958; Universal City, CA, Universal Studios, 1996. DVD.
Lang, Fritz, dir. *Metropolis*. 1927; Berlin, Germany, UFA, 2010. Blu-ray Disc.
Scott, Ridley, dir. *Blade Runner: The Final Cut*. 1982; Burbank, CA, Warner Bros. Studios, 2007. DVD.
Villeneuve, Denis. *Blade Runner 2049*. 2017; Burbank, CA, Warner Bros. Studios, 2018. DVD.
Wilder, Billy, dir. *Sunset Boulevard*. 1950; Hollywood, CA, Paramount Pictures, 2002. DVD.

Index

Note: *Page numbers in italics indicate figures.*

About the Author

CHRISTINA PARKER-FLYNN has a PhD in comparative literature from Emory University, specializing in French, psychoanalytic studies, and film. She is currently an assistant professor of film and literature in the Literature, Media, and Culture program in the English Department at Florida State University. A native New Jerseyan, Parker-Flynn now lives in Tallahassee, Florida with her husband and their two children, and enjoys going to the beach above all else—even watching movies.